Queer Subjects in Modern Japanese Literature

MICHIGAN MONOGRAPH SERIES IN JAPANESE STUDIES

NUMBER 96

CENTER FOR JAPANESE STUDIES

UNIVERSITY OF MICHIGAN

Queer Subjects in Modern Japanese Literature

Male Love, Intimacy, and Erotics, 1886–2014

Stephen D. Miller, Editor

University of Michigan Press
Ann Arbor

Copyright © 2022 by Stephen D. Miller
All rights reserved

For questions or permissions, please contact um.press.perms@umich.edu

Published in the United States of America by the
University of Michigan Press
Manufactured in the United States of America
Printed on acid-free paper
First published November 2022

A CIP catalog record for this book is available from the British Library.

Library of Congress Cataloging-in-Publication data has been applied for.

ISBN 978-0-472-07567-8 (hardcover : alk. paper)
ISBN 978-0-472-05567-8 (paper : alk. paper)
ISBN 978-0-472-22076-2 (e-book)

Contents

Digital materials related to this title can be found on the Fulcrum platform via the following citable URL: https://doi.org/10.3998/mpub.12296457

Introduction

Stephen D. Miller

> Queerness is not yet here. Queerness is an ideality.[1]
> —José Esteban Muñoz

Queer Subjects in Modern Japanese Literature: Male Love, Erotics, and Intimacy, 1886–2014 is an anthology of translated Japanese literature that covers more than 125 years of modern and contemporary Japanese history. It contains shorter works—stories, poems, and essays—about men behaving lovingly, erotically, and intimately with other men (and occasionally women).[2] It is not meant to be comprehensive or complete (no anthology could be), nor is it meant to establish a queer canon of Japanese literature. These selections represent a small compilation of works on this topic within the world of modern Japanese literature; I urge scholars and translators to continue to expand our understanding of queerness in Japanese culture.

The anthology can be roughly divided into two sections: chapters 1–7 correspond to the pre–World War II era, while chapters 8–16 fall within the postwar era. There are no entries here for the years between 1935 and 1960—roughly the period when Japan was pursuing a military agenda and the immediate postwar era when most efforts were directed toward rebuilding the country.[3] (Mishima Yukio published a

---

1. José Esteban Muñoz, *Cruising Utopia: The Then and There of Queer Futurity* (New York: New York University Press, 2009), 1.

2. Most Western readers would probably not consider something written in 1886 as "modern," but this is how Japanese historians characterize anything written after the Meiji Restoration (1868).

3. The exceptions to this are the three stories in chapter 5 by Inagaki Taruho that were written and published originally in 1924 and subsequently revised for republication in the 1950s and 1960s.

major novel in 1949, but this anthology is primarily focused on shorter, nonexcerpted works.)

I chose 1886 as the beginning date for the anthology because Yamada Bimyo's work, included here, evoked the version of *nanshoku* ("male-male desire") so prominent in the previous historical era, the Edo period (1600–1868).

As for 2014, the end date of the anthology, in that year Morii Ryō's "The Playroom" won the Newcomer's Award (*Shinjinshō*) from the well-known journal *Bungakukai* (Literary World). The story is a fitting finale to the anthology because it evokes the troubling, sad, beautiful present and perhaps future of Japanese queer literature.

Terminology

The use of proper terminology for sexual studies in English and Japanese is fraught with problems, in terms of both definitions and ideology. Here, I'll focus only on vocabulary in English. Japanese terminology will be discussed in the historical sections in which the vocabulary originally appeared.

The word "queer" is in the title of the anthology, so it's necessary to define how and why I'm using it.[4] The word was politicized in the late twentieth century, when it was intentionally reclaimed by queer people from being a pejorative slur. Many of the scholars whose work the translators and I depended on in this anthology *do* use the word in this political and activist sense.

For my own part, for the purposes of this introduction, I chose the word both for its primary meaning as "strange or odd from a conventional viewpoint,"[5] and its usefulness as an umbrella term that I believe can encompass many other LGBTQ terms.

The queerness of "subjects" in the title may be understood to refer to both topics and people, characterized by peculiarity, eccentricity, uncanniness, nonconformity, subversiveness, and even an embrace of "the forbidden." On the positive end of the spectrum, I intend the meaning "a pleasing and even necessary variation upon pattern," in the sense that the (heterosexual) pattern without (queer) variation is stultifying in both works of art and whole cultures.

---

4. The terminology used in reference to the texts included in the anthology was left to the discretion of individual translators.

5. https://www.dictionary.com/browse/queer

I use the word "queer" as an LGBTQ umbrella term deliberately, knowing that it's a contested term. Anticipating objections, I'll briefly describe the primary critique of applying the word "queer" retroactively and to phenomena of non-Western cultures.

In terms of chronology, there have been objections to applying the word "queer" to times before there was a coherent concept of queerness as a shared identity with a common political goal for improving the status of queer people in society. The date after which it's been judged legitimate to apply the word "queer" retroactively is itself contested: some would reference the early 1900s, or the early 1950s, with the creation of various liberation-oriented organizations, or 1969, the date of the Stonewall Riots, or the 1990s, with the rise of Queer Theory as a scholarly discipline.[6]

In terms of geography, there have been objections to applying a Western term to non-Western cultures, which has been thought to carry forward colonial and appropriative impulses, and a Western unwillingness to consider how non-Western phenomena may have a very different conceptual basis than seemingly similar phenomena in the West.

While noting and appreciating these very necessary warnings about the dangers of applying what we believe we know to phenomena we may not fully understand, it may be time for a looser approach to how we treat chronological and geographical distances. The warnings have focused on what is different between times, places, and cultures, and have seemed to preclude or disallow exploring what is similar between times, places, and cultures. To insist on difference may be as misleading as to ignore difference. I believe it's possible to find what a poet might call a "rhyming relationship" between queer phenomena of the past and present and of variant cultures, without overstating the similarities or claiming too much for them.

However, this introduction will only apply the word "queer" to phenomena occurring after 1868, the beginning of the modern era in Japan. In answer to the objection that non-Western phenomena may have a very different conceptual basis than seemingly similar phenomena in the West, 1868 is the date after which Japan rapidly began to adopt Western ideas in almost

---

6. "By the 1910s and 1920s, the men who identified themselves as part of a distinct category of men primarily on the basis of their homosexual interest rather than their womanlike gender status usually called themselves *queer*. Essentially synonymous with 'homosexual,' *queer* presupposed the statistical normalcy—and normative character—of men's sexual interest in women; tellingly, queers referred to their counterparts as 'normal men' (or 'straight men') rather than 'heterosexuals.'" George Chauncey, *Gay New York: Gender, Urban Culture, and the Making of the Gay World, 1890–1940* (New York: Basic Books, 1994), 15–16.

every discipline. It is understood that the word "queer" doesn't reach back to 1868, but a historical framework for male-male sexuality in Japan does reach back that far (and even further). "Queer" is a possible translation for the Japanese word *nanshoku* (male-male desire), a concept in use as far as the medieval era, and one that that has been radically transformed in the modern era. I believe as well that its use is justified by the need for an umbrella term to describe the phenomena of male love, erotics, and intimacy that we observe in the contents of this anthology.

Readers will encounter here a wide variety of other terms and phrases about same-sex-loving men—their practices, the places and events that concern them, their relationships with society in general—as well as terminology related to other kinds of sexual minorities. These include the word "homo" (the word of choice in queer magazines from the 1960s through the 1980s, but still considered pejorative in certain contexts), "homosexuality," "male-male desire," "male-male sex," "queer sexuality," "male-male love," "homosexual love," "male desire," "male-male sexuality," "connoisseurs of boys," "woman-haters," "same-sex desire," "queers," "queer sexuality," "mashers," "effeminate male prostitutes," "gay boys," "third sex," "male-male relations," "homosocial," "sadomasochism," "transsexualism," "marginal sexualities," "gay male population," "homo-hetero divide," "gay bars," "queer community," "gay boom," and "LGBT boom." This nuanced list demonstrates both the difficulty of using an umbrella term such as "queer" to encompass so many different phenomena, but also the seeming necessity of doing so.

The reader may find it useful to have a historical context of male-male phenomena in Japan that reaches back much further than the works in the anthology.

History and Background

The Imperial Court and Medieval Eras (ca. 784–1600)

The imperial court and medieval eras cover more than 800 years of Japanese history. These two eras (which consisted of the Heian [784–1185], Kamakura [1185–1333], and Muromachi [1333–ca. 1600] periods) began in relative peace and stability, but by the end of the Muromachi period, the country was engaged in constant warfare that lasted over a hundred years.

Examples of male-male sexuality in Japanese literature date back more than 1100years. In the imperial court era, instances of male-male love and sexuality may be found in a variety of genres and in five specific texts.

Kokinshū

Gustav Heldt has written extensively about the poetry in the *Kokinshū* (905), Japan's first imperial poetry anthology,[7] and has identified "homosocial desire" in poetic exchanges between Ki no Tsurayuki (872–945), the principal compiler of the *Kokinshū*, and two other noblemen of the same era. Heldt argued that "codes of poetic intercourse" in the *Kokinshū* allowed it to express "male-male desire" in a way "that was indistinguishable from the one they used toward women."[8]

The Tale of Genji

Rajyashree Pandey writes about the protagonist of *The Tale of Genji* (Genji monogatari, ca. 1008, attributed to Murasaki Shikibu), "Genji is perhaps the one whose beauty and radiance is most celebrated and commented upon by the narrating figures, the serving women, and the men who observe him."[9] "In depictions of Genji as an erotic figure, the text draws attention to the fact that the men observing Genji see him either as they would a woman or wish they were themselves women."[10] Reginald Jackson has gone so far as to claim that Japan's greatest work of prose literature "is a queer text"[11]—not just referring to an incident in chapter 2 ("Hahakigi") in which Genji, disappointed when a woman doesn't show up for an assignation, sleeps with her younger brother instead—but due to a certain subversiveness in Murasaki's entire project: "Queering a text . . . involves apprehending the extent to which . . . textual moments, in their uneasy adjacency to enduring social mores and hegemonic discourses, challenged the primacy or stability of such norms to suggest other modes of thinking, desiring, moving, living, and having."[12]

The Changelings and Partings at Dawn

Two tales from the second half of the imperial court era explore the topic of male-male sexuality. The first is *The Changelings* (Torikaebaya monogatari,

---

7. Gustav Heldt, *The Pursuit of Harmony: Poetry and Power in Early Heian Japan* (Ithaca: Cornell East Asia Series, Cornell University Press, 2008).

8. Gustav Heldt, "Between Followers and Friends: Male Homosocial Desire in Heian Court Poetry," *U.S.-Japan Women's Journal* 33 (2007), 3.

9. Rajyashree Pandey, *Perfumed Sleeves and Tangled Hair* (Honolulu: University of Hawai'i Press, 2016), 57.

10. Pandey, *Perfumed Sleeves and Tangled Hair*, 59.

11. Reginald Jackson, *A Proximate Remove: Queering Intimacy and Loss in* The Tale of Genji (Oakland: University of California Press, 2021), 1.

12. Jackson, *A Proximate Remove*, 6.

ca. twelfth century), which tells the story of an exchange of gender roles between a high-ranking brother and sister at the imperial court. (The title literally translates as "If Only They Could Be Exchanged.") Gregory Pflug-felder has written about *The Changelings* that "the tale has sometimes been cited as a locus classicus [for] the issue of same-sex and same-gender sexual practices and desires—'homosexuality,' in today's prevailing usage."[13]

A second tale, *Partings at Dawn* (Ariake no wakare, late twelfth century) is also based on gender exchange, in which (for very complicated reasons) a girl, Ariake, is raised as a boy. Ariake's real gender is discovered when the emperor falls passionately in love with him: "he [Ariake] was so indescrib-ably appealing that the Emperor simply could not restrain his feelings."[14] The twist in the tale is that what appears to be male-male desire actually isn't—though the hint of sexual unorthodoxy made Ariake "more attractive than any ordinary woman one could think of."[15]

Taiki

Finally, the diary *Taiki* (twelfth century) written in Chinese by Fujiwara no Yorinaga (1120–1156), a high-ranking member of the court, has received significant scholarly attention for its descriptions of how "sexual encounters with other men were pursued as a way of establishing political networks and alliances at court."[16] Gustav Heldt writes, "[W]hen the author is penetrated by another man, the act is often described as a 'ravaging' [*ransui*], a term that can also refer to confusion of the social order or inversion of social roles."[17] *Taiki* is one of many men's diaries from the late twelfth century that portrays male-male relationships of this nature.

Acolyte Tales

Moving forward in time, during the medieval era (comprised of the Kamak-ura and Muromachi periods, 1185–ca. 1615), known for its warriors and sho-guns, examples of male-male sex appear in literature about and within large Buddhist monasteries. In one genre in particular, *chigo monogatari* (acolyte tales), there are numerous instances of older monks serving as the sexual partners of young boys (*chigo*) who were their students and attendants. Sachi Schmidt-Hori has described how these relationships were sacralized

---

13. Gregory Pflugfelder, "Strange Fates: Sex, Gender, and Sexuality in *Torikaebaya mono-gatari*," *Monumenta Nipponica* 47, no. 3 (Autumn 1992), 348.

14. Stephen D. Miller, ed., *Partings at Dawn: An Anthology of Japanese Gay Literature* (San Francisco: Gay Sunshine Press, 1996).

15. Miller, *Partings at Dawn*, 29.

16. Heldt, "Followers and Friends," 28.

17. Heldt, "Followers and Friends," 28.

by means of specific rituals (*kanjō*) that converted the *chigo* into religious beings "in the flesh" (specifically Kannon, the bodhisattva of compassion). By means of the same *kanjō*, the older monks as well were permitted "to have intercourse with a properly consecrated *chigo*," but if the *chigo* had not been properly consecrated, the monk would be "sent to one of the three hells."[18]

Today's Tales of Yesterday

In the early seventeenth century, an anonymous anecdotal work, *Today's Tales of Yesterday* (Kinō wa kyō monogatari), took up aspects of male-male sexuality. (As translator Paul Gordon Schalow writes, the fact that there are fifty-four extant copies of this work from the Edo period "attests[s] to its widespread dissemination."[19]) The work's title suggests that the author wished to align it with a genre of Japanese literature known as *setsuwa* (brief narrative tales) from the Heian (784–1185) and Kamakura periods (1185–1333). Each *setsuwa* begins, *ima wa mukashi*, "now, it is long ago," which is echoed by the title of the anecdotal tales: *Today's Tales of Yesterday*, *kinō wa kyō*, "yesterday, it is today." Another way that *Today's Tales of Yesterday* reached backward is an emphasis on the *chigo* (acolyte) phenomenon, for instance in this bawdy story:

> "This acolyte lives in such poverty that to dress for formal occasions at the temple he must borrow everything he wears," said the boy's caretaker. "The only thing he owns is his cock. Poor boy!"
>
> The acolyte heard this and said, "To my great regret, not even that is mine."
>
> "How can that be?"
>
> "Because everyone who sees it calls it a horse's cock."[20]

Though, as we've seen, pre-Edo literary examples of male-male sexuality were sporadic, in the next period such texts will proliferate.

The Early Modern Era, Tokugawa (Edo) Period: 1600–1868

All evidence points to the fact that male-male sexuality was prevalent throughout urban areas in the early modern era in Japan.[21] Historian Iwata

---

18. Sachi Schmidt-Hori, *Tale of Idolized Boys: Male-Male Love in Medieval Japanese Buddhist Narratives* (Honolulu: University of Hawai'i Press, 2021), 10.

19. Paul Gordon Schalow, *Partings at Dawn: An Anthology of Japanese Gay Literature*, ed. Stephen D. Miller (San Francisco: Gay Sunshine Press, 1996), 55.

20. *Partings at Dawn*, 57. Scholars of Japanese literature categorize this work as a *kana-zōshi*, short vernacular tales written entirely in *kana*, a writing system free of Chinese characters.

21. See Gregory Pflugfelder, *Cartographies of Desire: Male-Male Sexuality in Japanese Dis-*

Jun'ichi (1900–1945) cataloged as many as 566 texts that concerned male-male love from the Edo period.[22] For our purposes, the developments of this period are primarily important for how they created the conditions of the following period, when the entries in this anthology began to be written.

The end of the medieval era can be divided into two different periods. The first period (1467–1568) was a hundred years of unrelenting conflict among the warlords who ruled over various areas of the country. Beginning in 1568, successive battles were fought by Oda Nobunaga (1532–1582), Toyotomi Hideyoshi (1537–1598), and Tokugawa Ieyasu (1543–1616), with the goal to establish rule over the entire country.

The years between 1568 and 1600 (the Azuchi-Momoyama era) were characterized by a cultural efflorescence, including the construction of massive and magnificent castle structures throughout the country, the flourishing of the tea ceremony under the guidance of Sen no Rikyū (1522–1591), monumental screen, door, wall, and ceiling paintings such as those by Kanō Eitoku (1543–1590), as well as smaller works on paper (ink painting and calligraphic scrolls) by artists such as Hon'ami Kōetsu (1558–1633).

The country was finally permanently unified with Tokugawa Ieyasu's victory in 1600 at the Battle of Sekigahara, which formally brought the medieval period to an end. The Tokugawa family took control of the shogunate (also called the *bakufu*) in 1603 and held control for the next 265 years, selecting Edo (present-day Tokyo) as its capital. The peace that began with the start of the Edo period came with a price, however. Ieyasu and his immediate successors instituted restrictions that quickly gave the period (and the shogunate or *bakufu*) an authoritarian nature.

A policy called "alternative attendance" (*sankin kōtai*) was instituted by the third Tokugawa shogun between 1635 and 1642, requiring that all 260 military lords (*daimyō*) of the country's various domains, their military attendants, and their male servants spend every other year in Edo. At first, this system caused the population of Edo to fluctuate, but over time the population steadily increased. By 1720 the population had reached one million, making it the largest urban community in the country. In the same year, Osaka's and Kyoto's populations reached 382,000 and 341,000 respectively. Then as now, the existence of urban centers meant that men attracted

course (Berkeley: University of California Press, 1999), and Gary P. Leupp, *Male Colors: The Construction of Homosexuality in Tokugawa Japan* (Berkeley: University of California Press, 1995).

22. Jim Reichert, *In the Company of Men: Representations of Male-Male Sexuality in Meiji Literature* (Palo Alto: Stanford University Press, 2006), 6.

to men would find more opportunities to make connections, sexual and commercial.

Society was divided by the *bakufu* into four classes: samurai, farmers, artisans, and merchants. Below these fixed classes were others who did not fit into any of these groups. Priests, actors, artists, prostitutes, as well as various outcastes such as the *eta* (a word meaning "much filth") and *hinin*, or "nonhumans," who "were forced to subsist on jobs such as ragpicking," made up the rest of society.[23]

A policy of national isolation (*sakoku*) was instituted by the third shogun and enforced by means of edicts. Foreign visitors were not allowed to interact with citizens of Japan, except in portions of Nagasaki (especially the port of Deshima).

The increasing growth of literacy and developments in movable-type printing triggered changes in other spheres of Edo society—making it more likely, for instance, that books on male-male sexuality would reach the public. (This may be described as one of several publishing "booms" in the history of male-male sexuality in Japan; those that occurred in the modern period were far larger in scope.) Marius Jansen comments about literacy at the beginning of the Edo period that "[A]fter the early decades of the seventeenth century Japanese had access to a steadily growing volume of books—devotional, entertaining, and practical—and grew up surrounded by print in a society that valued the ability to master that medium."[24] Speaking about both the urban and rural areas of Japan by the end of the seventeenth century, Andrew Gordon writes, "it seems that between one-third and one-half of Japanese men and perhaps one-fifth of women were literate by the early 1800s."[25]

Evidence of male-male sexualities may be found even in the evolution of Edo period laws and medicine.[26] But it's in the realm of literature—stories, anecdotes, and poems—that we really see a new flourishing of texts on this topic.

---

23. Andrew Gordon, *A Modern History of Japan: From Tokugawa Times to the Present* (Cambridge: Harvard University Press, 2000; Oxford: Oxford University Press, 2003), 16.

24. Marius Jansen, *The Making of Modern Japan* (Cambridge: Harvard University Press, 2000), 163.

25. Gordon, *A Modern History of Japan*, 26.

26. See chapter 2 of Pflugfelder's *Cartographies of Desire* about the legal discourse surrounding male-male sexuality, and chapters 4 and 5 for the medical discourse. During the Edo period, the primary goal of medical practitioners, still reliant on the Chinese medical system, was to maintain the physical health of men having sex with men.

The Great Mirror of Male Love

One of the most influential of these texts was a group of forty stories (in a genre referred to as *ukiyo-zōshi*, "tales of the floating world") called *Nanshoku ōkagami: Honchō waka fūzoku* (The Great Mirror of Male Love: The Custom of Boy Love in Our Land, 1687) by Ihara Saikaku (1642–1693). Paul Gordon Schalow argues (in the introduction to his translation of *Nanshoku*) that "[Saikaku] chose the topic of homosexual love because it had the broadest appeal to both the samurai men of Edo and the townsmen [merchants, or *chōnin*] of Kyoto and Osaka, his regular audience."[27]

The word *nanshoku* in the title *Nanshoku ōkagami* was one of the most common words indicating the sexual desire of one man for another. *Nanshoku* literally means "male colors," but the translation "male desire" is more helpful in indicating a mode of sexuality; the word is still used in Japan to reference male-male sexuality of the past. (The word *shudō*, short for *wakashudō*, "the way of youth," was also used during this period, emphasizing the age differential that was ubiquitous in all Edo male-male relationships.[28])

The forty stories in *Nanshoku* were divided into two equal halves: twenty stories about the samurai, and twenty stories about the boy prostitute culture of the kabuki theater.[29] According to Schalow, two types of men were depicted in the tales: connoisseurs of boys (*shōjin-zuki*) and woman-haters (*onna-girai*).[30] The first type had a "nonexclusive interest in boys" (and therefore slept with, or could sleep with, both men and women) while the second type "did not marry and . . . completely rejected women as sexual partners."[31] *Nanshoku* was not Saikaku's first foray into male-male love. His first published work, *Kōshoku ichidai otoko* (The Man Who Loved Love, 1682), depicted a man who had had almost 4,500 lovers, 725 of whom were boys.[32]

Sex was not the only important element in a relationship between a man and his youth. Schalow writes about relationships between samurai, "The adult male lover (called a *nenja*) was supposed to provide social backing,

---

27. Ihara Saikaku, *The Great Mirror of Male Love*, trans. Paul Gordon Schalow (Palo Alto: Stanford University Press, 1990), 13.

28. See Pflugfelder's *Cartographies of Desire*, 26–27.

29. At the time *Nanshoku* was published, kabuki—now regarded as one of three most important classical forms of theater along with noh and puppet theater—was in its early stages of formation.

30. Saikaku, *The Great Mirror of Male Love*, 4.

31. Saikaku, *The Great Mirror of Male Love*, 4.

32. Saikaku, *The Great Mirror of Male Love*, 16.

emotional support, and a model of manliness for the boy. In exchange, the boy was expected to be worthy of his lover by being a good student of samurai manhood."[33]

Other Literary Works on Nanshoku

In the early seventeenth century, Konoe Nobuhiro (1599–1649) wrote *Inu tsurezuregusa* (Mongrel Essays in Idleness), a satire of the famous fourteenth-century classic *Tsuzuregusa* (Essays in Idleness, 1331) by Yoshida Kenkō. In his introduction, Konoe wrote, "there is nothing that can compare with the allure of a handsome youth. . . . a few stray locks of hair frame his face. He greets you with a smile when you pass and winks with a knowing look. . . . He speaks only when spoken to, and then shyly and in a low voice. . . . he is friendly and anxious to please. . . . Such a youth is impossible to resist."[34]

Later in the seventeenth century, the anthology *Wild Azaleas* (Iwatsutsuji, 1676) appeared, edited by Kitamura Kigin (1625–1705), a scholar of *The Tale of Genji*.[35] About *Wild Azaleas*, Paul Gordon Schalow wrote:

> [the anthology] contributed to the overall process of historicizing male love by defining a literary past for it. . . . Kigin gathered thirty-four homoerotic love poems and prose passages from sixteen classical works of literature in order to show how men of the past . . . expressed their love for youths, usually their *chigo*, or acolytes. His purpose was to provide a [spiritualized] model of behavior for men and youths of his day.[36]

Wild Azaleas became the first example of a Japanese writer compiling a literary anthology of male-male sexuality. The opening poem by one of Kūkai's disciples (Kūkai [774–835] was the founder of the Buddhist Shingon sect), in which the word *iwatsutsuji* (wild azaleas) first appears, reinforced the errone-

---

33. Saikaku, *The Great Mirror of Male Love*, 27.

34. Konoe Nobuhiro, "Mongrel Essays in Idleness," in *A Kamigata Anthology: Literature from Japan Metropolitan Centers, 1600–1750*, ed. Sumie Jones and Adam L. Kern, with Kenji Watanabe (Honolulu: University of Hawaii Press, 2020), 373–85.

35. Paul Gordon Schalow, trans., *Wild Azaleas* in *Partings at Dawn*, 99. Kitamura completed the first comprehensive study of *The Tale of Genji* (Kogetsushō, 1673) three years before he compiled *Wild Azaleas*.

36. *Partings at Dawn*, 98.

ous idea that Kūkai had introduced same-sex love from China to Japan.[37] The poem also indicates the kinds of literary works collected in the anthology, which consists primarily of poems from priests to their *chigo*. Attesting to its popularity among readers, *Wild Azaleas* was reprinted numerous times throughout the Edo period.

Around 1702, Urushiya Ensai published a story called "How a Pledge of Undying Love Was Reborn" in an anthology called *Nanshoku kinomesuke* (Male Colors Pickled with Pepperleaf Shoots). Urushiya wrote, "Great metaphors like 'the mountain of swords' and 'the sea of rough beaches' are possible only in male love."[38]

Another *ukiyo-zōshi* author, Ejima Kiseki (1666–1735), developed a new genre called *katagimono*, or "character sketches." One of his works, *Seken musuko katagi* (Characters of Worldly Young Men), contains a scene in which there is a debate between women-haters (*onnagirai*) and young-men-haters (*wakashugirai*). One merchant's son in the sketch is described as "from the very first . . . a woman-hater: all his life he remained unmarried in the grip of intense passions for a succession of handsome young boys."[39]

Ueda Akinari (1734–1809), famous for his fiction, poetry, and scholarship, included in his collection *Tales of Moonlight and Rain* (Ugetsu monogatari, 1776) the story "The Blue Cowl" (Aozukin), which translator William F. Sibley called "one of the finest works in the classical Japanese tradition."[40] In the story, a popular Zen Buddhist priest in a mountain temple turns into a flesh-eating demon after his young lover (*chigo*) dies unexpectedly. On the boy's death, "[The priest] spent whole days with his face pressed against the boy's, clutching at his dead hand, and in the end went stark mad. . . . [S]ince he could not bear to watch the flesh decay, he fell to eating what was left, even licking the bones, until at last he had devoured everything."[41]

Many historians mark the end of the Edo period with the appearance of

---

37. The poem by Shinga Sōzu reads: "Memories of love reverie, / like wild azaleas bursting into bloom / on mountains of evergreen; / my stony silence only shows / how much I love you." "The Invention of a Literary Tradition of Male Love," *Monumenta Nipponica* 48, no. 1 (Spring 1993), 5 (translation by Schalow).

38. *A Kamigata Anthology*, ed. Sumie Jones, trans. by Gregory Pflugfelder, 387–91. There are illustrations from this text in *Partings at Dawn*, 20 and 127.

39. Leupp, *Male Colors*, 104.

40. *Partings at Dawn*, 125.

41. *Partings at Dawn*, 128.

Commodore Perry's "Black Ships" in Edo harbor in 1853. This event, with the demand to "Agree to trade in peace, or suffer the consequences in war,"[42] marked the forced opening of Japan to the rest of the world after 253 years of isolationist policies. This incident, by itself, wouldn't erase two centuries of *nanshoku/wakashudō* culture, but the world of male-male sexuality depicted by Saikaku and others would eventually be threatened by imported Western ideologies.

The Modern Era (1868–Present)

The Meiji (1868–1912), Taishō (1912–1926), and Early Shōwa Periods (1926–Late 1930s)

The most crucial date in the establishment of the modern Japanese state is 1868, the year that imperial rule was restored after more than half a millennium of military rule ("The Meiji Restoration," named after Emperor Meiji).

As Japan searched for a favorable position in the international community from which it had excluded itself for several centuries, it actively tried to "catch up" with Western manners, customs, infrastructure, and ideals. It instituted a program of modernization under the slogan of *bunmei kaika* ("civilization and enlightenment"). Japanese bureaucrats and intellectuals traveled to Europe and North America to educate themselves about what constituted a civilized country according to Western values. Based on what they observed, changes in Japanese society and culture were made rapidly. The socioeconomic system was reformed; universal conscription was established; the wearing of Western-style clothes and the consumption of Western food were encouraged; the Western calendar was adopted; a postal and telegraph system was implemented; a public school system was established; and Western ideals were introduced to the general public through the writings of public figures such as Fukuzawa Yukichi (1835–1901) and members of the intellectual society known as the Meirokusha (Meiji 6 Society).[43]

The importation of Western ideas in virtually every discipline eventually began to affect the long-standing tolerance for male-male sexuality. A law of 1873 "categorically proscribed, for the first time in Japanese history, the

---

42. Gordon, *A Modern History of Japan*, 49.
43. For the Meirokusha, see Marius Jansen, *The Making of Modern Japan*, 461–62.

practice of anal intercourse (*keikan*),"[44] an example of how male-male sexuality was viewed with increasing distaste during this period. (Because the law against anal intercourse was rescinded nine years after it was instituted and never reinstated, Taniguchi Hiroyuki argued that "there have never been effective laws prohibiting same-sex sexual conduct in Japan."[45])

How a stigma against homosexuality arose in Japan is sociologically complex. Prior to the Meiji period, Japanese culture had lacked a religious proscription against male-male sexuality, but this prohibition was familiar from some Western religions. During the Meiji period, such proscriptions definitely began to intrude, but the factor that most influenced views on this topic was the growing emphasis on *the family* as the primary societal unit, which in turn created a stigma against any kind of sex that was not procreative.

A critical aspect of the Meiji period, as it related to male-male sexuality, was the Westernization of the medical system, leaving behind a reliance on traditional Chinese medical views and practices. As Gregory Pflugfelder says, "male-male sexuality was viewed in the Edo period not so much as pathological in itself as an aspect of bodily experience that required proper management in order to preserve, or in some cases, enhance, health."[46] Deviation from the goal of procreation was judged to be antisocial, repugnant, and offensive to the establishment of a society that conformed to Western ideals of civilization.

From personal experience, I've seen how Meiji ideas about the centrality of procreation persist in Japanese ideology to the present day. After my husband and I came out at a presentation at the International House of Japan in Tokyo in 2014, an older male audience member commented that the legalization of same-sex marriage was contraindicated in Japan, because in his view the low-birth-rate[47] era already threatened the stability of Japanese society. (The audience member's concern seemed to be that if same-sex marriage were legalized, Japanese heterosexual men would suddenly choose to become queer and stop procreating.)

One aspect to the new medical system of the Meiji period was the introduction and dissemination of a pseudoscience known as "sexology." When Japanese students traveled abroad to study Western medicine (German in

44. Pflugfelder, *Cartographies of Desire*, 153.

45. Taniguchi Hiroyuki, "The Legal Situation Facing Sexual Minorities in Japan," *Intersections: Gender, History, and Culture* 12 (January 2006), 1.

46. Pflugfelder, *Cartographies of Desire*, 239.

47. Amanda Seaman, *Writing Pregnancy in Low-Fertility Japan* (Honolulu: University of Hawai'i Press, 2016).

particular), they acquired Western ideas about sexuality. The influence of sexology in Japan began with the introduction, and then translation in 1894, of a book by the German-Austrian doctor Richard von Krafft-Ebing (1840–1902), *Psychopathia Sexualis*, which began the pathologizing of homosexuality in modern Japan. On the opposite side of the debate, it was known in Japan that German lawyer Karl Ulrichs (1825–1895) had called for the recognition of male-male unions, and that German physician and sexologist Magnus Hirschfeld (1868–1935) had founded the Scientific-Humanitarian Committee for homosexual rights in 1897. Though these minority opinions were known to the medical community and the reading public in Japan through articles in journals and magazines, until after the Second World War it was the views of *Psychopathia Sexualis* that were the primary influence on Japanese attitudes toward male-male sexuality.

Another mechanism by which stigma against male-male sexuality advanced during the Meiji period was vocabulary drawn from Western medicine. Among these were *sei* ("sex"), *seiyoku* ("sexual desire"), and *hentai*, or ("abnormal," "strange," "unusual"—and, later, "queer"). This stigmatization continued into the Taishō period (1912–1926)—as we're about to see, the term *hentai* was introduced through retranslation of the title of Krafft-Ebing's book in 1913 (*Hentai seiyoku shinri* [Psychology of Abnormal Desire]). Mark McLelland writes that "from the end of the Meiji period discussions of 'perverse' or 'queer' desire (*hentai seiyoku*) . . . began to circulate in popular magazines that advocated the improvement of public morals in pursuit of 'civilization and enlightenment'" and was "discussed in the early years of the Taishō . . . period via popular sexology works such as Habuto Eiji and Sawada Junjirō's best-selling *Hentai seiyokuron*."[48]

Compared to the publishing boom of the Edo period, the size of the Meiji boom completely eclipsed its earlier counterpart, with the establishment of publishing houses, newspapers, and magazines, and with the increasing popularity of novels. Some of these novels met a continuing (though more covert) public interest in *nanshoku* (male-male desire) by evoking it as a phenomenon that was safely in the past. Keith Vincent has written that "male-male sexuality was relegated to and simultaneously preserved within the past, both on the level of national history and on the level of the individual."[49]

---

48. Mark McLelland, "A Short History of '*Hentai*'," *Intersections: Gender, History, and Culture in the Asian Context* 12 (January 2006), 4.

49. J. Keith Vincent, *Two-Timing Modernity: Homosocial Narrative in Modern Japanese Fiction* (Cambridge: Harvard University Press, 2012), 24.

However—echoing Taniguchi Hiroyuki—scholar and queer theorist Eve Kosofsky Sedgwick reminds us that though attitudes and policies may change, they also remain the same. In *Epistemology of the Closet*, Sedgwick argues that both the past and the present state of acceptance/nonacceptance of male-male sexuality in any culture "comprises . . . a space of overlapping, contradictory, and conflictual definitional forces."[50] Meiji-era attempts to eliminate centuries-old acceptance of male-male sexuality were only partially successful.

One particular novel of the Meiji period demonstrates how fraught the topic of male-male sexuality became. *Vita sexualis*, by the famous medical doctor/novelist Mori Ōgai (1862–1922), who had studied medicine in Germany, was banned a month after its 1909 publication as being "dangerous to public morals,"[51] although it had already been widely circulated. Ōgai's title echoes the title of Krafft-Ebing's book *Psychopathia Sexualis*, and the novel itself describes same-sex relations using the words *nanshoku* and *Urning*. Japanese readers were well acquainted with *nanshoku*, but *Urning* was new, a word invented by Karl Ulrichs to designate a male homosexual. By juxtaposing these two words, Ōgai reminded readers of a familiar concept in relationship to a modern concept. The novel concerned itself with two different types of college-age men, *kōha* ("queers") and *nanpa* ("mashers"):

> When I consider the question of sexual desire, my fellow students in those days consisted of the mashers, who were dandies and affected the elegance of dress and manner, and the queers, who were more manly and casual in their dress. The mashers belonged to that group which enjoyed looking at those strange drawings I've already mentioned. . . . The queers never looked at those books. The one thing they could hardly wait to devour, each waiting his turn, was a handwritten manuscript about a boy named Sangoro Hirata.[52] It was said that at private schools in Kagoshima, this story was to be the very first one read on the first day of the new year. It described the history of a love affair between Sangoro, who wore his hair in bangs, and an older man, his hair in the forelock style, shaved except for a small portion above each ear. It was about their jealousy and rivalry in love.[53]

---

50. Eve Kosofsky Sedgwick, *Epistemology of the Closet* (Berkeley: University of California Press, 1990), 45.

51. Donald Keene, *Dawn to the West: A History of Japanese Literature* (New York: Columbia University Press, 1999), 357.

52. For more on Sangorō Hirata, see Yamada Bimyō's poem in chapter 1.

53. Mori Ōgai, *Vita Sexualis*, trans. Sanford Goldstein and Kazuji Ninomiya (Rutland,

In this passage, Ōgai alludes to a late-sixteenth-century story about a love affair between two samurai (one older, one younger) from Kagoshima, an area of Japan long associated with male-male relations. (Yamada Bimyō's poem about this relationship is the first entry in this anthology.) Ōgai's entire discourse on this topic was unacceptable to Meiji authorities, which is why the novel was banned.

The rapid modernization of Japan's military was another important aspect of the Meiji era, catching the international community off guard. Within thirty to forty years after the Meiji Restoration, Japan engaged in and won wars against two nations with well-established militaries, China (1894–1895) and Russia (1904–1905). The military created and sustained yet another all-male environment in Japanese culture, and in *Vita sexualis* Ōgai describes the atmosphere in dormitories as being sexually charged. Gregory Pflugfelder writes, "It was widely acknowledged that male-male erotic practices were common in barracks life" and "the imperial navy . . . had by the early twentieth century earned a reputation as a breeding ground for 'same-sex love'."[54]

It may be helpful to draw a distinction between homosociality and explicit male-male desire: it was perhaps inevitable that in Japan, where genders were largely separated, homosocial atmospheres would result. In fact, several texts in the first half of this anthology may seem more emblematic of homosociality,[55] including "The Historian" (chapter 2) by Nishimura Suimu, and "The Whistle" (chapter 4) by Orikuchi Shinobu.

The Taishō period began in 1912, after the death of Emperor Meiji. The 1913 retranslation of Krafft-Ebing's *Psychopathia Sexualis*—with a completely new title, *Hentai seiyoku shinri*, (Psychology of Abnormal Desire)—caused its ideas and terminology to again become part of the discourse about male-male sexuality. The first time Krafft-Ebing's book was published in Japan, the discourse was focused on the morality of same-sex desire. The second time around, the focus was on a desire to understand *why* same-sex desire existed, and the conclusion drawn was that it was a medical abnormality.[56]

VT: Charles E. Tuttle Company, 1972), 62–63. Pages 61–66 provide more description on "queers" and "mashers."

54. Pflugfelder, *Cartographies of Desire,* 284.

55. The definition of "homosocial" depends on the text in which it is found, but according to Eve Kosofsky Sedgwick, "in any erotic rivalry, the bond that links the two rivals is as intense and potent as the bond that links either of the rivals to the beloved: that the bonds of 'rivalry' and 'love,' differently as they are experienced, are equally powerful and in many senses equivalent." Sedgwick, *Between Men: English Literature and Male Homosocial Desire* (New York: Columbia University Press, 1985), 21.

56. Around 1920, the terms *dōsei* (same-sex) and *dōseiai* (same-sex love) appeared.

If same-sex desire is a disease, then it might be cured. As Greg Pflug-felder explains, with "recuperative therapy" (*setsuyō ryōhō*) a subject might be "expected to regain a 'healthy' erotic desire by maintaining a regimen of moderate exercise, bland food, relaxation, change of scenery, and avoiding venues, such as schools or concerts where members of his own sex congregated."[57]

An early-twentieth-century phrase related to male-male desire was *ero, guro, nansensu*. Short for "the erotic" (*ero*), "the grotesque" (*guro*), and "the nonsensical" (*nansensu*), these terms were sometimes used together or separately in various kinds of writing, both popular and formal, to indicate anything out of the ordinary. Greg Pflugfelder writes:

> The celebration of the "erotic" in its myriad forms constituted a rejection of the Meiji dictum that sexuality was unsuited for public display or representation unless it conformed to the narrow standards of "civilized morality." The elevation of the "grotesque" betrayed a similar disregard for prevailing esthetic codes, with their focus on traditional canons of beauty and concealment of the seamier sides of existence. Finally, the valorization of the "nonsensical" signaled a discontent with the constraining nature of received moral and epistemological certitudes.[58]

Another term that developed out of *ero, guro, nansensu* was *ryōki*, "hunting for the curious or strange";[59] magazines such as *Ryōki gahō* (Curiosity-Hunting Pictorial) supplied interested readers with "full photos of the 'erotic and grotesque!!"[60]

As we move into the later Shōwa period, Mishima Yukio (1925–1970) is represented pseudonymously in this anthology by the short story "Worse for Love" (chapter 9), and it may be helpful to address here how Mishima represents homosexuality in his much more famous novel *Confessions of a Mask* (Kamen no kokuhaku, 1949).

---

57. Pflugfelder, *Cartographies of Desire*, 274.

58. Pflugfelder, *Cartographies of Desire*, 290.

59. One of the places such "hunting" took place was in the male-male cruising areas in Asakusa Park, where "it was common knowledge that men could purchase the services of effeminate male prostitutes (*kagema*) after eight P.M." Jeffrey Angles, *Writing the Love of Boys: Origins of Bishōnen Culture in Modernist Japanese Literature* (Minneapolis: University of Minnesota Press, 2011), 118.

60. Angles, *Writing the Love of Boys*, 113.

As we've seen, Japanese discourse since the late nineteenth century had gradually reached the conclusion that male-male desire was a medico-scientific condition, possibly amenable to treatment. Aligning with this idea, Mishima identified the inability of the protagonist to advance to heterosexual relationships as due to an unspecified psychological obstruction. As Keith Vincent puts it, "*Confessions* manages to straddle two very different moments in the history of homosexuality in Japan: one in which male-male sexuality has not yet been cordoned off as a separate and distinct identity, and one in which the homosocial continuum has ruptured for good along the homo-hetero divide."[61]

It would be several decades before a positive view of same-sex sexuality—on the part of same-sex-loving people, at least—would begin to emerge in Japan.

Late Shōwa Period (1945–1989) and Heisei Period (1989–2019)

According to Mark McLelland there was (another) "boom in erotic publications"[62] between the end of the war and 1955, three years after the Occupation ended. This boom was characterized by *kasutori* culture (*kasutori bunka*). This metaphor, derived from the term for the lees of saké left behind after the distilling process, refers to the huge segment of the culture left behind due to the shocks and deprivations of the war and its aftermath. Dower describes this period, writing, "the denizens of kasutori culture . . . exhibited an ardor and vitality that conveyed a strong impression of liberation from authority and dogma."[63] The literary expression of *kasutori* was a genre called "carnal literature" (*nikutai bungaku*), cheap novels written in a lower-class vernacular. This period also saw an outpouring of magazines sometimes called the "perverse press."[64] These featured discussions of homosexuality, sadomasochism, transsexualism, and other kinds of minority sexualities. "Sex-customs" (*fūzoku*) magazines such as *Ningen tankyū* (Human Research, 1950–1953), *Amatoria* (1951–1955), *Fūzoku kagaku* (Sex-Customs Science, 1953–1955), *Fūzoku zōshi* (Sex-Customs Storybook, 1953–1955), *Ura mado* (Rear Window, 1956–1965), and *Fūzoku kitan* (Strange Talk about Sex

---

61. Vincent, *Two-Timing Modernity*, 180.

62. Mark McLelland, *Queer Japan from the Pacific War to the Internet Age* (Oxford, England: Rowman & Littlefield Publishers, 2005), 45.

63. John Dower, *Embracing Defeat: Japan in the Wake of World War II* (New York: W. W. Norton and Company, 1999), 36.

64. McLelland, *Queer Japan*, 66–72.

Customs, 1960–1974) were all popular from the 1950s to 1970s.[65] (In addition, some men had access to pamphlet-like magazines on "sex customs" as part of their memberships in male-only organizations.) These magazines opened public discourse to topics about sexuality that had been prohibited before the war.

Another "boom"—which McLelland described as "Japan's 'Original' Gay Boom"[66] (*gei būmu*)—occurred when the mainstream press began to give substantial coverage to the rapid proliferation of gay bars (*gei bā*) in Tokyo between 1957 and 1958, after an antiprostitution bill closed those establishments to women.[67] This boom was, according to a popular magazine at the time, *Shūkan taishū* (Weekly Popular Culture), "the best in the world."[68] It's hard to know how the editors reached this conclusion, but one result of the boom was the appearance of a new term: the *gei bōi* (gay boy). The *gei bōi* worked at *gei bā* (gay bars), and often became companions to American servicemen who came to Japan during the war and remained there after the Occupation (1945–1952). The *gei bōi* dressed fashionably, wore perfume, and were referred to as a "third sex" (*dai san no sei*),[69] though not all identified as homosexual.

Access to writing on same-sex topics expanded dramatically in 1971 with the publication of *Barazoku* (Rose Tribe), Japan's first commercial "homo" magazine.[70] Despite some initial setbacks, the magazine continued to publish for another thirty-seven years, and its influence on queer people throughout Japan cannot be overemphasized. Though its focus was on entertainment, the very fact of the magazine's existence was evidence of greater public vis-

---

65. McLelland, *Queer Japan*, 69.

66. McLelland, *Queer Japan*, 106–11.

67. Shinjuku Ni-chōmei, the area of Tokyo where most of the *gai bā* opened, is now the most popular gay district in Tokyo.

68. McMelland, *Queer Japan*, 108.

69. Many other terms developed out of this subculture: *danshoku aikōsha* (young Japanese partners of Western servicemen), *danshoku kissaten* (coffee shops), *sakaba* (drinking spots), *mama-san* (men who managed the *gei bā*), *onēsan* (another word for the *gei bōi* who worked at the *gei bā*), *danshō* (cross-dressing male prostitutes), *okama* (passive male homosexuals), *kyaku* ("customers," referring to male partners of *danshō* and *gei bōi*). See McLelland, *Queer Japan*, chapters 2 and 3.

70. Pflugfelder wrote about the Edo period (though the same could be said for the modern era): "The salience of male-male erotic behavior within Japanese cultural ontology is illustrated by the fact that literally hundreds of categories and signifiers have emerged around it in the native languages over the centuries." *Cartographies of Desire*, 4.

ibility of male-male desire.[71] *Barazoku* may be understood to have laid the groundwork for many other popular commercial *homo* magazines in the twentieth and twenty-first centuries, including *G-Men, Bádi, Samson,* and *Sabu.*

From the 1960s forward, openly queer authors begin to appear in Japan. One such, the extremely prolific Takahashi Mutsuo (1937–)—who had been personally mentored by Mishima Yukio—is represented in this anthology by "Sacred Headland" (chapter 10). Many of Takahashi's books take homosexuality as their major theme, and he is widely admired by the Japanese literary community.[72]

Other authors who were open about their sexuality during their lives include Kasugai Ken (1938–2004) (chapter 12) and Fukushima Jirō (1930–2006) (chapter 13) (also influenced and mentored by Mishima Yukio), as well as Tanaka Atsusuke (1961–) (chapter 14).

Simultaneous to these instances of greater openness and absence of self-censorship, one sees examples of continuing prejudice in Japan against queer topics, including the hostility of the Mishima estate regarding associating him with any context they would have deemed "homosexual." When Fukushima Jirō (who had been one of Mishima's lovers, according to his own testimony) published *Mishima Yukio: tsurugi to kanbeni* (Mishima Yukio: Sword and Cold Crimson, 1999), which included descriptions of their sexual relationship, the Mishima estate forced the publisher to withdraw the book.

Jeffrey Angles (translator of Tanaka Atsusuke's poems in this anthology) has written, "In Japan, far fewer people are eager to take on a self-identifying sexual identity at all. It is generally more common to hear one describing one's sexual feelings and activities in terms of emotion or sexual play than in terms of something associated with an outward, political, social, or subcultural identity. Until recently, there was relatively little use in Japan of identity-based language that implied a continuity between one's sexual preferences and one's subjectivity."[73] It may be said that in the public arena a

---

71. *Barazoku* was, to my knowledge, the only gay Japanese magazine or journal to review my first anthology of Japanese queer literature, *Partings at Dawn*, which covered the Heian (imperial court) era to the early Heisei period.

72. On a personal note—during the somewhat uncomfortable discussion at the International House of Japan event I referenced earlier, at which my husband and I advocated for greater legal codification of queer people's rights in Japan, a female audience member—a friend, she said, of Takahashi—argued that Takahashi's success was proof that there was no prejudice against queer people in Japan.

73. Jeffrey Angles, "Translating Queer in Japan: Affective Identification and Translation in

tension between confident self-revelation and a reluctance to self-identify characterizes Japanese society to the present day, though queer men do privately identify as such with one another, especially in the context of various websites.

In the early 1990s, Japan began to experience yet another "gay boom"— sometimes referred to as the "second" such boom, even though many smaller booms had occurred previously. (Some of this awareness most certainly arose as a result of the HIV/AIDS epidemic in Japan in the late 1980s.) In 1991, *Crea*, one of Japan's popular magazines, published a special issue titled "Gay Renaissance," that focused on aspects of gay public life in Japan, especially those having to do with bars and the appearance of an online queer culture. In 1992, Japan held its first gay and lesbian film festival. Also in 1992, directors Nakajima Takehiro and Matsuoka Jōji debuted their queer-themed films, *Okoge* (literally, "the hard rice that sticks to the bottom of the pot," a slang expression for "fag hag") and *Twinkle* (based on the novel *Kira kira hikaru* by Ekuni Kaori), respectively.

The year 1993 marked the debut of *Dōsōkai* (Reunion), one of Japan's most influential television dramas. The writer of *Dōsōkai*, Izawa Mann, said to me in a private conversation that he felt the drama was as influential (both to queer people and the general public) as the Stonewall Riots in the United States. *Dōsōkai* was the first program to make a sincere presentation (rather than as the butt of a joke) of a male main character who resembles many other Japanese "salarymen," but who eventually self-identifies as gay. This may be contrasted with the almost farcical tone of the seven-episode TV series *Ossan's Love* (2016), in which a story with queer aspects is played almost entirely for laughs.

In 1994, Japan's first "pride" parade was held in Tokyo, attracting a thousand participants, and pride parades have proliferated in Japan since then.

The second boom may be judged to have ended with Hashiguchi Ryōsuke's 2001 movie *Hush!*, marketed as "gay," and released internationally to widespread acclaim. However, year by year, queer topics and people continued to increase in visibility in Japan.

Fushimi Noriaki, one of the most outspoken queer activists in Japan, published the Bungei award–winning novel *Majo no musuko* (Daughter of a Witch) in 2003, and a year later his nonfiction book *Gei to iu keiken* (It's an Experience of What We Call "Gay") appeared.

---

the 'Gay Boom' of the 1990s," in *Multiple Translation Communities in Contemporary Japan*, ed. Beverly Curran, Nana Sato-Rosenberg, and Kikuko Tanabe (New York: Routledge), 106–7.

Ishikawa Taiga is the first openly queer person to be elected to Tokyo's Toshima Ward Assembly (2011), and then to the Upper House of the National Diet (2019). Previous to his entering politics, he published the nonfiction book, *Boku no kareshi wa doko?* (Where Is My Boyfriend?)[74] in 2002.

To describe newer developments in contemporary queer culture in Japan is beyond the purview of this introduction, as the situation on the ground is an extremely complex interaction between global (primarily Western, but also Asian) ideals of having queer rights codified into law—especially anti-discrimination and marriage-equality laws (as in Taiwan, for example)—and the Japanese relationship to those ideals, which can be characterized as partly resistant but still making progress in small pockets of the culture.

I began this introduction by saying that no anthology on any topic could be comprehensive or definitive. Perhaps the metaphor of the "core sample," drawn from geology, can be useful—as drilling down in different locations will always produce different results. My intent here has been to present a useful, interesting, and artistically important core sample of texts that speak to the queer experience in Japan between the nineteenth and twenty-first centuries.

Over the last millennium, Japanese attitudes toward queer topics have taken a curious, winding, sometimes fraught path—one that *might*, in the present day, find its way back to a place resembling where it began.

Left to their own devices, the Japanese regarded male-male love as a legitimate and widespread minority sexual expression with a long tradition—though always there was some ambivalence about how this phenomenon fit into whatever was felt to be the "main project" of the day.

After the forced opening of Japan to the West, and during the Meiji rush to modernize, queer topics began to be regarded as an antique holdover, a diversion of important resources, an embarrassment, an illness or imbalance, and even a crime. It may be debated whether the West is entirely responsible for this situation—the country was forced open, but after that, Japan's headlong adoption of Western values amounted almost to an enthusiastic intellectual "self-colonization."

But then the West, beginning in the twentieth century, after participating in pathologizing queerness in Japanese attitudes a century earlier, made an about-face in its own attitudes toward queerness, arguing for its legitimacy

---

74. Fushimi Noriaki, *Gei to iu keiken* (It's an Experience of What We Call "Gay") (Tokyo: Pot Publishing Co., 2004), and Ishikawa Taiga, *Boku no kareshi wa doko?* (Tokyo: Kodansha Publishing Co., 2002).

and for tolerance and even support for sexual minorities on society's part. Now Japan finds itself in the ironic position of being pressured by Western countries to liberalize its stance toward queer people. Japanese queer people themselves are not of one mind about what they want or need from society in the present day, or how they wish to identify.

It's certain, though, that through the enormous changes and traumas of the years this anthology represents, Japanese literary artists—whether they were criticized or celebrated for doing so—persisted in describing male love, erotics, and intimacy as they saw it. In doing so, they have left a moving record for us to consider, delight in, and learn from.

ONE

"A Portrait of Young Sangorō"
(Shōnen sugata) by Yamada Bimyō (1886)

Translated by Nicholas Albertson

Biography and Introduction

Yamada Taketarō (1868–1910)—commonly called by his pen name, Bimyō—
was born in the Kanda section of what was then Edo and is now Tokyo. He
was the oldest son of Yamada Yoshio, a samurai gentleman from the Nambu
Domain in northeastern Honshū. The family lost their samurai status with
the political reforms following the Meiji Restoration (1868), which dissolved
the feudal system of the Tokugawa shogunate, but Bimyō still received a
privileged education and trained with experts in Chinese and Japanese
poetry. In 1885, while studying at a college preparatory school, Bimyō joined
Ozaki Kōyō (1868–1903) and others in founding the Friends of the Inkstone
(*Ken'yūsha*) literary society. Bimyō's work was widely published in all the
leading magazines and newspapers in the late 1880s and 1890s.

Bimyō's influence on modern Japanese literary forms, though now
largely forgotten, was immense. In his prolific writings, he led efforts to
modernize poetry, inaugurated the genre of historical novels with works
such as "Musashi Plain" (*Musashino*, 1887) and "Butterfly" (*Kochō*, 1889),
and experimented with diction as part of a widespread effort to make literary
language reflect the way people actually spoke—the *genbun itchi* ("unifica-
tion of speech and writing") movement.

Although he was a literary pioneer, Bimyō also drew inspiration from
towering literary figures of the past. Foremost among them was the fiction
writer Takizawa Bakin (1767–1848), author of the epic *Eight Dog Chronicles*
(*Nansō Satomi hakkenden*, 1814–42). At one point early in his career, Bimyō

even used the pen name Bakin II. A second literary predecessor for Bimyō was the satirist and poet Ihara Saikaku (1642–1693). Like Bimyō, Saikaku wrote of the love affairs of men and women—including male-male love affairs, as in his *Great Mirror of Male Love* (*Nanshoku ōkagami*, 1687). Prior to the Meiji period (1868–1912), *nanshoku* or gay male sexual behavior was considered quite compatible with a samurai's or a monk's honorable image, and writers portrayed male-male romances without ascribing any shame or threat to the masculinity of their heroes. Their stories of loyalty and sacrifice, typically between a man of higher status and his younger lover, endeared such gallant, aestheticized young men to readers of all stripes. With the criminalization of homosexual acts in 1873, increasing censorship of male-male erotic themes, and the negative portrayal of same-sex attraction in important works such as Tsubouchi Shōyō's (1859–1935) novel *Character of Present-day Students* (*Tōsei shosei katagi*, 1885–86), compulsory heterosexuality took root in literary discourse.[1]

Yamada Bimyō's *Portraits of Youths in New-style Verse* (*Shintaishika shōnen sugata*, 1886), from which this selection is taken, seems to repudiate Shōyō's insistence on both heterosexual heroes and modern settings in literature. The work also offers us glimpses of Bimyō's early experiments with long-form poetry, his interest in dramatizing historical episodes, and his graceful and robust language. Each of the seven portraits in this eighty-page work begins with a prose introduction to its heroes, proceeds to a story in verse (alternating units of seven and five syllables, though not lineated), and finishes with a thirty-one-syllable envoy that abstracts the mood of the story.

"A Portrait of Young Sangorō" is set against the backdrop of a samurai rebellion in Kyūshū in 1599, not long before the great general Tokugawa Ieyasu (1543–1616) consolidated power in the Battle of Sekigahara (1600), thus beginning over 250 years of hereditary military rule. Although the Kyūshū skirmish itself was of minor historical importance, the story of how Hirata Sangorō Munetsugu and his lover, Yoshida Daizō Kiyoie, died defending the Shimazu domain from traitors became a beloved tale in the well-known work *Humble Ball of Yarn* (*Shizu no odamaki*, date and authorship unknown). Here, their supreme devotion to each other is expressed through metaphor and hyperbole, as though their relationship existed on a plane separate from all other romances.

---

1. See Gregory M. Pflugfelder, *Cartographies of Desire: Male-Male Sexuality in Japanese Discourse, 1600–1950* (Berkeley: University of California Press, 1999); Jim Reichert, "Tsubouchi Shōyō's 'Tōsei shosei katagi' and the Institutionalization of Exclusive Heterosexuality," *Harvard Journal of Asiatic Studies* 63, no. 1 (June 2003): 69–114.

A Portrait of Young Sangorō

Hirata Sangorō Munetsugu was the eldest son of Inspector Hirata Tarozaemon Masamune, regent to the Shimazu family of the Satsuma domain. Though hardly more than a child, he was devoted to the ways of both the brush and the sword, and he was possessed of a manly disposition. The swaggering Yoshida Daizō Kiyoie, another vassal of the Shimazu family, was also young, but his fame had already spread to neighboring domains. The two had similar temperaments, and eventually they came to act like brothers, sworn to live and die together and always inseparable. They strove in their studies and refined their martial skills. Then, around the fourth year of the Keichō era (1599), a man named Ijūin Genjirō, who had long held a grudge against the daimyō, barricaded himself inside the daimyō's castle, constructed twelve strongholds, and raised the flag of rebellion. Daizō and Sangorō went to battle together, and they attacked the most valuable of the twelve strongholds. No one knows how many casualties there were on the traitors' side. Daizō had by this point fought in a number of battles and was a seasoned fighter, but in the end he was bested. Sangorō's grief at seeing him die on the battlefield was unspeakable, and he charged into the enemy's ranks to meet his own death and thus fulfill their pledge to live and die together. Sangorō was fifteen years old, and Daizō was twenty-six.[2]

In this story, Sangorō's long lamentations after Daizō's death may not seem to fit his urgency to ride into battle. But my intention was to portray what he felt deep in his heart at that moment, and even to do that has made it a long work. Well, then, given that their story is not unique, I have probably wasted superfluous words for people who won't even care to look at it.

> At Takarabe Castle in Ōsumi
> Where our forces clashed with the barbarians,
> Fighting fearlessly and without faltering,
> How hair-raising were those sounds
> Of roaring rifles and battle cries!
> In every direction blanketing clouds

---

2. By the traditional method of counting, a person was age one at birth, and one year would be added at the beginning of each new year. Thus, Sangorō was closer to fourteen years old and Daizō was closer to twenty-five.

Of gunpowder mixed together with drifting
Dust kicked up from horses' hooves.
And though the sky was cloudy, too,
The swords glinted as if in cloudless
Sunlight, and the nimble warriors still
Did not retreat from their samurai path
Amid the hail of bullets
That flew before and behind their steps.
If I am crushed and die, farewell!
I repay you with this slice of my heart!
Though my catalpa bow should snap,
May my name still hit its mark!
Pressing ahead to do battle
Amid the danger of the melee,
Overcoming his fear and standing still,
Was beautiful young Sangorō—
Yes, it was Hirata Sangorō,
Who made the fateful moon ashamed
To show its face at dawn,
And frightened the white chrysanthemums
And colorful deutzia flowers, menacing
In armor, and upon his head
Disdaining to wear a helmet,
He sported a crisp, white headband,
And he rode in the shell-inlaid saddle
Of a six-year-old palomino.
What splendid and graceful attire!
And *What a lovely samurai figure!*
Both friend and foe admired.
But his loving blood-brother Daizō Kiyoie
Had just been surrounded by the enemy.
What would become of him? That was
The one thing weighing on Sangorō's heart,
As he searched in vain for a trace of him.
At that very moment Satō Taketani,
A foot soldier for Daizō,
Not knowing whether Sangorō
Would linger there dumbfounded,
Had raced back on the road into camp,

And with astonishing speed
He hurried to his side
And tugged at his shoulder.
Sangorō-sama? he began,
And at this Sangorō turned round.
Taketani, is that you? How brave!
But where did Lord Daizō . . . ?
He said, but when he looked more closely
At the load that Taketani shouldered,
He could see it was Daizō himself!
His whole body was torn to pieces,
Crimson blood spilled from his wounds,
His eyes were dark and his heart snuffed out.
Unable to restrain himself, Sangorō
Leapt down from his horse and held him tight,
And Taketani, beholding this,
Shed tears he could not hide and said,
Though it will cause you grief to hear,
He plunged deep into the enemy's ranks
Until he was completely surrounded.
He held them off for a long time,
But finally his luck ran out,
And having suffered grave wounds
There he met his tragic end!
As Sangorō listened to this report,
His grief surfaced as in a clear mirror,
While the moon in his heart clouded with tears.
In my place as a samurai in this world
That witnesses the battles of demons,
To grieve would be womanly—
But still, should I have no feelings at all?
These days and years, like a big brother
To a little brother you gave me affection
Even beyond the bonds of blood relations.
I think on it—was it a dream? An illusion?
All that endures in the world
Is change itself, they say.
But now, my brother, Master Daizō,
What has become of your fleeting form!

At that moment when you left our camp,
"Strike! Strike at the only glory
To be found in this world!"
Said a nameless soldier, his mind and body
All aflutter as he grabbed you
By the hand. "Don't die in vain!"
I know now the solemn pledge you made
When your hand clutched his, resigned
To what this world and the next might bring.
Though you have died in vain,
And now how wretched you look,
Your figure soaked with the tide of blood,
Our past shall yet live on in me
Until my body and this world snuff out.
Surprising for one who was not my kin,
The exceptional depths of your heart bound us
Like a dewdrop or a jeweled powder case—
We two stuck together like glue and lacquer—
We never once betrayed anger—
We were a rarity in this world.
That's what people said with a smile,
As we passed the years bound together.
Neither the pain of the buck's antlers in autumn
Nor the heartbreak of the monkey crying in a ravine
Could surpass my own grief.
Oh, that it has come to this, Master Daizō!
Though not born the same year,
Month, or day, nevertheless
We will die on the same year, month, and day,
As we have sworn to do.
Oh, what joy could there be, my knight,
In going that tragic way?
You should have had a long life
In this empty shell of a world of unbearable grief.
I shall follow you momentarily!
And so saying, he wept.
How poignant the hero's determination!
He composed himself so that
He wouldn't be laughed at after his death

And galloped away on his fast horse.
With unwavering nerve he struck into
The enemy ranks like rice stalks,
And he raced unfettered in all directions—
His heart was an arrow and his spirit a taut bow.
It was here that he had determined
To die in battle,
With peerless bravery belied by his beauty.
He did not remove the arrows that stuck in him.
He did not weaken though he was pierced through.
In spite of it all, this was the body of a youth—
Such was the zeal in his heart!
But soon, even the weary horse
That he rode was injured,
And when it suddenly collapsed,
Its master could no longer endure, and he fell.
Seeing their opening, the enemy soldiers
Pounced on him from above,
And alas, his armor was smashed to bits
By dozens of thrashing swords!
But the spray of blood that surged that eve
Glimmers on in the far-off grove.
The dreadful sound of the mountain temple bell:
Impermanence—with whom at twilight
Like a bird returning to its roost
Does it hasten to the underworld?
That was the end of Sangorō.
As I write it out, it gets more intense,
My brush falters and even the written page
Wells up with the traces of ink.
Look, then, at tonight's evening landscape.
All you hear is the pitiless sound of the flute.
And yet, as matchmaker for heartbreak,
The moon has come out in the sky,
And a cold gale blows in the treetops.

*This text was written on a bright moonlit night in the middle of
October 1885.*

Because of a vow
    not to disturb the dewdrop on a leaf tip
      the jewel of a pure heart can still be seen

TWO

"The Little Historian" (Shō rekishika) by Nishimura Suimu (1907)

Translated by Kristin Sivak and Chelsea Bernard

Biography and Introduction

Nishimura Suimu (西村酔夢) was born Nishimura Shinji (西村真次) in Ujiyamada (now Ise) in Mie prefecture in 1879. After returning from deployment in China during the Russo-Japanese war, Nishimura worked as a journalist for *Asahi Shimbun*, as well as for a variety of magazines, most notably the student magazine *Gakusei*. Better known for his wide-ranging work in history and cultural anthropology—and particularly nautical history—than for his fiction, Nishimura's tenure and work as a professor at Tōkyō Senmon Gakkō (now Waseda University), where he had earlier studied under the literary critic and author Tsubouchi Shōyō (1859–1935), became foundational to the study of Japanese and East Asian history and culture. He continued to lecture and publish prolifically on these subjects until his death in 1943.

The following story, "The Little Historian" (小歴史家), was published in 1907 in the June edition of *Bungei Kurabu* (Literary Club) (vol. 13, no. 6). It tells the story—somehow both darkly humorous and movingly tragic—of the relationship between a schoolteacher, his wife, and his most promising and captivating student. The student, seventeen-year-old Kasai Sumio, sometimes referred to by his surname Kasai and at other times more casually by his given name, "Sumio," is described as beautiful, bright, and precocious in his knowledge and understanding of Japanese history. The teacher, referred to only by his surname, Mitsuya, is for his part admittedly obsessive in his devotion to the study of history, and thus attributes his fascination with Kasai to the boy's own youthful enthusiasm for and prodigious mastery of his beloved subject. Nevertheless, it becomes increasingly unclear whether Sumio's historical prowess is truly the driving force behind Mitsuya's affection, or just a convenient proxy for it.

Mitsuya perceives his master-student mentorship of Kasai as both perfectly innocent and blissfully fulfilling, but this idyll is shattered when he learns that his friend and coworker Teshigahara, also referred to only by his surname, has been suggesting to Mitsuya's wife, who also lacks a given name in the text, that the relationship between her husband and the young boy might go far beyond the academic. Coincidentally, even as he struggles with Teshigahara's insinuations and accusations, Mitsuya himself begins to fear that the relationship between his young pupil and his wife has become far more significant than he had previously imagined.

The drama unfolds thus on the threshold of competing institutions of sexual desire and domestic dispute. Mitsuya insists that his feelings constitute a wholesome and genuine concern for Sumio's future as he attempts to navigate the demands of a committed and respectable modern heterosexual marriage. This task, however, becomes increasingly difficult for Mitsuya as he also finds himself forced to confront the haunting, nagging specter of Teshigahara's reminder that the love of men and boys can neither be relegated to the past nor banished to the lawless realm of Teshigahara's native Satsuma—a place that by the time of the story's telling had become closely associated with its earlier embrace of romantically and sexually charged mentorships between men of the samurai class.

"The Little Historian" has a twist and a surprise for every one of its colorful cast of characters as Mitsuya, whose own retrospective narrative frames the story, both reflects on and deflects the ironies and tragedies of events as they unfolded, even as these events find a way of speaking for themselves. In the end, the reader is left with a highly memorable tale that pits differing ideologies and conceptualizations of domesticity, history, and sexuality in the Meiji period (1868–1912) against one another as vividly as it depicts the conflicts between its remarkable characters.

The Little Historian

I.

It happened when I was a secondary school teacher.

Kasai Sumio was one of my students, among the top of his fourth-year class. He was a good-looking boy around the age of seventeen—

pale-faced, but with thick eyebrows and piercing eyes, and always sharply dressed in a crisp uniform. He would occasionally visit me at home and grew close to my wife as well, until one of my male colleagues, a teacher of classical literary Japanese from Kagoshima, visited my wife while I was away and whipped up some ridiculous story about Sumio and me. That's when she started regarding our relationship with suspicion.

I had gone, on a whim, to Mt. Iwadono in Kōshū, and when I returned home four days later, my wife pounced.

"Where have you been? Can't you imagine what I was thinking?"

"What do you mean?" There was a fierce look in her eyes. *Oh, she's jealous!* I thought. *She thinks I've been off fooling around somewhere!* I softened my tone. "I was in Kōshū—just Kōshū."

"Kōshū?" She regarded me with disbelief. "What did you go there for?"

"Well, I was at Mt. Iwadono, so I went to see the statue of Takeda Katsuyori."

"A likely story! I know exactly what you've been up to . . ." She faltered, peering at me, her eyes full of distrust.

"Oh, and what exactly is that?"

"You've been off somewhere fooling around with Kasai-san!"

"No, I was in Kōshū—alone! Why would I take Kasai with me? No wonder you're so bent out of shape, imagining nonsense like that." I burst into laughter at the sheer absurdity of it.

"But that's what I heard! That you two went off to fool around together." She grew even more serious.

"That's ridiculous! You think I have that kind of time? You of all people should know how serious I am about my historical research."

"Well, yes, I know that, but . . ."

"But what?"

"Well, my dear, Teshigahara-san came by yesterday and informed me: 'your husband is off in the mountains fooling around with Kasai'."

"Well, that's completely unfounded! That's just some kind of silly conspiracy theory. The real problem is that you'd believe such ridiculous gossip! Ha, ha, ha!"

She glowered at me and said, "Oh, but what more proof do I need than Kasai-san's absence from school?"

"He's been absent?" This was a surprise to me. "He must have gotten sick or into some kind of accident."

"You certainly know how to talk your way out of something."

"If you're so suspicious, why don't you ask Kasai-san yourself? He won't know what you're talking about."

"Of course he'll say that—you're in on it together!"

"Don't be stupid!" I found myself snapping at her. But if she was that deeply suspicious, there was no use trying to vindicate myself, not after she had already whipped herself up into a frenzy with her misunderstanding and jealousy and lost the ability to think clearly. So I held my tongue and refrained from further argument.

I resolved, however, to demand an explanation from Teshigahara when I saw him at school the next day since it was he who had planted those ideas in my wife's head. It's not right to go stirring up trouble in other people's homes. *That guy's shameless even for a man from Satsuma,* I thought.

That night I fell asleep to the sight of my wife's sour expression, and she was just as sulky the following morning.

I had to wonder if my wife, who on the average day was so good-natured, often going to such great lengths to please me as to be overindulgent, had somehow grown less fond of me, given her uncharacteristically angry and jealous behavior toward me over the past month, and particularly since the previous night.

I tucked the books I would need for the lecture that day under my arm, *The History of the East* and *The History of the West,* as well as two or three other reference volumes, and headed toward the front entryway where my wife saw me off with her sour look.

"When I see Teshigahara-kun at school today, I'm going to tell him all about what happened last night and give him a piece of my mind. You okay with that?"

"Yes, that's fine. I know he was telling the truth."

"Okay, well I'm going to let him know just how much trouble he's caused with his stupid lies."

"But those 'stupid lies' happen to be the truth."

"I really can't stand that you keep saying that."

"Well, then you'll have to prove to me somehow that nothing is going on between you two."

"That's exactly what I'm going to do."

"All you have to do is prove it to me, and I won't mention this nonsense again."

"All I have to do is prove it to you? Easy enough." I left the house.

My wife had always been mercurial and deeply emotional, as if she became a different person depending on the time and place, like fire whenever she got heated up, and like ice water at her coldest. Meanwhile I, for my part, had gone and become a historian and gotten stuck in my ways, so much so that even our unyielding school principal would tease me for being stubborn. So it's no wonder our marriage was rocky. We weren't as bad as oil and water, though there was always a slight distance between us. But even assuming he didn't know about our marital problems, why would Teshigahara go shooting his mouth off like that? Maybe he was the one lusting after Sumio. *No, that would be absurd*, I thought, *and at any rate I'm going to confront him when I see him today and get an apology out of him.* I turned all of this over in my mind as I trudged my way to the school.

2.

I caught sight of Teshigahara as soon as I passed through the gates to campus. *Now isn't the time*, I thought, and decided to wait to confront him until after classes. Despite my unease, I managed to plow through my lecture with vigor.

Three o'clock came around, and those so-called teachers who treat lecturing as some sort of intellectual prostitution beelined for home as soon as the bell rang, as usual. I myself generally made a habit of staying behind and searching the library for reference materials for the next day's lessons, though that day I was going to try and catch Teshigahara and have a little chat with him, so I took up a seat in the teacher's lounge. Most of my colleagues had already gone home, my sole remaining companion leafing through the *Kogetsushō* commentary on *The Tale of Genji*, reading over this and that with a puzzled expression on his face.

It was early spring, the sun radiating a pleasant warmth that spread across my back while I lost myself in thought, and it wasn't long before I was spread out on the table, sleeping. Well, I say sleeping, but I was actually waking up every few minutes, falling in and out of consciousness, treading the line between dreams and reality, when I suddenly heard my name spoken at my ear.

"Mitsuya-kun."

And there, when I lifted my head, was Teshigahara standing at my side.

"Ah, well that felt nice."

"Wanna head home now? It's four, you know."

"Four?" Just as I glanced up at the clock, it struck four.

"Come on, let's go." Teshigahara repeated.

"Oh, but wait—I'd like to have a word with you first." It tumbled right out of me.

"About what?"

"About Kasai."

"Oh, you mean your boy?"

"That 'boy' nonsense is shameful. You need to start taking some things seriously, you know. No one fit to call themselves a secondary school teacher should even be talking about having 'boys'!" I raised my voice in anger.

"What are you so concerned about? I'm completely fine with it." Teshigahara sounded surprised.

"And this is why I say that you have no sense of dignity."

"Why?"

"Why? That shouldn't require any explanation, but it's beside the point. I hear that you visited my home recently."

"Yeah, I did."

"And when you did, you said some shameful things to my wife, didn't you?"

"Whoa, I have no idea what you're even talking about."

"But you've been talking to my wife lately, haven't you? Didn't you pay her a visit the other day to tell her that there's something fishy going on between me and Kasai?" Having thus broached the topic, I recounted the events of the previous night and reproached my friend for his thoughtlessness.

Teshigahara, however, looked unconcerned. "Okay, so I did. I did say that."

"Well, can't you see how it might cause problems to go running your mouth off like that?"

"But there's probably no avoiding it given that I was just telling her the truth."

"You idiot, how could something so stupid possibly be true?"

"But everyone's talking about it, saying that there's something abnormal about the relationship between you and Kasai."

"Unbelievable. Even silly rumors can go too far, you know. This is just too much . . ."

"So you don't think it's odd that you and Kasai are so close?" My friend fixed his eyes on me, staring into my face as if to see straight into my heart.

"Oh, but there's a good reason for that." I stared back at him and said, with utmost seriousness, "And I don't know anything about that 'boy' stuff. I should think the place you come from has the monopoly on that. Only Satsuma men understand the appeal of that sort of thing."

"Ha, ha, ha! I wasn't expecting that! Well, you've cut right to the chase now, haven't you? Be that as it may, how on earth did you and that boy end up growing so close to each other?"

"I'll tell you how. There's a bit of a history there."

And so I began to describe in detail the course of my relationship with Kasai, from the very beginning up until that day.

This is what I told him:

About five or six years ago, I was on my way home from Ueno Park one spring evening when I saw this beautiful boy. He was fair-skinned, tall and slim, his eyes glittering like stars, his whole look giving off an intellectual aura—it stirred something deep inside me. This boy was somehow different from ordinary children. Whether it was the sparkle in his eyes, or the tight set of his lips, an air of genius lingered about his beautiful face. I found myself feeling unbearably wistful, thinking about how this child would impact the future of the world. So I followed him until he entered a gated home atop Masagozaka. The nameplate, written in bold brush strokes on zelkova wood, read "Kasai Nobukatsu." I searched my memory, having an inkling that I had heard this name before, when I realized that Nobukatsu must be the younger brother of Professor Kasai, a known authority on Japanese history.

I was living on a backstreet in Yumi-chō at the time, and when I went to the neighborhood Taka-no-yu bathhouse the very next day, I saw the same boy talking loudly about something with another boy as they took turns washing each other's backs. My heart leapt at the thought that meeting him there was a sign that the gods were bringing us together.

As I soaked in the warm bath and listened to their conversation, I got the sense that the two of them were friends from school. The subject was the battle between the old provinces of Echigo and Kai, and Sumio waxed enthusiastically about the warlord Kenshin's character.

"But Shingen was a great man, too, you know? I mean, he was about to be struck down by Kenshin at Kawanakajima when he parried

Kenshin's sword with an iron fan." The other boy stilled his hand, pausing his washing, and looked at Sumio.

"Well, he was a military commander. That kind of thing comes with the territory." Sumio thought for a moment, dipping his washcloth in a wooden bucket filled with water. "What I'm really trying to say is that Kenshin was the greater man because of that time he sent Shingen salt."

"But it was just salt! How cheap can you get? There's nothing impressive about sending someone salt. I mean, even I could go ahead and send you some salt."

"And that's where you're wrong, Mikami-san. You just don't understand the value of salt." Sumio lifted his glittering eyes and trained them on his companion.

"Sure I do. I know how important salt is." Mikami pouted.

"Well, then hear me out. Kai was a province in the mountains, so there was no ocean, right? You can't get salt if there's no ocean. And Echigo was by the sea, so they could haul in plenty of salt. So that's why Kenshin sent Shingen salt."

"But he only sent salt because he had heaps of it. If Shingen had any extra salt, I'm sure he would have sent it to Kenshin."

"But at the time there wasn't enough salt in Kōshū, and that was a huge problem for Shingen. Kenshin caught wind of that and sent salt because he took pity on Shingen, and that's why he's a great man."

"I guess . . ."

"That's what I think. Shingen was his enemy, but it was just too pitiful to see him struggling just because the province didn't have enough salt. He was fighting Shingen on the battlefield, not over salt. So Kenshin figured he had to send Shingen enough salt so that Shingen wouldn't be troubled over rations for his men—that way they could take to the battlefield and see who was truly the stronger one. Now there's a real man for you."

"Okay, so Kenshin was a great man, too." Mikami made this small concession.

"You better believe it. Ten times better than Shingen." Sumio shot back, gloating.

Just then a drunk came in and broke into a loud rendition of a kabuki song. The boys' conversation ended abruptly. And I, having grown slightly dizzy from steaming in the hot water, soon left the bath. But I had taken quite a liking to Sumio, and although I tried, I couldn't put him out of my mind.

The two boys had taken off in the meantime. I too left the bath-house and returned home. After that incident, I saw Sumio on the street five or six times. And no fewer than four or five times over the course of a day, he would appear in my mind's eye, clad in a tight-sleeved, navy blue and white-speckled kimono with rib-knit trousers and wearing a French cap with an insignia.

But then I moved to Koishigawa and no longer had occasion to catch sight of the dear boy, although I did occasionally linger in front of his home, hoping that I just might see him.

Four or five years passed in a daze. I met the woman who would become my wife and managed to get a job teaching at the school. But I was in for a real surprise when I stepped up to the lectern. There he was, Sumio, leaning against a desk in the front row and gazing at me intently. He was in his third year by then, but this was the first time that we had the chance to speak to one another, and in that moment I realized that just as I had been yearning for him all this time, he too remembered me, and something in my heart told me that some incredible fate linked the two of us together.

"And that was how I came to be acquainted with Sumio. After that, he would come to visit me every now and then, so naturally I grew extremely fond of him." I brought my story to an end.

"I see." Teshigahara nodded.

"So you see, there's nothing unseemly going on between the two of us, and certainly not in the way you were thinking. I've always hated this stuff about pretty boys. Such an unnatural, exceedingly immoral thing has no place in this world."

"Hmm, I suppose," was Teshigahara's unenthusiastic reply.

"And all this about what's going on with Sumio all comes down to your misunderstanding, and as you know my wife is an extremely emotional person, so it's been a big problem for me—she's been angry and coming down hard on me ever since you told her all that when, if anyone's at fault here, it's you."

"Geez, well, I'm really sorry." Teshigahara interjected.

"Then I'd like you to come to my house and tell my wife that you retract everything that you said. Are you free tonight by any chance?"

"Tonight?"

"Yes, tonight."

"Oh, um . . ." Teshigahara thought for bit. "Okay, I'll make it work. This is my fault, after all."

"All you have to do is take it back—then we can put all of this behind us. So please, just spare me a little time this evening."

"All right, I understand. I'll come tonight."

"Please do."

Having reached an understanding, I parted ways with Teshigahara and arrived home to find that my wife was fuming, once again. Puzzled as to why, I asked what was wrong and she told me that Sumio had come over to visit just a little while ago. It just was just all too ridiculous for me to even respond, so I went to my study and began looking over *The History of the West* just as the sun was beginning to set.

3.

Teshigahara arrived shortly after my wife and I finished dinner. I was showing him in and offering him refreshments when my wife appeared, having finished her business in the kitchen.

"I apologize for not being a more generous host when you visited the other day. It's so kind of you to visit again this evening." My wife placed both hands on the floor and bowed deeply.

"No, I'm the one who should be sorry. But maybe you can make it up to me today?" Teshigahara spoke playfully as he stared fixedly at my wife, her eyes downcast. "How about you get us something to eat, hmm?" My friend asked, tilting his head as he looked at her.

"Oh yes, of course." She finally lifted her head. "What would you like?"

"I'd be happy with anything. Treat us to whatever you like." He paused, and shifted in his seat to turn toward her. "The truth is, I came here to apologize."

"To apologize? What for?" My wife looked at Teshigahara with a puzzled expression. "I really don't know what you could be talking about."

"Well, it's nothing really, but, um, you know all those things I told you when I came to see you the other day, while Mitsuya-kun was in Kōshū? I'd like to completely retract everything that I said."

"And just what did you tell me then?"

"About the relationship between Mitsuya-kun and Kasai—it was all just groundless conjecture on my part. And it seems as if I've caused you a great deal of worry by saying such absurd things."

"Oh, so that's what you mean." My wife looked at me and said,

"You told Teshigahara-san about all that? My, I can't believe you sometimes."

"Well, look, when I pressed you about it, didn't you tell me you didn't care if I said something to him?"

"Even so, don't you think it's inappropriate to be making others listen to such nonsense?"

"Sure, but what else was I supposed to do with you being so combative?"

"Truly, I cannot believe you." She buried her chin in her collar and fell silent.

"Hey, look, this is all my fault. I don't think before I speak, so sometimes I go and say something uncalled for and end up stirring up trouble in other peoples' homes." Teshigahara was apologizing in earnest, his right hand nervously rubbing his closely cropped head.

"Oh, I'm sorry that I even said anything. Now I'm the one who's gone and caused you trouble."

"Ha, ha, no, no, really, I'm the one in the wrong here. I wish I had never even mentioned that particular flight of fancy. As a matter of fact, I was mostly joking when I said it, so I never thought that it would become a source of conflict between the two of you. But I've learned my lesson. I'll never tell another joke again from now on."

I found myself pitying him and couldn't help but cut in. "Well now, there'll be no need for that—I think we're all clear on the matter. It's my turn to apologize for making you so anxious about it."

"Why, it won't even cross my mind anymore, so please, Teshigahara-san, don't worry about it," my wife added.

"Oh, I'm not worried at all. I mean, I'll be satisfied as long as there's no more misunderstanding between you two. How about, as a way to celebrate your reconciliation, you bring us a little treat?" My unrelentingly vivacious friend replied, half-joking.

"Why yes, I will . . . But surely you have something for us as well?"

"Hey, don't be rude!" I hastily reprimanded her before realizing that she had been joking, which left me feeling a little self-conscious.

"He's so serious I don't know what to do with him. Teshigahara-san, could you please teach this man how to lighten up a little?"

"You have my word. I'll do everything in my power. And that's all the more reason for you to give us a real feast tonight."

"Yes, of course, only the finest of delicacies will do. And your contribution?"

"Oh, yes, I'd forgotten about that." Teshigahara produced a paper package from the breast of his kimono and handed it to my wife. "It's a rarity of greatest renown."

"My, my." She opened the package, and a small doll emerged from inside. "My, how adorable. Thank you so much."

"You know, I went all the way to my hometown to buy it in the hopes that it would bring the two of you closer together."

"Oh, really? Well, thank you very much."

I joined in, saying with utmost sincerity, "That's very kind of you. We're delighted to receive such a wonderful gift." I took the doll from my wife's hands. "Wow, this is nice, very well-crafted. This clothing is from the Tenpyō era, I see. And the hair is arranged in the Nara fashion. The coloring is excellent, too. But there's something strange about the skirt . . ."

"Ah yes, it's just like a historian to notice what's strange about it." Teshigahara was poking fun at me.

"But of course! My heart never strays from history."

"What a dedicated scholar." My friend flashed my wife a smile. "And I'm sure you enjoy history, as well?"

"I hate it."

"Is that so?"

"This one hates anything having to do with history—I'm constantly under attack."

When I said this, Teshigahara responded with his characteristically derisive smirk. "No two peoples' tastes are ever quite alike, are they?"

"That's right." My wife agreed.

Just then, the front door opened—it seemed the maid had returned. The soba we ordered had finally arrived, and the three of us sat in a circle and slurped down our buckwheat noodles. The conversation was momentarily put on hold.

Eventually we finished eating, and the conversation resumed. This time we discussed Kasai: everything from his demeanor to his appearance to his performance in school, his parents, his uncle the eminent historian. My wife listened silently throughout, only tilting her head occasionally, though she seemed to be listening intently.

Before long, Teshigahara headed home, leaving me and my wife sitting opposite one another. We had the maid close the storm shutters to the veranda and tidied up the room before warming our hands over the dying coals in the brazier.

"So just how old is that Sumio-san anyway?" My wife asked unexpectedly.

"I believe he's seventeen."

"Wow, seventeen . . . And he's doing quite well in school, yes?"

"Oh, it's hardly a matter of whether he's doing well or not. I've only been teaching him since his third year, but the principal says that Sumio has received the top score on every exam he's taken."

"My, what an impressive young man."

"Yes, he is . . . I think I'd like to have a kid like that."

"I'm sure." Seemingly impressed, my wife became lost in thought for a moment before adding, "I guess he's what you'd call a genius."

"That's right, he certainly is." I confirmed, looking to my wife. The light of the desk lamp shone on her face so that her eyes were strangely bright, and there was a beautiful glow about her forehead.

"How marvelous." My wife sniffed and looked up at me, but the moment our eyes locked, hers darted upwards and then hastily to the side.

"Any parent would be lucky to have a kid like that," I idly offered.

"Absolutely. And any wife would be lucky to have such a fine man for a husband."

"I agree."

"I really wonder who he'll marry. Of course there's no telling now, but whoever he makes his wife will be one lucky woman."

Hearing her say this bothered me for some reason . . . The truth is, my wife spoke in that moment with a kind of tremble in her voice, her words seeming to surge up from deep, deep down in her heart, as if she had been seized by a vision or intoxicated by a dream.

I stayed quiet, and my wife also refrained from speaking again. We sat silently in front of the lamp, huddled around the now-cold brazier. It all felt indescribably desolate, as if it weren't a spring evening at all but rather a winter day, with the cold wind raging through the dying trees. This was a desolation like nothing I had ever experienced, a feeling exactly as though a sharp blade had been thrust into my chest. In all honesty, I have not once felt such disquiet as I did on that evening.

4.

Sumio came to visit the next day, after evening set in. When I asked him why he'd missed class the other day, he explained that he had come down with the flu. Hearing this further cleared up my wife's suspicions, and she was all smiles after Sumio went home.

Although Sumio's penchant for history became more and more pronounced, and his knowledge of the subject only continued to grow, he didn't do very well on his summer term tests, maybe because he had been busy reading too many reference volumes. And besides, the questions the history department writes are so cleverly worded that they could make even someone with a degree in the field doubt his knowledge . . . At any rate, Sumio had a particular talent for making penetrating historical insights, and his critiques never missed the mark— astonishing not only myself, but the other teachers as well.

In this way, my admiration for Sumio grew stronger by the day. On occasions when he would visit, we would debate about the character of famous figures in history, the likes of Nitta Yoshisada and Ashikaga Takauji. I would often teach him, and he was very engaged, showing an unparalleled interest in what I had to share. Sometimes my wife would join us, and we would discuss female writers of the Heian period or the like. She, too, was deeply surprised and moved by the sophisticated manner in which Sumio spoke for a boy of seventeen, and came to greatly respect him . . . She entertained our guest not just as a star student, but as a true genius, as a future historian. Sumio grew close to her as well, coming to visit her just to chat even when I wasn't at home. Soon, he came to seem no longer like my mentee at all, but rather more like a nephew or a cousin.

Despite this intimacy, Sumio continued to respectfully call me "Sensei" as he always had, even as I was already calling him by his first name and treating him like a little brother. He reminded me, in fact, of my nephew who had passed away. Occasionally we'd go out on walks together, or maybe visit the library, and sometimes he'd join us at the table for dinner to enjoy some of my wife's cooking, after which we'd end up maybe arm wrestling or playing a board game like *go*. But Sumio had erected a wall between us and didn't demonstrate either the intimacy one has with an older brother or the affection one feels toward an uncle, leaving me feeling like something was lacking. The other strange thing was that, for all his lack of intimacy toward me, he was extremely open with my wife, and had grown accustomed to calling her "sister."

"Why do you call my wife 'sister'?" I had asked.

He replied, "I know it's presumptuous, but I only call her that because we're so close."

"Well, then why don't you call me 'brother'?"

"Because, Sensei, you're my *sensei*."

"But if it's a matter of closeness, doesn't that create a disparity between my wife and I?"

"Yes, I suppose it does . . ." Sumio seemed reluctant to say more.

"That's right, so I guess that means you're closer to my wife." I pressed.

"That's not it . . ." Sumio thought for a moment. "I was calling her Mrs. Mitsuya before, but then she asked me to start calling her 'sister' instead."

"Ha, ha, ha! Is that right? That's what she told you, huh?"

"Yes, she did."

"Well, then how about you start calling me 'brother' from now on?"

"But that seems kind of disrespectful . . ." Sumio flushed red as he spoke.

This was as deep as our relationship ever became. As a matter of fact, after the summer break, Sumio started visiting less often than he had in the past, and even when I saw him at school he often acted as if he didn't know me particularly well. I couldn't imagine that it was because he had actually turned his back on me, but perhaps he thought that his own knowledge of history had eclipsed mine and so there was no longer any need for him to listen to my lectures. Thinking along those lines put me extremely ill at ease, and then one day I returned home late from school and heard some ruckus coming from inside the house. Curious as to what in the world could be going on, I went inside and found my wife shutting the closet. Just as she was about to remove her hand from the door, she saw me. Her face blanched.

"My, you're certainly home early today."

"What do you mean, 'early'? I got home two hours later than usual."

"Oh my, really?" She heaved a sigh. "What were you doing there so late?"

"Reading my reference volumes, as usual."

"Well, aren't you a dedicated scholar!"

"You should know that by now . . . And what have you been up to today that's got you so flustered?"

"Me? I'm not flustered."

"But I heard some ruckus coming from in here, so what was that? What was all that noise about?" I doubled down on my questioning.

"Oh, that? Well, that was . . . I was putting things away."

"What things?"

"The futon."

"The futon? You'd laid out the futon in the middle of the day?"

"No . . ."

"Well, then what was going on?"

"I was hiding something."

"The futon?"

"No. Something you'll like!" She spoke emphatically, staring at me with a glint in her eyes.

Finally starting to relax, I pondered for a moment what it could possibly be, but I couldn't even begin to imagine. "Books?"

"No."

"Oh, I know. Rice cakes."

"No."

"Okay, a kimono then." I wondered if she'd sewn a kimono for me in secret.

"No, not something so lifeless." Her eyes lit up with a smile.

"Something alive then . . . So an animal?"

"Sure, it's an animal, a large one."

"Oh, I've got it. It's the cat from next door."

"No, think a higher order species."

"Okay, so a dog."

"No."

"Oh, I know! It's a goldfish."

"Not even close."

"In that case . . . I don't know. There's nothing else that you'd put in a closet."

"So you give up?"

"I give up."

"Okay, then I'll show you." My wife slid the door open. "Come on out."

Sumio appeared.

"Sumio-san?! You've got to be kidding me." I muttered this to myself as Sumio stood there red-faced and hanging his head.

My wife, being the emotional person that she was, was like something from hell when she was feeling low but impossibly good-natured and vivacious when she was in a good mood—she would go about her business with a pep in her step and a liveliness to her speech, and she was sometimes even inclined to enjoy pulling a prank such as this.

Sumio joined us for dinner that evening, staying at our house until past 9 o' clock, and nothing seemed particularly different from usual. The one thing that I didn't understand was why my wife had hidden Sumio in the closet. It had to be a prank, but if that was the case, then why was she so flustered to see me? And even if the reason for her face going pale was that she hadn't been expecting me to find her there, that didn't explain why Sumio had turned all red and hung his head like that . . . The more I thought about it, the more it seemed like there might be a reason for the way my wife had been behaving ever since that spring, for why Sumio had been acting so distant, and especially for the fact that my wife, who so rarely ventured outside, had been going out quite a bit lately. It was enough to make me wonder if this meant there was some chain linking the two of them. Once that thought occurred to me, I couldn't let it go. Suspicion begets monsters—as the saying goes—and I became convinced that there was something out of the ordinary going on between Sumio and my wife.

And then came the end of summer. My wife left the house one afternoon, saying that she was going to visit a friend, and I, unable to withstand the heat, headed to the botanical gardens. My intent was to wander through the dense cedar thickets and cypress groves, breathing in the cool, damp air, but when I passed through the western groves on my way to the Hikawa fields, I saw a man and a woman in the shade of the trees on the far side . . . and I was certain of it—it was Sumio and my wife.

Now *this* was strange. I took cover behind the larger trees out of their sight and managed to get maybe fifty feet or so away from them for a better look, when I realized that I was mistaken, that the two were not who I had thought they were.

"What the hell."

I swore in spite of myself. I was glad to know that what I had been imagining was in fact unfounded . . . but even afterward doubts lingered in my mind, and I wasn't able to trust my wife as I once had. And although I respected Sumio's rare gifts, I could no longer love him as deeply as if he were my own dear, lost nephew. No, I was even inclined to despise him, to find him detestable.

"That insolent, ungrateful little ass!" I burst out unconsciously before coming to my senses, realizing that this outburst was the first time I had ever directed such harsh words at Sumio. I had even come to rue just how deep, how insatiable, was my attachment to Sumio, the suspicion and jealousy he made me feel. And although I could logically conclude that I should trust the two of them and that nothing untoward was going on between them, emotionally speaking, the arrow of doubt that I had slung at them had plunged deep into my own heart and left a scar that refused to heal.

5.

"Mitsuya-kun."

I was about to pass through the school gates when someone called my name. I turned around. That evening, everything was cast in a gray pall, and the skies were threatening rain, striking in me a resounding chord of loneliness.

"Hmm?" I squeaked out a nervous reply, but no one was there. Thinking it must have been my imagination, I was going to pass on by when someone said again,

"Mitsuya-kun."

"Who's there?" I turned around again.

"It's me." Emerging from the shadows of the doorway was none other than Teshigahara.

"Geez, you startled me—must you always be so tedious?"

"You were so lost in thought that I figured I'd give you a bit of scare. I've been waiting here for a while."

"Quit fooling around." I started off at a brisk pace. My friend fell in beside me. The sky grew even more menacing.

"Actually, there's something I want to warn you about. That's why I was waiting for you." Teshigahara broke the silence.

"Oh, not more of your lies. Every time you open your mouth it puts me on edge, you know, wondering if you're going to pull my leg yet again."

"No, this is god's honest truth. I'm completely serious about what I'm going to tell you."

"And what would that be?" I asked, doing my best to contain the anxiety roaring in my chest.

"Well, it's just that . . . Don't get mad, okay? I'm offering this advice out of the goodness of my heart."

"I won't get mad, so just tell me. Because if there's anything I'm doing wrong, I'll make amends for it immediately."

"Okay, here goes then."

"Oh, just come out with it already."

"So, you're not the one at fault here . . . It's your wife."

"My wife?" My heart leapt with a pang.

"Err, yeah, your wife . . ."

"Is something the matter with her?"

"Well, it's not so much that there's something the matter really, but she's been going out frequently lately, hasn't she?"

"Going out? Yeah, she has."

"She has, she has. So that's it, that's what I wanted to talk to you about." After that he fell silent, and we walked quietly for a while before he said, "It's a little odd."

"What do you mean by 'odd'?"

"Well, it's just that she's often walking with that boy Kasai."

"With Kasai? You've seen them together a lot?"

"Well, I've only seen them twice now, but apparently other people have seen them a lot, too."

"I see. And so has anything shady happened?"

"I haven't heard that. But it does seem strange, you know, them spending all that time on walks together." Teshigahara kept glancing at me from the side.

I made an effort to appear calm, but my heart was hammering an irregular beat like an alarm bell, and just walking was making it hard to breathe. However, I steeled myself, knowing how unbearable it would be if he were to see through me. "Well, she does love Kasai, so I don't think there's anything strange about them walking together, but I suppose it's negatively affecting their reputation?"

"Well I don't know about that, but . . . see, I met with Kuroki the other day . . ."

"Kuroki?"

"Yeah, he's that English teacher at that bankrupt secondary school. The flamboyant one, with the flashy silver watch on the gold chain, his name's Kuroki. So when I met with him, he was saying something fishy was going on with your wife, that he saw her strolling through Hibiya Park and carrying on with an attractive young man, that's what he said."

"I see."

"And if it were only Kuroki who was saying it, I wouldn't put much stock in it, but again, I've seen them already twice now myself, walking around holding hands."

"Where? When?"

"Four or five days ago."

"Around what time?"

"The sun was about to set, so probably around six?"

"Hmm. And where was this?"

"Along the Edogawa River."

"Hmm." I fell deep into thought.

"I can hardly put into words how friendly they were with each other—they would let go of each other's hands whenever somebody would come by, and then start holding hands again as soon as the person was gone . . ." Even the normally outspoken Teshigahara, having reached this point, now hesitated. Maybe he was thinking that he had said too much.

"But that doesn't mean they have some dodgy relationship . . ."

"Well, I can't say without a doubt that it's one way or the other, but it's the kind of thing that you wouldn't want attracting attention, so I'm thinking you might want to say something to your wife."

"Thank you, I'll be sure to ask her about it."

"Of course. And it's not like I think anything's going on there. In other words, I'm saying this out of concern, you know, prevention is better than cure and all."

"Oh, yes, of course, that's very kind of you."

Before long, droplets of rain began to fall. The wind wailed over the roofs of the houses.

"So I hope you're not offended by anything I've said . . . I'm such an outspoken person that I just end up saying everything that pops into my head, so take it with a grain of salt."

"No, no, I don't think badly of you at all. I'm actually very grateful."

"Well, I hope so . . ." Teshigahara said as we reached a crossroads. "Alright, I'll leave you here then." He removed his hat.

"Oh yes, this is where you turn off isn't it." I removed my hat as well.

My friend disappeared down the side street. Now alone, I felt like pulling my hair out as I hurried along home, getting soaked all the way by the drizzling rain. A northwesterly wind sliced through the air as the tops of the trees on the roadside rustled and swayed.

• • •

When I got home, my wife wasn't there. Wondering where she might have gone in all this rain, I called the maid to ask her, and she told me that my wife had gone out just a little while ago.

"Did she leave alone?"

"Yes, she did."

"Around when?"

"Just a little while ago."

"Hmm . . . Did she mention dinner or anything?"

"Yes, she said that you'd be arriving home shortly so I was to prepare you a hearty meal. She even dictated the menu."

"Oh, is that so? Well then, I could use something to eat."

"Yes, sir." The maid gave me a smile and withdrew to the kitchen.

I headed to my desk. The maid brought me a lamp. It dimly lit the room, casting my shadow on the wall.

I admit that as I sat there looking at my faint, feeble shadow, I was overcome with an inexplicable loneliness and sadness. The idea that my wife might have left me cast a pall over my mind . . . Surely I didn't have to worry about her doing anything with a kid like Sumio. But there was one thing in particular that I couldn't get past: my wife was so passionate and had such strong feelings that there was really nothing that she wouldn't be capable of if it struck her fancy. *At any rate, I'll give her a talking-to when she comes back. But how could a man really bring himself to voice an idea so stupid? Oh, what should I do . . .*

I continued along this line of thinking for a while, slumped over on my desk, feeling out of sorts and unable to collect my thoughts. I thoughtlessly picked up the newspaper at my side and skimmed through articles at random, but I hadn't the slightest idea what I was reading or what it was about. While I was whiling away the time like this, the maid brought in my dinner tray. I picked up my chopsticks, but I wasn't in the mood to eat. My thoughts were unsavory as I downed two or three bowls of food, but I felt somehow unsatisfied . . . as if I was forgetting something.

I soon sunk deep into thought. Outside I heard the wind shaking the branches, the rain trickling down the eaves. Through the commotion of the wind and rain I could hear a dog barking in the distance. I fell into a deep trance.

"Sir?" The maid called out.

Her voice entered my ears, but I felt as if I was hearing it from within a dream, so I remained silent until she repeated, "Sir?"

"What?" This time I responded.

"Are you finished?" She regarded me with a look of uncertainty.

"Oh, yes, that's right." I straightened up and lifted my half-eaten bowl. "I forgot that I was eating dinner! Ha, ha, ha!" I tried to laugh it off, but the maid nonetheless cast me a skeptical look.

Once I had finally finished eating and the maid had cleared my tray, the sound of the wind and rain abruptly intensified, the rumble of thunder reverberating through the air. Lightning flashed through the room, spilling through the cracks around the door.

As I continued wondering what my wife was doing, what kind of trouble she might have gotten herself into, I was gripped by a sort of loneliness, an overwhelming loneliness, that made me feel like my blood had frozen in my chest. The flickering lights dimmed, the temperature dropped, and I grew increasingly uncomfortable, no longer feeling up to sitting uselessly at my desk. I pulled out the futon and laid down on my side.

The thunder was increasing in intensity, sounding as if it might rend apart the heavens and the earth. The air was filled with loathsome sounds: the groaning leaves of the trees, the storm shutters and the fence—shaking in the wind, rustling and clattering. It felt as if my heart were being drawn down into a dark, lonely chamber deep underground . . . And then, before I knew it, I had fallen asleep.

It wasn't long before the maid was shaking me awake, and no sooner did I open my eyes than she anxiously said, "You have a telegram."

"What, a telegram?"

"Yes." I took it from her and broke the seal. It said, "MIYOKO ILL. STAYING THE NIGHT." It was my wife, of course. She had sent it from her aunt's house, which managed to finally put me at ease. The maid looked on with curiosity.

I was greatly relieved to know where my wife was, but now I was concerned about Miyoko's illness. She was my wife's only cousin, and it was heart-wrenching to think of the budding young girl, this year on the cusp of blooming into an eighteen-year-old woman, helplessly ravaged in the storm of a sudden illness. *Maybe I should go and visit her as well . . . Oh, how wrong I had been to doubt my wife under such circumstances. But I suppose if I'm going over there I should say something to the maid first. In any event, I have to move quickly.* I abruptly got up and sat on the futon.

"Are you getting up, sir?" The maid appeared from the adjoining room.

"Yes, I am."

"Are you going somewhere?"

"My wife's aunt . . . I'm thinking I'll drop by her place."

"Because of the telegram . . . Has something urgent come up?"

"Mm."

"Was it from the missus?"

"Mm, she said that Miyoko has fallen ill and so she'll be staying the night. I'm heading over now myself." I explained as I got dressed.

"My, is it that bad?" The maid looked deeply concerned.

"I'm not entirely sure, but it can't be good if she had to send me a telegram."

"That's true."

"Actually, did my wife receive a telegram or something before she left?"

"Yes, not a telegram, but I do believe something came in the post."

"Hmm." It must have been from her aunt. I summoned a rickshaw and hurried to her house, where I found my wife nursing Miyoko. The girl had come down with acute pneumonia, which had developed as a complication of influenza. At one point her condition did take a critical turn, it seemed, but within four or five days it cleared up as if it had never happened, and my wife came home.

6.

Sumio came to visit us five or six days later. It was a chilly, moonlit night. We opened up the door and went out onto the veranda, where we discussed the epics of history while gazing up at the moon. Once I got started talking about history, my passion would take over, and I was prone to forget about absolutely everything else. Tonight was no different, and the relationship between my wife and Sumio didn't even enter my mind.

"And there's one more thing, Sensei, that I'm just not sure about." Sumio broached a new topic.

"And what would that be?"

"About what became of Emperor Antoku."

"I see."

"I don't think Emperor Antoku perished during the naval battle at Dan-no-ura."

"I see."

"The account of the war in *The Tale of the Heike* is almost entirely false. It's interesting in a novelistic way, and is written with a great deal of pathos, but it's not a document to place any trust in."

"I see."

"And I especially don't believe the part about Dan-no-ura." Quoting from numerous works, Sumio argued that Emperor Antoku did not in fact end up in a watery grave at the bottom of Dan-no-ura.

The moonlight shone down through the leaves of the trees, casting the young man's face in a pale light. His brow quivered, his eyes were sparkling, and his mind radiated sweet brilliance. Each word he spoke struck me deeply.

While I listened to him talk and thought of the potential this boy had, I couldn't suppress a smile on behalf of historians everywhere. Whenever he would make a particularly insightful comment, I couldn't help but mutter to myself about what a shining star of the field he would become.

My wife had announced that she would be treating us to some sweet agar jelly and accompanied the maid to the kitchen. I could hear the commotion of bowls clattering, cooking tongs, something falling onto the cutting board. As the night wore on, the neighborhood grew quieter, and the sound of insects could be heard off in the distance. My kimono was damp, perhaps from the settling dew, and a slight chill crept over my skin.

"Sensei," the boy called out suddenly. His eyes shone brilliantly.

"What?"

"If I died, would you look into the Dan-no-ura matter for me?"

Although I thought this was an odd thing to say, I replied. "Of course I would. I'd look into it, but you're hardly at an age where you should be thinking about death."

"No, Sensei." The boy blinked. "That's not true. For some reason I can't help but feel as if I'm going to die."

"That's the silliest thing I've ever heard. You don't even have health problems." I searched the boy's face.

"Well, it's not that anything's wrong in particular, but I just have this feeling that I won't even last another month."

"That's the silliest thing I've ever heard." I repeated myself, but after a closer look, there did seem to be a gloomy shadow hanging about the boy's face. Somewhere between his brow and his eyes there was an indescribably odd gleam of sorts. Up until this point I had thought it the sparkle of genius, but on that night, whether or not it was my imagination, it seemed to me the shadow of death.

"But if I *am* going to die, there's nothing I can do about it, so I might as well study as much as possible in the meantime." He spoke forlornly, looking directly into my face.

"That's right, death is up to fate, and we can't escape it even if we want to."

"And it's so poignant when someone dies young. Especially when they were full of ambition and on the verge of making something of themselves . . ." The boy trailed off and his eyes fell to the ground. For some reason, hearing him say that made my heart beat so fast that I thought my blood might stop circulating.

"I wonder why the heavens don't bestow a long life upon those with promise . . ." The boy continued.

"Far be it from me to begrudge talent, but it really does seem that geniuses always die young. Maybe it's just that the heavens don't bestow two gifts on one person."

"That could be . . ." The boy sighed, and I too was overcome with melancholy, a sigh escaping my lips as well. This wouldn't do at all, and so, attempting to change the subject, I said, in a deliberately loud voice, "How old is your uncle, again?"

"On the Kasai side?"

"Yes, Professor Kasai."

"He's forty-five."

"Ah, so he's still young."

"Yes, he is. Three years younger than my father."

"Oh, really?"

"My uncle is strong, which is great, but my father's weak and useless . . . And sure enough, I'm just as hopelessly weak."

"Enough of this pessimism! Just get plenty of exercise! You'll get much stronger."

"But I'm hopeless at baseball and all that."

"Well how about tennis or something, then?"

"I can't do that, either. I lose my breath." He coughed. "It's, r-really pathetic, just how weak I am."

"It's the way you think that's the problem. You've got to keep your spirits up!" I tried to encourage the boy.

He restrained himself while he listened to what I had to say, and then said, "But, Sensei, I just can't seem to do that."

"I find that hard to believe."

"Every little thing makes me anxious . . . I'm distressed by everything I see, everything I hear. I'm incapable of being unaffected."

"Well, that won't do. You just need to invest yourself in something else."

"But, you see, my most cherished wish is to be felled for the sake of history."

This declaration was followed by a cough. He clutched his chest, and the next moment a spurt of fluid was dribbling from his mouth. There was scarlet on his chest. He had coughed up blood.

My wife came in to attend to him, then put him in a car and escorted him away. She had accompanied him as his attendant, and after she returned, she blinked back tears as she told me about how his parents had tearfully thanked her and said that he had coughed up blood once before.

I soon found myself tearing up, thinking about the limited time left in this promising boy's painfully short life, and I cursed the gods for failing to grant longevity alongside genius . . . My wife finally let out a sob and started weeping. After exhausting all of my words trying to console her, I said, "Hey now, crying won't help him," but she cut me off.

"But how could I not cry! With Sumio as sick as he is!"

Hearing her say this brought another wave of emotion over me . . . I abruptly held my tongue and sat before my wife as tears streamed down her cheeks, mulling over the ephemerality, the melancholy, the injustice of it all.

7.

Sumio was absent from school for a long time, as he was naturally in need of further medical care. My wife went to visit him three or four times, and I went once or twice myself. The last time I went to see him, he had largely wasted away. His mother was saying that if his fever subsided within the next two or three days, she was going to send him to Shōnan for a bit of fresh air, but I remember thinking to myself that that probably wasn't going to happen.

It was past the point of mid-autumn, and little by little the sky had turned the color of ash and the air had begun to feel not just chilly but bitingly cold—one of those fiercely windy days when all I want to do is just bury my hands in my pants pockets. It was early on this cold morning when a single postcard arrived to inform us of Sumio's death.

"Oh, how terrible! After all that, Sumio-san has died." I said to my wife beside me.

"What, he died?!" She took the postcard from my hand and stared at it, tears already coursing down her cheeks.

"It's so sad, he was only what, seventeen? Eighteen? If only he'd made it to even thirty, who knows what he might have achieved . . ."

"Yeah, it really . . ." But she couldn't say anything further, was looking down at the floor. She flung herself onto it face down, unable to bear the rush of emotion, and cried her heart out, beginning to sob and wail.

I was feeling pretty shaken myself, but I was just about to leave for school, so I said, "Well, please go give them our condolences. I'm heading to school now."

"You're going to school?!" My wife asked through her tears.

"Yes, I am, I certainly can't take the day off."

"You're so heartless!" She flung herself back onto the ground and burst into tears.

"Okay, I'll leave it in your hands then." I pulled out my watch and, seeing that I was running out of time, left the house in a hurry.

When I arrived at the school, Teshigahara saw me and told me that he'd received notice of Sumio's death. "You got the news as well, yeah?"

"Yeah, I did."

"I'm sure you're going to pay your respects, since you were so close and all."

"Yeah, I sent my wife, since I have class . . ."

"Oh?" He paused. "Well, it's terribly sad, of course, but the kid's death was only to be expected. The heavens don't grant two gifts to one person, after all." He was giving me an odd look.

"Why must they take the prodigies away from us, while they let the scoundrels live?"

"You know, I really wonder . . ." He yawned. "Well, he may have been talented, but he was certainly a cheeky bastard."

"Sumio?"

"Yeah."

"Maybe *you* thought so, but I thought he was extremely mature. He was such a good kid . . ."

"Well, that's because you loved him. Even pockmarks look like dimples when you're in love! Ha, ha, ha, I give you my deepest condolences, Mitsuya-kun." Teshigahara flashed me a smile that was not so much light-hearted as it was flippant.

At that moment, shocked by Teshigahara's complete lack of feeling, it occurred to me that I would be happy to never exchange a word with him again. Not only that, but I realized that he was in fact an aggravating man, a man hardly worth speaking to. Not to mention the fact that my friend very well may have been the one in love with Sumio—perhaps it was he who harbored for the boy that strange desire so peculiar to Satsuma, and maybe when the boy didn't reciprocate, that's when Teshigahara started speaking ill of him.

The funeral was held two days later. I went to say my final goodbyes, as did my wife, of course. She grieved even more deeply than the boy's mother . . . But it wasn't just grief so much as a deep-seated pain. The tears truly rained down her cheeks . . . Seeing that gave me a strange feeling. To put it bluntly, the relationship between the two of them seemed ever more suspicious. But I restrained myself, and did my best to put that pointless suspicion out of my mind.

"You really cried like a banshee today, eh? Were you that upset?" I questioned my wife after we arrived back home.

"But isn't it just awful? He was always coming over to the house, he was so at ease with us . . ." Recalling this, she covered her eyes, which were swollen from crying. But I still didn't understand why she was crying so much.

It was the afternoon of the seventh day after Sumio's death, the day on which the second memorial service is customarily held. It was a Saturday, so I had come home from school to grab lunch. I had just picked up a newspaper that had earlier escaped my notice and was browsing through it when my wife started talking at my side.

"I'm stepping out for a moment now, all right?"

"You've been doing that a lot lately. Where are you headed?"

"To the gravesite."

"Whose?"

"Sumio-san's."

"To pay your respects?"

"Yes. I haven't been yet."

"You have a ridiculous amount of feeling for that boy."

"Yes, I do . . ."

"Why do you miss him so badly?" I asked her pointedly.

"Hmm, why indeed . . ." She lifted her eyes to look at me, but I suppose my expression was disagreeable because she asked, "And what's got you so bent out of shape?"

"I'm not bent out of shape."

"Then why are you in such a huff?"

"That's your imagination."

"My imagination? Oh, well, I wonder why I'm imagining such things, hmm? What do you think?" She shot me a terrifying glare and then took the newspaper from me and tore it to shreds. There was a glint in her eyes that I'd never seen there before.

"Hey, there's no reason to get this upset . . . If you want to pay your respects, by all means, do so."

"You were the one making a big deal out of it."

"I said I don't care if you go! It's not like I tried to stop you or anything."

"Oh, but you . . ." We continued bickering like that for a while until she finally got dressed and left the house.

I was alone after that, and started to imagine the gravesite in Nippori, the route there, the trees alongside the road, the way the blighted leaves slipped through and fell from the branches. Suddenly, a thought about the relationship between Sumio and my wife popped into my head, and I was reeling.

I cried out at once—"the letter box!" It had occurred to me to take a look at the diary my wife ordinarily kept stashed in there. Barely conscious of my own actions, I stood up and went over to the black-lacquered letter box and lifted the diary out from inside. Thinking that now I just might figure out what was going on between them, I leafed through a page at a time, finding frequent mention of Sumio, starting from that past summer.

June 2: *Such a clever young prodigy, such a beautiful boy. At first glance I thought he'd make a wonderful husband for Miyoko. The closer we become, the more these feelings deepen.*

July 30: *Today Sumio and I went to the banks of the Edogawa River. The moon was lovely, the wind refreshing—oh, if only we were husband and wife, I thought, how wonderful that would be.*

August 2: *Sumio came over. I dispensed with formalities and tried addressing him by his first name for the first time. He didn't respond, so I was afraid I may have offended him, but then later he called me "sister," and my affection for him grew even more. I wonder what it would be like to have such a sweet young thing for my husband.*

August 22: *Oh, Sumio—why don't you ever visit anymore? Each day feels like a thousand years. Don't you know that I'm waiting for you?*

October 12: *My one hope in this world, my one comfort, my little brother Sumio is dead. Oh, better for me to die as well, overwhelmed as I am by my grief.*

October 15: *I was unable to visit his grave yet again today—oh, this wretched, unjust world . . .*

There was an unceasing stream of entries like this. I read frantically, not wanting to miss a single word, but eventually my displeasure overtook me, and I hurled the diary across the room with all my might. It smashed against the wall and ripped apart, falling with a thud onto the tatami flooring.

"That's more like it!" I cried out, but my cry didn't dispel the distress in my heart. I folded my hands together and started to mull it over.

. . . Did my wife merely love Sumio for the genius that he was, or did her affection for him spring from another connection between them? In the end, I just could never be sure. Not only was the question there then, but even now it remains, a deep agony carved into my chest. Every time that I remember it's there, my head swims and I feel dizzy, as if I'm about to faint.

THREE

"Is This Love?" (Ai ka) by Yi Kwangsu (1909)

Translated by Janet Poole

Biography and Introduction

"Is This Love?" (*Ai ka*) was the first published work of fiction by Korean writer Yi Kwangsu, appearing toward the end of 1909 in the *Shiragane gakuhō*, the school newsletter of the Meiji Gakuin where Yi was then a student. Those familiar with Yi's reputation as a founding father of modern Korean literature will be surprised to see that he began his writing career working in the Japanese language. Equally surprising might be Yi's focus on same-sex love, given that his later long novels so often detail the love triangles of enlightenment-era youths, where the male protagonist is confronted with a choice between a so-called new woman and one embodying a traditional past in an allegorical quest to modernize the Korean nation. The indeterminacy of both language and sexuality are perhaps related in this earlier body of work, produced before both state monolingualism and a strictly policed divide between homosexuality and heterosexuality had been fully established on the Korean peninsula.

Born in 1892 in northern Korea to an impoverished but educated family, Yi's mother and father both died of cholera when he was ten years old, leaving him to fend for himself. With the support of members of the Tonghak ("Eastern Learning") religious community, he first traveled to Japan in 1905 and then attended Meiji Gakuin from 1907 until 1910. He returned to study at Waseda University in 1915. The protagonist of "Is This Love?" shares this situation, having been orphaned, but burning with a great ambition. When Yi wrote "Is This Love?" his own precarious social existence seemed mirrored by that of the nation in which he was born. Yi had first traveled to Japan in the wake of the Russo-Japanese War and a Protectorate Treaty that had wrested control of Korea's diplomatic affairs into the hands of the victorious nation, whose army was still stationed on the peninsula; just months after the story appeared, Korea was annexed as a formal colony of the Japanese empire. A decade of guerilla insurgency and brutal military crackdowns followed, but at the same time there was renewed intellectual and cultural discovery as a generation of young Koreans increasingly attended new schools and traveled back and forth to China and Japan, as did Yi. These educated youths were largely bilingual, and so the early experiments in what was to be later canonized as modern Korean literature emerged from a heterolingual context. Just eight years after "Is This Love?" Yi began the serialization of *Heartless* (Mujŏng), later hailed as the first modern Korean-language novel and in whose first pages the characters speak Korean, Japanese, and English. Such heterolingual writing was to continue throughout the colonial occupation, with the Japanese language providing a major medium for colonial rule, but also for creative expression. It is only from the retrospective viewpoint of the modern, postcolonial nation-state that a story such as Yi's can be assigned to either Japanese or Korean literature. Most frequently such works are omitted from both categories.

In the first decade of the twentieth century the teenage Yi was vigorously rejecting everything that he associated with what he saw as Korea's Confucian past and chasing after a new ideal of civilization. Writing in Japanese was surely part of his journey, but so was the version of young male subjectivity seen in "Is This Love?": the suffering, introspective literary male overwhelmed by the discovery of his emotions. Such characters had not been seen in previous literature written in Korean, in which the short-story form too was only beginning to emerge. Both the form and the subjectivity surely reflect Yi's reading in contemporary Japanese fiction. Yoon Sun Yang has termed such characters "sensitive young men" and argues that they arose from the internalization of the ideology of progress in Korea, where they began to populate literature in the decades that followed. Love—separated from the traditional arranged marriage—immediately gained traction as the most important emotion discovered by the sensitive youth.

In Yi's early fiction love most frequently took the form of same-sex relations, whether male or female. Later, as the parameters of modern Korean literature solidified, same-sex love tended to disappear from print pages, along with the interethnic love seen in Yi's story. In fact, in colonial-era Korean literature there is a decided lack of Japanese characters of all kinds. In the annals of Japanese literary history, after the loss of Japan's empire, the likes of Yi, who had always been marginalized as colonials in Japanese culture, disappeared into the silence that fell on Japan's imperial history. For these various reasons, Yi's brief first story shines light both onto what was to emerge as a dominant literary form of subjectivity in Korea and onto what became repressed as part of that subjectivity on both sides of the straits. Thus Mungil's failed love affair in all its fragility suggests to the reader today what has vanished in the interstices between metropole and colony. Yet its few pages offer a memorable depiction of the fraught experience of the young Korean subject studying at a prestigious institution in the imperial metropole on the eve of the imposition of colonial occupation.

Is This Love?

Mungil went to Shibuya to see Misao. He was full of boundless joy, happiness and hope. Feeling the need for some kind of excuse, he visited a couple of friends on the way. It was late at night and the road was muddy, but Mungil paid no heed to such things as he made his way toward Misao's house.

Words could not describe his feelings as he reached the front gate. Whether from happiness, sadness, or simple embarrassment, his heart pounded and his breathing grew heavy. Yet within a few minutes this moment had already vanished from his memory.

As he walked through the front gate and up to the lattice door, his heart began to pump more rapidly and his whole body quiver. The shutters were closed and everything was dead quiet. Maybe he's already asleep . . . no, he can't be . . . it couldn't be much later than nine o'clock. And it's the examination period so he couldn't possibly have gone to sleep already. It must have been so quiet around here that they decided to close the shutters early. Should I knock? They'd be sure to open the door. But he could not bring himself to do so. He stood there, stilling his breath, like a wooden statue. What was wrong with him? How could he come so far to visit a friend and then not be able to even knock on the door? It was not as if he would get told off simply for knocking, nor did he have to restrain his own hand from reaching toward the door, rather he simply did not have the courage. Oh, Misao must be busy studying for tomorrow's exam. He wouldn't imagine even in his dreams that I am standing here right now. No more than a double wall separates us but our thoughts are ten thousand miles apart. Oh, what should I do? All hope and happiness seemed to disappear like melting spring snow. Oh, do I have to leave here like this? Disappointment and agony boiled up in his breast. With no other choice, Mungil turned around and quietly walked away.

By the time he reached the well he had sweated so much it felt as if his cotton jacket had been soaked in water. He exhaled a deep sigh while a summer-evening breeze lightly brushed his burning red cheeks. His legs would not move any further. This time he tried walking around the back, but the shutters there were also closed; only a dim lamp pierced the darkness. That was it. There was no other possibility. Having apparently made some kind of resolution, he walked away without so much as a sideward glance. Coming out through the gate, he headed down the hill, but this hill, which he had walked up without any difficulty at all, now threw up obstacles on the descent. Two or three times he stumbled. At the halfway point he abruptly stood still, as if a thought had struck him. He did not want to give up. He suddenly had a good idea. In the street below, a red lamp flickered all alone before an electric pole, heightening the quiet of the summer night.

He stood thinking. I'm going home tomorrow, and once I've gone I won't be able to see his face again until next semester. Oh, what should I do? What! Who would be stupid enough to come all this way only to go back without seeing him? I'm such a weakling. I know I am, but if I can't even do this, then what's to become of me? I must try to become a little stronger. All right, this time I will definitely knock on the door. Of course, once inside there were no particularly interesting stories to tell or business to accomplish, but he would be able to gaze upon Misao's face. He turned around again. This time his step was light and quick, as if full of courage. He walked so quickly that he ended up passing the gate altogether. He was really laughable. He retraced his steps and entered the main gate. This time he deliberately stamped his way across the stepping-stones. Yet although to him this seemed to be one method, it was one that no one else recognized. He had hoped for success from this alone, but there was still no sign of anyone by the time he had reached the lattice door. Even if he wanted to stamp some more, there was no space left to do so, and he could hardly walk on the spot like in gym class. Oh, another failure. This time he really had no choice but to turn around again. He exhaled loudly once more. However, just as they say that when in need there's always a way, he had the idea to make even more noise as he left. If he did so, then someone inside might just hear and come to the door. It was really his last hope. At last he heard a drowsy voice that must belong to the servant girl, who sounded as if she were calling, "Misao." This turned out to be a vain hope for success. He stood still for a while, holding his breath. If he were discovered by a policeman, he might well be accused of being a thief. He took his last risk. Yes, it was a risk. This time he did not try to soften his footsteps, but walked confidently toward the rear garden where he found some real light. This was truly light in the darkness! Like a crystalline spring to a thirsty tiger!

"Who is it?" Someone called out from the back porch.

"It's me." His voice trembled as he replied. He pushed his face into the light so that it was clear who he was and added,

"I was worried you might have already gone to bed . . ."

"Oh, it's you . . . in this darkness . . . well, don't just stand there, come in."

He removed his shoes and stepped up onto the porch as the landlord bade him. A cushion was proffered but Mungil hardly seemed to appreciate the gesture.

"Did you finish your exams?" the landlord asked, putting the magazine he had been reading back on the shelf.

"Yes, I finished this morning. What about here?" This was no more than the exchange of formalities. He did not like these kinds of conversations; in fact he detested them. He wanted to come to the point and ask whether Misao was in. But he could not and did not want to reveal the workings of his heart. And yet, they say that the face acts like a spy looking into the mind; no matter how hard he pretended to be relaxed, everything was surely apparent. The landlord was gazing at his side profile with suspicion.

"We still have a while to go. At least until this Saturday. I'm getting tired of it." He frowned. A swarm of mosquitoes came in for the attack. Sweat dripped.

"It's certainly unusually hot this year," Mungil said as he thought to himself, "I want to let Misao know that I'm here, but I'm embarrassed to be found out." He hoped that Misao would realise by himself rather than have to be told directly. Just one sliding door separated the two of them now. Mungil pictured Misao in his head and thought, "He must know by now, is he really not coming out even though he knows I'm here?"

After a while a student staying in the same room returned. Mungil was overjoyed and deliberately raised his voice to ask, "So are you studying hard?" "Yes," the student replied and went to his room. Probably to tell Misao that I'm here, Mungil thought. And so he was happy, but then nothing happened. He wondered whether Misao was not there after all. Yet clearly he was. That was whispering he could hear. He is here. So is he pretending he doesn't know? What's going on? Can people really be this cruel? It was really too cruel.

He trembled. His breathing gradually grew short and his eyes grim, as if boiling hot water had been poured over him. Still the landlord stared; his suspicions seemed to be growing. Mungil couldn't bear it any longer. Oh, may this heart burst open, this blood spurt out, and this body turn cold! I shed blood for you, and you will not even show your face to me?

It was just past ten o'clock when he brushed aside the landlord's efforts to make him stay longer and left.

He started home in a half-crazed state due to his disappointment, grief, and anger. The streets were quietly sleeping in the misty darkness and only the discordant whistle of a poor masseur selling his services rattled the humid summer-evening air.

Mungil had lost his parents at the age of eleven and faced all the trials of the world on his own ever since. He had some other relatives, good-time relatives who had not given him a second glance since his downfall. On account of the god of poverty swooping in he had experienced the world earlier than most. By the age of fourteen he was already an adult and all traces of fresh innocence were fading from his face, which should have shone instead with the rosy bloom of youth.

He was bright, so bright that his father had sometimes even forgotten the pain of their poverty-stricken life on account of the great joy brought by his son's rapid mastery of the Lesser Learning and other books. For two to three years following his parents' death Mungil had drifted and life had been truly tragic. During that time he had continued to borrow books from friends, although he had not been able to receive a normal education. But he did not fall behind others his age. Due to the influence of his family and poverty he was a gentle youth. Or rather, he was a weak youth. And yet, he possessed a strange ambition. He wanted to surprise the world just once by doing something that would make generations to come adore his name; this wish was always deeply buried in his heart, and he was all the more troubled because of it. He was terrified that he might die having achieved nothing. Then one day a ray of light shone on him and he was able to go to Tokyo to study with the help of an official. He was delighted and danced with joy, as if he had found the gate to all his dreams.

Without any delay he came to Tokyo and enrolled in the third year of a middle school in Shiba. He earned good grades and was considered by everyone to be a promising student; one might say that he had moved from darkness into the light. But in truth he was not happy and gradually began to feel more and more lonely, for although each day he met tens, even hundreds, of people not one of them could be counted as a friend. He cried. There are many different kinds of sorrow, but he believed there was none as painful as the sorrow of lacking a friend.

He searched frantically for someone to befriend, but no one came to him. Occasionally someone would appear, but no one who brought the satisfaction of listening to his inner thoughts. His thirst grew more extreme and his mind more troubled. Of the more than a billion and a half people on earth is there no one who understands me, he wailed. Gradually he grew more and more weak and depressed, to the point where he began to avoid meeting people even though he generally enjoyed talking. The only comfort he found was in writing down his thoughts in his diary. He thought of giving up altogether, but this was also something of which he was not capable. Such was the source of his endless suffering. Two years passed in this way.

Then, at a sports event in January that year, he had caught sight of a youth from whose face the colour of love overflowed and in whose eyes the smile of an angel floated. Entranced, Mungil had forgotten himself for a moment and poured oil onto the flames burning in his heart. That youth was Misao. This was the one, he thought.

He wrote down his feelings in a letter, asking for Misao's love, and Misao sent a reply telling of his own loneliness, of understanding Mungil's love, and stating that he too loved him back. How did Mungil feel when he received this letter? He was happy, so very, very happy, and yet the suffering in his heart remained while new worries now emerged. Misao was a man of exceptionally few words. This was most exasperating for Mungil. He felt that Misao did not really love him, that Misao acted too cold, and so sometimes Mungil doubted his love. Then Mungil began to so fear these doubts of his that he had to force himself to conclude that Misao must indeed love him. Here lay new worries. Misao had come to seem like life itself. In fact, there was no time day or night, or even during his classes, when he was not thinking of Misao.

Whenever they were apart he would think about Misao and then fall into despair, with each new thought that despair would grow and spawn yet more thoughts. From January on, his diary contained nothing other than his thoughts of Misao. And when he saw Misao he felt so happy. What was this? Why was this? He could not understand it himself. "Why do I love him? Why did he love me? Even though I have no right to ask anything of him." These were the phrases he wrote in his diary. Whenever he met Misao, he could not even raise his head or speak and would appear totally reserved, as if he had walked before the emperor. He could not talk about these incomprehensible, instinctual things but would write about them. Three days previously he had cut his finger and sent a letter written in blood.

The first semester examinations had finished and he would be returning to his country the next day, and so he had summoned all his courage to visit Misao tonight.

Deep in thought, he forced his feet onward with no sensation whatsoever. Oh, I wish I could die. I don't want to stay in this world any longer. Aren't those the Tamagawa tramline tracks? It's eleven o'clock at the earliest, so there'll be no more trams tonight. But, there's still the train. One more rumble of the train and I'll be able to leave this world. I've always despised suicide and even spat whenever I saw an article reporting on a case. Isn't it strange? Now I'm about to do it myself. My only regrets are that I'll die without realising any of those great ambitions I once harboured, and my old grandfather and younger sister will grieve for me, but at this moment there's nothing to be done, no one who can stop me. Whether I live or die is completely beyond my power.

He hurried toward the crossing of the Shibuya rail track. The shrill shriek of a whistle sounded through the darkness. Great, he thought, and ran toward it, when someone dressed in black appeared and closed the crossing. This was too much. Some evil spirit was thwarting him even in his attempts to die. The train rumbled past unawares. Mungil stepped onto the track, walked about five yards up to a spot where he lay down his head on the east-facing rail to wait for the next train, which should come along at any moment, and then he gazed up at the stars peeking out between the clouds. So the eighteen years of my life have come to an end . . . I hope with death I disappear, or at least can't feel any more. What will happen to all of those dreams that I once held here, inside, now that this is all over and this is the end of me? Oh, I'm so lonely, I just want to be held by somebody, just once. The stars are heartless. Why is there no train? Why doesn't it come quickly and crush this head of mine? Hot tears flowed without end.

FOUR

"Whistle" (Kuchibue)
by Orikuchi Shinobu (1914)

Translated by Joseph Boxman

Biography and Introduction

Orikuchi Shinobu (1887–1953) gained notoriety as a scholar of anthropology, ethnology, and folklore as a professor at Kokugakuin University, and then at Keio Gijuku University (later to become Keio University). While he was an outlier in many senses, having studied with (but later broken with) renowned folklorist Yanagita Kunio (1875–1962), Orikuchi was a successor to the tradition of "nativist" (*kokugaku*) learning concerned with using Japan's past (real or imagined) to define its character as a modern nation. Often such literature had a focus on the role of the emperor, and his scholarship and some poetic works were part of the ferment of imperialist and nationalist thought, prominent in the early twentieth century as Japan expanded its colonial holdings. Orikuchi was also a highly regarded poet and critic of poetry as an adherent of the Negishi school of poetry which included Itō Sachio (1864–1913) and others from Masaoka Shiki's (1867–1902) Negishi Tanka Society, members of which went on to produce the poetry journal *Araragi* (active from 1908 to 1997). He eventually left the Araragi group and became involved in creating the tanka journal *Nikkō* along with Kitahara Hakushū (1885–1942) and others from 1924 to 1927. Under the name Shaku Chōkū, he wrote both tanka and poetry in newer forms and produced one novella and one novel—*Kuchibue* (*Whistle*, translated here) and *Shisha no sho*,[1] respectively—in addition to the voluminous array of essays, lectures, and other nonfiction writing he produced under his own name.

Today Orikuchi is perhaps best remembered by tanka poets, with one of the most prestigious tanka awards in Japan still bearing his pen name, but he is also well remembered as a man who was attracted to other men. He is said to have faced some opposition because of this—there is a well-known anecdote in which Yanagita cautioned a student of Orikuchi's that he must not accept his teacher's advances.[2] It is important to note, however, that while male-male desire was perhaps waning in acceptance and popularity in comparison to earlier times, when *Whistle* was published its depiction would not have been considered especially shocking, given that such relationships between schoolboys were well represented in that time. Orikuchi was relatively open about his attraction to men and later adopted a follower as his "son" (a method used at the time to effectively take a spouse of the same sex).

Whistle first appeared in twenty-five installments from March 24 to April 19 of 1914 in a short-lived Osaka daily paper called *Fuji Shimbun* run by boundary-pushing writer and journalist Miyatake Gaikotsu (1867–1955). Serialization stopped when Orikuchi moved on to more urgent projects and was never resumed. The short novel was not published again until Orikuchi's collected works were released shortly after his death. This translation is based primarily on the 2010 paperback edition from Iwanami Shoten, because that is the most recent and widely available version and because it contains helpful annotations and commentary from Andō Reiji, a leading scholar on Orikuchi.[3] Together with Andō, the work of Tomioka Taeko and Mochida Nobuko has been especially helpful, not to mention Jeffrey Angles's translations and work on the subject, among many others, and this translation owes everything to the rich body of work on Orikuchi that already exists. Andō and Tomioka have written extensively on the experiences and influences that form the background of the work, including the theory that it is based on a real-life relationship with a young man a few years older than

---

1. For the first full English translation of *Shisha no sho*, see Orikuchi Shinobu and Reiji Andō, *The Book of the Dead*, trans. Jeffrey Angles (Minneapolis: University of Minnesota Press, 2016).

2. Details about this exchange and a chronicle of life as one of Orikuchi's live-in students were first brought to light in Katō Morio's 1991 book *Wa ga shi Orikuchi Shinobu*, which describes many episodes of unwelcome advances Orikuchi made toward the author.

3. Orikuchi Shinobu, *Shisha no sho, Kuchibue* (Tokyo: Iwanami Shoten, 2010). The version of the text in the later version of the author's complete works was also consulted. (Orikuchi Shinobu, *Orikuchi Shinobu zenshū*, vol. 24 [Tokyo: Chūkō Bunko, 1975]).

Orikuchi called Fuji Muzen.[4] Mochida suggests that in its context *Whistle* was written in large part as a reaction to and replacement for Mori Ogai's *Vita Sexualis* (1909), which Orikuchi saw as too patently normal and simple a story of sexual socialization—he hoped to write a version that was truer to his own experience.[5] Still other scholars writing in Japanese and English have discussed the themes of purity, degradation, sexual awakening, and poetic sensitivity, especially as they relate to the invention of the modern self in Japan, but *Whistle* itself has not been central to scholarship on Orikuchi, and until Angles's 2016 translation of *The Book of the Dead* there was little engagement with his fiction.[6]

Considered heavily autobiographical, the story follows Yasura through a few months of his fifteenth summer, starting near the end of the school term. The target of the romantic advances of an upperclassman, Yasura wrestles with guilt and anxiety as he weighs his complicated attraction to this boy a few years older than himself against his feelings for another boy closer to his age, Atsumi. As soon as his mother allows him to experience the freedom of traveling alone for the first time, Yasura risks everything to be with Atsumi. Readers should be advised that this text contains references to sexual harassment and assault, suicide, and derogatory terms for communities historically subject to discrimination.

Orikuchi's text pays careful attention to local ways of speech in the region and reflects these in the dialogue, but this translation works to convey these nuances in numerous other small ways rather than attempting to recreate the differences in spoken language. The text is also locally focused in its orientation around specific, real landmarks, these often being mapped out in terms of distances. The original text expresses these distances in units now rarely used even in Japan, but they have been roughly converted to imperial units to be more familiar to North American readers. These are rooted in a real landscape through which Yasura is traveling, but the most important function of these distances usually seems to be to create a visual scene. For other

4. See Tomioka Taeko's *Shaku Chōkū nōto* (Tōkyō: Iwanami, 2000) and Tomioka and Andō's *Orikuchi Shinobu no seishun* (Tokyo: Pneumasha, 2013), for example.

5. Mochida, Nobuko. *Uta no ko, shi no ko: Orikuchi Shinobu* (Tokyo: Genki Shobō, 2016), 60.

6. See for example, Andō's *Orikuchi Shinobu* (2014) and *Hikari no mandara* (2016) in Japanese. More background about the cultures and norms surrounding these themes historically in Japan is discussed in Keith Vincent's *Two-Timing Modernity: Homosocial Narrative in Modern Japanese Fiction* (2012) and Angles's *Writing the Love of Boys: Origins of Bishōnen Culture in Modernist Japanese Literature* (2011).

cultural references and the large variety of flora and fauna named throughout, Japanese terms are retained in some cases where English vocabulary falls
short or where it is useful to do so, with notes added as necessary. Feeling
was prioritized over strict scientific accuracy, and a few smaller, less-relevant
details, related to clothing and buildings for example, have been glossed
over slightly for readability in English, but the translation on the whole
aims to retain bring the reader into the work's context, rather than the other
way around. This translation has benefitted from the advice and feedback of
many, especially Davinder Bhowmik and Ted Mack, Tomoko Shirota-Jones,
Doug Given, and Ami Tian; any shortcomings, however, are my own.

Whistle

I

May came, crisp and refreshing. The acacia trees behind the school-
house were in bloom and the students no longer wore their knit
sweaters.

Lately, Yasura Uruma was often mystified by the extraordinary fatigue
he felt in spite of the season. He wanted to stretch his body out against
the ground like a lazy dog. He had no name for this feeling, and there
was certainly no way he could ask his aunt what to call it.

He was more than careless about his own appearance. In fact, he
tended to take pride in his incredible nonchalance.

At school, a few teachers became concerned enough to caution him
that he must take care not to cut too sloppy a figure. Whenever this
happened, he felt a shiver of some pleasant sensation for which he had
no name. His mother and his aunt were both too preoccupied with the
shop to extend their care and attention to Yasura. This set the tone of
his early childhood, which was average if somewhat lacking in structure, and he eventually came to enjoy this sort of patchwork upbringing
he had at times.

He plodded impatiently up the stone steps that formed the path.
On either side of the path up the hill were graveyards enclosed by
bamboo fences. In a few places, bamboo shoots thrust vigorously up
through the layers of old leaves on the ground.

Turning his eyes toward the bright morning light that filtered into
the grove, he came to a stop.

Once again, he had found himself pursued by the same peculiar feeling from the moment he awoke. This had become a common occurrence for him lately. He forced his eyes open wider and wider, straining to make sense of that feeling, to clarify it. But it was fleeting, and eventually, as always, it would run its course and settle into a kind of daze. Remembering that he had to get to school, he set out walking without waiting for that to happen.

The road passed through a cluster of temples at the top of the hill. The school was another five or six blocks past that. Just as the school was coming into view, he heard the first bell ring. With redoubled force he hurled himself forward and straight up the stairs to his classroom. He did not see the teacher yet. All the other students were either in their seats or standing near other students' desks talking noisily. When Yasura came running in panting, the entire class erupted into laughter.

He could feel a hot blush spreading across his face. Gathering himself narrowly, he sat down in his assigned seat.

"Looks like Uruma's head's on fire," shouted one boy, drawing the attention of everyone in the class to Yasura yet again.

Yasura's hand went immediately to his head, finding his hair soaking wet. He realized that he was practically steaming with sweat. The way he looked, the way he felt—the moment his hand touched his head he felt like some clown pantomiming his own regrets, making him wish even more fiercely to disappear completely.

After a short while, a calmer and cooler state of mind returned to him.

The teacher never did show up for that class. This put the students in high spirits, and they spent the time cavorting, some chasing a ball around the expansive yard.

Yasura splayed out on a bed of clover, taking the full force of the morning sun on his back. He watched white clouds slowly appear in the blue sky for what seemed like forever.

The next day it rained.

The warm, wet wind brought the scent of new baby roses, as if to remind him of how close the meadows were. The fine mist that came in on the wind dampened Yasura's jacket and he enjoyed the sensation of its wet pressure against his skin. He was prone to heavy sweating. His sweating was especially intense from late April through early May.

Even when he was able to feign a calm expression, he had often felt the sweat welling up like pure spring water just under the surface of his skin. Today, his skin had felt sticky and slack since morning, so he had shown up to class not wearing his usual undershirt.

The teacher, seeming to be enjoying himself, said loudly, "And so at this point, Fritz was left with no choice but to hurl the wolf against the door with all his might." From the outset, Yasura had no interest at all in the content of his textbook. He had been excited by the stories of Iwami Jūtarō and Perseus at first, but after two or three years, he had abandoned any interest in them.

Yet now, he imagined the story ending with Fritz's vibrant blood spurting out of his white chest and onto the softness of the snow. Next to his dreamlike premonition, the story's actual resolution, which was predictably tame and (he supposed) meant to evoke the power of humanity, seemed tedious to him. When the lecture was over, the other students competed eagerly to ask questions. For Yasura, however, no doubts remained.

Third hour was physical education. Yasura started to feel short of breath.

On the platform in the gymnasium stood the large teacher the students called "the Toad." He began to unbutton his jacket in a leisurely manner.

The students began taking off their jackets. All the blood in Yasura's body rushed to his head. Finally, he heard the call to attention.

"Stretches! Exercise one, first set!" the teacher boomed. "The jacket, Uruma."

No words came to Yasura. He was aware of all his pores opening at once.

The Toad hopped down from the platform. "Why won't you take it off?"

The teacher began grabbing at his chest, but Yasura remained slumped over, his face bright red. The Toad proceeded to undo the first button, then the second, and finally the rest. One button was rent loose and flew.

Suddenly, a cold-blooded look crept across the teacher's face. "All right, you. Get up there. You'll be leading the exercises today."

Yasura trudged toward the platform as if in a trance. His jacket was still in the hands of the teacher. He appeared up on the platform with not a single stitch on the upper half of his body. His face was pale. The tender contours running from his high-set shoulders to his collarbone, the soft, wavering recess that extended from his collarbone to his chest, then from his chest down to his navel: white like February snow, in front of all the other students—

He stood weakly on the platform, feeling that snowy whiteness wish it could melt away.

There was one boy in his year who looked at him with pity in his eyes.

"Stretches! Exercise one, first set! Arms up!"

The clarity of his voice penetrated the ears of the other students.

He eventually came back down from the platform with a pained smile, looking like some sort of captive.

When he walked home, the clouds had cleared and swallows flitted about, showing their white underbellies.

Yasura felt renewed and lighter of heart as he trod soil freshly washed by thunderstorms. After five or six hundred yards, the path went into the tea fields.

At the top of the low hill stood a stone stupa, bathed in the afternoon sun.

A bird flew up out of the thicket of tea leaves, the sound of its wings loud.

Standing on top of the hill, Yasura watched the bird as it flew away. He felt a sort of itch deep behind his nose and his eyes lost focus.

Fated as I am to have come here to the bay of Naniwa,
I look to the setting sun over the waves for salvation[7]

The stately, trailing rhythm of the words had been called up from somewhere in the deepest recesses of his mind. That same young mind was in some sense already beginning to fathom the bleakness of the later years of the poet from the *Shin kokinshū*.[8] This was the poet to whom a memorial still stood on the same hill where Yasura was now standing.

---

7. A "deathbed poem" (*jisei*) of Fujiwara no Ietaka (1158–1237), here in a slightly altered version.

8. Formally *Shin kokin wakashū*, this is the eighth imperially commissioned collection of poetry. It contains mostly *waka* and was completed in 1205. The above poet was one of the compilers. The memorial in the next line refers to the stone stupa mentioned above, and the poem included here comes from a collection of didactic Buddhist tales (*setsuwa*) called *Kokon chomonjū* (1254). It reflects a Pure Land Buddhist outlook, in which paradise lies always to the west (see Orikuchi, *Shisha no sho, Kuchibue*, 300).

Just then, he felt something come into contact with his cheek. A single leaf from the thin branches above his head had fallen in front of him.

Turning his eyes upward, Yasura saw a softly plump, gray pigeon change branches.

Saw its heartbreakingly red legs. Saw the eyes of the small bird watching him in the unstable light.

For a week it rained and cleared in turns, keeping the air sticky and hot. The purple petals of the paulownia blossoms scattered white.

Near one corner of the sports field, there were some forty square yards where Yasura had made rows and planted his garden. This time of year he had to water it twice every day, morning and evening. It was into this garden that he had lowered the seeds he had kept in the fall, produced by what he had sown in the spring.

When he transplanted the small plants in rows, a little further apart each time, he had a childish sense that he was watching himself impart his own strength to the lives of these hundreds of plants.

Many were already sprouting. He watered them relentlessly and they continued to quickly soak up what he gave them.

He dashed out after an hour-long class period to work in his garden, but he seldom found any part of the garden dried out. Without fail, he bent to his work every morning before the start of classes and after dismissal every afternoon, intently scrutinizing every individual seedling. Soon, watering the garden morning and night was not enough to satisfy him. He began giving water to his garden whenever it occurred to him. His natural history teacher told him that the roots would not hold out if he continued to water it so much, but this only solidified Yasura's juvenile opposition toward such advice.

The invisible desires of plants and trees manifest themselves in the hearts of those who care for them. When it occurs to that person that the garden should be watered, it is the plants communicating that desire to their care-taker, he thought. Just as he had hoped, all his plants continued to grow rapidly. Before long, he had begun to see reddening, yellow-striped buds appear.

In the now rather slanted light of the sun, Yasura fervently worked his rows, his downturned face wet with sweat. After about an hour of this, he took a quick, deep breath and stood up straight. Suddenly staggering as if he would fall, he leaned against a nearby fence. His ears began ringing terribly and his nose stopped up, which made it difficult to breathe. At the same time, he felt a cold sweat surfacing, carried by indescribable chills. He laid himself down on the grass.

As he lay there, he tried for some time to take deep, regular breaths to bring his breathing back to a steadier pace. He thought he felt something like the sensation of ice sliding down the muscles of his back. Just then his sweating stopped abruptly. He could feel the blood throbbing throughout his entire body.

His cheeks burning red, Yasura returned to where he had been working between the rows in his garden.

"Hey, Uruma!"

From the dim hallway that led from the bottom of the stairs to the science room, someone called to Yasura, who was the last to leave his classroom on the second floor.

"What?"

"Come down here for just a minute."

The instant he heard the voice, he pictured the face of the boy it belonged to. The shiver he felt made him suspect something might be afoot. "Let's talk again later—there are still things I need to do in the yard there," he said all at once, running straight down the stairs and out into the yard.

"Hey, hold it!"

The boy chased Yasura into one corner of the schoolyard where pines and willows had been planted. His menacing made Yasura wither in terror. Still, Yasura didn't listen to what the boy said. The bell rang. The students flowed like the tide into their classrooms. Yasura turned and ran.

The ferocity in the boy's voice stayed with him: "Don't you forget!"

He made no real attempt to run away or hide. Again at lunchtime, Yasura was out in the schoolyard pulling weeds.

Makioka, the boy from earlier, had been joined by two others who now circled around outside the fence threateningly, eruptions of dark red acne on their faces.

The supple white outline of the shoulders of his summer clothes were bathed in sunlight. It was June.

It was a dry Sunday following five or six days of rain. Yasura left the house around five, and walked eastward, eastward. After an hour of walking, he came into an open meadow. Without a glance to either side, he walked straight up the single dusty path through it. He passed countless ox carts that were headed to town.

The sun shone on the blue and white patterned top kimono he wore, filling his nose with the scent of its fresh indigo.

He came to a little collection of buildings. There he bought peaches and apricots, which he stuffed into his bag. Turning south from there, he passed graveyards, coming to a village alive with the work songs of women weaving. He passed rivers, he passed deep groves, and he passed more than that, until he had walked just over two miles. The walls of a temple complex came into view.

He felt as if he could hear the opening words of Kazan-in's poem about purple clouds emanating from some corner of the inner recesses of the complex: "A visit to Fujii-dera annihilates all desire . . ."[9] He began the motions of pulling a fortune, shaking a thin wooden rod out of the metal cylinder. It said twenty-eight. He couldn't see anyone who would give him the associated paper fortune.[10] Yasura felt as though his eyes had suddenly met with the gleaming eyes of the Buddha that sat in the shadows behind the thick pillars and heavy curtains steeped in the scents of sandalwood and aloeswood. In his core, he began to want nothing more than to throw himself completely on the mercy of that presence.

A chicken came up the stairs and over the tall enclosure and crowed under the latticework of the main hall.

Two people who appeared to be a father and son on the Saikoku pilgrimage were standing near the temple's small fountain.[11] The father was drinking water out of a ladle. The child, who must have been around ten, used his small hands to hold a bucket from which he poured water little by little into the father's ladle. The sight of the pair affected him deeply. Yasura left through the front gate. Vegetables hung from the eaves of each of the houses withered in the midday sun. A dry wind blew through, kicking up sand.

---

9. This can be found in Orikuchi's tanka collection (Orikuchi Shinobu, *Shaku Chōkū kashū*, ed. Tomioka Taeko (Tokyo: Iwanami shoten, 2000) 69), as part of the 1925 collection *Umi yama no aida*; a version was also attributed to Kazan-in when he visited the Shingon temple as part of his journey to re-establish the Shikoku Thirty-Three Kannon pilgrimage as depicted in Orikuchi's play *Kazan-in engi* (Orikuchi, *Shisha no sho, Kuchibue*, 301).

10. *Omikuji* fortunes often work by drawing a stick in the manner described here. Each stick has a number written on it, which is exchanged for the corresponding fortune.

11. *Chōzu*, a stand with running water and ladles for washing the hands and mouth before entering sacred places.

Since earlier that day, Yasura's stomach had been aching in a way that put pressure on his ribs. It soon became unbearable. Bending over at the side of the road where the grass grew thick, he tried pressing on his chest. A bitter liquid suddenly rushed up his throat. He spat out something thin and yellow.

Yasura stayed in that position for a short while. A man wearing a bright white sedge hat, likely on his way home for an afternoon nap after working in the fields, came trudging toward him. The man stopped for a moment to observe him and then continued quietly on his way. In that moment Yasura felt a peculiar spasm run through the base of his jaw. It was somehow melancholy but it also gave him a pleasant sensation of comfort.

Yasura rose. By that time, the man's white hat had become a dim, far-off blur at the other side of the nearly endless expanse of barley, all heavy with grain. He was a man of medium build with a face that was slightly dark but delicately formed. His hitched-up sleeves revealed two arms that seemed incongruously pale and plump. The man's gentle gaze, directed at Yasura with sympathy, left a deep impression on Yasura's heart.

There was a narrower road to one side. Slumped over, he journeyed westward, westward. Innumerable haystacks passed him by on either side as if in a dream. It was only after practically collapsing in the shade of one of these haystacks that his mind, which had been completely scattered up to then, began to regain focus. When he opened his eyes again, directly in front of him, one flower of a Chinese milk vetch waved gently in a breeze that was almost too soft to be felt.

His breath sounded ragged to his own ears and his flushed cheeks were hot to the touch. Once again raising himself up, he focused his eyes intently. Still, he saw nothing but the sunlight that flooded the barley, and he heard nothing but the voices of the larks drifting toward him on the gentle breeze.

By the time he had slowly dragged himself all the way back home, the sun had set completely.

It was hard for him to make it to school with a cheerful countenance for more than two or three days in a row.

Mornings he woke up early. Though he was late nearly every day, he was never absent under any circumstances. Most days he was listless and seemed to be walking around half asleep from the time he left his bed.

More and more of the rare flowers from the West bloomed in his garden every day, evidence of his devotion. Time and again he would find himself standing in a daze, stock-still amid the flowers, his eyes drained of strength.

Aizendō was a temple on the way to Yasura's school. There stood the newly restored Tahōdō pavilion and the Kondō with its darkened vermilion, all before a background of birches, rare for the area.[12] There was an old man who maintained the temple and lived on the grounds. In the light of early morning and then again in the twilight hours, Yasura would see him raising and lowering the lattice shutters here and there. The clearing was always covered in layers of leaves. Yasura's path took him over the leaves and out the exit to one side of the temple grounds.

Once again, one morning near the end of June, he turned his face up toward the light filtering through the thin branches and wondered whether he might in fact be somehow ill.

That day as well, class had already begun by the time he reached the classroom. With an ironic smile, his mathematics teacher upbraided him for his tardiness. Yasura reddened to the ears. His teacher bore down further and further on him, but he would not raise his head. Only after dumping some veiled insult on him did the teacher finally let up.

As soon as students started going up to the board to solve geometry problems, the bell rang. The teacher complained so that everyone could hear.

"Thanks to Uruma here, we've gotten nowhere this whole hour," he sneered.

It was now peak season for fourth- and fifth-year boys to chase after the younger boys who had pale white cheeks and delicate, slender frames. All the younger boys were dreading the overnight class trip that drew nearer with each passing day.

Yasura did not concern himself with such matters, for his was a path that belonged to him alone. In order to keep his path undisturbed, he kept his true thoughts quiet at school.

---

12. Aizendō is a complex of temple buildings, the two mentioned here being the main ones. The Tahōdō is a two-story pagoda, and the Kondō is the bright red and white central hall. The complex appears in Ihara Saikaku's 1687 *Nanshoku ōkagami*, a work centered on tales of male-male affection.

Summer break dangled just in front of the students' eyes. It was the last day of the nearly weeklong stretch of final examinations.

By the time he left for home, Yasura's body was soaked in sweat and drained of life. As he left the schoolyard, an unexpected cool breeze caressed his cheek. Houses stood quietly on one side of the road. On the other side were tea fields. The bright noon sun shone glistening on the white sand. A large, colorful beetle flew out in front of him. It flew, then stopped, then flew again, keeping just two or three paces ahead as if to lead the way.

He suddenly felt someone's breath on the nape of his neck. All at once, Yasura was caught in the flushed embrace of a body that seemed on the verge of igniting.

Gasping, he felt sweat stream down the contours of his back like a waterfall.

It was a boy in fifth year, about eighteen or nineteen. His face was dark and severe, his hair bristly and black. He was known as a tennis ace and a model student.

"Say, Uruma. Why don't you stop past my place on your way home? It's just there. Come on, there's something I need to talk to you about. What's the matter—if you don't want to, then come meet me at Aizendō," he said. His voice had a wild edge to it, but it also had a certain ring of intimacy that seemed to somehow draw one in, and quiver.

Yasura could not harden his heart against that voice.

Crunching through old leaves fallen from the birches and oaks, Yasura climbed up to the base of the two-storied Tahōdō, Okazawa fluttering along behind him. Yasura drifted into a depressed, hopeless frame of mind. He lowered his eyes when he felt the reddened eyes of Okazawa staring at his forehead when they faced each other.

"Why's your house so far, Uruma? Mine isn't but two hundred yards from here. Since you've already come this far, there's no reason for you to go all the way home and come back again."

Okazawa had tailed him on purpose. Yasura merely slumped.

"So, the thing I needed to talk to you about: you know Kurokawa in our class, right? Well, he's got it out for you. Has had for some time. But what was it that Umeno tried with you lately? Well, so—do you recall two weeks ago, we had that little tennis tournament? And when it was down to just the tennis players, as usual, Makioka and Umeno were trying to start a fight over you. So naturally I got between them. I told them that was no matter they'd be able to settle by arguing. Whoever makes it first will have bragging rights, no underhandedness or ulterior motives. Only, I see now that was a pretty rotten thing to do to you. You never quite know what those two imbeciles might try. And now with exams coming up, I knew I had to tell you, I just had to. I thought they might set to you once the exams are through and so I was afraid I might be too late. So that's why I knew I needed to talk to you right away—today—and that's why I followed you. People are starting to say some pretty strange things about me, you know. Ever since all that happened, they've started to talk about how *that damned Okazawa is crazy about Uruma.*"

He added this last part as if it were particularly vexing to him.

In that moment, however, Yasura was able to steal a glance at Okazawa's face, which betrayed his words.

His hot breath, his bloodshot eyes, the sensation of his close, squeezing presence. Yasura glanced around him.

Not a soul passed by the midday forest.

"I'll be going now, Okazawa. Thank you. I'll be as careful as I can. Good-bye."

In a dreamlike state, he turned to go.

"Uruma—will you read this? Just read it, and if you're moved to write back, then please do."

Yasura could not look the other boy in the face.

After setting off at a clumsy trot to the front gate, Yasura stopped and leaned on the trunk of a mast-straight tree, feeling a sadness well up within him when he looked back to see the lonesome hunched shoulders of the boy who had watched him go.

2

Several times, just as Yasura was about to open the letter the upperclassman had given him, he hesitated. His mind was in turmoil, weighed down by a desolate melancholy shot through with rich imaginings of pleasures that might soon be his. When he returned home, he stepped through the gate with the feeling that he was smuggling in contraband. This made him wary of the eyes he imagined were watching him from every dark corner in the house. He finally made it up to the loft of the storehouse. In the dim light that came through the screen door, his eyes followed the hurried scrawl across the lined pages.

He stood staring blankly for a few moments, once again in a state of mind he had no name for. The large leaves of the phoenix tree in front of the screen door gave off a gloomy light as the sun shone through them.

He pulled the heavy sliding door closed and descended the dark stairs.

3

Yasura gave in to the lethargy he had been struggling against since April or May, and did not do a single thing all day, starting first thing every morning. Loathing the light, he even moved his desk to a darker room. Then once the sun had nearly set, like a bat he would go out to the front of the shop. There, under the electric lights, he would catch any boy who visited the shop and talk to him in a loud and interested-sounding voice.

On what was said to be the hottest night of the summer, he was sitting on the veranda at the side of the shop, his legs dangling off the edge as he watched the people in the streets. Though in the house it had already been dark for an hour, outside the sun's light had yet to disappear completely. The pale white glow of the sky in the west brought to mind the frozen skies of February.

"Yasu. Yasu."

It was his aunt calling him from inside the house.

"Heard there'll be some *jōruri* on down at Miya's place tonight. Why don't you go?"[13]

"Amateurs?"

"Amateurs."

"Must be the usual local lineup. Seems like a hassle on such a hot night."

"Don't you be like that. I'm telling you because I wanted you to go see it. It's not the usual lineup, it's Kihō and Kijaku and the rest. Still don't want to go? Fine. In that case, you can stay here and look after the shop."

---

13. *Jōruri* is a type of dramatic narrative performance often put on in conjunction with *bunraku* puppets. Here no puppets are mentioned, so this may not involve that element. The art form was created in the Kyoto and Osaka areas and matured throughout the Edo period, but was still very active in the period in which this story is set.

She wore a yukata that seemed too stiff and angular for an evening out. She started to leave, taking the maid along with her.

"Hold on there. I'm coming," Yasura said.

"Well, we have to go now—just wear that, don't bother changing clothes."

Yasura jumped onto his geta and took off. He was wearing only a thin, short-sleeved cotton kimono that barely went past his knees.

Enveloped in the stifling smell of the sweat and steam of all those gathered under the poor light of the lamps, everyone worked their fans in the same way.

They laid out the cushions brought from home by their maid. Each act brought a succession of local stars out in front of the audience. Yasura was immediately entranced, focusing intently as soon as one of the younger men, a performer called Rikishi, began to tell his story in his softly masculine voice.

The story was the Juraku-machi act of one of those Ume no Yoshibei the Swindler stories, from something called *The Hidden Well of Nonaka*.[14] This was the first time Yasura had seen it. In it, Chōkichi's sister tips him off to the fact that Yoshibei had begun to steal money from her husband; Yasura began to feel an intuitive sadness as Chōkichi's guileless plot goes on falling apart. When it came to the part where Chōkichi goes off to boil the water, Yasura watched him intently as he left for the kitchen. It pained his heart.

Chōkichi is eventually killed by his brother-in-law. The moment it finally happened, Yasura let out a sigh of relief, feeling somehow as though he, too, had at long last also accomplished something necessary.

Chōkichi's feelings at the moment the sword came down on him entered Yasura's own heart and became a part of it.

The scene where Chōkichi searches for somewhere to die and looks down into the well left Yasura briefly feeling as though he had been doused with water. The audience lauded the storyteller's looks, his upbringing, and his technique, some even speculating that he would be the one to take over after Kihō. Everyone clearly saw him as a cut above all the other young performers. Though surrounded by such raucous praise, Yasura found himself alone, still peering at his own reflection down in the bottom of the well.

---

14. *Akanezome nonaka no komori ido* is a *jōruri* text dating from the Edo period (Orikuchi, *Shisha no sho, Kuchibue*, 301).

After that, two old, white-haired storytellers told abbreviated versions of stories, and then the one they called Kihō took the stage. He told *Horikawa* in a voice as fresh and endearing as it was frank.[15] Some men shouted things like, "Not even Koshiji can top him!" Eventually, everyone was shouting something.

"That's the leading man of Suō-machi!"

"The best in Japan!"

"The *bunraku* champ!"

Met with praise like this, Kihō, the headliner that night, launched into *Terakoya*. Yojirō and Oshun, and even Genzō and Matsuō and the rest, all elicited fragile, tearful emotions.[16]

Yasura left the venue holding his heart as though it might shatter at any moment. Long, thin strands of cloud were stretched across the misty early summer moon.

It was his habit to fall into a deep sleep right after going to his room for the night, but that night he had many dreams.

4

To Yasura's eyes, still sticky with sweat from sleeping, the glistening colors of the morning glories were cool and refreshing.

Because it was the day of the commencement ceremony at his school, Yasura rushed to leave the house. As he stepped onto the road that went up and in front of Aizendō, he realized abruptly what the day would mean.

Now the day had come. He had not forgotten about Okazawa and his feelings, but he still had no intention of writing a response to the letter he had received. And yet, he could not forget that pitiful, forlorn expression that overtook the youth's manly features when he said he would be waiting for a reply.

He walked on the spring grasses in a marsh made of melted snow. By putting his unquiet thoughts to rest here, he managed to enjoy a calm and relaxed state of mind until he was once again torn from his revery and thrown instead into a state of confusion. He had truly no purpose or direction at all about what he should do.

---

15. "Horikawa" is short for *Horikawa nami no tsudzumi*, a *jōruri* piece by Chikamatsu Monzaemon first performed in 1707.

16. "Terakoya" refers to the fourth act of *Sugawara denju tenarai kagami* (first performed in Osaka in 1746) based on legends of Sugawara no Michizane, as well as Chikamatsu Monzaemon's play *Tenjinki*. (Orikuchi, *Shisha no sho, Kuchibue*, 301.)

Breathing heavily between the trees, he sank deeper into his thoughts as he walked along listlessly.

A poem he had seen somewhere sprung to mind: "Are you keeping your thoughts to yourself then, toad?"[17] Yasura tore a sheet from his small notebook and scrawled this across it in purple pencil.

5

Yasura took the road to swimming practice at high noon, walking the entire three and a half miles to the Ōkawa River. His face darkened from exposure to the sun with each passing day. The lukewarm water was always slightly turbid. Directly after a rain it would turn yellow. Although he had come to practice every day throughout the summers of both his second and third year, his body still refused to stay above water. He had spent three summers practicing treading water, grasping the bamboo poles stuck in the riverbed.

The surface of the river at times rippled a strange silver color and would fall to below Yasura's armpits, flowing with the current. Occasionally he would release his grip on the bamboo and let himself sink to the bottom of the river. When he stood up again, however, he would find that the water only came to his chest. Other times he would narrow his eyes and stand completely still to feel the intimate lapping of the viscous, stagnant water as the sun beat down on him from above.

He ducked under the rope, and then set out at a sprint to where the others were doing a hundred-yard swim. After three or four steps, he found that the river suddenly became much deeper. When he pulled back in surprise, the water undulated deeply and flowed into the treacherous, hidden depths at his feet as though it were pulling him downward. At last, he reached the edge and breathed a sigh of relief as he clung to the border rope.

Then, ten or fifteen yards out in front of him, Yasura detected a strange motion in the surface of the water. As he watched, whatever it was shot toward him like an arrow leaving a bowstring.

He stood cowering. The movement in the water came to a stop directly in front of him, and at that same moment he felt warm hands grab hold of his feet. A head appeared slowly from the surface of the water and all at once the water turned to foam. It was Okazawa.

---

17. This is a haiku by Suganuma Kyokusui (1659–1717).

Okazawa looked around and behind him, and then pulled hard. Yasura's waist was no longer under his own control. The rope stayed slack, trailing loosely a foot or two behind him. The riverbed there dropped off sharply. Yasura felt his body suddenly upended and then tightly cradled in Okazawa's strong, masculine arms. He felt the well-developed muscles of Okazawa's chest against his back. Suddenly, he heard the loud sound of a kiss on his cheek.

Drifting over to a shallower part of the river, Yasura let out a tortured breath. He felt as though his crazed pulse might tear his heart apart.

"Hm? I would never hurt you. Try to control yourself. Thought you were done for. That really was close," Okazawa said in a hushed voice.

"And what you wrote back the day before yesterday—I really couldn't get a word of it. I worked at it for two days, but you know literature isn't something I know anything about."

Just at that moment, the bell that signaled the end of swimming practice rang out noisily across the surface of the water.

To relieve some of the boredom of the trip, he made a full circle around the intersection at just about every block. Today there was much he needed to think about, so he broke away from his usual crew of friends and walked along alone, slumped under the sun high above as it baked the glistening sweat seeping from his fresh and untroubled skin. His heart was filled with soft utterances and velvety sensations.

Recalling Okazawa's nearness to him and his daring behavior in front of so many others made Yasura tremble. He felt like giving himself a sound thrashing for not being able to escape from a boy like that, even if it had all been over in an instant.

It was just as he had said himself: Okazawa knew nothing of literature. And yet everyone said he was an excellent student. Nevertheless, given the way he carried on with Makioka, Umeno, and the others, Yasura couldn't help but feel that somewhere in his nature, deep in his heart, Okazawa was something of a brute. Since he was small, Yasura had always had certain prejudices about other people. He had never understood the reasons behind them, but for the first time today, he realized that he was most attracted to people with a certain sophistication and delicacy of heart. Yasura felt that Okazawa lacked this. But then why was he so taken with him despite that? He examined the depths of his own heart. He had until this moment thought it beautiful, but he started to think that sordid episodes like the events of that

afternoon (of which he had until only recently been completely innocent) had begun to soil it. Thoughts like these stirred everything inside
of him around until he was dizzy.

Every time he heard Okazawa's name, a spasm much like that
strange sensation he once felt ran through the base of his jaw.

He thought his heart would spill over. Everything pure and good in
the world and everything vile and depraved in the world swirled like
fire inside his small head. Lifting his eyes, he saw the wild blue of the
clear and gaping sky threatening to suck him in. The light of the setting
sun seemed to sway gently.

He was dizzy.

"Look out!"

A cart struck his elbow with terrible force, catching him off guard,
and then kept going.

The awnings of the buildings that lined the narrow street had been
pulled across toward each other, creating a rather effective makeshift
shade for a number of blocks.

He came to the front of the big Hachiman shrine surrounded by
houses. Feeling a desire to pray, he stood in front of the shrine, gathered
his thoughts, and bowed his head. And yet he had no idea for what he
should pray.

The sultry and desolate weather continued.

Waves of heat rose like a mirage from the freshly watered and turned
dirt road. The sun glittered on the broad, copper-red back of a fisherman carrying the morning's catch to market. Along the rows of houses,
here and there flowerpots were lined up with pride. The big morning
glories in them opened each morning.

Out where the road was entirely deserted, he could hear people on
the Shikoku pilgrimage. They would be dressed in white. He could
hear them filling cups with cold barley tea from a jug set out next to
the lattice of an old house, drinking them, and filling them up again,
clicking their tongues at the heat now and then. He thought he heard
the rumbling of a cart coming to pick up beef from the slaughterhouse
set back from the road. Then indeed the heavy cart passed him by with
a tremendous shaking of the ground. He saw a thin sunshade of white
and pale yellow stripes that fluttered now and then as if it had just
remembered the wind.

Since starting elementary school, Yasura had been taught that naps came with deleterious effects. Those lessons had left a deep impression in his mind, and now, he considered the practice of napping to have a moral dimension.

From early July to late August each year, his late father had the habit of going into the storehouse after finishing his noontime meal to sleep through the afternoon on a rattan lounge chair. Then, after four, once the sun had fallen to a degree, he would come out of the storehouse. Yasura and his older brother quarreled on a practically daily basis. Yasura was a crybaby and his brother was mean, so the younger boy cried plenty. If his cries became loud enough, the lacquered door would slide open and the boys' father would appear before them. After standing and glaring at the two brothers from inside the door, he would go back into the house once his nap had been disturbed. On such days, he was sure to be in a bad temper. Thinking back on such times now, Yasura could still see his father's bloodshot eyes.

Compared to the average person, his mother was corpulent in the extreme. When the radiant, scorching afternoon sun came around, she would have Yasura mind the shop. "All right, I've had it," she would say, and then she would run back into the private part of the house and go to sleep. After lying down for no more than twenty minutes, she would come back out looking fully rested.

The naps of both his father and his mother were outside the bounds of any moral critique on Yasura's part. His father was a scholar who had amassed piles of books from Chinese men with difficult names like Zhu Xi and Wang Yangming.[18] His mother had gone to a women's college, and their educations gave them a certain beauty in the young boy's eyes. Owing to his father's stoic discipline, Yasura never bared his shoulders to wipe his sweat and cool off.

Yasura was leaning idly against the register at the store, staring into the dazzlingly bright street out front.

"Why, hello there. Haven't you gotten big!"

Just as he was beginning to doze, he was awakened by a woman's crisp yet fluid Kyoto accent. Lifting his face, he saw the woman who had once been his nanny. She had left for Kyoto to be married some four or five years ago. He was flustered and confused, and the right words did not come to his lips.

---

18. Neo-Confucian thinkers who had been influential in Japan since the early nineteenth century.

"Where is everyone else?"

Before she finished saying it, she had made her way through the shop to the entrance to the house. He couldn't contain himself. "Auntie from Kyoto is here!" he yelled.

From the interior, he could hear his nanny's voice as she talked excitedly for a while, the laughter that came to him somehow tangible.

"Well, I wondered what you would say. I'm telling you, there is nobody out there who has had worse luck than me. After all this worrying, I'll end up getting it in my veins and my lungs and I'm sure I'll die. And now you, young man, mean to tell me that you're already in your third year of junior high? Oh, time just rushes by!" He shut his eyes and listened to her speak.

He recalled the way she had told him how her family was among the oldest in Kawachi. She told him stories of the depths of feeling of the great lover Narihira, which he had heard many times, and the story of Shuntokumaru's karmic retribution, and other stories one after the other came rushing back to him, making him feel as though he were an infant folded into her arms, pawing at her soft bosom again.[19]

He was suddenly transported back to a day in his memory: the cavernous, empty house stood in front of him. Inside, the tops of its tall beams shone black with soot. He could clearly see a yellowed paper charm on one of the rafters. He examined it and concluded that it must be meant to prevent fires. Above the wide earthen-floored area near the door, there was a raised floor with room for six tatami mats surrounding a large sunken hearth in the middle of the room.

In the next room, a dim light spilled in from a horizontal window with no *shōji* or *fusuma*. Against the front wall of that room was a tall Buddhist altar. When he first arrived, he was inordinately giddy, but once he had calmed down, he saw that there was a woman lying on her side with her back to him. Her hair was done in a style called "new butterflies," which made Yasura sure it must be his nanny. A white-haired old woman was spinning thread on the other side of the hearth. Yasura felt a great deal of interest in her, since she had been the nanny to his nanny. In her small face, browned by the sun, her eyes were open wide

---

19. Probably referring to a *waka* poem by Ariwara no Narihira (825–880), featured in the *Ogura hyakunin isshu*, and originally appeared in the second imperial poetry collection the *Gosenshū* (vol. 11, Love poems 3, 776).

and her mouth was drawn up tight. She worked the spinning wheel
gently without saying a word to Yasura. Her pale blue kimono was
pulled down far enough to free one shoulder, so that he could see her
loose, wrinkled skin. Her reticence allowed Yasura to reach a relaxed
state of mind in her presence. After neatly folding his legs under himself, he began to doze.

The old woman's focus was absorbed by the creaking wheel she was
spinning. From time to time, she took up her scissors and snapped
them across the thread. His nanny didn't get up, even after he had
waited quite a long time. Now he felt utterly abandoned. First twenty
minutes, then thirty, and then forty passed in this manner. The old
woman raised her eyes now and then to glance at him. This caught him
off guard every time. Then he noticed that he could hear the distant
crowing of a cock. He could tell by what he saw when he arrived at
her house that there were no other houses for some distance around it.
It reminded him of the stage in one of the cheap productions that his
nanny had taken him to over at Sennichimae. It was set, after all, in
a house in the middle of an open field like this one, where an elderly
woman lived. A dashing, handsome young samurai and a beautiful
woman come seeking lodging for the night. Then the samurai suddenly
remembers something he had forgotten completely, so he leaves the
woman and heads intently down the *hanamichi*.[20] The young woman is
pregnant. After a short while, the old woman who had led them inside
reappears and begins sharpening a large kitchen cleaver on a grindstone.
When finished, the old woman grips the freshly sharpened blade in one
hand and peers into the interior room with a grin. Cat ears could be
seen on the top of her gray head.

The moment the old woman dashes into the other room, a scream
is heard, and the young woman comes running out, hair flailing,
her quilted winter kimono halfway pulled off, leaving a trail of thick
blood. The old woman comes out after her, pulling at her obi. As the
obi unwinds, the young woman is spun around and around. Mor-
tally wounded, the young woman collapses where she stands. The old
woman bends to one knee at the younger woman's side and begins
slashing at her belly. The young woman's limbs twitch a few times. A
smile festers on the old woman's face as she pulls the baby, covered in
blood, from the woman's body. He could see it all happening so vividly.

---

20. Part of a *noh* stage similar to a catwalk, extending into the audience area.

There was a ferocious fire burning in the hearth. The ends of a pair of thick fire tongs jutted out of the ash pile. His nanny was still sleeping, curled up like the murdered woman. The old woman spun her thread as before, her hands never stopping. The handful of hairs that stuck forlornly out of her head suggested cat ears. One after another, the stories of Kurodzuka, the ghost stories of Hitotsuya, and stories like Arima and Nabeshima that made all the hair on his body stand on end paraded through his mind. He tried closing his eyes. From time to time he would timidly peek through his eyelids to look at the old woman. He realized that at any moment now she could come tearing after him. This made his heart beat faster. Why wouldn't his nanny wake up? He felt sure that before the next half hour had passed, he would be reduced to nothing but bones. Desperate tears welled up in his eyes. He focused his entire being on listening in order to make sure he didn't miss any of the old woman's movements. When he raised his eyes, they were met squarely by those of the old woman, which gave him a chill. Yasura's fear mounted. Unable to stand being in the room any longer, he began to consider his options for escape.

Just outside the doors, which were open to the width of the room, a scarlet flower trembled.

And yet he couldn't help but picture her claws sinking into his back the instant he tried to leave the room. As if to appeal to any shred of sympathy she might have, he worked to be as still and pitiful looking as he could manage, sitting blank and expressionless. He felt that sitting in such a way was the only hope he had. A brittle cold like embracing a block of ice came over him and stayed there for more than an hour.

By the time the nanny at long last stretched her arms and legs out and rose, Yasura's terror had already reached its peak. As soon as he began to relax, the sadness that he had been holding inside came spilling forth at once, and he started to sob. His nanny came running over to him in surprise.

This had all happened the year just before his nanny went to Kyoto to get married. He had once gone back with her overnight to her hometown. His memory of that hectic time was as fresh as if everything had happened just yesterday.

"You just take it easy this evening, now, and then you can take Yasu for a nice stroll on the Dōtonbori and the Sennichimae and all that. I'll bet you'd like to see one of those plays at Fukuen that you liked so much!" He heard his mother's voice.

"What a way to be talked to! Don't be absurd. I'll have you know that I have not been to one play yet since moving up there. Everything since moving there has been an abject tragedy in any case, and I never even make it down to Fourth Avenue; we're left there working with all this dust from morning to night, and wouldn't you know, my husband had trouble with his lungs. And on top of that my stepson does nothing but get into trouble with the weavers, and he's only eighteen. I tell you he just chases those weaver girls everywhere, no way to stop him."

Her voice was strong but somber.

"But you know, the world isn't exactly something that's meant to be enjoyed as entertainment," his aunt said as if in consolation.

"That's exactly it. We come into this life only to suffer, and I think I'll suffer as much as I need to now so that I'll be saved in the next life. Lately when I have the time I've been going to Rokujō-san.[21] Early in the morning when I stand there in the wide, silent expanse of its grounds, something comes over me, and I start invoking the name of the Buddha without even realizing I'm doing it."

"That really does sound like something."

The voice of his grandmother, who should have been in her own room detached from the house, was also among them.

"You know—the head of the temple said the same thing. It's only after that point that you can get started. And you can't let that get away from you. You've got to strive if you want to hang onto it, is what he says. Oh yes, had I told you that the year before last I took my vows there? Now they call me Sister Myōjun. Can you imagine, like a real nun? Ah, now I've worn myself out jabbering on. I'll take a little tea, please."

This time he heard a voice coming from the kitchen. "I'll tell you we just barely made it with the one-year anniversary of my husband's death, things were so hectic. I was thinking you could perhaps write down his Buddhist name in the temple's death registry for me. He was such a scholar I can barely even write the characters correctly."

Yasura's aunt chimed in. "It's true, at the time it was just the two of us here, and we didn't have the first clue about what to do. Even when the first forty-nine days of mourning were up and we had to send around gifts, there were some nights that even after the day was over, instead of shutting the store, the two of us sat there and stared at each other. We'd sit there all night, wouldn't we?"

---

21. The nanny is referring to a temple.

"We did, that we did. That's about the way it was. Back then even when I tried to eat it wouldn't go down. I just couldn't imagine how I would go about raising five boys, I was just scared to death to even think about it. Oyana, I don't know how many nights I would have spent gnashing my teeth and crying in the bedroom if it hadn't been for your Oiku here staying on instead of going and getting married sooner," answered his mother.

"Oh, how silly. Can you just picture it? I will say that business has been good, but the truth is, his older sister was responsible for most of it, and his brother was there for us, too. I depended on him, but then he up and died, and now it's all come to rest on my shoulders. I didn't know what I would do. So many times I've thought to myself how much better things will be once my Ryu finally finishes school. And here I am a whole two years later, just now starting to get a handle on things. But then I remember that he's still two years away from graduating. It's enough to rob an old woman of her will to live."

"Why don't you take off your jacket, come up into the house and tell us all about Kyoto," his mother offered.

"Thank you kindly." His grandmother had taken the other old woman away with her.

Toward the back of the house, a Japanese robin (on loan from the *geta* shop across the street) incessantly repeated its high-pitched cry.

Hidden in the shadow on the other side of the glass door, Yasura watched the front of the shop that was open to the street.

The nanny did not want to waste any precious time taking the scenic route through her stories. Instead, Oyana stayed in the whole night, talking about everything she had stored up over five years, hardly stopping for air, to anyone in the house who would listen.

As they spoke of the past, she began to relax and to feel much as she had when she was in the house five years earlier. Osakan vocabulary and a Kawachi lilt crept back into her speech.

"They're only a year apart, but there's such a difference between our boy and your Yasu. Yasu puts everything into his schoolwork. But ours seems to have gotten interested in girls a little too soon, really."

"We don't have that problem with him, but you should see him eat—oh, it would astound you. Every time I turn around, he's in the cabinets or the pantry looking for something to eat. If he's got anything it's an appetite. It's not easy keeping him fed," said his mother, shutting her eyes tight.

"Even when he was seven or eight, whenever he would play with Osumi and the other children from along the river there, if they would get too close to him, he would start yelling and carrying on about how they were 'icky,' just like a little baby. Are you ever going to start liking girls, little Yasu?" his nanny teased.

"I don't know what you're talking about."

Yasura's face turned red as he stood up to leave. Then he went quietly up the stairs to the second floor. He went out onto the balcony that was now covered in dew and wallowed in his wish to simply crawl into a hole and disappear.

6

Once the break started, Yasura went to the school two mornings to water his garden, but after that found it impossible to find the motivation to continue. At first, he might think of it every few days. He could clearly envision the plants drying out, drawing nearer to death every second, but feeling helpless, he merely fumed in his futon. The real issue was that he couldn't bring himself to go to the school. After four or five days the feeling was no longer as strong as it had been. But then one morning he saw a bracing vision in his mind of the way the dew glinted on the white sand with the grass grown long on the sports yard. All at once, he felt the desire to stand in the center of the still schoolyard, so he left the house before the main gate had even been opened. Just as he had pictured, two stray dogs were running around the perfectly silent schoolyard. He went into the shed to take out the gardening tools.

There was no sign of anyone in the night watch room, but a kettle of water boiled insistently. The scent of brick clay imparted an indescribable nostalgia to the interior of the building. After a quick look around, he put his hands softly onto the floor of the corridor, and lying flat on his belly, breathed in fragrances he had never before known. He began to think that he was hearing a succession of sounds that might indicate someone approaching from afar. Yasura stood up. He had only imagined the sounds. Nevertheless, he could feel that his face had turned red.

After half an hour, he found himself standing idly again amid the dried-up flowering plants in the garden.

A few streaks of green still clung to the stems among the leaves here and there. The strawflowers alone had retained their color, but they made a dry noise when his fingers touched them. He felt the wretchedness of shame and regret welling up inside him. *These honest, hardworking flowers have all dried up and died while I was burning with filthy thoughts and desires.* His beautiful, fragile heart withered and died with those flowers. The trampled brown plants bore the distinct footprints of a young boy falling into a life of dissipation.

His vision grew clouded, and soon he could contain it no longer. Tears splashed down onto the leaves of the flowers.

Yasura had been given a space on the second floor as his own room. It was little more than a storage space that had been tidied just enough to make room to put his desk in it. Bags of citrus peels, heartleaf, and other strong herbal ingredients were piled up there to be sold in the shop. Their fragrances permeated the quiet room.

To one side of Yasura's desk stood his aunt's full-length mirror. The women of the house, consumed with the family business to the point that they had no time to bother much with their appearance, had left this mirror on the second floor. Once in a while, however, his mother or one of the others would come up to where the mirror was, holding her hair like a bird's nest in one hand, and would announce that she was going out to pick something up. Whenever this happened Yasura would go out onto the balcony because he hated to see the dandruff flying. After about ten minutes had passed and he felt it was likely that it was all over, he would come creeping warily back into the room. There were even times when, sitting and reading a book, he would stare enchanted at his own face reflected in the mirror. Then he would hear someone come thumping up the stairs. Flustered, he would drop his eyes to the pages of his book, pretending to be reading any random line. The mirror reflected nearly his entire upper body. Southern exposure and a low ceiling kept the second-floor room stuffy and humid even at night.

His two older brothers had gone away to school, one to the northern provinces and the other down to Kyushu, meaning that aside from Yasura and his younger brothers (twins who had just turned seven), there were no males in the house. This allowed Yasura to enjoy the same treatment a full-grown man might expect in his home. The maid prepared the bath every day throughout the summer, and he always went in first. After him his aunt bathed, and then his mother.

Yasura had already been soaking in the bath for nearly an hour, remaining almost motionless as he enjoyed the water playing tenderly against his skin. When he opened the small vent for light, cooler air came rushing in to revive him. From the space between the house and the storehouse, he could see the clear blue sky.

As he soaked, Okazawa crossed his mind. It appeared to him lately that everything he thought and everything he did was somehow linked to Okazawa. Yasura felt this was something to despise.

"Yasu, what *could* you be doing in there? Have you melted?"

When he heard his aunt call from the house Yasura recoiled, as if his sinful thoughts had been suspected.

Making only a hurried reply, he flew out of the tub and up the stairs.

Long, tilted shafts of light from the summer sun shone down low from the propped-open windows, gently warming the fragrance of the tatami.

Sweat rolled in beads down Yasura's skin. He opened the windows and the *shōji*. The leaves of the varnish tree shook and then all at once, wind rushed in. Looking backward, he saw himself reflected in the tilted mirror, waving up and down. The sunlight seemed to shine right through his skin, which was smooth as marble. Lately he would spend time staring with feigned disinterest at his shoulders, which had started to become thicker and more muscular, and at the soft curves of his chest.

He raised his arms slightly and brought them together near the nape of his neck. The flesh of his shoulders was snowy and supple where it met his slight arms. He felt his heart fill and stretch with curiosity, as though he had found something mysterious hidden within himself. Adjusting the mirror to face downward onto himself, he posed with one leg thrust straight out and the other bent inward. The curves of his midsection folded together into an array of tense lines that extended down to his shins. Facing backward, trying to see himself from behind over his shoulder, he struck a few more poses. Each of these revealed to him the pulsating of his various muscles through his skin, and he was enthralled by an indescribable pleasure.

All at once an emotion that he could describe as neither sad nor happy cut across his heart. Unmoving, [text missing]

Yasura's grandfather on the Uruma side had already been dead for some years by the time Yasura was born. This grandfather had been adopted into the Uruma family, but the grandfather's mother could not bear children and his father died early, so she raised him on her own, all while running a sizable enterprise.[22] Yasura's great-grandmother had arranged for her adopted son to take a distant relation as a wife.

His grandfather had been born to a family in Yamato that was involved in official religious ceremonies. He had died twenty years ago already, but his name still came up often where he had lived. The people spoke highly of him, saying he was as broad-natured as the sea in spring, and they had countless anecdotes that attested to his compassion.

Around that time his grandfather's brother was running the main house and all of the family's affairs in Yamato, but this brother's wife was a wicked person who often offended Yasura's great-grandmother. Yasura's grandfather, growing worried, made various efforts toward a reconciliation between the two, but once the families were separated, their members continued to grow further apart. Then in the summer of 1885, there was an outbreak of cholera. Yasura's grandfather was a doctor, so he spent his time doing everything he could for the people in the area, working through every night. By the time autumn arrived, the disease had lost much of its momentum. It was just then that the doctor himself, who had only begun to have some reprieve from the hardest part of his work, contracted the illness that ended up claiming his life. This person, who had lived a life so full of compassion, finished it writhing in agony, throwing the covers off no matter how many times they were put back on him. When people heard that he had died, wailing could be heard ringing out from the eaves of the nearby *eta* village.[23]

Many people there lamented his death, recognizing the fact that now that he was gone, there would likely no longer be anyone willing and able to tend to the sick in their village.

When Yasura's grandfather died, Yasura's willful father took his place. Having been adopted from a rural but respectable and relatively well-to-do family, his father, never one to bow down to anyone, was not interested in troubling himself with the burdens of socializing with his

22. It was common for the husband of a woman to be adopted by her family if the husband was to inherit the family business or occupation.

23. This refers to a section of town or a completely separate community of people traditionally considered "ritually unclean" (originally due to occupational associations with butchery, tanning, and undertaking) and thus placed in the lowest caste in society, the so-called *burakumin*, who are still subject to discrimination to the present day.

new family. This led to him eventually falling completely out of contact with his own father's main house.

Meanwhile, on the other end, Yasura's father's aunt, older brother, and nephew from his birth family all died, leaving few with blood ties to Yasura's grandfather. Then in the Uruma family, his father had succumbed to a heart attack three years before. This meant that on both sides, only women remained, along with a considerable number of children.

As soon as Yasura was old enough to understand what was going on around him, he had heard that he had such relatives in Yamato and had often wondered why he did not also get to go anywhere like other children did on holidays—why was it that no one came to visit them from his father's side, be it Obon or New Year, or even memorial days for anyone in the family? Both his grandfather and his father had composed poetry of various types and had been rather well versed in the classics, so much so that the stories of ages past, and places like Yamato and Nara began to excite him to no small degree, though Yasura himself knew nothing of them. In Asuka, in Takechi, Yamato province—his home, land of antiquity—lay the origin of his ancient family with its two thousand years of history. That was where Yasura's grandfather was from. When he thought about this, he became aware of his entire body ringing, as if some mysterious power were radiating outward from the tips of his fingernails and the ends of his hair.

Before this year, he had never been allowed to take any kind of overnight trip by himself. Last year and the year before as well, during spring and late summer vacation he entreated his aunt and his mother, but they refused. They said it was too dangerous. This summer, however, he would finally be allowed to go. When they asked where he would go, he replied without hesitation: "Yamato." Then they asked who he would go with. That was when he knew he was trapped. Betraying nothing of this in his answer, however, he said: "Saitō." He felt sweat seep outward from his armpits. Saitō was a boy he had known since elementary school, and now they went to the same junior high. This was how he finally received reluctant permission for one night away from home. Yasura was walking on air. He climbed the stairs to his room. After a short while, however, that pleasant feeling began to flag, as though caught on something, and he became more and more dissatisfied. He turned pensive, wondering what had possessed him to lie. He pictured his own face as he looked his aunt in the eye and said,

"With Saitō." He could not abuse and revile himself enough for having made his face into a mask of sincerity to deceive his aunt and look polite while he told her an obvious lie.

That was it. There was only one way that he could make up for the lie he had told. He had to be sure to compel Saitō to accompany him on this trip. As soon as he decided this, he felt as though all the tension left his shoulders at once. He dashed the half-mile over to Saitō's.

"Is Itchan around?"

Saitō's older sister, forming package after package of miso in bamboo skin as she talked with a customer, turned toward the house and said, "Itchan, Yasu's here to see you!"

"Oh yeah?"

Although he was in the same year as Yasura, Saitō was taller than the average adult. He always had a trail of snot down to his upper lip. Now and then he would make a stopped-up slurping sound. That's the type of boy he was. Yasura pulled him just out into the front of the house and whispered to him to play along.

"I really would love to, but my mother's so awful sick, they have my sister and all of us staying up to take care of her every night."

"So you really can't go?"

"I do want to, but if I ask now, I'll get in trouble."

"I see. Sure. In that case, I suppose I'll have to go by myself."

"I do wish I could go with you. Send me a postcard, will you?"

"You bet."

Yasura wanted to cry.

After Yasura had walked no more than a hundred yards away, Saitō came chasing after him.

"Uruma, you don't have a map of Yamato, do you? Take this with you."

He handed him a map dingy from handling.

7

It had been a steamy, hot day since morning. Wearing his stark white, wide-brimmed straw hat, Yasura rushed to the train platform. Nevertheless, his mood was dark and gloomy. His mother and his aunt were satisfied, since as far as they knew, he would be going with Saitō. Tremulous excitement in his heart had not allowed him any sleep at all the night before. Now and then clouds cast a pall over the joyful anticipation he felt about his first unchaperoned trip, which he had been nursing so dearly. Once day broke, however, the thing that had kept him occupied with worry the whole night through seemed like nothing more than a dream. When he left the house, he was once again trapped by an intractable anxiety. He was caught off guard by the realization that he might be heading toward some dreadful fate that now awaited him as punishment for having deceived his mother and aunt. The locomotive pulled through the meadow, trailing layered streaks of summer mist. At last he suddenly realized that he was now beyond the reach of his aunt, his mother, and all the rest, and finally got a taste of what it is to be at ease, free of obligations.

The fact that Saitō was not with him began to make him seriously worry that someone at home might find out that he had gone alone. He tried to envision various scenarios in which someone from Saitō's place and someone from his own house might encounter one another. He worked himself into a panic and then silently prayed that no such scenario would arise between today and when he returned home the next day. He wondered if any deity would answer such a wicked prayer, but his doubts did not stop him from praying that no one at home would find out.

After two hours, the train stopped at the station he had been waiting for. Where the road ended at the edge of this country town, there was a large stone well cover littered with willow leaves. Next to it, a decorative canna stood withered. A red dragonfly flew dizzyingly through the low sky.

He came out on the bank of a dry river that was deep and wide. From time to time he heard the sound of vibrating wings from the thick stands of new bamboo.

The three Yamato mountains stood facing one another at some distance with Yasura standing between them. They seemed to command him to recall romantic competitions of the age of the gods. That spring he had gotten someone to buy him his first copy of *Man'yōshū*, and in the beginning he only felt somewhat uncomfortable with the competition between the poets Naka Oine and Ōkiama, but now he had become more able to recognize the legitimacy of the feelings of the two princes.[24]

---

24. The *Man'yōshū* was the first Japanese poetry collection, and the oldest collection writ-

When he finally turned away, the lush green, rounded curves of Miminashiyama, the swaggering, masculine figure of Unebiyama's shoulders, and Kaguyama in the shape of a woman past her prime, stirred up an indescribable feeling of pathos within him.

The green fields extended far out beyond the completely silent meadow, and the sun burned slowly. From time to time the wind stirred dust up under the noontime sun. He came to a place where there was a large gutter for collecting rain. A big, old hackberry tree cast a wide shadow over it. Lately Yasura had begun to feel somehow that he was beginning to see the world with a terrifying clarity. Just then, he found himself enchanted by his own visions of a terrific power that grew and spread throughout dead grass now come to life, that life force rushing through it like water swirling down all at once through a full rain gutter the moment it becomes unclogged.

The sun had burned off the clouds and the deep blue sky stretched on endlessly.

He climbed down onto the gravelly bank of the river and urinated freely to his heart's content. The light shone directly on his pale lower abdomen, making it shine. In that instant, he felt an extraordinary power well up within him.

He ran like mad over the riverbed in a short straight line.

I wish they would leave the brush uncut high on the Saho's banks
so that in it we two could hide from prying eyes

He strained his voice to sing a *sedōka* with such force it seemed he would rip apart.[25] A little further down was an *eta* village. Looking at

---

ten in Japanese (albeit using Chinese characters), completed around 785. Orikuchi and the Araragi school with which he was affiliated for many years were devoted to reviving poetry of the style and tone found in this collection, often seen as more masculine, folksy, and raw as opposed to the more feminine, courtly, and refined sensibilities of later collections. As such, Orikuchi wrote extensively on the *Man'yōshū* and its poets and was heavily influenced by it in his own poetry.

25. This *sedōka* (an ancient form of Japanese poetry) is based on one found in the fourth book of the *Man 'yōshū* mentioned in the previous footnote. *Sedōka* is one of the least common forms found in the collection, longer than tanka and more open than longer forms in the collection, but still features a 5-7-7-5-7-7 meter. This one has been modified by Yasura. The original poem reads: *saho kawa no / kishi no tsukasa no / shiba nakarisone / aritsutsu mo / haru shi kitaraba / tachikakuru gane.* Yasura's version rewrites the penultimate *ku* (*haru shi kitaraba*—because spring is now here) as *kimi to futari ga* (together with you).

the roof of the temple, which was large for the village, from where he stood on the stone bridge, he saw the hides of four or five dogs spread out on the rather wide riverbed. On the veranda of a small house that had been left open, a young man wearing only a red loincloth was sleeping. The veranda faced a thicket. In front of the house the lever of a mortar hung its head in a lonesome looking way.

Near the ruins of the Toyura Palace and the temple where the stone tablet is kept, the rocks fell sharply, forming a natural promontory in one place.[26] When he came to that area, water babbled as it ran over the rocks. Under the promontory, there were two boys—one sixteen or seventeen, and the other perhaps eleven or twelve, catching little fish with a net-like basket.

Sensing that someone was standing up on the embankment, the older one looked up at him.

His hair at the hairline had grown out to just about half an inch, softly framing the top of his round white face.

Lifting his clear eyes, he stared at Yasura.

Yasura felt as if he had been suspected in some way, and his face began to burn. He hurried away, feeling the eyes of the boys watching him as he walked quickly.

The road followed a stream that cut across the lower part of the mountains.

He knew that he had seen that face somewhere before. It seemed like it must have belonged to someone he had seen often before but had not seen lately. He tried the face this way and that in his mind. No, this was not a face he had ever seen before in this life, he realized. It was a face he had first seen in a past far more distant than that. Or could it be some trick of his immature mind, as if he were dreaming while wide awake? He wondered. When he realized where he was, he could see a small hill rising out of the middle of the fields about two hundred yards in the direction of the mountain. With the help of the map, he found what he supposed was his grandfather's shrine. The village during nap time was completely still like the middle of the night. The smell of roasting rice bran hung in the air. Cedar sprigs gathered into a large *sakabayashi* wreath were hung from the eaves of one house.[27]

---

26. A palace once used by Empress Suiko (554–628).

27. The spherical evergreen wreath known as a *sakabayashi* typically indicates that the

He heard footsteps come running up behind him noisily. When he looked back, he saw the smaller boy carrying a net running up behind the older boy, who had a fish basket on his shoulder. Both boys had their hems tucked up high in their belts and walked barefoot on the hot earth. The bigger of the two stared at Yasura as they passed him by.

The mountains he had seen earlier revealed a stone stairway that went some thirty steps up from the eastern end of the village. At the foot of the mountain stood a house surrounded by a crumbling white wall. He could just vaguely make out the surname, the same as the name of the village, written on the plate at the front gate. Yasura stepped cautiously over the threshold. He walked tensely across the stone floor between the gate and the entrance.

"Hello?"

When he was finally able to call out, the relief he felt at still having a working voice led him to believe that the most critical part of his ordeal was over. Once he had calmed down, he was able to make out more of the house's appearance. This relief, however, was scarcely different from the vague feeling he had had before of what was to come. It didn't seem that anyone would appear.

"Hello? Is anyone here?"

This time his voice came out with ease. He heard steps on a wooden floor from far away. Someone was coming.

"Who is it?"

A woman of perhaps fifty opened the poorly fitted *shōji* to reveal her face.

8

The imposing grand shrine that once featured in the background of the classics was now an old shack in the middle of a field, leaning in a way that made one think of the end of the older Shinto ways. Behind it, the mountains connected to Tōnomine extended toward the south. The soft curves of the green mountains drifted across a meadow lying out to the side that shimmered with the heat of the sun.

He crouched down and closed his eyes in front of the shrine of his ancestral deity. As he was doing that, the mind of that deity merged with his, warm. *The things you do now are no different from what has*

---

building belongs to a brewer of sake.

always been done. None of those things can be considered a sin before me.
He felt as if a voice were whispering to him that what he must do was
in fact right in front of his very eyes.

What you must do. But what could that be? He considered it as he went
down the stone steps. Far below, he could see chickens scratching in
the yard of the house where his grandfather was raised. He could see it
as clearly as though he might grasp it in his hand. He realized that he
needed to restore the ties between the two sides of his family, which had
been growing further apart, to what they had formerly been. He ran
swiftly down the steps. When he arrived once again in front of the gate,
Yasura froze. The woman from earlier must be his aunt. Why hadn't he
just told her who he was then? He couldn't help regretting that when
she asked where he came from, he had said Osaka and left it at that,
only to receive a purifying blessing and run away. What could he possibly say at this point to her to get her to let him in? And who knows
what terrifying sorts of people might be there in addition to the first
old woman he had seen. Just imagining what it might be like to have
a conversation with and explain himself to people like these, people he
had never met before, was agony for him.

He was surprised to hear someone come running out after he had
left. After walking about fifty yards, he looked back and saw the bigger
boy from earlier. He had been watching Yasura as he went.

When he came out of the village on its south side and went across
the fields, he found a small temple called Ango-in.[28] Yasura peered
at what was behind the lattice. A mosquito flew at him from out of
the darkness, brushing against his eyelashes. His eyes gradually grew
accustomed to the darkness, and little by little he began to be able to
make out what the inside of the hall looked like. Only the eyes of the
large, jet-black statue of the Buddha glinted with a golden light. The
egg-shaped stone memorial for Soga no Iruka[29] stood on the built-up
division between tobacco fields. He looked around himself, in front
and behind. Then he kicked his legs up high. His tall *geta* made a thick
wooden sound. The sun shone red, and the earth withered below, yel-

---

28. Ango-in is a remnant of Asuka-dera, one of the first Buddhist complexes built in
Japan, which dates back to the end of the sixth century.

29. The Soga family was one of the most important political families during the Asuka
period (sixth to eighth centuries). Iruka was assassinated in a coup in 645.

low. He could see frayed and tangled-looking bamboo thickets here and there. The few small shacks that stood in the meadow seemed about to collapse, dizzy with exhaustion. He came to the river. On the riverbank, the green grasses had fallen over and the bindweed bloomed faint white.

After visiting two other temples, called Tachibanadera and Okadera, Yasura climbed up toward Tōnomine. Sweat dripped down his back.

Soon after the *aburasemi*, concentrated in the thin branches, fell silent, the *higurashi* began with their cries like a bell being struck.[30]

"How does one get to Hase from here?" he asked an old monk standing in a grove of cedars. The sun's light shone through the trees at a rather sharp slant.

"Take the main road down a quarter of a mile to get to a place called Kurahashi, and then from there you'll want to cross over to a village called Ossaka. The sun will set before you get there unless you really hurry."

When he left for Ossaka it was twilight. People's faces became less distinct. The last light of the sun hit some peak he did not know the name of, and the children of the village were throwing stones and chasing each other. Purplish smoke from a fire for the bath rose from one house. The smell of green wood burning reminded him painfully of the loneliness of his journey. An hour later, when he arrived at Hase, the sun had already sunk below the horizon. Several times he went up and down the street lined with inns. At long last, he took the plunge and went into one of them. It made him sweat to go into one of these in a town so deep in the mountains. He left the room full of the smell of oil smoke and climbed up toward the main hall of Hasedera. The long corridor leading up to it wound and wound up the steep incline. Coming to a platform, he saw the moon, draped in mist, spilling hazy light on its floorboards. From the time he had come up the mountain until he had arrived at where he was now, he hadn't encountered a single person. He went over to lean on the railing and looked down over the town. Though lights still burned in many houses, there was not a sound to be heard. He closed his eyes and soon found himself enraptured. His feelings were much like those of a woman coming to stay at this temple on a pilgrimage from the Heian court. When he opened his eyes just slightly, he saw that the moon had come out from behind the clouds, brightly illuminating the folds in the sides of the mountains. The sound

---

30. *Aburasemi* and *higurashi* are two types of cicadas with distinct calls.

of his *geta* on the boards echoed across the peaks and valleys. The night quietly grew late.

Round pillars stood here and there, creating dim corners. Yasura walked reverently around the hall without making a sound. He circled around it once and returned to the platform. Looking back for a moment as he walked away, he saw a white figure glide toward the hall's heavy lattice shutters. Yasura fixed his eyes on it and did not move a muscle. Then, cautiously, Yasura drew closer.

The outline of the white figure melted away and disappeared like a dream.

The shrill cry of a bird could be heard from the wild side of the mountain behind the temple.

The road gradually climbed higher and higher. Beneath him lay the hills, the rivers, and the forests. The sun shone brightly. The morning was quiet—not a single insect stirred.

At the end of the road far to the south behind the mountain, he continued up a steep slope until he came to a flat area where he could see another steep slope up ahead. There were various small groves and stands of trees on either side of the slope. Now and then birds would unexpectedly take flight from the branches above him. His white shins were now wet with dew. Where the trees were thinner, he could see through to a small mound. As he stepped up onto that mound, he froze where he stood. His hair stood on end and he broke out in a cold sweat. It was a snake. He felt fear surge up within himself. In the next instant, however, he was calm again. Yasura fixed his eyes directly on the snake. It was a thin line of coral pink stretched out atop the grass. His heart was still racing. He stood on tiptoe and watched the slender pink line slip peacefully into a dewy clump of overgrown grass. His eyes burned with hatred for it.

The crickets began to chirp and the weather turned ill-tempered as it had done the day before. The path split into two. One went up to the pines above the far side the mountain. The other went straight down to the houses that could be seen at the foot of the mountain. Looking around, Yasura saw that just ahead, there was a shack in the middle of the mandarin orange orchards. He walked cautiously toward it. Peeking inside the raised shutter, what he saw startled him enough to knock him back two or three steps. From within the shack, a sturdy man of about twenty was looking back at him with a lewd grin that dominated his dull face, crawling toward the door on his hands and knees, surprised.

Time and again, Yasura looked behind him. He even crouched down and tried to prick up his ears. He couldn't hear anyone in the depths of this cypress forest. When he closed his eyes, he saw a vivid image of the ruddy pink snake tangled around the naked arms and thighs of the man keeping watch over the mountain.

Later that afternoon, he found himself standing at the entrance of the grounds of Miwa Shrine, where a huge cedar cast its shadow over the burning white sand. The wind from the top of the mountain blew down from the peak that he had just come over.

He traveled along the far-reaching paths through the fields as he ruminated on the love story of Odamaki-dzuka Sugisakaya. Just about the time the lights were being lit, he took his exhausted body over toward a bench near a railway station. Twilight hung blue. Suddenly, a young man walked up beside him.

"You come from Osaka?"

"Yes."

"Whereabouts?"

"The south."

"You go to school?"

"Kudara Junior High."

"You know somebody named Atsumi there at your school?"

Atsumi . . . Atsumi . . . he felt as though he were being dragged to waking from the depths of a deep sleep.

"Atsumi . . . yes, there's an Atsumi."

"You know him?"

"We're in the same class."

"Well, that's something—truth is, he's a relative of mine. He's my little cousin. We haven't seen each other for a long time, though. Can I ask what year you're in?"

"Third."

He began to feel as if he were choking.

"You still have a little time. How about we step out? It's so hot I can't stand it in here."

The young man cut across the middle of the field and continued out toward the bank where he could see fifty yards out in front of him. The moon floated upward. The stream, thinner from the dryness of summer, flowed past the dry ground he stood on, only a foot or so across.

The bush clover was just beginning to bloom. The two were enveloped in its exciting fragrance. The young man sat down on the dry riverbed.

"Oh, the crickets! You know that one? It's called an *umaoi*. And that one coming from way over there—that's a *matsumushi*. There's a *suzu-mushi*, too![31] Don't they sound nice? You try bringing a little lantern out here some night. It's really something to see—they'll all jump right onto it."

Yasura knew he needed to respond somehow. The more he thought about it, though, the tighter his chest felt, and he couldn't get a single word out. When he heard the name Atsumi, he had felt a strange trembling in his heart. The fact that he had met Atsumi's older cousin in a place like this inspired in him a feeling he was at a loss to describe.

"I'm going to the First High School. You know, I haven't seen him for three years already. I'll bet he's grown a lot, right? How's he doing with his grades?"

"Seems he does all right. He always makes the honor roll."

The bush clover swayed, glimmering in the tender light of the moon and somehow reminding Yasura of Atsumi's face.

The young man took a watch out of his obi. Its glint penetrated Yasura's eyes through the nighttime fog.

"You ought to head back to the platform. The train for Nara will be here in no time. And when you see Atsumi, you tell him that studying is important, but he needs to make sure to get some exercise, too. You tell him that's what Yanagita in Tambaichi said."

The train came. The young man came to the window to bid him farewell before walking off, dragging his walking stick along the platform.

The young man had an angular, almost diamond-shaped face.

When he returned home, it was as if nothing had happened. His aunt, mother, and everyone else seemed to want to hear stories from his trip. They pressed him with questions: *how was Tōnomine* and *was Hase nice* and so on, making him feel frustrated with the depth of their investigation. He was afraid that some question about Saitō might arise at any moment, but they showed no sign that they knew or suspected anything.

"We were really worried about you, though. We know how care-

---

31. Different types of crickets and grasshoppers.

less you are all the time, and then you go off to visit those shrines." Thinking he had at last perhaps found a way out, he began talking about visiting his father's family's shrine, detailing everything from the completely dilapidated condition of the shrine to the appearance of his father's family home, talking so much that it seemed odd even to him.

"Right, I almost forgot—I brought back a charm."

He brought it out of his bag and handed it to his aunt.

That night, all alone in the large mosquito net, he lay still but irritable. He could still see the pink snake, softly glinting as it slithered through the dewy fields of grass right in front of him. He fanned himself in intermittent bursts but that did not stop his pajamas from getting soaked with sweat. He crawled out of the mosquito net and tried sitting in a chair on one end of the veranda. The sound of the night shift pounding soybeans in a mortar could be heard from the tofu maker's shop next door. The wind began to howl. Feeling rather refreshed, he rolled into his bedding on the floor. He put the comforter over his head and shut his eyes tight underneath it. The covers soon filled with warm, moist air as he sucked on his upper arms, staying perfectly still as though he were coagulating. Once enclosed in this pocket of steam and sweat, he fell into a deep sleep.

9

Because in this town they held Tanabata and Urabon celebrations according to the old lunar calendar, the white of the Milky Way could still be seen stretched across the sky. When the sun went down, he would bring a blanket out onto the balcony nearly every day. He would lie on his back to sleep and count each of the stars as they appeared in the dark blue sky above—it made him feel like flying away just like that.

"The balcony's already cooled off nice, hasn't it? I was thinking I'd probably better lay off, but when it's time for the bats to come out I end up getting wound up and coming out here with a bottle of sake." Nisaburō, the eel monger next door to the east, was a lively man of fifty or so. He was shirtless and talked to Yasura almost as if he were another adult while he sat at a small table drinking and snacking on chilled tofu.

"You'll be called up before too long, won't you? How old are you this year?"

"Fifteen."

"Fifteen, huh? I thought you must've been all of seventeen!"

He let out an exaggerated moan.

"Well how about you climb over the roofs to me here. I'll show you a couple of things."

He had known Nisaburō since he was small enough to be carried around on his nanny's back. His nanny took him with her like that to go visiting at Nisaburō's all the time—so often in fact that people began to talk. Though Nisaburō had rather begun to decline, to Yasura, he still appeared as he did then when he was in the prime of his manhood, seeming more youthful than he actually was.

The moon rose, large in the soot-smeared eastern sky.

"I tell you, boy, when I was your age, when Bon came around you just couldn't keep us indoors. We'd put on yukatas and go chase the girls around. Yessir, that was all we thought of once we turned fourteen or fifteen. You must think that's crazy, huh? But that's fine, after all you're sharp when it comes to school. The bottom line is, you've got to see to your studies. You better be sure to watch yourself—even a boy like you, you can blunder just once and it might throw everything off— that's why I'm telling you that where you start out is important. You just remember that and keep yourself in line. But what do you think? If you want, I could find somebody for you."

He cackled and talked on and on like a buffoon.

"Don't listen to his nonsense. Your aunt and them would be furi- ous," said Nisaburō's wife said suddenly. "Oh, Yasu, what's the matter— has he upset you, too? See how nasty he is. You can see for yourself the sorrow a lack of schooling brings," she said. Then she turned to her husband. "But really, what do you do out there so long? Don't you think you'll catch a cold being half naked? Minamoto from Naniwa is here saying he wants to talk about what he bought from you earlier today. We'll call it a night."

She sent Nisaburō downstairs and then followed him down after clearing the table. When Yasura put his back against the nighttime cold that had settled on the boards and shut his eyes, he felt that his body and mind were settled and clear. He could hear the chattering of people coming and going to the front of the house. The stars were drowned out in places by the light of the moon, but the zodiacal light gave the sky above the horizon a blurred, faint glow. The leaves of a varnish tree reached toward the balcony. They looked blue in the dark.

The next day he stayed in the upstairs room all day, slung across his desk, eyes closed, not moving. Every day, between one and three, the wind seemed to stop completely. The daytime moon could be seen faintly in the depths of the burning, wide-open sky. The foundation stone of the old temple and the huge stone doors that seemed to be looking upward glittered in front of his enraptured eyes. Soon, groups of five or ten people began to come down from the mountain using the red fans they had gotten at their lodging in Yoshino somewhere, and pass him by as they gossiped in loud voices about the fields back at home. His body was completely exhausted, and his senses were nearly entirely asleep. His heart alone, however, was awake within his closed-off body, observing things with full clarity. A clock struck three, making a sound like an old-fashioned oil press being worked. On his desk, a typeset edition of *Sankashū* was open.[32] His late father had known a bit about haiku. From about the time that he moved from nursery school to elementary school, his father would always call him to his bed when it was still dim outside—*Yasura, Yasura*. He would go running clumsily through the two rooms separating his father's bed and his own. His father would pull him into the comforter and teach him the one about the old pond, the one about the withered branch, and so on. He would have Yasura memorize them by repeating.[33] From that time on, the vague light of this bright and unknown land of poetry had shone on his undeveloped mind. Even now there were likely a dozen or two that he had memorized less than perfectly. More and more, Yasura felt that in his heart there was a world where he belonged more than he had ever belonged even with his own family.

"Tell me of the sadness of this mountain, old yam digger."[34]

The lines of poetry that came back to him one after the other only brought tears to his eyes. When he dropped his eyes to the text, he saw the tanka that starts "As I go into the mountains in Yoshino with no intention of coming back . . ." Lately he had begun to be able to envision very vividly the worlds that poets like Saigyō and Bashō had inhabited. Often, he felt that it made no sense for this to be the case, however. The world at such times looked altogether too fragile, too illusory. Sometimes he felt like he wanted to hide from all his friends

---

32. A collection of tanka by Saigyō (1118–1190).
33. Both refer to well-known haiku by Matsuo Bashō (1644–1694).
34. Also attributed to Bashō.

so that he could burst out from somewhere to startle them. The path that poets like Saigyō and Bashō had walked now lay unmistakably before him. Whenever Yasura tried to take this road, a coral-colored snake would come slithering from out of nowhere and block his route. He writhed in frustration. It made him so frantic he wanted to pull out every hair on his head.

"Yasu, there's mail for you."

When he glanced over, rather than coming all the way up the stairs, his mother was standing there, holding it out to him.

"How about that."

Two pieces of mail had come for him.

One was a picture postcard. Over the printed photograph of lines of pines standing in front of a large Mount Fuji were the words:

Will be climbing Fuji soon. Will share details upon return to Osaka. Begging your affection more than ever.
The East Gate, August 20

This was without a doubt the work of Okazawa. Yasura burst out laughing. He couldn't help but laugh at a level of vanity that would prompt this young man to write something as nonsensical as "begging your affection more than ever." He felt a sort of vague satisfaction with the idea that he had finally been able to free himself from Okazawa, who had held him captive for so long. He resisted the urge to mock his own shallowness and looked at the back of the other piece of mail. He glimpsed the sender's name and location: Taizō Atsumi, in the mountains west of Kyoto. All at once he felt like he wanted to bury himself in a hole in the ground. He felt his face turn red. His mind was full of grandiose hopes. And yet here he was with this letter, unable to make up his mind to open it. He paced anxiously around the room.

He wanted to read the letter from Atsumi in a calmer, less frantic state. He thought that it would be best to approach it with the same frame of mind he did whenever they talked. He tried to think of where he could read the letter with no noise to interfere. Stifling the sound of his steps, he held onto this feeling with the utmost care as he descended the stairs. There was a narrow space that led to the outhouse just behind the storehouse. The amaranth here had grown to a considerable height, but now withered, defeated by the late summer heat. Yasura put his *geta* on in the yard and went around to the back. He was afraid to even touch a letter written by someone so pure as Atsumi, having a mind as soiled as his own. He broke the seal on the letter with trepidation.

⸺While it is lonely lying here by myself in the moonlight that shines into this quiet study, it gives me a real taste of what it feels like to be apart from the world. I want with all my heart for you to come here, but at the same time I feel that you should pay no attention to that, because even if you were to come I would be unable to tell you even a tiny fraction of what is in my heart. So, I shall write it here after all. How can I tell you what has befallen me? When I am talking with you I get like this; I can't seem to stop my mind from racing. Even as I write this here now, I am already losing my patience with this letter. What am I to do? I cannot ask you to come here. Because I've already written everything here. Nevertheless, if you do not come, I can make no promise that I will not hate you very much for it. I am no longer capable of making any decision, so there is nothing I can do but follow my heart. I will treat your decision on this matter as my own. I am certain that you must think me a very strange person to write such incomprehensible things⸺

Once Yasura found himself in such a state of elation, it was hard for him to get his feelings under control. And yet, just then, he became aware of a glimmer of resentment against Atsumi passing through his mind.

He read the letter over and over again. No matter how many times he did, however, there was something in this letter that did not sit well with him. Then the feeling he got whenever he talked with Atsumi came back to him. His bright and cheerful words that called to mind the crunchy, springy texture of a wood ear mushroom—how could a person who could say things like that with clear eyes write a letter like this? "When I am talking with you I get like this; I can't seem to stop my mind from racing." The truth was that Yasura always felt the same way when he was talking with Atsumi. He felt it must be some sort of prank, some vague insinuation, but Atsumi didn't seem the type to do something so mean as that. Why did he get this feeling then? How could Atsumi talk about such things so casually? Since the time they were in first year, whenever he heard Atsumi's name, he would feel a pleasing sensation like being caressed with soft fluff. Even Yasura

himself had no idea why this always happened to him. He had tried
thinking through the cause carefully on the train coming back the day
before. He realized, however, that no matter how he looked at the situation, it wasn't so different from his feelings toward Okazawa. He then
felt trapped by this uncomfortable thought. He had a vague fear that
for him to visit a pure person like Atsumi with a heart rooted in such
unclean soil as his would be to sully Atsumi somehow. It was impossible for him to believe that Atsumi could feel the same way he did.
He thought that if he could only go visit that temple in the mountains
to the west, everything would at last be resolved. As he had just come
back from his trip yesterday, however, he would be denied as soon as
he asked. Atsumi seemed difficult to get close to. Yasura thought of
himself as much more like Okazawa—the type to write something like
"begging your affection more than ever"—which made him sad. In the
quiet afternoon, the way he looked squatting here where no one would
see him, sweating, absorbed in his own miserable sadness, he thought
he resembled a beast curled up in a ball in some kind of cave. He began
to feel the pounding of the mill on the back street: its reverberations
approached and then went through him. Around the foundation of the
storehouse bloomed two clumps of heartleaf with pallid flowers. Yasura
stretched out his hand to pluck one. A strange smell like moldering,
rotten flesh struck his nose. He flung the flower against the ground.

Then he stepped on it and twisted it into the ground until he felt
satisfied. Its smell, however, clung stubbornly to his fingers.

10

The twisted path crossed the valley and then doubled back. Once the
path began to ascend again, Yasura saw the top of a large gate between
the trees that had grown thick, obscuring the remaining hundred-yard
stretch of cliff. Rather than being relieved, he grew even more impatient
about that stretch, feeling as if he were walking up a steep incline for
the entirety of it.

When he arrived at the foot of the gate and sat himself down on
the tiles under it, he felt his consciousness, which had been focused,
suddenly dissolve and release him into a state of mindless rapture. At
last, he caught sight of the light of sunset hitting the pines at the top of
the summer-dry mountain, as if it had been hung from the top of the
gate. Thinking that he was probably now close enough to see the white

walls of the monks' dormitories where he would find Atsumi, he set out walking in a hurry, as though pursued.

Crows flew so low in the sky over Yasura he was afraid they might swoop down just above his head and make a commotion with their flapping wings. He continued to trudge up the path to the tower to his left. The tower looked out over the ornamental ridge tiles on the roof of the main hall. Through the low gate of the main dormitory, he saw the black outlines of the large comb-shaped windows in the white walls of the building inside. One summer chrysanthemum swayed in the breeze unassumingly over the packed clay of the yard. The earthen storehouse in one corner of the yard and the evening mist that began to envelop it made for a peaceful nightfall.

He learned that Atsumi had been taken out by his uncle Kazunao on a tour of the nearby peaks. They had gone all the way to the "temple of flowers." The monk on duty, whose shaved head looked so blue it seemed painted, showed Yasura into the study.

The mere fact that this was the place described in the letter was enough to induce in him a feeling of nostalgia for it.

The mountains were completely silent, and would soon be completely dark as well. He thought he could hear the distant noise of twilight from the port town that broke the peaceful air. The noise proved to be a figment of his imagination.

Having been invited by the monk to have a bath, he went around the long veranda and into the bathhouse. He heard the thin buzz of a mosquito from the shadow of the tub.

A pipe of green bamboo supplied water to the tub. Thinking about how that water had probably come from up that mountain now wrapped in the evening fog, he poured the hot water over himself in cascades. At times he stopped momentarily, his eyes fixed on the darkish color of the water falling behind him into the tub.

No matter how he tried, he simply could not recall what path had brought him here or imagine how he had traveled it. He had no memory of receiving permission from his aunt or mother or anyone else. A light anxiety passed him by at a close distance. After reflecting on several different things, his thoughts settled on Atsumi. Wouldn't Atsumi end up becoming a monk eventually if he stayed here? What if he came back from the flower temple with his head all shaved like the monk he had seen on duty earlier? As soon as he started to consider it in this way, he began to think this may indeed be Atsumi's fate, given his perfectly quiet demeanor.

After the sun had set, the sound of the wind blowing across the darkening thickets of bamboo below him reached his ears. Yasura sat down at the small table, enjoying the pleasure of the cold air on his freshly bathed skin.

Then once it was nighttime, alone at a low writing desk in the room, the large lamp brought out the moths, and he could hear the far-off sound of voices in the kitchen and the distinct sound of brushwood crackling in the fire.

As the fatigue from the events of the day set in, he began to doze. Sensing something, he opened his eyes. When he looked over, he saw Atsumi's slight figure as he shut the sliding door without making a sound.

Caught off guard, Yasura straightened his posture. Atsumi gently motioned for him to relax, then sat down gracefully.

"I'm glad you came."

"Sure."

"Did you get my letter?"

"Yes, thanks."

Nothing he had said struck Yasura as out of the ordinary. His even and casual tone was completely different from what he had expected. And what about him, now—how could he be so flustered?—he couldn't even look up once he realized it. He stared down at the new tatami.

"My uncle is the principal here. Whenever I have any time off from school, I come here. You can see how quiet it is now—this is how it always is. And hardly a mosquito to be seen."

As the other boy spoke, Yasura raised his eyes furtively to steal a look at his face. Yasura knew that Atsumi tended to lose weight in the summer, and so was not surprised to sense a loneliness in Atsumi's pale, sunken cheeks. And yet, as Yasura dropped his eyes to Atsumi's pitiful knobby knees, lined up so properly, he thought he saw them shaking faintly. He couldn't be sure.

"Uruma, sometimes coming out here makes me think I might like to try being a monk."

Could this possibly be the same person who wrote the letter he had received? A letter like that? He began to feel that he had been tricked somehow.

He felt as though Atsumi must have known already how elated he had been when he read the letter, and that he even knew that Yasura had made up some reckless lie to tell his mother and aunt in order

to come to the temple. The smooth rise and fall of Atsumi's intona-
tion made Yasura's heart flutter gently. Before long, he had forgotten
everything else. In his mind, he may as well have been bounding across
a green meadow.

"How old are you going to be this year? Oh, that's right, you'll be
fifteen—I'm a year older."

Then Atsumi ceased talking. When Yasura cautiously lifted his eyes,
he noticed Atsumi's thin-looking chest.

Yasura had let Atsumi go on talking by himself, responding from
time to time merely by nodding or making a vague noise. It occurred
to him that this must be terribly unsatisfying for Atsumi, but the more
he thought about it, the more aware he became that he was evading the
heart of the conversation.

He was filled with an urge to somehow let Atsumi know that his
words had indeed penetrated to his very depths. He began to wonder
how a person like Atsumi could think about something so deep as that.
He felt somehow as if his body were closing in on itself.

They heard footsteps on the boards of the veranda that wrapped
around the outside of the building. Someone was approaching, coughing dryly all the while.

"Here comes my uncle," he whispered.

"What's this, a visitor? First time we've had one of those. It's good
that you and Taizō here are friends. You can stay as long as you like, and
then the two of you can go back together. Oh, it is lonely in a temple,
so even one visitor, even for a little while, really does liven things up so
much."

Without forcing any response from Yasura, who only nodded his
head limply, the man made himself comfortable, sitting cross-legged on
the floor. He went on to talk for some time with the boys about gossip
from Osaka, and as far as he thought children might understand, told
them stories about himself when he was in a smaller temple on the
grounds of Tennōji some fifteen years ago. When he coughed, he would
have Atsumi pat him firmly on the back. He stroked his white eyebrows
with the outside of his index finger continuously. After an hour, he
stood up.

"Tai, you ought to go on to bed. Make up a place for your friend to
sleep, too. I'm going to turn in as well. Today we went all the way to the
flower temple, and boy am I worn out."

A young boy monk quite a bit smaller than Yasura appeared and began to noisily pull the shutters closed.

"Kōkyō, it's a bit hot tonight, so why don't you leave them open just a hair."

"Very well."

The boy left the shutters alone and sat briefly near the threshold, placing his hands on the tatami. He bowed his head, revealing its deep depressions, said goodnight, and went off toward the kitchen.

"Shall we go to sleep?"

"Yes."

Yasura curled up in the bedding that Atsumi had laid out for him and remained stiff, unmoving. Once the lamp was blown out and the room was darker, he felt his mind suddenly begin to settle again.

"Uruma?"

"Yes?"

"You know how grown-ups are always so concerned with avoiding death? The way I see it, dying doesn't really seem like anything special. I have no issue with death itself. But I do think that if there were even one person who, if they were to witness my death, would cherish me as worthy of pity forever, I would be willing to die in front of that person right now. Without that, it does seem like it would be a bit lonely, no matter how you look at it."

After this he fell silent for a short time. He was waiting for Yasura's response. Atsumi's words weighed down upon Yasura's heart with terrific force. He had just barely been able to stop the words that had risen to his lips from coming out. It was then that an inspired thought swept through his mind.

He had sensed what Atsumi was trying to get him to say: *I would die with you.* Nevertheless, the fear that he might be wrong about it pinned his tongue down and prevented him from opening his mouth. His lips quaked with a sad spasm.

When he opened his eyes, the shutters that had been left open let the blue light of the moon through to illuminate the shoji. The chilly mountain air pressed against his skin. He heard a sound like running water, and thinking it might be rain, he listened closer. It was the sound of the river far away in the valley.

Atsumi was sleeping, and Yasura could hear the thin vibration of his snoring. When he turned over he could see the light of the moon shining clear and white directly onto Atsumi's forehead.

In Kawachi as well, going north from there were three houses belonging to relatives of his on his father's side. His father's birth home was now practically connected to the homes of his father's two younger sisters, so that he had an aunt, an uncle, and other relatives in each of those houses. Older than any of the five boys was their eldest sister, who went to be married in the town their father grew up in. Whenever he and his older brothers got some time off, they would go see her, all three of them piling into a two-person rickshaw and heading out. They would stay for up to a month at a time, spending the days fishing and swimming in the river, their eyes shining from the outdoors and activity. Now, even with his two brothers gone away to study, Yasura had still not outgrown his shyness, and he did not want to think about spending a summer with relatives. Nevertheless, the day after he returned from Yamato, his aunt was finally able to convince him to go by conceding the condition that it would only be for ten days. Now he spent nearly two hours tumbling through meadows full of ascending larks. Using the map, he had reckoned that the temple where Atsumi was would be to his left, but then he realized that in fact he could even see it. He had a terrible scheme in the works. He knew he was making his way toward a far more deeply rooted sin than that of having deceived his aunt and mother when he had gone to Yamato. Despite that, his mind was mysteriously calm. After three days at his sister's house, Yasura suddenly announced that he would be returning to Osaka, and there was nothing anyone could say to stop him.

Going further up the road toward the old capital northward, he crossed three big rivers. Once he had left the main path for a smaller one, he had kept his eyes on the mountain and strayed no more from the path toward it.

Now, his eyes were open wide as he lay in the bedding Atsumi had brought him. Thinking that he would soon grow more and more used to doing wicked things like this and would eventually fall into an abyss from which he could no longer be saved, his mind was filled with vivid images of that fateful day when his depravity would become complete. He became sad, feeling it would not be enough even to flagellate himself in front of this Buddha-like person. He broke into tears, aware that he was alone in the world, with no refuge to cling to in all of heaven and earth.

"Atsumi."

Yasura tried calling to him softly, but was startled by the sound of his own voice. Atsumi, who Yasura thought had just been asleep, was awake after all.

"Can't you sleep?"

He felt as though somehow Atsumi had been able to read him completely. He wanted to disappear.

II

The next day, Yasura announced suddenly that he was going home. He was once again drawn in by Atsumi's pleading eyes, which rendered him incapable of leaving. Throwing caution to the wind, he decided to stay one more day. Anxiety flitted ceaselessly across his heart. At noon, the three of them grilled tofu skin and ate together. Its light, simple flavor invoked an unparalleled nostalgia in Yasura.

"Tai, how about you take Yasura down the valley?" said Kazunao, holding his chopsticks.

"Yes—what do you say, Uruma? Should we go down to the river?"

"Oh, yes."

The boys put on their straw hats and set out. Once they got about two hundred yards down the slope, they were in the valley. The two split up to strip off their clothes, as if they were each ashamed of the other seeing them nude. Then in the water, the boys kept ten yards between them. Yasura pretended not to look at Atsumi standing over there with only his head above water. Not knowing how to swim, Yasura lamented the blue light that played on the flowing water from his knees in the shallows. He looked on as the redness intensified on the excited flesh of his arms when he rubbed them. Covered in goosebumps, he realized that he was more alone than he had thought. When he looked up to see what Atsumi was doing, he saw that he was trying to climb up onto a large rock. The rock stuck out a yard above the water and the water around it was still and deep. His friend now stood on the rock, watching the surface of the water strangely. Atsumi's expression reminded him of a cluster of silky wisteria flowers crawling weakly across the earth.

"Should we go to the temple?"

At this, Yasura awoke from his reverie.

Now clothed again, Atsumi sat down next to Yasura. Together they looked out over the deep pool. This friend, who had since morning said very little to him, sat slumped over and trembling sadly, one pale cheek supported by a hand, and looked at the color of the deep pool as though it drew his gaze to itself. He shuddered with sadness. His eyes were clouded as if he were dreaming of the blue light of the moon. Now and again, he lifted them toward the sky. The sky was just visible through the tips of the pine branches.

He suddenly began to feel abnormally agitated. When he looked at his friend, he saw tears were streaming down Atsumi's downturned face.

"Let's go then."

The sight of Atsumi going up the steep slope from behind moved him to tears. They left from a different direction than the one by which they had come. The roads between the mountains to the west of Kyoto and Anao-dera in Tamba followed the rustling of the leaves on the trees, rising narrowly up and up.

Between the mountains jutting out on either side, the tall peaks dissolved into the reddish brown of the afternoon light.

"Shakagatake—that's what that one's called."

He stopped and pointed at a peak that rose out of a sharp ridge.

"I wonder if it takes an awfully long time to get there from here."

"There was a monk a little older than Kōkyō, called Kōchō. Now he's at seminary, but he went up there with somebody once. Said it wasn't too bad."

Even in the temple with its very few inhabitants, he was unsatisfied that the two of them could not be alone together.

"Should we try to climb it?"

He was startled by these words from Atsumi. Their meaning had become terribly clear to him.

Between the cedar trees that made up the forest he could see gaps in the underbrush that looked like paths. Atsumi continued to climb up the rolling slope with careful steps. They went some distance further into the woods, their footsteps echoing loudly as they walked through the striped bamboo bushes. He thought he could hear the heavy breathing and pounding heart of his friend walking just a few paces ahead of him.

When the boys came out of the woods, the blue sky was bright and clear. The trail kept going up. It went around the edge of the mountain. He heard something rustling toward them through the field of pampas grass. Imagining some ferocious beast, he became terrified. In the next instant, however, he decided that they were together, and so even if they were both killed and eaten right there, he would have no regrets. Once he had made that decision, he began to wish for that terrible death to come to them as soon as possible. What came through the grass at them just then was a middle-aged man wearing the white clothes of a pilgrim, his face streaked with purple sores.

"Is this the way to Yoshimine?" he asked.

"Thank you."

He went down the path that Atsumi had shown him. The two stood there for some time watching him go. The path continued like the sharp edge of an axe. Yasura climbed up the steep slope, his breath ragged. Atsumi stopped and pointed wordlessly at a grassy plain that could be seen through an open space in the undergrowth. Yasura crumbled to the ground and sat there. He felt his violent heartbeat against the palm of his hand, feeling as though it might tear right through his ribs. He decided that his heart was bad. In his mind he could still clearly see the pale face of his dead father in his coffin. He quietly put his hand to his chest, and in his heart, he felt a longing for the hand of a friend that would rub his chest in his pain and sadness. Then out of nowhere he heard Atsumi's voice.

"You're having palpitations? Let me give you a rub."

This surprised Yasura even more. He bared his chest, wet with sweat, and allowed Atsumi to do what he would, offering no resistance. At last, the darkening sky cleared to reveal a striking blue, and the sun's light faded. The delicate, white fingers of Atsumi's long hand fluttered over his chest.

"I feel better now. Let's get up to the peak."

With that, they set off walking again, Atsumi walking ahead and looking back from time to time with concern at Yasura. Each time Yasura seemed about to collapse, Atsumi would take his hand and the two would climb further. Yasura was almost sure that his aunt and mother and the rest already knew about the two of them walking here together like this by now. The cold light that he imagined in the eyes of his family struck him through the heart. He felt that this moment was what everything depended on—the thing that could upturn heaven and earth—and had the power to return the world to what it had once been. The young pines appeared to continue into the limitless depths of the sky. Neither Atsumi nor Yasura said a word. They weaved in and out of the pines unsteadily, seeking the peak. Atsumi tripped on a tree root and fell—Yasura got right down by his side. The boys stayed perfectly still. Yasura felt as though all the blood in his body had turned to sweat and left him. He could no longer support his swimming head.

By now, however, a force invisible to the two boys had overtaken them, allowing no room for resistance. The two drifted forward slowly. When they made it to the peak, they stared hard at each other's exhausted faces. The dim blue wind of twilight howled.

He buried his head in Atsumi's chest as they held each other tightly. Atsumi stood straight up. Then, he crossed the grassy plain as if carried by wind which seemed to lift his thin heels off the ground. Yasura followed him until the two stood at one edge of the peak.

The dark cedar woods sloped down toward the distant floor of the valley. The white rocks bared themselves here and there, visible to the two boys. The wind rose up from the valley around them, making their clothes seem ready to fly off and away.

"Uruma."

"Atsumi."

Their voices shook.

The idea that they would in fact die created an enormous excitement in both of their hearts. The colors of sunset had sunk past the horizon. The valley fell dizzyingly below their eyes, and as soon as they thought they might be able to step out into it, melancholy struck them hard again. With their palms pressed tightly together, their hands seemed to possess a strength that would prevent them from ever being pulled apart.

A violent shudder shook both boys through their entire bodies. A spiral of icy flame surged over them, and they ran full force, each groaning from the core of his being. They took their first step out off the rocky edge.

FIVE

Three Stories by Inagaki Taruho

Translated by Jeffrey Angles

Biography and Introduction

Literature lovers frequently remember Inagaki Taruho (稲垣足穂, 1900–1970) as a modernist innovator. One of his admirers, the novelist Mishima Yukio, wrote in *Sakkaron* (On Authors) that in the literature of the Shōwa period, Taruho was a rare genius who held a place equivalent to the astronauts in history; one could divide literary history "into the world before Taruho and the world after Taruho." This high appraisal is grounded in Taruho's stylistic experimentation, his sensitive and introspective nature, and his associative style of writing, which blurs the boundaries between reality and fantasy, fiction and nonfiction, and even poetry and prose.

Taruho began writing in the 1920s when the new, cosmopolitan, hybrid culture of modern Japan was giving birth to numerous new artistic trends. As I have written elsewhere in a more thorough look at Taruho's homoerotic writing, he believed that modern life provided numerous opportunities for poignant aesthetic experiences, and much of his early writing celebrates small, random encounters with the "new" that might momentarily liberate a viewer from the constraints of mundane reality.[1] In particular, he focused on a number of common themes. Later, when reflecting on his career, Taruho was sometimes known to quip that he had spent much of his life writing about three subjects in particular—the "three As": astronomy, airplanes, and anal eroticism.

---

1. Jeffrey Angles, *Writing the Love of Boys: Origins of Bishōnen Culture in Japanese Modernist Literature* (Minneapolis: University of Minnesota Press, 2011), 193–224.

Despite what this statement might imply, Taruho rarely wrote explicitly about male sexual activity, but he was a fan of fashionable, attractive adolescent men (*bishōnen*) since at least his days as a grade school student, and some of his earliest work, which is translated in this volume, deals with the ways that sort of special beauty might inspire writers and artists. In the crucible of the prewar all-male schools where boys like Taruho were feeling the powerful pangs of adolescence, it was not uncommon for boys to develop strong friendships in which homosocial bonding spilled over into overt homoeroticism. Taruho's early writings describe a system of age-graded sexuality, with older upperclassmen admiring younger students as objects of desire; however, unlike other earlier authors, such as Mori Ōgai (1862–1922), who describe this as a predatory manifestation of masculinity, Taruho carefully links the admiration to the cosmopolitan, increasingly internationally inclined aesthetics of the 1920s. In Taruho, *bishōnen* are not simply schoolboys; they are avatars of the fashionable beauty that he valued above all else.

Many of Taruho's early *bishōnen* stories appeared in magazines for women, which were less likely to frame their stories and literature with the kinds of sensational rhetoric about homoeroticism one finds in magazines geared toward boys and men. Taruho's use of nonpathologizing, flowery modes of writing about male-male desire in women's magazines is historically significant—he seems to be the first major writer in Japan to have conceived of love between boys as a subject that would interest female readers. One reason Taruho is so deserving of critical reevaluation today is that his florid, romanticized depictions of male-male desire were forerunners of the florid, romanticized *shōjo manga* (graphic novels written for young female readers) about same-sex desire that became so popular in the 1970s. In fact, Takemiya Keiko (1950–), one of the most important manga artists of the time, has credited Taruho as inspiring her to write her masterpiece *Kaze to ki no uta* (The Song of the Wind and the Trees, serialized from 1976 to 1984), which features a flowery love story between boys in a French provincial school. Not only did this long-running manga sell wildly, it inspired countless other manga artists to write about similar subjects, turning male homoeroticism into one of the most common tropes in contemporary girls' manga. Taruho, in short, is the literary ancestor of this genre, which remains so popular today.

Another reason Taruho is so deserving of critical reevaluation has to do with his contributions to the rise of the cultural trend that started in the 1920s and that would later come to be described using the term *ero guro nansensu*. Nowadays, the term *ero guro nansensu* appears as a fixed expression that almost invariably appears in academic discussions of the cultural obsessions of the prewar era; however, the individual elements of this term (which come from the roots of the English words "the erotic," "the grotesque," and "the nonsensical") started to circulate independently as fashionable "modern words" (*modango*) in the 1920s. During that time, the words *ero* and *guro* sometimes appeared together, but it wasn't until later, toward the end of the 1930s, that the word *nansensu* was brought into the constellation to form a set phrase that described the particular interlocking set of cultural obsessions that shaped so much Japanese writing, art, film, and poetry in the years preceding the outbreak of warfare in China in 1937. As mentioned above, Taruho's writing isn't especially sexually explicit or grotesque, but a strong erotic flavor underlies much of his work. His writing is, in a sense, "nonsensical" in that it deals with the small and seemingly insignificant details of modern life that do not necessarily always make their way into the halls of high art.

Finally, it is worth mentioning that Taruho was obsessed during his youth with the new medium of cinema, which he enjoyed with his schoolmates in the theaters of Kobe, an important port city that was one of the few places outside of Tokyo that was especially quick to import Western culture. Not surprisingly, much of his early work is highly cinematic in nature. Numerous scenes in early works like "The False Mustache," presented here, or the often-anthologized short story "Astromania" (*Tentai shikō-shō*), take direct inspiration from scenes by early filmmakers such as D. W. Griffith and Georges Méliès, who impressed Taruho's active young imagination with their dramatic and groundbreaking camerawork.[2] Even when Taruho is not explicitly describing scenes from specific films, the influence of cinema is clearly visible throughout his early work. He tends to present a good deal of visual detail even when scenes do not have a lot of internal movement, producing writing that sometimes feels more like a series of poetic, cinematic stills that linger in the imagination long after the film that contained them is over.[3] As William Tyler noted, by "avoiding plot-driven narrative

---

2. Inagaki Taruho, "Astromania," trans. Jeffrey Angles, in *Three-Dimensional Reading: Stories of Time and Space in Japanese Modernist Fiction, 1911–1932*, ed. Angela Yiu (Honolulu: University of Hawaii Press, 2013), 69–84.

3. For instance, "The Story of R-chan and S" (R-chan to S no hanashi) contains a series of scenes in which the narrator obsesses over the clothing and looks of a younger student with whom he is in love. Little in the way of plot happens in some of these scenes, but Taruho enjoys lingering in an almost cinematic fashion over the appearance of his beloved. See "The Story of R-chan and S," trans. Jeffrey Angles, *Modanizumu: Modernist Fiction from Japan,*

and highlighting the episodic and cinematic," Taruho "put his early character sketches or *contes* in service of an agenda that prioritized heightened emotional and artistic receptivity as a key tenet of *modanizumu*," the unique Japanese take upon modern literature.[4]

"Karl and the White Lamp"[5]

1924 (revised 1954)

Among the things that Karl likes are clarinets, airplanes, and movies.

My older sister in the city and some of my friends maintain that he's a delinquent, but I wonder why Karl is on their list of people marked as "requiring special attention." All you need to do is say a single word to him, and his ears will immediately flush bright red. There isn't anyone among my sister's church-going crew or their followers who think of him as a "blue flower," to borrow the turn of phrase from Novalis.

Karl looks best in a green overcoat. His girlish eyelashes and fashionably stylish eyes give him an especially charming look, as if he were wearing a thin layer of makeup. His expression makes him look like he might have been crying the previous night—in fact, one of my artist friends said that he had a "distressed" look, "like a delicate, white surface of a hard-boiled egg that had been slightly soiled by someone's fingerprints." That's how transcendental and Krafft-Ebingish he is.

Come to think of it, whenever I see the white light of a streetlamp twitching in the evening twilight as if all the sorrows of the twentieth century are intertwining, for some reason, I can't help but think of Karl with tears running down his face. The futurist artist A. had this to say: "That boy vibrates at the same frequency as the tungsten filament in a light bulb. In terms of atmosphere, there's no real difference between them." Once when I was walking home from a movie with Karl, I pointed to an electric streetlamp radiating white light, and said, "It

---

1913–1938, ed. William J. Tyler (Honolulu: University of Hawaii Press, 2008), 358–75.

4. William J. Tyler, "Making Sense of *Nansensu*," *Japan Forum* 21, no. 1 (2009), 9.

5. Taruho had a habit of making changes to his work, sometimes quite significant changes, each time a piece was republished. This short story, which is hardly much longer than a contemporary piece of flash fiction, was first published in the magazine *Fujin gurafu* (Ladies' Pictoral) in 1924, but he revised it on republication in 1954. This translation is based on the final version, which appears as Inagaki Taruho, "Kāru to shiroi dentō," *Inagaki Taruho zenshū*, vol. 1 (Tokyo: Chikuma Shobō, 2000), 69–70.

looks just like you." The attractive young man let out a slightly forlorn chuckle and stopped to stare. As he looked up at the lamp, his face appealed to me greatly.

If you're the kind of person who loves movies and feels your heart dance at the sobbing of the violins in an orchestra, or if your eyes fill with tears at the sight of the red taillights on the back of an automobile, then no doubt you'll understand what I'm trying to describe here. You are the type who, as twilight gives way to the blue of night in the city, will hear Karl's lament coming from the trembling white streetlamps that stand on the street corners under the sycamore trees.

"Pince-Nez Glasses"[6]

1924 (revised 1958, 1969)

Back in my college-prep school days, I used to commute by train from Maiko to the eastern part of Kobe where my school was located. At Suma, just a couple of stations from where I boarded, one of my schoolmates, an underclassman with the initials K.Y., also got on the same train.

I first got to know K.Y. one day in late spring. I was in my third year of school at the time, and I happened to be riding the train home alone. We'd just left Takatori Station, and fortunately, there were only a few other passengers so I stuck my hand in my pocket and started rooting around for my small box of Golden Bat cigarettes, but before pulling them out, I stood up and looked around to make sure the coast was clear. Right then, a voice started singing behind me.

I hear their
gentle voices
calling Old Black Joe

The song was in English. The singing boy took great care in pronouncing the words, but his ability to carry a tune was quite good. Although his voice was quiet, it was gentle. I took a furtive glance to see

---

6. This piece was first published in 1924, then revised twice in 1958 and 1969. This translation is based on the final version, which appears in Inagaki Taruho, "Hana megane," *Inagaki Taruho zenshū*, vol. 1 (Tokyo: Chikuma Shobō, 2000), 169–77.

who it was. Back-to-back with me on the other side of the seat was a boy. His uniform indicated we attended the same school. He'd slumped down so far that he was almost lying on his back, and he looked as if he was about to slide off the seat altogether. On his chest rested an open musical score, and from it trailed a purple ribbon bookmark. The nape of his neck caught the rays of sunlight pouring through the window. The sunlight illuminated the curve of his neck, and the sight struck me as unusually elegant. I hadn't realized there was a new underclassman who took the same train, and I sat up tall to see his face. At that very moment, he looked up at me, and our eyes met. We both smiled, but he hurriedly grabbed his music and covered it with the white bookbag by his side.

He got off at the next station, and I watched with interest through the window as he walked away. His appearance was completely above reproof—the hair above his ears was neatly trimmed, his collar was white as snow, his trousers were neatly creased, and his shoes had been carefully shined. I realized that even if his parents fussed at him, any freshman who groomed himself that meticulously must be doing so voluntarily.

What really caught my fancy, however, was his face with its rough-hewn chin. He was so fair that he reminded me of the foreign students at the Canadian mission school that stood behind our school, surrounded by poplar trees. His lips were the color of a rose, and his eyes were adorned with lovely, long lashes. Most interestingly, the space between his eyes was creased, almost as if he was worried about something, and these creases distinctly reminded me of a pair of pince-nez glasses.

The next morning, when I arrived at the station near school, I kept my ears open, hoping to overhear what the friends of the mysterious boy, who looked like he might be of mixed ethnic background, called him. Still, try as I might, I didn't catch his name. Just as he was going through the ticket gate, however, I did overhear a tall, gangly student who appeared to be the same age yell "*Très chic!*" at the boy's back.

Two or three days later when I was on my way home, I again ran into the "*chic*" boy at the station. He was sitting on a bench on the platform. He was talking in a low voice with someone. The other fellow was a young man, perhaps a college student boarding at the boy's house. Maybe he had brought the young man along with him on some errand that day. In any case, whatever the boy was saying to the young man did not seem to be getting through. The young man asked,

"What? . . . What? . . ." several times, before the boy finally sprang from his seat. Some of our schoolmates were standing nearby, and he seemed embarrassed about what they might think. As the two started to walk toward me, I saw him repeat something quietly in the ear of the young man, who leaned over to hear him better. The boy looked very self-conscious.

After witnessing this scene, I couldn't resist. As the music sounded to signal the arrival of the train, I grabbed hold of a gangly underclassman I'd met the other day, and I asked the boy's name. He said it was K.Y., and as an afterthought, he added, "You know, that guy is really king of the castle at home . . ." As soon as I got back to my house, I flipped through the phone book and, sure enough, I found a listing for someone in West Suma with the right name.

His classmate had also told me that I'd been right when, a few days before in the train, I had guessed he was an only child. I had figured anyone groomed that properly had no siblings, and must be a child of a relatively young mother at that. When I confirmed that, I felt like smiling. It wouldn't be long before I caught a glimpse of his mother.

When July rolled around, the Western teachers left for summer resorts to escape the heat, so we only had classes in the morning. Summer vacation started in the middle of the month. It was one morning a few days after the formal start of the vacation. I'd gone to Kobe on a small errand and was on my way home when the train stopped at Suma Station. There, standing on the platform for the eastward-bound trains, was K.Y. He wasn't wearing his uniform of black and white speckled cloth; instead, he had on cream-colored shorts and a pith helmet. He was standing there with the same college student I'd seen before. Next to them was a middle-aged woman in a wisteria-colored kimono. Behind them were two trunks. "Ah-ha!" I thought, but right then, an eastward-bound train rushed between us and cut them off from view.

There's a break in my memories of K.Y. after that. To be honest, the only reason I'd paid attention to him in the first place was mere momentary curiosity. When the new term started, my interest naturally slid since I wasn't really making any attempt to become friends. That was all right with me. Still, I do remember finding the creases that formed between his eyes when he furrowed his brow especially charming—they had all the charm of a tri-colored pansy. Wasn't that proof I bore some feelings for him that went beyond casual interest? I can't say with certainty.

In any case, the vision of him in shorts on the platform is the last of

my memories of him before he hit adolescence. From the very beginning, he'd struck me as more like a little brother than anything else.
His foppishness and bashfulness made him too much like me and so he
never struck me as having the right qualifications to be a lover.

Still, I didn't find him disagreeable. Every time I saw him on the
train or in school, I'd think, "Gosh, I'd like to see him in a pair of
pince-nez glasses," or "He'd probably look really good sitting on one of
those chairs in the music room," or something of that nature. Or when
a friend started talking about him, I'd think, "If someone is going to ask
him out for a stroll, it ought to be me . . ." But that's about the extent
to which he entered my thoughts.

Almost two years went by with virtually no interaction between us.

During that time, I became pals with a bunch of the young freshmen who entered school after K.Y., but why did I keep my distance
from him and him alone? At first, I couldn't act frankly because of the
feelings I described previously. It also seems clear to me that part of my
reluctance to talk to him had to do with an aloofness that I sensed on
his part as well. At school, I rarely saw him, so I never knew where to
find him, and on the train, he was usually by himself. When he wasn't,
however, he was always with a certain pale, sickly looking student who
got on at Hyōgō Station. The two of them had been hanging out since
their freshman year, and they would always sit alone, as far away from
everyone else as possible.

When I was in my fifth and final year of college-prep school, he was
already in his third year. He'd grown a great deal taller, and his whole
body seemed to exude a youthful freshness. Perhaps he had come close
to his "spring awakening." I suppose one might say that he was putting on airs. His choice of clothes never violated school regulations, but
after his freshman year, he started wearing flashier clothing that made
him stand out even more than before. He outfitted himself like certain
upperclassmen, wearing a short overcoat of special material. His pants
were extremely loose about the hips although the legs tapered near his
ankles. In addition, he started fastening his textbooks and notebooks
together with a thin leather strap, and he let them dangle by his side.
One could see the gold clips of the fountain pens lined up in his breast
pocket, and sticking out beside them was the shaft of a pencil topped
with a glass bead cut to look like a jewel. When winter rolled around,
the red wrists of a scarlet sweater sometimes poked out of the sleeves of
his jacket.

Like the other young boys undergoing similar transformations, he never bowed to us upperclassmen when he and his buddies spied us out somewhere. At the station I occasionally saw him go from the second-class car toward the back of the train where the girl students sat. When I saw these things, I realized with a touch of sadness that he had reached the mellow ripeness of adolescence and would probably lose his saucy stylishness within a year or so.

That reminds me . . . I once happened to see him standing on the tennis courts by our school. It was the time of year when the forest by our school was beginning to cloak itself in fragrant young leaves. Blinding sunlight poured over his face, making him so alluringly fair that I thought of the beautiful girl from Arles in Bizet's ballet. I remember being overcome with strong emotions unlike anything I'd ever felt, and everything seemed to go black before my eyes.

However, one day during the second term, K.Y. looked me straight in the eye and smiled.

I was in the train station going down the stone stairs in front of the waiting room when I saw him coming up toward me. That was when it happened. Wondering if there was someone else behind me, I turned around to look. Later at the station as we were getting ready to go home, it happened again.

"Well, well!" said one of my classmates standing beside me. He gave me an earnest look, but I had no way of knowing how to interpret K.Y.'s odd smile. The next day, and the day after that, K.Y. gave me the same little grin.

It wasn't so much that I wondered what was going on—I just felt embarrassed. Even so, I thought it'd be rude not to respond so I smiled back. Every time I did, he got a look like he wanted to say something, but he never said a word. The more time I spent staring in his direction, the less hesitant he seemed to return a coquettish gaze. Finally, one day when no one else was there, I furtively beckoned him to come over. He flushed bright red, and he took off, disappearing behind the school as if trying to run away.

One day toward the end of autumn, something happened on the train home. I was talking with my friends when, quite unexpectedly, I sensed a hand rubbing my side and making a quiet rustling noise. Needless to say, the hand belonged to K.Y., who was seated directly behind me. Much like that first day with the musical score and the bookmark of purple ribbon, our seats were back-to-back, but he'd turned his upper body to the side, put his back to the window, and stuck his left hand between the seat dividers to touch my side.

By this time, I was accustomed to his smile and his girlish flirtatiousness, but this was so sudden and unexpected that I was more than a little taken aback. I had a flash of instinct—maybe he was trying to steal something from my pocket! The possibility wasn't entirely impossible. I was aware that only the other day, another boy named M. had been expelled from school for the same thing. M. had a reputation as a good-looking kid, but he had a habit of pilfering things. Some of the guys were saying that it was so bad that when you went to the movies with M., you had to put your wallet on an inside pocket where only you could get to it. K.Y. was a refined fellow, but perhaps he had an eccentric streak to him too. It wasn't out of the question. If so, what a splendid aesthete he was—beauty and a willingness to break the rules, all in the same package!

But it was my own aesthetic sensibilities at work that made me imagine such things. I needed to clear my muddled mind. I tried to remember what was in the right-side pocket he'd put his hand on, so I quietly moved my own hand to the outside of the pocket on the opposite side to feel its contents. What would happen if he slipped his hand inside? I was filled with curiosity. Acting as if nothing was happening, I leaned forward, widening the gap between me and the back of the seat. What happened next really gave me a start. The sensation of the boy's graceful, searching fingers told me that since I'd moved, he didn't take the easy route into my right pocket. Instead, his fingers shifted downward and slid under the bottom of my jacket. He was reaching inside. Startled, I wondered if he wasn't trying to get hold of the top of my trousers!

That made me uncomfortable. I got up and stuck my head out of the window. I snuck a glance downward. Because I'd stood up so quickly, he'd lost his chance. For a moment or two, his white fingers toyed with the edge of the seat as if engaging in an innocent, absent-minded diversion. Suddenly, his fingers withdrew through the partition between the seats, disappearing on the opposite side. A moment later, I heard the young, pale upstart begin talking quietly.

I realized I'd been wrong. He wasn't trying to pick my pocket, but what could his behavior have possibly meant? I couldn't even guess. The thought struck me that the best course of action would just be to look him straight in the face and ask, but I never got up the gumption. Instead, I fretted my days away aimlessly. I wanted a clear, definite explanation. The opportunity, however, never presented itself. The remainder of the school year passed quickly, and by the time graduation rolled around, there wasn't any more time to confront him.

When I reflect on it now, I regret losing the chance to talk to him. Even now, long after graduation, I sometimes blame myself for letting the situation go unresolved. The second and third terms of my last year in school, however, were taken up with thoughts of another boy. My heart was so clouded with feelings for the other boy that I couldn't help feeling that, in the words of Wedekind's *Spring Awakening*, "I had drawn a bad lot." Sometimes, I even considered imitating Moritz, the main character of the play who stood deep in a forest of willow trees, held a pistol to the side of his head, and pulled the trigger.

The day the results of the graduation exam were posted, I was leaning absentmindedly against a pommel horse in a corner of the exercise yard when K.Y. walked in front of me. He was clutching his white bookbag and walking as if he was trying to skip out of school early. He turned his fair countenance in my direction and smiled. I smiled back, and the casual thought occurred to me that this would be the last time I'd ever see him under those circumstances. He seemed to know what I was thinking, for he gazed at me much longer than usual. We continued exchanging smiles across the distance as he crossed the exercise yard. The granite gravel strewn over the yard sparkled so brilliantly in the sun that it almost hurt my eyes. We kept smiling until he finally disappeared into the grove of trees nearby.

Five years went by.

Not long ago in February, a friend asked me to go to the opening night of a performance by an Italian opera troupe that was touring Japan, and so we got tickets.

Before the curtain went up that evening, I was standing in a corridor of the Imperial Theater, which was so full of swirling eddies of cigar smoke and perfume that it seemed like some enchanted palace. All the sudden, I spied a group of three or four people emerge from the shade of a potted palm tree, and sure enough, who should be standing right in the middle of the group but K.Y.?!

I blurted out, "Oh my!" He immediately saw me and approached with quick steps. Then pulling back slightly, he made a generous bow, which seemed slightly affected, but not at all inappropriate given those circumstances. What struck me like a bombshell, however, was not his high-society greeting, nor the neatly parted hair atop a head that now stood so much taller that he appeared to be a different person altogether, nor the collar of his black, tuxedo-cut jacket shining in the blue light. No, what struck me was the pair of thin pince-nez glasses with thin, white tortoise-shell frames that now sat over the creases between his eyes—the same creases that had reminded of pince-nez glasses all those years before.

I thought, "Well, I'll be . . . !"

As we started chatting in what was the first real—albeit short—conversation of our lives, a feeling of relief welled up inside my heart and replaced the old set of feelings lingering there. After graduation, I'd hardly ever thought about him, but on those rare occasions when I did, I reflected sorrowfully on how each passing day no doubt carried him one step farther away from boyhood toward adulthood. The young gentleman I ran into that night was no longer the K.Y. of the past, but I was pleased to find he was in no way inferior to the boy I'd known all those years ago. If anything, he was the same, old K.Y., only with an extra, added layer of elegance and refinement.

Once when he was in school, he got in a car and took a ride with a female student. When I realized that in the years since graduation he'd exchanged his schoolgirl companion for the socialite ladies of the capital, I felt a slight sadness over how things pass away. At the same time, I couldn't suppress the somewhat affected smile that rose to my lips.

"So that's how he turned out . . . No use fretting about him anymore." Feeling like a mother who'd just married off her daughter, I heaved a sigh of relief. With that, the bell sounded to announce the beginning of the performance. I returned to my seat, and before me, the curtains rose to reveal the dazzling stage of *Rigoletto*.

"The False Mustache"[7]

1927 (revised 1954, 1969)

Even though the boy was already in middle school, he was still terrified to strike a match, so much so that in fact, he was never quite sure if

---

7. This story was first published in the magazine *Shinchō* (New Tide) in 1927. He revised the story first in 1954 and again in 1969. This translation is based on the final version, which appears as Inagaki Taruho, "Tsukehige," *Inagaki Taruho zenshū*, vol. 1 (Tokyo: Chikuma Shobō, 2000), 189–97.

he'd succeed in lighting it or if he'd accidentally throw the matchstick from his fingers.[8] That's why when he saw two samurai clash and draw their swords in the movies, he couldn't even raise his head to look at the screen. And yet, the boy would find himself in seventh heaven whenever a band of soldiers in tight formation or mounted on horses started firing their rifles and pistols, letting out phantasmal puffs of white smoke. Such things brought to mind something he'd seen once in a movie somewhere.

The scene featured a group of soldiers next to a bunch of tents set up in the flat land beside the foot of some mountains.[9] Around the soldiers was a group of mounted Indians on the attack. The soldiers had formed a large circle around the tents to try to fight off the Indians, who were concentrating all their firepower on them as they spurred on their horses and rode around. The soldiers fell one after another. Behind the clouds of white smoke, one could catch glimpses of the Stars and Stripes fluttering as if trying to alert everyone to the unfolding disaster. The fluttering flag struck the boy as so beautiful that he hardly knew how to put it into words, and much later, he could still easily summon the vision of it before his eyes. But the scene that really captured the boy's heart was the short one that followed it.

The attack was over. The flag had been ripped from the flagpole, and the tents had been pulled down and trampled, leaving everything in disarray. Meanwhile, the moon shone overhead as if nothing were the matter—the film had been colored to give it a bluish tinge—but there in the flat land between the hills, in the middle of all the confusion, which was so terrible that it was almost impossible to understand what he was seeing at first glance, there were heaps and heaps—yes, that's right—of corpses of nude soldiers, none of which were wearing even a single stitch of clothing.

---

8. In prewar Japan, "middle school" was the equivalent of college preparatory school. The narrative identifies him as a "boy" (*shōnen*), but he is fourteen years old, right about the age when he would be experiencing puberty.

9. The scene that Taruho describes appears to be from the 1914 silent film *The Massacre*, directed by D. W. Griffith and released by Biograph Studios, although there are some differences between the actual film and the narrator's recollections of it. (One should remember that Taruho wrote this story during an age when films were not readily available on DVD or other streaming services, so his need to reconstruct the scene from memory may account for some of the differences.) Taruho was a passionate lover of film and wrote a great deal about it. Both his essays and his prewar, modernist stories often describe scenes from films that he loved, including several by Georges Méliès, D. W. Griffith, and Ben F. Wilson. Taruho's homoerotic short story "R-chan to S no hanashi," written in 1924, also describes some bodies acting out a homoerotic scene involving a wounded soldier. See Taruho, "Story of R-chan and S," in *Modanizumu*.

When the boy realized what he was seeing, he stared at the screen with eyes wide open in surprise. Was it okay to film something like that? He did his best to take in the entire pile of soft, white things as quickly as possible, while trying to figure out which part belonged to which body. What had happened to that hand? Why was that leg over there? How were those parts between the trunks of the bodies connected? The naked corpses were piled together in utter confusion. There was no rhyme or reason at all.

The boy felt anxious as he rushed to take it in. The momentary scene on the screen was so confused that he couldn't make heads or tails of it at first. But a few seconds later, he finally understood—the white lump on the left edge of the vivid mountain of flesh was actually a head and a body; two-thirds of the body had been exposed, and it was lying face-down. The way the head folded under the body made it look like the soldier was taking a deep bow, practically folding in two. The pale moonlight on the scrren alone was enough to make the exposed curve of his hips sensually beautiful. Even after the film moved on to show a rescue party departing, even after the film ended and the lights went up in the theater, and in fact, even as the boy was on his way home, he found himself completely unable to think about anything but that curve.

But even though he remembered the scene vividly, he didn't think he'd be able reenact it at home when he was alone, like he had done after seeing the detective tied to the railway tracks, the young girl trapped in the box, or the pilot crushed underneath his smashed airplane . . . Those other scenes had also made his heart race, but this time, merely imagining the scene and adopting the deep bow of the soldier wouldn't be enough to satisfy him. It wouldn't be enough unless he tried to replicate the feel of a cold, moonlit night in the mountains by taking off half of his clothes and exposing his skin. Still, he didn't think he could go all the way. What would happen if someone walked in on him and saw him acting so strangely? Before long, however, he realized he could strip completely naked in bed, especially after the lights had gone out. He tried it that very night, but still it wasn't enough to satisfy him.

This went on for some time before one evening, when he noticed a figure of someone pressed against the side of the spiral staircase. Here's what happened. Earlier that evening, he had crawled out of his futon and had tried two or three times on the cold tatami mats to imitate the soldier who had died deep in the mountains, bathed in moonlight, but that was not enough for him. The boy pricked up his ears. There had been no sign his family was near, but he confirmed just to be sure the coast was clear, then turned his attention toward the interior of the dark, camphor-scented room directly across from his. Of course, no one was there either. The only thing he saw there was the faint, melancholy sparkle of the nickel and glass objects in the room catching the last light of twilight trickling through the window.

A light was on in the hallway, however, and across from it there was a pair of frosted glass doors that slid to either side. To open them, one would have to first come through the door by the front entrance. If someone did, he would hear and have plenty of time to get some clothes on. Even so, there was no way he could take off all of his clothes right there in the hallway. He rolled up the bottom of his kimono exposing his body from the hips downward, and he stuffed the underwear he had removed into his pocket. Perhaps with his lower half exposed, he could experience at least half of the sensation of the defeated soldier who had been stripped naked and thrown aside after his defeat, deep in the lonely wilderness of the barren mountains.

He kneeled on the hallway floor, folded his hands behind his back, leaned forward, and stuck his bottom out behind out him. He turned his head to the side, and with his mind resolutely made up, he fell forward so that his shoulders pressed against the floor in front of him—he imagined he'd been thrown down and abandoned by the feather-adorned Indians after they had repeatedly used him as their toy. The floor was covered in linoleum, and he pressed his body against it. Wanting to feel as much of its hard coldness as possible, he placed his cheek flat against the floor. Wondering how he looked, he tried to check himself out in the large mirror on the wall, but he was so low on the ground he couldn't see himself. He lifted his face and checked to see if he could make the line of white skin from his lower back to his thighs resemble the curve of the fallen soldier. With effort, perhaps—he had to hold his lower body still since the position immediately become extremely uncomfortable. Once he had ascertained that he had succeeded in forming the right kind of curve, he once again pressed his cheek against the linoleum to imitate the soldier's form. In the process of doing so, he turned his head to the side and glanced upward. The base of the spiral staircase was right by his feet, and as he glanced up, he saw that right above him, on the second story, a young man was leaning against the railing and staring down at him below.

Surprised, the boy froze for a moment, then, as he stood back up, he felt his own face flush bright red. The young man he had seen was a smart, college-aged student who had come from the same province as the boy's father, and he had been living with the boy's family while studying in medical school. The young man would have graduated in the spring of that year, but according to a surprising story that the boy heard from the nurse who also boarded with them, something bad had happened. The young man had been visiting someone's house and was cavorting with the wife when her husband suddenly came home and found them together. It caused a huge fuss, and the husband threated to bring a lawsuit against the young man.

The story would have been in the papers before long if the boy's father had not stepped in to keep a lid on the whole affair. The young man was temporarily expelled from school, but he was trying to get back in the school's good graces by spending time at the boy's house studying under close observation. Until around two years ago, the young man would sometimes go out with the boy to play in the park or do other things, but the boy was still young at the time, and there were many things he still didn't understand. His impressions of the young man were not all that remarkable—the young man was a person of few words, he was pretty, and his fingernails were always well manicured, but beyond noticing that, the boy didn't think much about him. He didn't especially like him, but he didn't dislike him either.

Still, when their eyes met, the boy sometimes acted oddly and followed the young man back to his room on the second floor. The young man tended to hole himself up awkwardly in his room, and so the boy would accompany him. There, the boy gazed at rare and unusual fragments of things through the young man's microscope, and the young man gave him small bottles of cobalt blue and brown glass with stoppered lids. But that was all, at least until that fateful evening.

The young man seemed to have moved closer to take in the boy's behavior, which the boy now realized was too embarrassing to explain. He felt so humiliated he wanted to burst into tears. He ought to run away as fast as he could. But even running away wouldn't solve anything. As the boy stood up, he looked up once again at the young man, and noticed he was smiling slightly.

That helped break the ice. With a smile creeping onto his face as well, the boy started climbing the stairs toward him. The movements came on their own accord, as if he wasn't even aware of what he was doing. But, what else could he have done? The boy passed the young man by the stairs and quietly walked through the door into the young man's room.

The lamp with the blue umbrella shade on the mahogany desk was still on, and it cast a circle of light on the thick German book beneath. The boy walked up to the desk, sat down, and began staring at the book's colorful red and blue anatomical drawings as if trying to lose himself in them. He still felt ill at ease. He had been feeling terribly awkward since he had noticed the young man's presence a few moments ago, and he still wasn't entirely sure what to do. Old memories were bubbling up from the depths of his brain, only to be replaced by others right away. The young man lingered by the staircase in apparent surprise, but after a few moments, he walked back into his room where the boy was waiting, and sat down beside him. Then, he placed an terribly soft hand on the boy's shoulder.

"Does that interest you?"

"What . . . This?" The boy's voice sounded somewhat hoarse as he said this.

"Tell me. What's going on?"

As he spoke, the young man turned and pulled the boy into an embrace. Then as if nothing was out of the ordinary at all, he pressed his cheek against the boy's, then turned his gaze on the boy to take in his entire countenance. Holding the boy's face between his hands, the young man turned the boy toward him and kissed him on the lips. The boy was motionless, unable to do a thing. Just then, he heard the nurse calling out from the bottom of the staircase. The young man called back energetically, "I hear you . . . Coming . . ." but before walking down the stairs, he swiftly wiped the boy's lips with the sleeve of his *Kurume-gasuri* kimono.

After the young man left, the boy was all alone on the second floor. He felt relieved, like he had passed through a checkpoint, but at the same time, he noticed in the small round mirror sitting on top of the desk that both of his eyelids had a deep, second fold running horizontally across them. He tried blinking and rubbing his eyelids with his fingers, but they didn't return to normal.

A new, different type of worry began to well up inside of him. Without a sound, he crept down the stairs from the second floor, entered his older sister's room, pulled a brush out of her mirror stand, and began tapping his cheeks with it to coat them with white powder.

It was at night about one week later that the boy received an order from the young man as he brushed by him—there was a Boy Scout uniform hanging on the wall behind them, and the young man told him to change into it. The order had come out of the blue, as unexpectedly as if it had come from a stranger passing him on a staircase or hallway, but still, the boy didn't feel like he had any choice but to obey.

That first night, when the young man embraced the boy from behind, he had placed the boy briefly on his lap. The next day, he had sat the boy on his lap facing him, and the day after that, they were doing the same thing again, this time rolling around on the tatami floor, when the boy found himself sticking out his own lips as if he were just about to smile. In doing so, he made it clear to the young man that he enjoyed their games together, so that's why he felt little choice when the order to change into the uniform came.

That evening brought more games. After the two sat down together, the young man commented that the boy had made a strange face for a moment when, after listening to the footsteps upstairs, the young man's schoolfriend came down. Then there was the time the young man picked up the boy in both arms and was carrying him down the stairs. The boy was feeling nervous and excited when, just as he had feared, the door to the pharmacy at the front of the building swung open to reveal the pale face of the nurse who boarded with them.

"My goodness, I thought everyone was out. What're you two up to?"

The young man, however, never lost his cool. He just said, "Boy! This would look bad if he was a girl!" With these words hanging in the air, he walked heavily down the stairs, with the boy still in his arms as if nothing was the matter. He didn't put the boy down until he reached the sink.

It was a perfect spot. Although the electric light was on, the spot where the young man's hand was touching was bathed in shade, and so there's no way the nurse would have noticed.

Sometimes when the boy came home from school, he'd go upstairs and take off his clothes as if it were a summer day. The young man had suggested to him that they try wrestling, but time went by and he didn't come up the stairs, so the boy began to think he wouldn't be coming. The games they surreptitiously shared continued until one evening about a week later when everyone was out of the house. The boy had changed into the Boy Scout uniform, just as the young man had requested, when the young man brought up the awkwardness that had transpired that first night. The boy had almost forgotten about it.

Someone looking down from the top of the stairs shouldn't have been able to figure out what the boy's strange behavior meant. That's why the boy was so astonished when the young man said, "I'll go the second floor. Try falling over like you've been shot." The young man carried the boy over and laid him face down. He had the boy bend his knees to take the same posture as that first night. He immediately turned off the tabletop lamp and switched on the overhead light so the boy was bathed in bluish shade instead. Dim light washed over the room like in the nighttime scene from the movie. The young man went to the *genkan* and brought back a pair of shoes from the shoe cabinet. He put them on the boy's feet and carefully tied the laces himself. The young man was clad in what seemed to be a military uniform from some foreign country: a sky-blue uniform with red piping. On his feet were a pair of red leather boots so shiny they practically twinkled. He was also wearing a military helmet on his head. It was the real thing—on the top was a short spear point. The young man told the boy that a friend had recently brought it for him in Germany. Later that evening, when the nurse came home late and opened the door from the *genkan* only to find the young man wearing the demonic-looking thing on his head, she was so taken aback by the odd vision that she slammed the door shut with a *wham!* After that, the helmet became one of their favorite toys.

In addition to the helmet and the uniform, the young man had a saber to make his outfit complete. The boy had no idea when the young man got all these things, or why exactly he had them, but when the young man stood there in the blue light, the outfit looked so good on him that the boy began to fall under the illusion he really was an officer in some foreign military. Before they became close, the boy had been full of anxiety, thinking he should stop his odd games, but now that another person had started playing with him, the surprised boy felt curiosity bubble up within him. Where would these games lead? He wanted to see them through to the very end.

The helmeted officer started delivering a monologue like he was narrating the action of a film.[10] "*A virtuous young soldier has fallen. He is lying on an embankment on the front lines in northern France, as the light*

---

10. During the era of silent film, it was common in Japan to have someone at the front of the cinema to describe the action of the film while it played on the screen. This person, called a *benshi* ("orator"), would explain what is happening, provide dramatic narration for the film, and even act out the dialogue of the characters. Here, the boy is pretending to be one of these narrators.

*of the moon shines down on him. Overhead, the searchlights swing back
and forth, forming shifting stripes of light in the sky, which is filled with
white smoke from all the exploding shells . . .'* We'll have to use fireworks
for that. I'll look into that sometime . . ."

Next, he blindfolded the boy with a handkerchief, removed the boy's
hat, put it back on, and loosened the strap below the boy's chin so it
was about ready to fall off. He tugged on the boy's neckerchief, twisted
the tips of the boy's shoes slightly to the side, spread the boy's thighs
so that they opened at a wider angle, then lifted the boy's lower back
so that his derriere stuck out a little more . . . The young man adjusted
the boy, tinkering with him in all sorts of ways as if giving him a rough
physical exam. Then, from what the boy could tell beneath his blind-
fold, the young man stepped back to admire his handiwork.

He gazed at the boy for what felt like quite a long time. After a
while, the boy heard the rattling of a saber and the squeak of the young
man's boots. They were coming from outside the room, probably
partway up the staircase. Then, slowly, the young man began creeping
stealthily back toward him. The boy could hear his own heart pounding
loudly in his chest as he felt the hard tip of a boot press firmly against
his shoulder.

The young man pushed him imitating a light kick, and the fallen
soldier's slender body rolled to the side. A little more, and the boy
found himself facing upward. The young man's knees pressed in
between the boy's thighs, which were wearing nothing but shorts, and
as he did so, the boy sensed the officer's aroma—a combination of
leather and wool—envelop him. Right then, the officer took one of
the boy's arms and placed it over his shoulder. As he was lifted into the
officer's arms, the boy felt like a fourteen-year-old bride. He trembled
slightly but remained limp as if he really were unconscious. As he felt
the blue, electric moon on his eyelids, he closed his eyes all the tighter.
The enemy officer had approached him from near by his feet, drawing
close as if wanting to take in the scent of the fallen soldier. Then, when
the fallen soldier felt the officer kiss him on the lips, he couldn't help
wondering for a moment if the bushy thing he felt brushing against
him hadn't been there from the very start.

SIX

Two Essays by Hamao Shirō (1930)

Translated by Steve Dodd

Biography and Introduction

Hamao Shirō (1896–1935) was born in Tokyo, the fourth son of the eminent physician Baron Katō Terumaro. After studying at Tokyo's First Higher School (Daiichi kōtō gakkō), he entered Tokyo Imperial University in 1918, and graduated from the Law Department in 1923. In 1918 Hamao married the daughter of Viscount Hamao Arata, a former president of the same university. Since he was adopted into the Hamao family, he followed the usual practice of taking on the family name.

During his literary career, which lasted no more than six years, he produced twenty literary works. He also carried out research related to theater and criminal psychology. From 1924, he was employed as a public prosecutor in Tokyo, but he also contributed essays on criminality to *Shinseinen* (New Youth), a magazine that specialized in matters such as criminology, sexology, and detective fiction during the 1920s and 1930s. He gained a reputation as an outstanding writer of detective fiction, his first such story appearing in *Shinseinen* in 1929. His writing is generally associated with the group of literary and artistic works categorized as *ero-guro-nansensu* (erotic grotesque nonsense). He took up a position as a lawyer from 1928, and he became a member of the House of Peers (Kizokuin) in 1933. In 1935, he died of a sudden brain hemorrhage at the relatively young age of forty.

Hamao was a man of many talents, with a strong interest in theater, *raguko* (comic storytelling), Western music, *joruri* narrative performance (*kiyomoto*), and even mahjong. He also carried out historical studies into traditional male same-sex relations (*shudō*) in cooperation with his close friend, the famed author Edogawa Ranpo (1894–1965). Some of Hamao's stories contain references to male same-sex relationships.

Introduction

These two articles first appeared in the magazine *Fujin saron* (Women's Salon). Writing in 1930, Hamao addressed a readership that was a world away from the late Tokugawa/early Meiji period when the male same-sex tradition of *nanshoku* was still viewed as relatively uncontroversial. This can be seen through the word *dōseiai* that Hamao frequently uses in his discussion of same-sex practices. The term only entered the Japanese vocabulary near the end of the Meiji period, and is a direct translation of the Western word "homosexuality" (German, *Homosexualität*), which emerged out of late nineteenth-century sexological studies such as Richard von Krafft-Ebing's *Psychopathia Sexualis* (1886).

Nanshoku was a term that centered exclusively on male-male relations, but *dōseiai* also addressed female-female relations. This allows Hamao to refer to both sets of relations in his articles. However, the word *dōseiai* also points to a new, Western-inspired and largely negative understanding of same-sex desire in general. As a result, any Japanese writer bold enough to address the subject positively in the late 1920s or early 1930s was forced to confront a newly emerged consensus in Japan—in imitation of other modern, "civilized" cultures—whereby homosexuality was considered a perversion, a taboo, and a topic that should generally be avoided in polite company. For this reason, the significance of Hamao's two articles should not be underestimated.

Hamao draws from pre-Meiji Japanese literary works and even the *Analects of Confucius* as a means to highlight an indigenous East Asian tradition of same-sex desire, but his articles also display various factors that place them very much in a modern Western-influenced frame of 1930s Japan. For instance, he describes homosexual activities that take place not in the home, but rather in peripheral public spaces like the impersonal busy streets of Ginza or in dark parks after nightfall. In other words, queer encounters are relegated to sites outside the realm of "normal" everyday life. Moreover, while Hamao's writing certainly stands out as a heartfelt plea for tolerance and understanding regarding homosexuality, the mood of the times dictates that he can only begin his discussion from a "common sense" acknowledgment that homosexuality is generally viewed as a form of sickness. A man of his age, Hamao can hardly be expected to articulate the more assertive and confident form of queer identity that many would expect in our present age. On the other hand, he makes full use of his legalistic training, drawing on Western sexological studies as an effective means to encourage a more compassionate understanding of homosexuality among his readers.

Hamao's account of queer life in Tokyo exhibits a mixture of both scientific rigor and prurient attention to detail in a way that echoes the interests of a skillful writer of crime fiction. On one level, his lurid accounts of hidden desire in the underbelly of the big city perfectly meets the interests of a readership whetted with an appetite for *ero-guro-nansensu* journalism. And he certainly does not hold back when it comes to titillating details. For instance, Hamao professes shock and revulsion that one feature of the *nanshoku* tradition—namely, that the younger partner should "naturally" take the passive role—threatens to be upturned by at least one eager older punter. But we might also take his account of an older partner keen to ignore the old rules as confirmation that a new and more flexible set of sexual relations had opened up in the modern world. It is hard to avoid the conclusion that his at-times salacious insights into queer life aim to shock and delight the readers in equal measure.

When trying to determine precisely how Hamao personally fits into this account of same-sex desire that he seems so passionate to spell out, we are left with a large degree of ambiguity. Indeed, it might be argued that this very lack of precision is only to be expected: after all, ambiguity has frequently served as a safe way for those of a queer disposition in unsympathetic cultures throughout history to recognize each other with a degree of safety. On the one hand, references to historical detail and scholarly texts in these articles create a kind of intellectual distancing that allows the author to avoid any suggestion of personal involvement. And yet, there exists between the lines a strong sense of knowingness that is difficult not to pick up. For example, Hamao identifies himself as an amateur researcher, but his readers must surely have wondered how his interest was first whetted, how he knew about the best places to meet other men, or how his friends included young men who pick up punters on the streets. Quite possibly Hamao's articles produced a spike in visits to these very same cruising grounds by other equally avid amateur researchers!

Finally, there is an interesting development between the two articles. While the first article concentrates on various details about queer life in Tokyo, the second emerged (we are informed) as a response to numerous letters that the author received. In that sense, Hamao is simply reflecting broader trends in the publishing industry during the Taishō and early Shōwa periods, which saw the emergence of mass magazines to which the readership began to contribute, often through letter columns, and share their concerns and opinions about various social matters. Particularly prominent among these matters were concerns about definitions of sexual normality and perversion. In that sense, Hamao's articles are not so much a simple exposé of a hitherto unreported aspect of urban life, but serve instead as the sign of a constantly developing social conversation about complex sexualities. In the second article, Hamao's contribution to this debate is to argue openly and forthrightly for "Urnings" to accept their true sexual natures, even in the face of a society that he believes mistakenly views homosexuality per se as an illness, rather than understand that the problem lies in a 1930s Japanese society that is unforgivably uneducated and ignorant on the subject.

"Thoughts on Homosexuality"

(Dōseiai kō)

Let me offer a few random thoughts about what I have picked up through conversations and reading on the subject of homosexuality (*dōseiai*). Of course, since I do not have any academic expertise in the field, I have no intention of making a scholarly argument. However, the very fact that I speak from outside of the scholarly field might, on the contrary, add some extra interest to what I have to say.

In general, almost all scholars who discuss matters of sex show no sympathy toward homosexuality. Notwithstanding the ideas of Krafft-Ebing and Albert Moll, which were introduced relatively early into Japan, it seems inconceivable to view homosexuals as anything but sick. Of course, if one starts from the assumption that homosexuality is abnormal, this view makes complete sense. However, it is surely an interesting phenomenon that many people who are not scholars in the field have so much to say on the matter. One example is Edward Carpenter, who seems to take the whole thing very seriously.

Putting aside the more egregious arguments of scholars, it is commonly believed that the word "homosexuality" can be clearly classified into two meanings, namely, "homosexual love" (*dōseikan no renjō*) and "homosexual desire" (*dōsei seiyoku*).

In the world at large, many people have no interest whatsoever in homosexuality. These people assert that even the mention of such a subject is unpleasant. One could not expect them to have any interest in a topic like the present one. But since this article is a matter of the written rather than the spoken word, there is even less likelihood that they will come across it, so I have no concerns about upsetting them.

The first thing to note is that, in any group of men, it appears that as many as seven out of ten will be uninterested in this topic. I am not sure of the situation among women since I have not made a detailed study of them.

Secondly, there are people who assert that they can understand "homosexual desire" but they cannot see how a man could love another man. On the other hand, there are also people who claim that, while they comprehend "homosexual love," they have never even thought of "homosexual desire."

People like this are keen to argue that homosexuality can only be defined according to the individual interpretations they put on it.

Those who can sympathize with both definitions probably have some experience of this particular form of love.

People who say they understand "homosexual desire" can be divided further into two groups. One group consists of so-called situational (*daiyōteki*) homosexuals. That is, fundamentally they like to eat rice, but they get so hungry that they make do with bread. This activity arises between men in places where there are no members of the opposite sex, such as dormitories, barracks, and prisons. Since these people immediately go back to eating rice once they escape from such places, they are obviously not real Urnings.

Consequently, there is no love as such between these men.

The second group consists of Urnings, who are stimulated by members of the same sex as much, if not more than, members of the opposite sex. I will return to this matter later.

People who are sympathetic to homosexual love (*dōsei ren'ai*) can also be separated into two groups. The first is made up of people who can be described as embracing their own sex before they develop an interest in the opposite sex; in other words, males still at the stage of young manhood who feel a vague, fleeting love toward their friends. (Of course, as I mentioned earlier, there are many who show no inclination toward their own sex during their whole lives.) Members of this first group interpret their feelings of love as friendship. During high school days when they discuss the nature of "friendship" and clasp each other's hands, they feel some kind of mutual affection. However, before long it reaches the point where they are stirred by love for the opposite sex, and show some letter they have received from a girl to their closest friend, with the comment that "this is my *Geliebte* (Beloved)." By that point their homosexual inclination has already faded away.

I think there are a considerable number of men who are familiar with this degree of homosexuality, but more passionate feelings seem to develop among women. Since women tend to prefer being the recipient rather than the instigator of love, it seems to be mostly a matter of younger women who direct their affections to older ones. This is in contrast to male homosexuality where the older partner frequently initiates the courtship.

Let us now move to homosexual love, which is of an entirely different nature than temporary or friendship-inspired forms of homosexuality.

We are talking here about the feelings of people who never lose their susceptibility to the beauty of the same sex, just as regular males always feel love for the opposite sex no matter how old they become. In other words, these are true Urnings.

There are quite a few people who have been acknowledged as true Urnings. Various literary works attest to the fact that Michelangelo, Shakespeare, Tchaikovsky, Whitman, Oscar Wilde, Montaigne, Schubert and Bacon undoubtedly fell into the camp.

It is noteworthy that many such people hail from artistic families, but they can also be counted among heroic figures. Examples include Alexander the Great and Julius Caesar. I leave it to the expert books in the field to set out the most appropriate examples, but one such book by Havelock Ellis suggests that virtually all the great figures appear to have been members of the homosexual fraternity. One book I have read indicates that Goethe was numbered among them, but he seems not to have been a great expert on the matter. There is certainly an element of truth in the book that treats Christ as sharing the same proclivity, but I think it strange that Confucius has never been thought of as someone who followed this particular path.

One volume of the *Analects*, in which Confucius's words and actions are recorded, is imbued with the distinct possibility that he was homosexual. It is to be regretted that this point is missing even from the writings of Carpenter, who so revered the practice.

When his beloved disciple Yan Hui died, Confucius wept bitter tears. Of course, this may be due to his fear that the death of his favorite meant that his teachings would fail to be passed down. But surely it makes greater sense to ascribe the cause not simply to such a practical reason, but rather to the exceptional love that Confucius felt for Hui. Would not such an interpretation reveal Confucius's utter humanity? Whatever the cause, the degree of Confucius's lamentation was certainly unusual.

In any case, until recently the word "homosexuality" was so misunderstood that it became an abomination and a taboo in society. For this reason, to interpret Confucius in such a way might well be considered a kind of blasphemy. However, I cannot overlook the fact that this tendency is evident in parts of the *Analects*. (There are a number of examples from the *Analects* that I would like to pick out, but I will omit them here.)

Since there is inadequate research in the field related to figures from our own Japanese history, it is not possible to be sure of the facts.

Even in books written on the subject by Japanese scholars there is no distinction between homosexual desire and homosexual love, so we cannot quantify these terms.

According to one document, "the practice of *nanshoku* became very stylish from around the time of the Warring States period (c. 1467—c. 1603)." Ihara Saikaku[1] asserted that it was rooted in the distant past, and Takizawa Bakin[2] joked that Kōbō daishi[3] imported it from China.

Notable examples include the third Tokugawa shōgun Iemitsu (1604–1651), Oda Nobunaga (1534–1582), and the samurai warrior-poet Ōta Dōkan (1432–1486), but it is not possible to say how deeply they were actually involved in the practice.

The "Report on Catamites" section of Anraku Sakuden's (1554–1642) *Laughs to Wake You Up* (*Seisuishō*, 1623) claims that it was a common practice among the community of Buddhist priests, but it is difficult to be certain of this.[4]

It is well known that the emergence of the theater led homosexuality to gain ground among actors. The fact that the expression "how can you squeeze something big into a narrow space?"[5] had its origins in cer-

---

1. Japanese poet and writer of "floating world" prose (*Ukiyo-zōshi*), 1642–1693.
2. Author of *gesaku* fiction, 1767–1848.
3. Also known as Kūkai, founder of Shingon school of Buddhism, 774–835.
4. A few words are missing from the original text here. This is probably due to censorship.
5. Again, some words are missing, probably due to censorship, which means I have had to guess the full expression.

tain kinds of behavior among theater actors indicates that the practice was an integral part of theatrical life.

However, the great pity is that among these details hardly any practical examples of actual love have been passed down to us.

There is just one story to mention. *The Humble Man's Bobbin* (*Shizu no odamaki*),[6] which tells the tale of the young man Sangorō, describes ardent feelings of love. I would say that the two young men in the story have such tightly knit feelings for each other that it is probably correct to describe them as full-blown Urnings.

There has been quite a lot of discussion about Matsuo Bashō (1644–1694). Some literati have vehemently denied that he had any such interest, but these people appear to have had a jaundiced opinion of homosexuality. It makes a great deal of sense to view Bashō as a homosexual.

So what is the situation in our country in the present age?

Of course, homosexuals have not ceased to exist. I have made no statistical study, so I cannot say if there is any increase or decrease in numbers, but it is undoubtedly true to assert that quite a few people are inclined this way.

However, it should be noted that many such people have not given thought to the social significance of homosexuality in the ways raised by Carpenter. They simply give in to the idea that they are sufferers of sexual perversion (*hentai seiyoku*), they consider their own acts as shameful, and as far as possible they hide everything they do from others. Consequently, in cities even as big as Tokyo these people walk in the shadows with their heads down.[7]

It is worth noting that there is presently no (official) system of legal punishment for homosexual sexual activity.

Tales of Yushima teashops that offered young rent boys (*kagema jaya*) and teashops in Yoshichō where you could do the business (*machiai jaya*) are nothing more than dreams of long ago.

According to laws on the European continent, even with mutual consent, homosexual "unnatural obscenity" is subject to punishment. (There is a justifiable debate about the propriety of calling homo-

---

6. Author unknown. Versions of the story circulated in Satsuma (present-day Kagoshima prefecture) during the Meiji period, and a version was serialized in the Liberal Party newspaper, *Lamp of Freedom* (*Jiyūtō*), from July 19 to August 16, 1884.

7. I have omitted the sentence following this because the original is such poor quality that it is impossible to read.

sexual sexual activity unnatural, or *widernaturlich*.) Though quite a few critiques from various quarters have been raised against these legal provisions, the fact remains that they are still clearly part of the German penal code. It seems that even in Britain it is punishable by law. If it were otherwise, there would have been no need for Wilde to write *De Profundis.*

On this point, homosexuals in Japan can be thankful for the law. Our law views the question of same-sex relations in the same way as it views adultery between men and women. Bearing in mind the opinions of people such as Urlichs, Weininger, and Carpenter, in this case our penal code might be appropriately described as more civilized than that of Europe.

Incidentally, the system of male prostitution might be totally out of bounds in Europe, but it does exist in the form of unlicensed prostitution.

Whatever the form of prostitution, homosexuals do not necessarily feel a sense of privation in Japan.

As I mentioned at the beginning, of course even at the present time as a matter of common sense it is necessary to distinguish between love and desire among members of the same sex.

Buds of love certainly seem to sprout most among groups in which young men abound; in particular students, shop assistants, and actors.

It is my opinion that one very remarkable difference between "homosexual love" and "heterosexual love" is that, in the case of love between members of the same sex, the intellectual level between lovers is generally balanced. (Of course there are cases when the balance is missing.) Generally, in the case of relations between men and women, there is no such meeting of minds, with the result that it is hard to find any intellectual constituent to such love. Among people of the same sex, it is different. For example, some fellow students not only fall in love with each other, but also find it possible to stimulate their intellects. This is a case in which the possession of a homosexual lover promotes serious study. Alternative examples include sportsmen who, having fallen for each other, both go on to excel in their fields. In other words, homosexual love produces a situation that always makes it possible for a couple to go to battle together.

If it is the case that homosexuality is considered loathsome and dirty, then present-day educators need to expand the horizons of their attentiveness a bit more. All these educators do is to guard against juvenile delinquents and regular students getting close to virtuous young men, but this is a mistake. They should probably pay more attention to preventing older gifted students from approaching lower-grade students. The reason for this is that there are numerous examples of students with homosexual tendencies who show signs of real smartness during the period of middle and high schools. Actually, this is not just a matter of student years. While not always reaching the heights of the great artists I mentioned earlier, the fact cannot be overlooked that there are an extraordinary number of intelligent people among those with Urning tendencies.

We should not be taken in by groundless Japanese books, which suggest for instance that senior students are normally masculine, whereas junior students who are the recipient of loving affections are feminine. The very opposite can be the case. There are numerous examples of people who are the recipient of affections being far more masculine than those who instigate the affair. Just one thing to note is that, when love arises between students of different ages, the older one may garner respect for some kind of accomplishment. He might, for instance, excel in scholarly abilities or in his irreproachable conduct, or he might be an outstanding baseball player or swimmer.

Among women, the depth of love can be extremely intense. Of course, this also necessitates an element of respect, but with women we tend to find more examples of relations between student and teacher rather than between two students.

More female couples commit homosexual lovers' suicide (*dōsei shinjū*) than male couples, but it would be wrong to infer that female couples are more sincere than male couples. There are generally lots of additional elements why women might commit homosexual lovers' suicide. When a particular area of someone's life becomes miserable, that wretchedness can quickly affect other parts of life, and the person plunges into sentimentality. Ultimately, it is relatively easy for the companion to be affected too.

Here are some typical examples of homosexual love:

Shakespeare's sonnets dedicated to Mr. W. H.
Whitman's poem, *Leaves of Grass*
Michelangelo's sonnets dedicated to Tommaso dei Cavalieri

Reihant's student memoirs[8]
Fletcher's poems lamenting his deceased friend

These last poems reveal some truly ardent passion.

What are the trends today for those who experience homosexual desire?

As noted above, many of them walk in the shadows so it is very hard to be entirely certain, but what is indisputable is that within Tokyo some people are engaged in related work.

It is common knowledge that this gang haunts the corner of XX and XXX in Asakusa Park at around 8 p.m. at night. People generally have no interest in matters of love, but are able to indulge in sexual activities. (This is especially true of men.)

None of the customers who frequent the red-light district every night can possibly have feelings of love toward the prostitutes.

It is exactly the same with those who pay for so-called rent boys (*kagema*). As long as people consort with these professionals, they are oblivious to sensuality and love, and the only matter that concerns them is money.

People say that, just as women give themselves up to licentiousness in order to fill their stomachs, men do the same thing because they want the money.

How pitiable to hear that people are reduced to doing this in order to eat.

But people who have no interest at all in such things could not do such a thing even if it was to earn a living. They would at least choose another route. Therefore, a lot of the people who enter this work lead lives in which to a considerable extent the surrounding environment has fanned their interest.

So what sort of people make up most of the customers?

One would assume, of course, that they are people who are born with feelings of homosexual desire. But this is not necessarily true. Some people who have played the field hard and grown weary of women's charms get started from curiosity. Moreover, some types have been spurred on to action by the recent fad for bizarre tastes.

Incidentally, the customers are naturally of no fixed age, and the same is true of the professionals.

---

8. I cannot identify the name. The katakana reads *reihanto*.

I expected to see nothing but beautiful sixteen- or seventeen-year-old youths, but I ended up falling into a mood of real disappointment.

Most people will assume that the clients are always active, but that is not actually true. Surprisingly, it seems that there are visits by stately gentlemen who say that they would like to be passive. How very convenient for these men who operate in the dark since, whatever their preference, their desires can be satisfied.

Now, I have heard a story that these people have recently expanded into the ultra-fashionable streets of Ginza. A beautiful young man with whom I am acquainted told me he was subject to some amorous glances in that district by a respectable looking gentleman of about forty-five or forty-six. One could understand the point if that older man were active, but the young man explained to me that, when they passed through some back streets and got as far as a dark spot next to XX bridge, the older man came out with a strange request. It turns out that he was actually passive.

"What on earth did you do?" To my question, the young man gave a little laugh and replied, "Well, I managed it somehow." At this, I could not refrain from frowning. What a frightening place the world is!

It seems that the professionals are most welcoming to foreigners. In general, a lot of foreigners who come to Japan tend to be objectionable, but the word is that this group of regular patrons is generous with their money. For this reason, when foreigners come out on the prowl (apparently on certain days only), Japanese clients are given the cold shoulder.

Since Europeans have tacit permission in Japan to do what is banned in their own countries by law, they are even more forward in their activities. Let me say how things are by way of a humorous anecdote.

A young policeman was walking through XXX Park, when a foreigner addressed him with the words, "*keikan, keikan.*" When he went to see what the problem was, the foreigner was behaving strangely, repeatedly flapping a five-yen note in his hand.

At this point, the policeman realized for the first time that the foreigner was not using the words "*keikan, keikan*" in the sense of "officer, officer."[9]

---

9. *Keikan* is also a legal term meaning, "sodomy." So this expression might be correctly translated as "bugger me, bugger me!"

This article has gone on for too long, but just before I stop, let me finish by spelling out one thing clearly. I am speaking particularly to all homosexuals and those who study the subject.

First of all, you need to be absolutely certain about what homosexuality is. Moreover, simply to feel ashamed of your selves to no purpose, and to hide away and carry out acts of stupidity is no good at all. You must clearly grasp the social significance of homosexuality.

Equally, those who count themselves as critics ought to first grasp its essence, and then recognize its value.

To be misled by groundless books published in Japan, and to say things that are unfounded simply will not do.

Here I mention some books that I think both these groups of people should definitely read:

Edward Carpenter
Intermediate Sex
Ioläus (An Anthology of Friendship)
Havelock Ellis
Sexual Inversion (*Psychology of Sex*, 2nd volume in the series)
Hirschfeld
Homosexualität
Gleichen-Russwurm
Freundschaft
Placzek
Freundschaft

Moreover, a final word to the lawyers. In Japan, homosexuality is not a legal problem, but it is a considerable legal problem in Europe, with the result that there are all kinds of articles.

All the works on homosexuality such as Wulffen's *Sexualverbrecher* are old, so reference should be made to the likes of Krafft-Ebing.

In addition, as far as I am aware, quite a few doctorate dissertations have been published in Germany. A large number of them are to be found in the Japanese Supreme Court (*Daishin'in*) library. Many of them carry the title, *Ueber widernaturliche Unzucht*.

The reason why I have not mentioned Japanese documents is certainly not due to any *pedantisch* (pedantic) reason. It is simply that there are no documents worth reading in Japanese.

(27th June, 1930)

"More Thoughts on Homosexuality"

(Futatabi dōseiai ni tsuite)

1. Why return to the subject?

Since the publication of my short article, "Thoughts on Homosexuality," in the September edition of this magazine, I have received various letters from readers I have never met. Letters have come all the way from outside of Japan. Other letters have reached me from closer at hand, from people who live in Tokyo just like me. These letters were all written by men. All these men appear to be quite extreme Urnings (homosexuals).

Now, every letter sent to me contains an account of personal experiences and a record of their concerns, and ends with a search for remedies that might possibly work out ways to resolve these worries.

These people do not know me at all, and yet (at least as far as I can believe what they say) they offer frank disclosures and totally clear accounts of what is usually a shameful part of their natures. This surely requires considerable courage and determination. At the same time, it is not hard to guess how deeply these people have suffered in their pain.

Probably only one or two people out of ten, or more likely out of a hundred, possess such courage, but the letters I have received from dozens, possibly hundreds, more of my fellow countrymen mean that I cannot help but feel keenly how, to varying degrees, they too have tasted the same bitterness. It was this compelling, hidden demand that led me to pick up my pen again.

2. The undeniable facts

All the letters I received add up to virtually the same thing. Of course the way every human life develops differs according to education and age, but they all pose the same questions and thoughts. Let me enumerate the common points shared by these letters:

1) Each Urning believes he is the only one. That is, they are always assailed by feelings of loneliness, believing that they are the only person in the world who feels love for the same sex.

2) They think of themselves as deformed, considering themselves to be sad cripples unable to speak out to others (particularly their parents). Or else, they lament that they are sick people cursed for life.

3) They are ashamed of themselves. Every letter was filled with comments such as "I am extremely embarrassed," and "I cannot mix with anyone."

4) Many of them are under the examination of doctors, but they have no possibility of receiving a positive outcome.

5) Some of the people who wrote to me noted that they are completely indifferent to the opposite sex, or feel loathing toward women. I put this down to the fact that they are all extreme Urnings. However, the reader should be aware that, due to a widespread lack of sympathy as well as ignorance of the part of the person concerned, some of these people get married. Some actually want to get married. Once married, they produce children but they then experience the bitterness of marital separation.

6) Some people have been so oppressed by feelings of loneliness and a widespread lack of sympathy that, in throes of agony, they have attempted suicide more than once. They note feelings of misfortune in having failed to accomplish the deed.

The compelling honesty with which these letters are written has convinced me that there is nothing fanciful about them.

What sort of questions do these facts present us with?

3. The importance of homosexuality as a social question

I have first set out the above facts to my readers as a basis for discussing the essential nature of homosexuality. Now, I am particularly hopeful that these facts will allow us to consider its importance as a social question.

About how many homosexuals exist? I have not looked into any of the statistics on this point, but let me quote here some words by Carpenter:

Contrary to the general impression, one of the first points that emerges from this study is that "Urnings," or Uranians, are by no means so very rare; but that they form, beneath the surface of society, a large class. It remains difficult, however, to get an exact statement of their numbers; and this for more than one reason: partly because, owing to the want of any general understanding of their case, these folk tend to conceal their true feelings . . . and partly because it is indubitable that the numbers do vary very greatly, not only in different countries but even in different classes in the same country. The consequence of all this being that we have estimates differing very widely from each other. Dr. Grabowsky, a well-known writer in Germany, quotes figures (which we think must be exaggerated) as high as 1 man in every 22, while Dr. Albert Moll (*Die Conträre Sexualempfindung*, chap. 3) gives estimates varying from 1 in every 50 to as low as 1 in every 500. These figures apply to such as are exclusively of the said nature, *i.e.*, to those whose deepest feelings of love and friendship go out only to persons of their own sex. Of course, if in addition are included those double-natured people (of whom there are a great number) who experience the normal attachment, with the homogenic tendency in less or greater degree superadded, the estimates must be greatly higher.[10]

If we tentatively accept Albert Moll's calculation of a minimum ratio of 1 in every 500 and apply it to the population of Japan, what does the number of Urnings in this country come to? This deserves some thought.

If 1 in every 500 of the total Japanese population harbors the kind of pain and distress mentioned above with no one to offer teaching or guidance, and if they have an intense hatred of their own bodies and the world around them, then what is to be done?

This is not a question of whether they exist. They certainly exist; of that I have no doubt.

4. The situation for men in society

I make a plea on behalf of all such men in society. Among our fellow countrymen, there are enormous numbers of people (or at least far more than the average person thinks) who are tormented throughout their lives by shame, anxiety, loneliness, and pain.

---

10. I have taken the original Carpenter quote from http://www.edwardcarpenter.net/ecint2.htm#urnings

As I mention later on, Urnings are certainly not all just sentimental-ists. They are not simply men who resemble women. If these people really had a stronger sense of self-awareness, they would have the talents and potential to contribute to the world and to promote culture. How-ever, since they both misunderstand themselves and are misunderstood by the world at large, they suffer from being unable to make their mark on society, and eventually get to a point where they contemplate sui-cide. How can we allow this to go on without comment? Is it right to remain ignorant and simply hold them in contempt as sexual perverts?

Even if, perish the thought, we were to allow for a moment that every one of them is indeed a cripple, then would not that be even more reason for healthy people to offer them help? It cannot possibly be right to remain contemptuous of these people without due cause.

The question is: how can we help? To answer this, firstly we need to understand what Urnings are. I have no desire to subject every male to a study of their sexual proclivities, but I would like people to realize that one of the most pressing problems in contemporary society is to gain a true understanding of Urnings.

The importance of homosexuality as a social question should at least be studied along parallel lines with the women's problem in society. Questions relating to women have already been raised in the past. Numerous magnificent warriors from the ranks of women have emerged to challenge contemporary society.

The study of homosexuality should certainly not be left entirely to the doctors. It demands to be debated beyond the confines of a study of sexual desire.

Even less should it be led by a prurient journalistic interest driven by erotic and grotesque tastes.

The question really deserves serious consideration, and is worthy of discussion in all earnestness. What other choice have I but to raise the subject of homosexuality as the most pressing problem of the present day?

5. The situation for women in society

The subject I have taken up is that of the male Urning, so let me venture to offer a warning on how women are affected by this phenom-enon. (If, on the other hand, we were discussing the subject of female Urnings, our comments here would be directed toward males from the opposite perspective. Obviously, if we were considering the female Urning, then it would make sense to change "the situation for men in society" in the previous section to "the situation for women in society.")

Some extreme Urnings feel a loathing for women, while others have less intense feelings, but in either case they tend to show total indifference to women. The result is that, as long as they have a complete lack of relations, however we define it, with the opposite sex, no problem should arise with women. Or at least, this is what might be expected.

However, society is complicated and things are not so easily settled.

Urnings do actually get married to the opposite sex. They become someone's husband, and even attain fatherhood.

Though these words of mine may sound unbelievable, I know this to be true from no less than three letters that I have personally received. Moreover, Carpenter's writings include the following comments on similar examples produced by Krafft-Ebing when he says that "such men, notwithstanding their actual aversion to intercourse with the female, do ultimately marry—either from ethical, as sometimes happens, or from social considerations."

A few of the letters I have received describe someone who has been thinking of getting married recently, but has concerns about it.

I am sure that the reader can imagine such cases among people from the countryside who are far from centers of culture, especially among people who are uneducated. In other words, when people close by such as parents or relatives say that the time has come, and then force them into marriage and select their spouses, these men lack the courage to make clear their true natures. The result is that, no matter how painful, they end up living together with women. They even dream of miracles, supposing that things will work out once they have moved in together!

Of course, it is not hard to guess what happens to marriages like this. They become extremely unfortunate affairs, with the result that they produce a cold household, which they have to endure for the rest of their lives. Or else, it all ends in divorce.

In a situation such as this, let us consider the responsibility of the Urning males. To what extent should they be blamed? Certainly, the man bears most of the responsibility. But surely the mistake results from ignorance on his part.

There is no doubt about what makes him so ignorant. The whole of society has no experience of the matter, and no one in society has taught him about his own essential nature.

It strikes me that even when addressing the question of marriage, the problem of Urnings is hugely important.

For a variety of reasons, I have almost never heard of an example of homosexuality being raised as a cause for divorce in the courts.

But any number of cases have arisen in society where this has been the real cause leading to divorce.

Most lamentable is the fact that there are women who still have no idea about the real cause for the family discord even after they have separated.

I have heard that unions short of marriage have been formed in the past with men who have a venereal disease.

Of course there is some question about the value of forming such unions, but there may be some benefits in marrying a man who has such a disease.

However, what possible desirable benefit could there be in marrying an extreme Urning?

After all, a venereal disease is treatable, while there is no chance of changing the nature of an extreme Urning.

The most suitable thing for a confirmed Urning is not to marry. However, if the male is not going to inform anyone or make any such announcement, the woman should work out the most suitable means of protecting herself.

I clearly acknowledge that, in such a case, the male has responsibility. However, as I mentioned earlier, it is conceivable that even the male may be unaware of his own past (because he may not comprehend his own nature). For this reason, I think that the woman must guard against becoming a victim in any such marriage.

How, then, can she plan such a countermeasure? Surely her only option is to make a study of male Urning psychology in order to familiarize herself with it.

6. The situation for Urnings in society

In order to avoid having to provide the same response over and over to each of the lengthy letters I have received, let me write out a single answer here.

I am of course perfectly aware of the impropriety of writing what should be a private response in the pages of this magazine. On the other hand, I can fully imagine that people with a similar disposition far outstrip those gentlemen who wrote to me. For this reason, I dare to act in an inappropriate manner.

The first thing we should bear in mind is the question of how far we ourselves are homosexual. In other words, we should grasp the extent to which we personally have the aspect of an Urning. Simply to use the single word Urning fails to address various degrees of feeling. As mentioned earlier, in extreme cases people even feel a sense of loathing toward the opposite sex. But there are also moderate people who are capable of equal feelings of love for both opposite and same sexes.

For this reason, the first question relates to gaining a good knowledge of our selves.

Secondly, as I have frequently noted, homosexuals are certainly not few in number. Armed with this fact, people should first shake off their sense of loneliness. This is an important matter. A sense of being alone is a core cause for loneliness and suffering in the world. Urnings, who remain hidden and silent in the world, must begin by freeing themselves from their sense of loneliness.

Thirdly, in my own opinion (and of course, this does not come just from me, but is a common view in foreign writings), *homosexuality is not a sickness*. It is human nature. There are differing opinions among medical writings on this point. I am not a scientist, so if the scientific viewpoint stubbornly insists that homosexuality is *pathologisch* (pathological) then I certainly have no objection. But for the present, I do not consider it a sickness. I believe it is human nature. For this reason, I insist that there is no reason to cure what is naturally given.

In part, the conclusion I have come to is entirely hopeless (although I will mention later on how this is not necessarily grounds for pessimism).

Homosexuality frequently goes hand in hand with mental illness and nervous debilitation (*shinkei suijaku*). But it would be rash to conclude from this that homosexuality results from mental illness and nervous debilitation. There are many examples of the opposite being the case.

For example, all the people who sent letters to me believe that they suffer from nervous debilitation because they are Urnings. The most extreme example of this is attempted suicide. But we should understand that people fall into nervous debilitation as a result of there being no understanding about homosexuality.

Fourthly, I have a question I would like to throw back at all those who sent me their letters. *Why are you ashamed of being homosexual?*

Why do you feel obliged to experience such shame? Why does an inability to love the opposite sex result in a source of shame?

More than anything else, you should feel ashamed of your own shame.

I have already said that homosexuality is not a sickness.

And so, I do not recognize any need to cure it. (Even if it were necessary, the present state of medical science makes that very unlikely, but that is a different question.) I say that you should stick to your own natures, and find the courage to improve human life. As for those who are extreme Urnings, I say to you that you absolutely should not marry.

This may sound exceedingly coldhearted, but I feel a need to give special emphasis to this point. The reason for this is that when an Urning marries, not only does that person fall into new levels of unhappiness, but the hapless member of the opposite sex also becomes a victim.

Fifthly, just as homosexuality is not an illness, homosexuals are not deformed. According to my thinking, I do not believe that even extreme Urnings should necessarily be described as cripples.

Since we are in possession of sexual organs, people always consider it our mission to produce descendants. However, while our organs were originally invested with that purpose, they are not necessarily geared toward that purpose these days. For some people, it is conceivable that they have been charged with a different mission. It seems that, instead of producing descendants, these people have another way of contributing to society from a different angle. (I would especially like to recommend that you look at what Carpenter has to say on this subject.)

If people are called cripples because they cannot marry, it would also be necessary to describe as cripples ordinary men and women who, though they have married, are not able to produce children.

Sixthly, what about the sexual lives of people who cannot have relations with members of the opposite sex?

I believe this is probably the point that Urnings are most interested in, but due to the nature of this article, I must avoid providing a detailed explanation. Here, I only want to offer some critical comments about foreign laws in foreign publications.

In both Great Britain and Germany, "unnatural obscenity between men" is penalized under the penal code.

This law is open to criticism in at least two senses. First of all, why should intercourse between members of the same sex be deemed a crime? In addition, if such an act between members of the same sex is to be penalized, why should it be restricted to men alone? It should be said that this is clearly unfair. (In the German penal code, there is a clause that specifies acts between men.)

I believe that, in this matter, our own legal code is above reproach.

Let me offer a few final words. No matter how much attention the world pays to this question, if the Urnings, who are the main players here, continue to conceal themselves and dodge the question, I will have failed in my mission.

I hope that homosexuals find some means to make a clear announcement of their situation to the world.

Of course, this will require extraordinary courage.

I look forward to some brave spirit emerging from the community of Urnings in the future.

7. Regarding homosexuality

It is only very recently that the world has really begun to take note of homosexuality. It first came to the attention of scientists. Since the first group to be recognized were abnormal Urnings, the belief emerges that all Urnings were abnormal. It is even more recently that people other than doctors have begun to take up the issue.

Apart from the fact that the object of their love differs from that of ordinary people, homosexuals are no different from ordinary people. (There are of course completely abnormal exceptions.)

Consequently, generalizations relating, for instance, to Urnings having no self-respect or Urnings being smart should be avoided. Just as some ordinary people are distinguished while others are not, it stands to reason that Urnings also include a large number of types.

Various distinguished people can be found among them. As far as artists are concerned, we find Shakespeare, Michelangelo, Leonardo da Vinci, Tchaikovsky and Whitman. Among kings there are Alexander the Great, Julius Caesar, Charles XII (the King of Sweden who was called the Mencius of Northern Europe), Frederick the Great of Prussia, and Edward II, James I, and William III (all of England).

(On this matter I would like to recommend the writings of Ellis and Hirschfeld.)

In Japan, we do not find many examples of homosexuality being taken up as a social question.

If my memory is not mistaken, when I was a student at the First Higher School, I saw a copy of Carpenter's "Homosexuality," translated by Mr. Yamakawa Kin (? I may be wrong with the name here, so I am open to correction),[11] in the shop front of a bookstore on Hongō-dōri.

Carpenter's writings certainly take up the matter as a social problem. I particularly encourage people to take a look at his work. Probably the only Japanese translation is by the aforementioned Mr. Yamakawa.

There are so many things to be said about homosexuality that it is a matter of regret that I am restricted here to a few pages. I still feel that I have not yet provided a clear, detailed account of homosexuality. However, there are so many things I want to say in order to give a full explanation that, unfortunately, even writing a whole book would not suffice.

Let me say this clearly. I am not a specialist researcher in this subject. As a result, there may be many mistakes in the points I have mentioned. I am open to receiving corrections from any quarter. If there are points of error, my intention is to correct those mistakes immediately.

Why then, despite my lack of confidence, have I taken up my pen twice to address this subject?

The short answer is that I wanted to draw the world's attention to the question.

Despite the limits to my knowledge, I firmly believe that the matter is extremely important as a social problem. I merely invite you all to pay attention to this fact.

In this article I have set out a few markers. With my complete lack of learning and ability, I have recklessly dared to reach base. I have simply performed a sacrifice hit.

I earnestly beseech one of you to reach the home base!

8. Reference materials

Finally, once again here are some works related to homosexuality.

- Krafft-Ebing, *Psychopathia Sexualis*
  This is a famous but quite old book on so-called sexual perversion. There is an English translation. A Japanese version has been

---

11. He must be referring to the socialist feminist Yamakawa Kikue (1890–1980), who translated Carpenter's *The Intermediate Sex* (1908) into Japanese. An abridged version was published in the magazine *Safuran* in 1914. It appeared in book form in 1919. See Michiko Suzuki, *Becoming Modern Woman*, p. 164, n. 16.

published by Bunmei Kyōkai as "Hentai seiyoku ron." This is not a complete translation. (I cannot be exactly sure because I don't have a translation at hand right now.)

- Havelock Ellis, *Psychology of Sex*, 2nd volume, "Sexual Inversion"
  This book consists of six volumes in total, and the 2nd volume is all about homosexuality. It stands out with its numerous examples and quotations. There is a text German, with the title *Homosexualität (Die sexuelle Inversion)*. I think there is a Japanese version, but I don't remember clearly.

- Gleichen-Russwurm, *Freundschaft*
  Eine psychologische Torschungsreis and notes are appended to this. This is a substantial, luxurious book that came from before the Great War. What is interesting about it is that, unlike the two books above, it lacks the scientific approach. It is a scholarly book that contains lots of quotations. I am not sure about English or Japanese translations.

- M. Hirschfeld, *Die Homosexualität*
  Extremely detailed. A large book of over 1,000 pages. I have not been through the whole book, so I cannot say anything about the contents. But I can say that that it appears to take a very medical approach.

- Erich Wulffen, *Sexualverbrecher*
  A legal and scientific book. It contains a section on *Homosexualität*. I do not believe there is a Japanese version. The author has written various other interesting books on literature and the law.

- Otto Weininger, *Geschlecht und Charakter*
  Both Japanese and English translations exist. I have read this book and can personally vouch for its high value. It touches substantially on the social angle.

- Edward Carpenter, *Intermediate Sex*
  This is the book that deals most effectively with the social angle. I would like to recommend it.

There are other works, but they inevitably quote from some of the books listed above.

As I mentioned in my September article, the reason why I have not mentioned Japanese books is not for pedantic reasons, but because there is nothing worth looking at. Most are basically abridged translations of the works mentioned above.

(24 September, 1930)

SEVEN

"Squalid Alleyways" (Rōkō)
by Kataoka Teppei (1934)

Translated by Mio Akasako and Amanda Seaman

Biography and Introduction

Prewar Japan, plagued with the growing pains of a newly founded capitalist culture, was a particularly strong breeding ground for the political ideas sowed by the 1917 Russian Revolution. With bourgeoning social unrest among the Japanese working class, the proletarian movement blossomed into one of the major political driving forces of the 1920s and 30s. This was the political and cultural milieu in which Kataoka Teppei (1894–1944) emerged as a prominent voice in the proletarian literary movement. After dropping out of Keiō University, he worked various odd jobs until one of his works, "Tongue" (Shita), was recognized by the literary community. He was originally a member of the "New Sensationist" (Shinkankakuha) group, which explored new literary methods of expressing subjective perception and sensation, but subsequently cultivated an interest in left-wing ideals and committed his efforts to the proletarian cause. His works during that time include "A Living Doll" (Ikeru Ningyō) and "This Time Surely" (Kondo-koso). He was thrown in jail during mass arrests of left-wing thinkers by the Japanese government but was released on parole after recanting his socialist ideas in 1932. "Squalid Alleyways" (Rōkō) was written shortly after his release.

In "Squalid Alleyways," Kataoka describes the struggles of two young homeless men, Sugita and Yamazaki, battling to survive in the vast, unforgiving metropolis of Tokyo. They are the poorest of the poor—they cannot afford to entertain the lofty ideals of the "intelligentsia," or participate in the organized struggle of their proletarian class. They must struggle simply to *be*. Ultimately, this work pushes the importance of class-consciousness and commitment to social obligation at the expense of human desire. In this case, this desire is one of "same-sex love."

To promote the socialist agenda, proletarian literature often used "same-sex love" as a sign of unrest and inequality in society. In "Squalid Alleyways," Sugita and Yamazaki meet on a bench in Asakusa Park, which is notorious for being a cruising spot for men seeking other men. They begin an "unnatural relationship," living together in the most dismal conditions, until Yamazaki leaves with a woman named Masuko. Upon their separation, Sugita and Yamazaki both embark on their own struggles to find their place and meaning in society. Sugita succeeds in finding honest work as a steel-factory laborer and becomes an exemplary member of the proletariat, but, curiously, remains engaged in "same-sex love."

Sugita's association with "grotesque" and "erotic" perversions of inner-city subculture reflects a popular notion at the time that male-male sexuality went hand in hand with criminality. Sugita's relationship with Chiyo-chan, a male prostitute, and his friend Hana-chan, roots him in the context of then-current events. Hana-chan refers to the notorious Shaji Hisaichi, a cross-dressing entertainer by the stage name of Hanayagi Biraku, who gained infamy in Japan for murdering a former lover and carrying his decapitated head around in a jar. Despite these ties, Sugita no longer languishes in the dregs of society as he once did—he has lifted himself up and is hardened by his work. By juxtaposing Sugita's sexual preferences and his successful pursuit of a meaningful purpose in life, Kataoka incorporates the subtleties of human emotions into a discourse that predominantly used "same-sex love" as an emblem of societal dysfunction.

Squalid Alleyways

Part I

The streets of Hirokōji in Ueno were rumbling with the sounds of trains and cars under the setting sun. A young man descended the hillside of the park, and on reaching its base, started walking along the crowded pedestrian walkway, wearing something that resembled a shabby overcoat over his kimono. His head, bare of any hat, was covered with lusterless hair left unattended and growing long. And yet, his run-down appearance did not seem to diminish him in any way as he wove confidently through the crowd—no, in fact he seemed rather elated, looking up at the crepuscular sky almost triumphantly. Life had taken a toll on his skin, rough with wear, but his rosy cheeks concealed no dark shadows; further, there was even a hint of a smile in his small, gentle eyes as he walked forward, unwaveringly.

"Oh, Sugita"—at the sound of his name, he stopped suddenly as if pulled back from the edge of absentmindedness. A tall, bulky woman stood with her shoulders hunched forward, leaning on an umbrella pressed firmly into the ground.

Sugita's mild eyes narrowed for an instant, and he flushed.

"Well, this is a—where are you off to?"

"Sugita, are you still writing those novels?" said the woman in a deep, manly voice. She rounded her big eyes, set close together in her swarthy face.

"No, right now I'm working as an amazake[1] seller."

When she heard this, she laughed heartily.

"My friend and I, we're renting the second floor of a place in Izumibashi. It's a dirty place, but you should come over sometime. What's going on with you?"

The woman mentioned that she commuted from her brother's home in Ikebukuro to a shipping agency in Shitaya every day. "I guess I'm a working woman!" She laughed.

People stared at them suspiciously as they passed by. The two went their separate ways, seemingly encouraged by the crowds of people looking their way. The man, evidently excited by this encounter, bounded off.

His tone was a little off—indeed, there was a certain peevishness in the way Sugita began to describe his encounter with the woman.

"It gives me the shivers that you're thinking about the likes of women," Yamazaki said, as he shrunk deeper under the single flimsy, threadbare quilt in the room that they shared. "Think of more important things like earning cash and come to bed!"

Ha, that would make me much more cheerful!

Sugita thought, yet eagerly proceeded to talk about his afternoon encounter with the woman in Hirokōji as he was coming back from the

---

1. Sweet rice spirit.

library. "I'm gonna invite her over to our place. She's a hot ticket, man. You'll be surprised."

What had up until that point been a vague image of a "woman" in Sugita's story suddenly acquired the heavy weight of human flesh and came crashing down on Yamazaki's gut with a thud. The young man felt such a strong desire he wanted to reach out and grab her with his hands.

"Really? Are you sure she'll come?" He didn't even attempt to hide the new glimmer in his eyes.

"Oh, for sure she'll come, she'll come alright. I'll write her a letter now. Just wait," replied his companion. He was in good humor, but he also had such an air of confidence and reliability that it made Yamazaki want to throw himself at his feet. Yamazaki's spirits suddenly rose of their own accord.

"We can't sell our sake when it rains so feel free to come by our place on your way back from the shop. Even if it's not raining, if you say you'd like to stop by, we'll take a break from work." As Sugita was writing this, Yamazaki burrowed into the quilt and filled it with his pleasurable fantasies. Breathing heavily in excitement, his heart cried, "She's gonna fall for me. She's gonna be mine!"

Sugita was twenty-six, and Yamazaki was twenty. Since meeting on a bench in Asakusa Park almost two years earlier, they had been living together among the dregs of society—tied inescapably to each other like an object and its shadow. Using park benches and cheap guesthouses as their nests, they were drawn together by a peculiar sort of love, even though they could barely manage to make ends meet. Today, they were living on the second floor of a dirty building in the back alleyways around Izumibashi in Kanda. Every night, they would go out to sell amazake.

Sugita once had ambition. He had a burning desire to make a living from his writing. Reaching for this goal, he traveled to Tokyo from distant Kyushu. But with no funds and no connections he soon found himself starving in the middle of Tokyo. Even though he had just turned twenty, he was pondering his own death as he walked along the edges of the pond in Asakusa Park. Death escaped him only because he still had twenty sen in his pockets, and with this, he managed to stay in a cheap inn. It was there that a street performing charlatan picked him up.

He then began working as the street hypnotist Sakura (Cherry Blossom), but before long, a strange incident occurred, and he was thrown out of the entourage with a few members of his Sakura crew. Next, he turned to newspaper delivery. During his breaks from this painful labor, he wrote two or three short stories and plays.

It was around this time that Sugita paid a visit to the home of an author by the name of Tanno Orizo—although he did so without first getting an invitation. Tanno read Sugita's play and told him that making a prophet say things in the style of "I shalt do so-and-so" was not his type of play and warned Sugita that he should put his energy into employing more realistic material and techniques. Despite this discouraging advice, Sugita began to live in Tanno's home as a houseboy.

Tanno, however, was fickle, and though he allowed Sugita make a small bed in the entryway, he offered him no help at all with the crucial task of literary composition. On those rare occasions when they met face to face, their conversations lasted less than ten minutes, and Sugita began to wonder why he was staying at Tanno's home at all. After half a year, he came up with some excuse to depart.

Once again he found himself living a vagrant lifestyle in Asakusa. He felt as though he had escaped a swamp and now found himself in a crystal-clear stream—it was liberating. One day, he discovered a boy on a park bench, looking dejected and at his wit's end.

"Hey, what's wrong? You look quite troubled." When Sugita came close, the boy looked up at him with a grim, guarded stare. However, Sugita had an odd charm. Indeed, he had the mussed-up hair of a bookworm that was thinning so much that it might come right out if pulled, and his skin was weather-beaten and lusterless. Sleeping on park benches and in cheap guesthouses had turned him into this grimy man. And yet, under his wide forehead, his small, gentle eyes made him always look cheerful. Nor had his difficult circumstances whittled away the flesh on his cheeks; when he smiled with his almost childlike features, his gentle eyes seemed to sparkle delightfully.

"Got anything to eat?" asked the boy. He told his story clearly—of having left his hometown five days earlier to come to Tokyo, and of having not a single sen to his name. His stomach was so empty that each time he uttered a word he sounded like a deflating balloon.

Sugita was strongly drawn to the boy's porcelain skin and lively dark eyes. He wrapped his arm under the boy's shoulder to help carry him toward an eatery, all the while having the strong impression that he was reeling in a carp. At the cafeteria, the boy showed no reservations and ate vigorously. "Good grief, what a wild child!" Sugita thought with surprise. Though the boy owed him a debt of gratitude, Sugita found himself utterly infatuated by his lack of manners. Why did he come to Tokyo, Sugita asked, and the boy replied that he'd simply wanted to find success. He had recklessly abandoned his parents' home in the Kansai countryside in the interest of "pursuing fame and fortune." He said this with the same intensity that he now directed toward his food. As Sugita watched, he felt pity, a feeling that freed him from the heaviness of his earlier infatuation.

He brought the boy to his lodgings and laid him down on bedding much softer than the park bench. "I'll take care of you," he promised tearfully, "I will never let you starve." This was the beginning of his unnatural relationship with Yamazaki.

Three days after Sugita wrote the letter, the woman replied. In the morning, while Sugita was alone drowsing in bed, his body aching from peddling sake the night before, Yamazaki came bounding in. "It came, it came!" he yelled, and holding a postcard over his head, he jumped up and down near his bedside. The gist of her message was that it would be a pity for them to skip work especially for her, so the next night it rained, she would visit. The two men started clapping.

The fact that Yamazaki became exceptionally cheerful was enough to make Sugita suddenly feel jealous. Yamazaki, even when he wasn't excited, possessed a particularly strange voice. In his high-pitched voice, he pestered Sugita about the kind of woman she was.

The woman's name was Torii Masuko, and in Sugita's words, he and she had "shared rice from the same bowl." Which is to say, when Sugita was acting as houseboy for Tanno Orizo, the woman was Tanno's maid. After graduating from a girl's school in Tosa, she had come to Tokyo with the help of her brother and was given the chance to work as a maid in Tanno's home. While she was living in the maid's quarters, she managed to do no work. Cooking, laundry, cleaning, almost all of the work she left for her fellow maid, while she herself sang songs in the maid's room from dawn until dark.

Yamazaki would lean toward Sugita, drinking in his stories of the woman. Every night he carried the weight of amazake and would sigh, "Oh, I wish it would rain soon!" Yet the more one wishes the rain to fall, the more it refuses to do so. They could do nothing but make money. Every day, they would get a batch of amazake from the Shitaya wholesale shop. The store let them borrow containers to carry the load. A twenty-sen box of stock became 12 cups of amazake; one cup was sold for five sen. They would take three boxes of liquor to sell, but other than that, all they had to pay was three sen for charcoal and the saccharin fee. If they sold three cups, then they were able to eat well. It was not as if they could not carry more, but it would put a strain on their bodies if they did, so they limited themselves to three boxes of stock. Sugita went out to the back streets of Shitaya toward Kanda, then to Renjakuchō, and finally to the back alleys of Kanda station. Yamazaki sold his amazake around Yanagimachi by the edges of the lake. The voices that called out "Sweeet sake, sweeet sweet sake" were glum.

However, amazake was falling out of favor with the dainty tastebuds of the gradually westernizing populace. Soda water and that suspicious-looking "coffee" flooded the marketplace, even in the rustic back alleys. "Sweeet sake. Sweeet, sweet sake." Their voices were timorous and sounded more like screams of despair. To sell even three cups was no easy task. The load they carried never became lighter. On the contrary, the rods increasingly dug into their shoulders, leaving their bodies drenched in greasy sweat. "Sweeet sake. Sweeet, sweet sake." Grinding their teeth and enduring, they wore out their voices. And then—this heavy burden be damned—rage bubbled up from inside them, urging them to dump all the saccharin onto the side of the road, container and all.

Born out of rage, it was a desire, still, that could be easily quelled. Oh, why won't it just rain!

Every time this frenzied despair came bubbling up, they remembered the lives they had lived before taking up this business. It put their minds at ease to reassure themselves that their lives were much more stable now than they were before. There had been hard times. On one such occasion when Sugita and Yamazaki had nothing to eat, they passed the midday heat of summer in a haze, sitting idly on a park bench. The sun set and night came. They slept outdoors and were repeatedly shooed away from the park benches by the police. At dawn, their yukata-clad bodies would shiver in the bitter cold. Gradually the sun would come up, and it would swiftly become hot. Their hopes were pinned on a five-yen letter sent a few days ago begging Yamazaki's bankrupt parents for help. They went to their usual cheap lodging place, weak and dazed from hunger. But the letter from his parents had not come. They clearly felt that they were going to die of

· hunger, but Sugita tried to raise Yamazaki's spirits, suggesting, "Let's go to Fukagawa!" Apparently, Sugita's friend was employed as an attendant at the Fukagawa bathhouse. The two hardly remembered how they traveled from Asakusa to the back door of the spa's kitchen. Their weakened bones and worn-out limbs must have somehow carried them over there like wraiths. As they stood before the kitchen door, they were met with a dinner scene—steam was rising from dinner box-sets and pickled blue baby eggplants were piled high in serving bowls. Greeting them in just his underwear, Sugita's friend said, "I haven't got any spare change." Turning to the steaming rice and blue pickles, he added with a sigh, "Also, this isn't mine to give away . . ." His sigh was a heartfelt one. But he eventually softened, adopting the philosophy of a virtuous thief, one who steals from the rich and gives to the poor. "I guess stealing this little bit won't get me into any trouble," he smiled sadly, taking two of the pickled baby eggplants, and giving one each to Sugita and Yamazaki. "You two must be starving."

Thank you, they said, and wandered off. The flavor of the eggplants they chewed as they walked down the street—oblivious to people's stares—was so savory they could feel a tingle go down their spines. Yamazaki ate his in a single gulp then stared jealously at the half-eaten eggplant still in Sugita's hand. "Okay, you can have it," said Sugita, handing it over as Yamazaki pounced on it.

Given that there had been days like these, the urge to toss their sake on the side of the road was an impulse they could not give in to so readily.

At long last, it finally rained.

That day Sugita was at the library. He needed to regain the self that was different from the self that sold amazake. That day in particular, his trip to the library had an exciting objective. Tanno Orizo had published a new novel in a magazine and Sugita wanted to read it.

Regardless of what had happened between them, Tanno Orizo was a writer who stirred up a sense of nostalgia in Sugita. Recently, Tanno had changed drastically in a way that surprised Sugita. While it was easy to imagine how the political situation in 1927 might have shaken the progressive intelligentsia,[2] Sugita still found himself shocked to learn

---

2. Political liberalism in Japan flourished in the mid-1920s due to economic prosperity caused mainly by trade with the West. However, the economy declined into a recession in

that a writer like Tanno—who had always sung the praises of capital-ist culture—had shifted his alliances so radically to a leftist position. As one who knew Tanno very well, Sugita was of two minds as he examined Tanno's reversal of positions: one made him suspicious of Tanno, the other drew on his affection and good will toward him. Even as Tanno was trying to cast himself into the ranks of the proletariat, Sugita—ostensibly proletarian by birth—was embarrassed by the fact that he continued to pass his time just like any old vagrant. Sometimes he felt like throwing everything away and joining the ranks of some kind of political organization. That impulse was easier to suppress than the urge to toss his sake out on the roadside. Though he turned up his nose at those "damn intellectuals," he was also instinctively distrustful of organized struggle. Strangely, however, even though he resisted, he was often plagued by the illusion that Tanno disdained him. He became more interested than ever before in Tanno's works.

All this aside, that day at the library, when he opened a magazine and started reading Tanno's work, he involuntarily gasped.

"What?! How dare he steal my work!"

The color rapidly drained from his face. Tanno's story was clearly one that used references from Sugita's novel. Sugita had entrusted Tanno with two or three of his short novels. There was no doubt that he'd drawn on one of those manuscripts for his own work. He had cleverly complicated events and changed the order of the plot. The only difference was that it was now twice as long.

"Doing something like this without asking me, what a way to destroy me!"

Until now he had felt indebted to Tanno, feeling affection and good will toward the writer; thus, the deceit was that much more painful.

"This isn't a matter of money," he told himself on the verge of tears.

God knows that his emotions had not bubbled forth out of greed. He was angry beyond words that he had simply been ignored. "Instead of stealing from me, why couldn't Tanno nurture me, so that I could make my work come alive with my own hands!"

Here he was peddling sweet sake while covered in dust, barely fill-

---

1926—unemployment rose, factories closed, and starvation became rampant in rural areas. A financial panic arose in 1927 (now known as the Shōwa Financial Crisis) in which numer-ous banks went under. A new prime minister rose to power, who persecuted communists and socialists based on their "dangerous thoughts."

ing his stomach in a public cafeteria while the popular writer Tanno Orizo swaggered along the flashy streets of Ginza. The distance between them became palpable. Tanno was swindling an astounding amount of manuscript money by claiming to be a member of the proletariat while exploiting the talents of Sugita, who was struggling at the very bottom of society. Realizing this made Sugita indignant once again. At the same time, he told himself, "Anger makes me greedy. I must not give in to such a thing," and he tried to suppress his fury. With a sinking heart, he thought, "Nevertheless, that man is trying to contribute something to the cause of the proletariat. But me—I live day to day, contributing nothing. I've just got to pull myself together . . . I've got to pull myself together!"

Ah, the weakness! As soon as I try to pull myself up, I crave something even farther out of reach, and once again my resolve breaks. This is my habit. Did something that transcends emotions—some consciousness that stopped him from pursuing resentment—did it take away his ability to be angry when it was the right time to be angry? As he shuffled home to their second-story room in the back alleyway, the much-anticipated rain started falling onto the roofs of the slums.

"Wait, it's raining, it's raining!" Sugita yelled with excitement and bounded up to the second floor.

"It sure is, which is why I've started practicing telling funny stories." Yamazaki jumped up from the bedding he had never once put away, grabbed Sugita's hand and shouted, "She's coming, she's coming. Tonight she's actually going to come!" But then suddenly he grew worried. "But is she really going to come?"

"Don't be silly, that woman is not the type to break her promise. Poor people like us—we're always trustworthy," Sugita reassured him.

Even if there came a time when Sugita and Yamazaki would forget what happened, the soot-covered ceiling, the ripped tatami, and every single dust particle in the room would be ingrained with the memory of that day. Torii Masuko was indeed a wonderful woman, just as Sugita had described to Yamazaki every day. A spirit of fearlessness flowed through her five-foot three-inch body. In her rather long and tanned face, her two narrowly set eyes were lively. The scent of a lake in far off Tosa emanated from her body and reached the men's noses.

"How much do you make monthly at the transportation service?" they asked.

"Eighteen yen," she replied, shrugging her shoulders slightly. The feast consisted of apples and steamed potatoes. Yamazaki became thoroughly excited, wildly pouncing on the woman chewing on her un-skinned apple, and tore her food away.

"Oh my," she said, opening her eyes in surprise. After gazing at the tooth marks on the apple for a second, Yamazaki sunk his own teeth in to overlap with the bite marks and started eating.

"Such a savage!"

"It's good."

Seeing this, Sugita remembered that day long ago when Yamazaki wolfed down his half-eaten eggplant.

At the end of the night, she decided that she would teach them a song. It was an old-fashioned song—the first line started with "I know not what spell is o'er me." Yamazaki ruined the melody with his strangely piercing voice, and was scolded, "You are terrible at singing." For today, she was only going to teach one line, "I know not what spell is o'er me, that I am so sad today." When she would come to visit later on, they would learn the rest little by little. "This is Heine's original,"[3] she said. Sugita was deeply inspired and started to try harder.

"I'm thirsty. Do you have any amazake left?" she asked. They warned her that although there was leftover amazake, it was laced with sac-charin and so she should avoid it. The woman shivered at the word "saccharin," and they returned to singing practice. It was the happiness of youth; no, this *was* youth!

Eventually the time to part came. "Goodbye." She looked at her black-banded wristwatch, much like a working woman, and cried, "Eleven o'clock! I've stayed for quite a long time." Sugita leaned against the wall, closed his eyes, and kept repeating the melody under his breath. "For some reason, I can't memorize it."

"Sugita, I'm going to walk Masuko to the train."

When he opened his eyes at the sound of Yamazaki's cheerful voice, the two were already out of sight. The ripped *shōji* trembled at the sound of their footsteps going down the stairs.

---

3. A famous poem later combined with music called "Die Loreley" (The Lorelei), by Hein-rich Heine. The English translation of the poem used is one by Emma Lazarus. Heinrich Heine and Emma Lazarus, *Poems and Ballads of Heinrich Heine. Translated by Emma Lazarus. To Which Is Prefixed a Biographical Sketch of Heine* (New York: Worthington, 1881). Project Gutenberg. Web.

After that first night, Masuko came by now and then to this soot-covered room. It wasn't just on the days when it rained. If they gave her a call at her workplace telling her they were taking a break from business that day, she would always visit. When she came, the atmosphere around the two lightened up, and they would be in tremendously high spirits. Yamazaki was a rough lad. He did not give a single thought to social convention. In front of Sugita, he would grab Masuko's firmly built arm, and even put his arm around her shoulders without any shame. She did not reject him. Sugita would reluctantly manage a thin smile, saying "Hey, you two suit each other pretty well."

In front of Sugita, Yamazaki would whisper something into the woman's ears, and she would nod back at him, and then, Yamazaki would suddenly become two times or three times more cheerful, getting rowdy.

"Come now, Sugita, let's dance, let's dance!"

"Stop, hey, stop!" An embarrassed Sugita recoiled, his face reddening, but he was taken by the hand and forced to stand up. The woman provided accompaniment, singing with her mouth filled with potato—"La, la, lan." Claiming it was a dance, Yamazaki clumsily dragged Sugita around the whole room. "Idiot, idiot," Sugita laughed, slapping his hand away, and fell onto his backside in the corner of the room. He retreated, while Yamazaki let out a wild high-pitched laugh and toppled over onto the tatami, using the woman's plump thighs as a pillow. Then, he pulled away a half-eaten potato from the woman's hand and tossed it into his mouth while she continued singing "La, la, lan."

One time, Masuko did not appear for one week, then two weeks. The normally cheerful and talkative Yamazaki became completely silent. The two of them both had the long hair of bookworms, but at the time, Yamazaki's jet-black hair, carefully tucked behind his ears, lost its shine, and his fair skin grew dull. Seeing this, Sugita would be filled with sorrow. When they were living on the benches in Asakusa Park and they did not have anything to eat, Yamazaki would become silent and pale exactly as he was now. Sugita had a longer and more varied experience with the vagrant lifestyle than Yamazaki. Thus one day of fasting was nothing new to Sugita, but seeing his younger friend sink into depression made his heart sting, and he couldn't sit still. He did whatever he could at any time of day to search for food for his friend.

Not seeing the woman and not having food harmed Yamazaki in the same way. Sugita's heart ached, and he blamed himself for not wanting to fix his friend's misfortunes. However, he could not allow her to come over because their amazake sales had not been going well, and they did not have the time or money for company. Skipping one day of work meant the next day, they must skip going to the public cafeteria. When fleeing from constant starvation, Yamazaki's face would cloud just like this, and he would become silent. To Sugita, watching this was more painful than his own empty stomach. In times like these, finding some sort of food for his younger friend was the only happiness that could sate his own hunger.

That is why it meant so much for him to be able to give even a small amount of pleasure to this friend of his, who had become depressed when he could not see the woman. Yet, that he could not see her was unavoidable. In other words, because the amazake sales had not gone well for the last few days, they had no means to welcome her. Taking a break from work one night meant that they could not get the supplies for the amazake the next day. They had to put more distance between themselves and starvation. They could not afford to be lazy until they had increased this distance. If it were to rain today, they were in grave danger of suffering.

The depressing cycle continued. The two went to sell in separate directions after getting the supply of amazake, melting it in boiling water, and adding saccharin. Yamazaki's territory was around the Shitaya pond. Setting down his load in an alleyway of the red-light district, he would call out in his half-muddled, peculiar voice, "Sweeet sake, sweeet sweet sake." Usually, two or three brothels would order some. He was known as the "merry amazake seller." "I am a writer by the name of Tanno Orizo," he would say to the women of the brothel; he was also called the "amazake-selling writer." He had been dragged to see Tanno Orizo two or three times by Sugita but kept the fact that he was using his name as a pseudonym a secret, even from Sugita. "Why are you selling such a thing like amazake when you're a writer?" he would be asked, and he would answer, "An advocate for the proletariat must know about the slums of modern society, so I am disguising myself as an amazake seller." The brothel ladies and the hostesses would have no idea of the significance of the name Tanno Orizo, the proletarian writer, but Yamazaki was proud, and he would joyfully call out in his peculiar voice, "Sweeet sake, sweeet sweet sake." He would go on his rounds, saying things like "My lady, have you read my novel published in this month's *Chūō Kōron*?"

However, as the period without seeing the woman grew longer, his cheerfulness faded. "Wait just a minute, amazake seller. If you're a writer, why don't you come into the house once in a while? A romance with a prostitute would most definitely be a great plot for a novel," some women would flirt. Usually he would say, "Okay, okay" and playfully slap a forehead or two, but now he did not even have the energy to do so.

One night, as he lay sleeping in their second-floor room after taking off early, a vision of Sugita, who would usually still be hauling his load around Kanda, popped into his mind. Ashamed, he started tearing up. However, Sugita, who came back late, was in rather high spirits, cheerfully stripped down to his knit undershirt and dove into the futon. Facing Yamazaki's back, he said,

"Yamazaki, we can rest tomorrow."

Yamazaki suddenly brightened but remained silent, suspicious of this unexpected announcement.

"I took four times the usual load and sold all of it. It's going to be okay. We can rest tomorrow."

Sugita waited for Yamazaki's response. It was a lie that he had sold four times his normal load. Sugita merely decided to take the day off tomorrow to cheer up Yamazaki. There was no doubt about it. That was why Yamazaki could not immediately show his excitement. He felt Sugita's love pour down on him like rain and was bewildered. Despite knowing that they were able to take the night off and invite the woman over, he could not even put on a show of genuine happiness. This wouldn't do, he thought, if I can't be happy, Sugita's gesture would be for nothing. He shrugged his shoulders, feeling like his body and soul were squeezed tightly by some irksome power. When Sugita's body temperature had warmed the cotton of the futon, Yamazaki jumped up as if he were escaping, and bounded down the stairs. He went in and out of the bathroom and went back to their room. He smiled, "Tomorrow, I'm gonna make the call!" and roughly dove back under the blanket.

The next day Sugita was also happy. It was not just because, at long last, he was able to see Yamazaki happy. Sugita also felt himself become merry at the thought of the woman's arrival. He readied some crab-flavored rice crackers and roasted potatoes. Meanwhile, Yamazaki went to the pay phone and called her at her workplace. "She said she'd come, she said she'd come!" He seemed delighted. The anticipated night came, and she looked dashing. Everything was back to normal. The only thing was that Sugita looked a bit melancholier than usual. He leaned against the farthest wall, talking little while watching his two friends and scratching at his dull swept-back hair. Yamazaki sat shoulder to shoulder with Masuko and genuinely appeared to be enjoying himself. The woman was telling stories about Tosa, such as nostalgic stories of a trip to Iso's Dōgo a few years ago with her father. On the way back, they had braved the bordering mountain range with fellow travelers. From the high peaks of the mountain passes, they went down to the valley on a path that curved like a flowering fern and passed through mountain villages. The moment her father proclaimed, "This is Sagawa," as they were passing by a storefront at dusk, a single pot of flowering white cherry seemed to flash across the car window like a phantom. It was still February. Sugita could almost see that white flower from the window of a car driving fast like an arrow. It was a vision too beautiful for his melancholy heart—but it was immediately erased by Yamazaki's strangely high-pitched laughter. Yamazaki started to talk about his father. He was living out in Osaka after his family disintegrated, but according to a recent postcard, it seems he had started a gravel business. "I'm thinking of heading back to Osaka. If I end up at my dad's place and can help him with the gravel business, I wouldn't have to worry about eating anymore."

At that point, the woman asked why anybody would buy gravel. Sugita restrained his feelings of sadness, and began to explain the relationship among infrastructure, concrete, and gravel.

After listening to half his explanation, the woman said, "Concrete is very popular at the moment, isn't it? So, demand for gravel should be high. Your father, he probably has good business."

"I also think that, for sure," Yamazaki got excited and suggested that Sugita should come with him to Osaka. Sugita had looked after him unconditionally, in every way possible, so surely his father would do something for Sugita—he wheedled in his uniquely impertinent way.

However, how likely are rumors of good business to be true in times like these? Sugita attempted to distract himself with these thoughts. For some reason, he got the sense that the day he would part from Yamazaki was coming soon and could not distract himself from these worries. Unexpectedly, he could feel hatred and resentment toward Yamazaki stirring in the pit of his stomach. He could just feel it . . .

Please let it be impossible for Yamazaki's father to succeed in his gravel business. And make Yamazaki feel despair. It was incomprehensible that Masuko loved Yamazaki, but still, she was too good-natured and so was just going along with Yamazaki. If she ever revealed her true cold indifferent self, that would shut up Yamazaki. Let him fall from his conceited perch. Let all possible misfortunes cascade onto his snotty nose at once! He never would have guessed that he would feel such animosity toward Yamazaki. But this situation was a mess! Sugita felt remorseful and whispered to himself, "I've become a beast." Nevertheless, this loathing was not something that would just fade away.

Sugita became miserable. He had resolved to eat less for two or three days beginning tomorrow so that they could take a break from today's business. If he refrained from going to the public cafeteria two or three times, the hole in their earnings from today's break would somehow be filled. Of course, even if he fasted, he fully intended to let Yamazaki eat as much as his stomach would allow. "This is how much I've wanted to see Yamazaki's cheerful face." The thought made him quite sentimental. Caring about Yamazaki to this extent had produced in him a wretched feeling of hatred. I should have gladly sent the woman away and had her existence disappear from our midst forever. I should have never had her come over. Sugita cursed Yamazaki with endless regret.

It passed eleven o'clock, and the woman said her goodbyes. Once again, only Yamazaki walked her to the Manseibashi station. For close to twenty minutes, Sugita waited for Yamazaki to come back. It was terribly painful to be left behind. If it were going to be this painful, then why didn't I go walk her with him, he thought as he blamed himself. While he was engaged in self-condemnation, the fact that nobody was beside him filled him with terror. I cannot let Yamazaki go, he screamed silently. Yamazaki may have already fallen for that woman, but it was not too late. Conjuring memories of all the joys and sorrows they had shared together should ensure that Yamazaki would not abandon Sugita, out of sheer obligation. If even that didn't work, Sugita would beg at Yamazaki's feet. "I'll become your slave," he would promise.

"Haven't I already become his slave," Sugita laughed bitterly. It was a laugh that distracted him from the terror of the moment, just for a split second. Then, Yamazaki came home with his usual rough vivaciousness.

"Yamazaki!" Sugita yelled, finally done waiting impatiently for Yamazaki. "Leave that woman alone. Promise that we both never lay a hand on her. Right now!"

He was speaking wildly. But Yamazaki merely lowered his eyes and replied, "Okay." Skins from the roasted potatoes were piled on top of the newspaper. They were small mementos left behind by the woman who, until a moment ago, was sitting just there.

The morning after, Yamazaki alone went to the public cafeteria for breakfast since Sugita did not get up, complaining of a pain in his stomach. The morning after that, Sugita again said something similar and stayed behind. For the first time, Yamazaki became suspicious that Sugita was consciously making an effort to eat less. Yamazaki knew perfectly well what the point of this was. He felt a heavy burden on his shoulders. Sugita was being kind to him, so he must be thankful. In the past Yamazaki had continued to feel honest gratitude, but this time around Sugita's love felt more like a heavy burden. Feeling unhappy, he came back from the cafeteria and was greeted with the sight of Sugita sleeping with his broad forehead peeking out from under the blanket. He must be pretending to sleep.

"How's your stomach?" Yamazaki tried asking, but he got no answer from the sleeping Sugita. His long, brittle hair hung over the edge of the dirty pillow, but that hair had recently started to fall out, and bald patches could be seen on his scalp. His skin was dusty brown and slack, stained with the grime from his long and arduous daily life. To be loved by this man! Yamazaki felt a shudder pass through him. He was already betraying this pitiful man. He was dreaming of a new life, released from this man's love. And it was not a dream. The night before the last, while taking the woman to Manseibashi, he got a clear answer from her. "I also want to live with you. Yes, it's true. I do love you . . ."

It was two or three nights later. Sugita finished selling the maximum load his shoulders could carry—three loads of amazake—relatively early. The last customer was a man in his forties he stopped in Kijima-chi. He stood underneath an overhang and sipping the cup of amazake Sugita was serving him, he let out a cry of wonder, "Ah, this—this isn't saccharin, no, not saccharin." But of course, the amazake contained saccharin, so Sugita scratched his head and thought, I guess he is being sarcastic. However, he soon realized that it was nothing of the sort. The customer had the serious tone of a connoisseur looking for praise for his sensitive taste that allowed him to distinguish between sugar and saccharin with the tip of his tongue. The world has its fair share of naïve folk. Walking home with a significantly lighter load, Sugita laughed heartily for the first time in a while. If I tell Yamazaki about this, he would also laugh loudly. Sugita felt merry. What a welcome surprise to have such an amusing incident occur in his everyday life!

Yet despite the fact that he came back so early, he could hear Yamazaki's high-pitched laughter from the second-floor room. Did Yamazaki already finish selling his amazake? He climbed up the dark stairs, feeling puzzled, as it seemed as if positions were hastily being changed in reaction to his footsteps. Precisely as Sugita suspected, when he opened the shoji door, Torii Masuko, who had just now jumped away from Yamazaki, was gathering her fallen hair into a bun. She still trembled from the vibrations of words spoken a moment ago.

"Damn it, you did it."

He experienced a flash of anger, but too embarrassed to reveal his bewildered emotional state, he quickly covered it up.

"Traitor!" He yelled, seemingly in jest.

"Come on, don't get mad. It was a coincidence," Yamazaki said, sneering.

"Coincidence my ass. Explain."

The woman was silently laughing in his face. Yamazaki also did not try to explain, and as was his habit whenever Sugita scolded him, he looked up at his partner flirtatiously. Engulfed in an awkward silence, Sugita felt a sadness that flayed him to the core. As if he were trying to push away this sadness, he shivered.

"Today, my head was hurting. And then after selling half I just couldn't do it anymore and came back. This one came right around then—"

"I thought today you two wouldn't be here and stopped by. I wanted to clean the room while you two were gone. But then Yamazaki was here, I was quite surprised," Masuko said.

Masuko glanced briefly at her black ribbon wristwatch—it's eleven already, I'll excuse myself now—and left. Yamazaki yelled at her retreating back, "I'm not going to walk you today!"

When it was just the two of them, Sugita asked, "Just tell me the truth, you two planned beforehand and met, didn't you?"

"Don't snoop around like that." Yamazaki avoided the question, but his response increased Sugita's worries further. After asking the same question two or three times, Sugita became completely full of despair.

"You bastards, when did you become a couple?" He angrily glared.

"Don't threaten me!" Yamazaki retorted fiercely, bracing himself.

They glared at each other, looking like they would go at each other at any moment, but Yamazaki suddenly went limp, lowered his eyes, and said, "It's my fault. I deceived you. There's no question about that. But I made a promise to her."

"What did you promise?" Sugita inquired hoarsely.

"Forgive me, Sugita, I must leave you. I promised to live with the woman."

"Does the woman love you?"

"She will love me, she said. I . . . I also love her."

"Is there no way to abandon her at this point?"

"I can't abandon her. She's entrusted herself to me."

"Is that right?"

That woman! Sugita trembled. Entrusted herself—for some reason, he could not think this without a feeling of dread. And this was reality. He grew pale as his desire to punch his adversary waned. This is the end. Don't panic! He suppressed the feelings that came bubbling up. And then, a vast emptiness spread.

I don't want to think about anything.

"How is this man going to live separated from me?"

An unwelcome thought, one he did not want to think about, popped into his mind. Yamazaki's father in Osaka had just sent word that nothing good would happen if he came home now. This young man, what does he think he could do to keep on living in Tokyo? Supporting a woman with the amazake business is just not feasible. But, the woman has a job. They would live on both incomes. But wait, if they did that, Yamazaki's life would be much easier than if he stayed together with Sugita. When he realized this, Sugita experienced a strange sort of despair. Why, there was no excuse for him to stop Yamazaki from leaving him anymore.

"Leaving me results in this man's happiness."

That was his conclusion. "But letting him leave doesn't mean I can't go on living. I must study. I must study with everything I've got!"

His literary ambitions rose once again. He remembered Tanno Orizo. Then he thought of how he was being stepped on even by Orizo, and how big of a shock that was. He rekindled his hostility toward Orizo once more.

I will not trust anyone again. He shouted silently again and again, so that he would never forget it. The key to living well is to never forget this. He trusted people too much, loved them too much. But he felt sorry for himself when he thought of what people had done to repay him for his selflessness, even if he did not particularly wish for any sort of repayment or appreciation.

"Hey, Yamazaki, before you leave me, go beat up that good-for-nothing son of a bitch Orizo," commanded Sugita.

Standing up, Yamazaki replied, "Okay."

Sugita said, "Let's see, if I had thirty yen, I could set up a used book stand in the night market."

Sugita had told Yamazaki that Tanno Orizo had used the manuscripts that he had left in the man's possession, without permission, to write a novel in a magazine titled, "It Will Get More Interesting." Yamazaki was amused by Sugita's blackmail attempt and started off to Tanno's house, located in the far end of Mejiro.

When he was taken into the reception room in the cheaply built residence, Yamazaki suddenly blurted out, "Sensei, I'm going to marry Torii."

Clad in a green dressing gown over pajamas, with sleep in his eyes, Tanno laughed, "Oh my, is that so?"

He had learned that Masuko had been frequenting Sugita's place the last time Sugita visited, but his curiosity was piqued by hearing now how fast things had progressed.

In response to Tanno's inquiries, Yamazaki gradually explained the events that had unfolded. "Sensei, it's really a mystery why she fell in love with a man like me. She says things like, I'm a man who'll do something big in the future, that right now I might be poor, but in the end, I'll become someone—and besides, somehow women seem to gravitate toward me."

After a while, Yamazaki got ready to leave, but at the front entrance, he shouted,

"Sensei. Sensei, Sugita is going to complain about your novel called 'It Will Get More Interesting,' so be careful. To be truthful, I came here to shake you down under Sugita's direction, but when I saw your face, I knew I couldn't do any such thing."

The color of Tanno's face changed slightly, no doubt due to the sensitive subject matter.

But he replied without hesitation, "Oh really. I admit I indeed stole material. But as far as that's concerned, I plan on seeing Sugita and talking to him about it."

"It's probably better if you don't see him. Since I've stolen a woman from him, Sugita has already developed something of an inferiority complex. I'll take care of it."

"But then, you'll be on bad terms with Sugita."

When pressed, Yamazaki said sadly, "Sugita and I aren't going to stay in contact anyway."

Tanno's heart stung for Sugita. There was no way for Sugita to save face like this. Glancing at Tanno's pained expression, Yamazaki left through the front entrance. He returned straight to Sugita's gloomy room.

"How did it go?"

Startled by Sugita's flashing eyes in the dark room, he replied, "It didn't work. Lay off the blackmail already."

"Damn it! You betrayed me again, didn't you!"

Everything that he had suppressed erupted suddenly and exploded. To learn that everyone who approached him, without exception, would bare their fangs at him made Sugita burn with a desire to beat something into a thousand pieces.

"Get out! A son of a bitch like you, even looking at your face is dirty!"

"Fine, I'll leave."

That was it. He didn't bother getting up to see Yamazaki's retreating figure carrying a bundle of rags not even worth calling belongings. Sugita laid down limply, staring at the ceiling. Now I feel better. Now is the beginning of my new life, he tearfully told himself, and summoned within his heart a yearning for a more noble meaning of life.

But the next day, when Yamazaki came by and coolly informed him of his new address, Sugita's sadness had calmed down a great deal. Yamazaki was living two to three cities away, again renting a dank and dirty second-floor room in the slums. That room was three tatami mats removed from sun compared to Sugita's, but in exchange for sunlight, the woman was coming to live with him starting that night.

"Does her brother approve of this?"

"Well, I didn't tell you, but I went to her brother's place and met him the other day. The woman took me there." Yamazaki answered, blushing.

"Is that right? Good for you." Sugita said calmly, and then solemnly added, "I'm going to study hard. I'm going to go to the library more often. My only hope is literature now!"

"Hurry up and write us something good. Whatever anyone says, she and I will always believe in your talents."

"Thank you."

Sugita couldn't stop thinking that if there were even a morsel of good faith in Tanno, then things could have been a little better. He had shown Tanno one play and three novels, but Tanno did not give any of them a good review. Especially the dialogue in the play between a prophet and the devil was showered with scathing criticism. The novel was a tale about a starving boy who was wandering around a pond, and while he gazed at a toad resting on a lotus leaf, he hallucinated that there was a coin-filled pouch there. This novel, Tanno said, was a barely readable joke. The other novels were also disappointing, Tanno said, and yet he stole the material. Tanno probably received a huge sum for the manuscript, but in reality, Sugita did not care about the money. He merely wanted Tanno to use his talents to get him closer to higher literature. Never mind literature! Tanno had once experienced living the life of a lower-class citizen—living one step away from starvation, struggling daily at the very bottom of society, abandoned even by the pleasures of everyday life. Had he ever looked back after leaving that life? The more he thought about Tanno stealing another's work so readily, the more he became infuriated. He called himself a proletarian intellectual, but other than displaying a passion for journalism, where was his own proletariat lifestyle? Even if stealing a poor man's talents could be forgiven, the poor man he'd stolen from will never regain the purity of his trusting soul. This is a harsher blow than having a day's worth of food stolen. To give such a heavy blow to Sugita's soul and yet failing to feel anything, Sugita wondered, was such an inhuman person qualified to be a writer? When he thought about this, he could not hate Yamazaki. Sugita did not have the right to prevent Yamazaki from leaving him and becoming happy. Sugita thought he would probably love Yamazaki more than any woman in the world would. But I am a poor man, he admitted, sadly. He could not make Yamazaki happy. The only thing he could give him was a fifteen-sen meal, and at times even that wouldn't satisfy his hunger. In this world, a helpless man's love would never lead to happiness. Sugita knew that. But even so, wasn't it his deepest, darkest desire to drag Yamazaki down to his own scummy lifestyle and lead him astray? No, he thought, I'm going to rise someday. I have literature. He attempted to struggle with his own thoughts, but he was already steeped in society's ruthlessness. The thought of going against the world's cold currents made everything go black.

That day, Yamazaki mentioned Tanno's wish to see Sugita once more. He had forgotten to bring it up yesterday because Sugita was so angry.

Hearing this, Sugita replied, "I don't want to," and turned away.

In that moment, Sugita decided that he too was going to move out. This room had too many memories; he did not want to stay any longer. But, his desire to move out had much more to do with avoiding a visit from Tanno. The next day, he gave up the room.

"If you tell Tanno about the next place, this time I'm really going to punch you." Sugita threatened Yamazaki.

It was a room that was brighter than the last—no, it was an almost *too* bright, empty, south-facing room. It was a big building where laborers and blue-collar workers lived; you could even say it was a sort of apartment.

He mysteriously attracted small children, especially boys. When the young boys of the apartment inhabitants saw him, they would immediately exclaim "Sugita!" If he had a bit of extra money, he would buy candy and give it out to the gathered children. Spring was in full bloom, and days of clear skies continued. Since moving in with the woman, Yamazaki still visited now and then. When the two came together, Sugita struggled. Yamazaki had found a job at Honjō. That is to say, he would work from home painting celluloid toys. However, since the woman still worked at the transportation agency, their life seemed a comfortable one.

One sunny day, Sugita bought candy and shouted, "Heey, everyone come on over," and all the children came running from their rooms in an uproar. At that very moment, Tanno Orizo suddenly appeared in the entrance of the room.

"This is—" Sugita's face shone, and he shooed the children away with a wave of his hand.

"Thank you for coming. How are you?"

Looking at his face, Sugita was filled with happiness and forgot his grudges. When he had said he did not want to see him, it was only because he was ashamed that he had sent Yamazaki to threaten him.

"Today, I came to apologize to you." Tanno said, his nervous face pale as paper.

"No, it's over, it's done with. You don't have to say anything."

"I should have told you beforehand, but the deadline was coming up, and I had to write it. And then, I just left it. It's a bad habit of mine—there's no excuse for it."

If Sugita's misgivings weren't dispelled, Tanno had resolved to plead that he borrowed the manuscript, but he didn't steal his writing style.

Since it was his fault the least he could do was apologize; he knew that was his obligation. The money he had gotten for using the manuscripts was, without doubt, an enormous sum of money for Sugita. On top of that, he hadn't given Sugita even a little bit of the money. Morally and economically, he could not justify what he had done. Despite all this, when he met him face to face, Sugita did not appear to hold a grudge.

"I want to give you some money. I do need a little for tomorrow though." Tanno said, in awe of Sugita's vast good will. Tanno put away all his excuses. It wasn't that he used the money he obtained from the novel based on Sugita's manuscripts for his own expenses. In addition to carrying a debt too large for his social position, with the money from that novel, he had to pay for the costs of two copyright fees and dues to the Labor Union and the Association. However, it was dirty using such excuses and was not something to talk about to an outsider.

Sugita was Sugita. He was so embarrassed about sending Yamazaki over the other day that he wanted to hide in a hole. He became flustered when hearing that Tanno was going to pay him.

"Bah, money, let's stop discussing that sort of thing," he said, dismissing the topic with a wave of his hand.

There was an exchange of words. Tanno attempted to force him to accept his offer, because he would have no peace of mind otherwise. Sugita thought that if he had fifty yen now, he would be able to turn around his life, but feeling guilty about it, he said, "Well then, just ten yen." He had left the previous second floor room without paying his back rent. The grandma downstairs forgave his leaving, even letting him borrow seven yen and ten sen. Sugita wanted to pay her back in any way he could. He decided to accept a sum of money four times lower than what Tanno was offering. Tanno was not happy about Sugita taking such a small amount of money and prodded him to be more assertive for his own well-being, but it was no use.

Sugita brought out all the old manuscripts he had accumulated. Placing them in front of Tanno he said, "Take these. If there is something you can use, please use it at your convenience."

Sugita accompanied Tanno to the Okachimachi Station, drank tea at a small café outside the station and left. "Ah, that man, no matter how far he falls, he possesses one thing he will never lose!" Tanno lamented on the train ride home. Yet, Tanno could not bring himself to acknowledge Sugita's talents. He thought, while the man had such a wealth of experiences, he could not make them come alive because of his weak character. He was battling starvation and oppression while at the same time trying to protect a certain kind of purity. Even if he managed to protect this purity, his talent and skill would be destroyed by the cruelties of his poor life. This was the reason why his literary talents did not develop one bit beyond a cheap street novel. What a tragedy this was. What sort of literary life could such a pure, genuine man have, without the power to express his life experiences? What distracted him was his grueling, aimless lifestyle. Sugita must throw away this life and create a new one that, although maybe more difficult, would bear fruit. Tanno imagined that if Sugita became a metalworker and straightened out his life, his passion toward literature would nurture him into a writer. This was probably an unattainable daydream. Because no matter what he advised Sugita, it was unthinkable that he would change his life. With the recession, Sugita probably would not find a factory job. And Tanno knew too well that no matter how hard he worked, his lumpen character,[4] seeped deep into his skin and bones, would never fail to cancel out his efforts.

Tanno was unable to finish the manuscript he was planning on finishing that day, so he went to the magazine company in the Osaka building of Uchiwaichō and borrowed ten yen. He asked a company worker to send a telegram and a ten-yen money order. In Uchiwachō, the telegram station that handled money orders was located inside the Imperial Hotel. When Sugita received the money order, he initially appreciated Tanno's good will, but suddenly noticed that it was marked "The Imperial Hotel."

A sudden explosion of anger made him dizzy.

"That man is holed up in the Imperial Hotel writing a novel!?"

Standing in the squalid alleyways wearing a frayed threadbare cotton overcoat over a kimono, he tossed away the money order he held in his hand. He felt Tanno trampling on him, again and again. The man who had run him over was now handing him a crumb in the slums from inside the Imperial Hotel. Is that how someone who claims that he is an

---

4. The term "lumpen" is used to define individuals, typically in the lower classes of society, who are uninterested in improving their socioeconomic situation. It is derived from "lumpen-proletariat," a term coined by Karl Marx to describe the lowest stratum of the proletariat, who lack awareness of their socioeconomic class and role in revolutionary struggle toward a class-less society. Members of this class include those outcast as unemployable, beggars, prostitutes, criminals, and other "degenerate" individuals.

ally of the proletariat should behave? What is this deception, this horrible falsehood!? Sugita grew feverish.

"I no longer hold you in any esteem. You will forever be the target of my hatred."

He swiftly wrote a postcard to Tanno. When he came back from putting it in the post, Yamazaki came along.

"I just wrote a letter cutting off all ties with that Orizo bastard. He was staying at an extravagant hotel. He humiliated me!" Sugita explained what happened over the last few days. Upon hearing this, Yamazaki flew over to Tanno's place, where Tanno wore a gloomy expression.

"What a horrible misunderstanding." He did not even dare to justify himself. Nonetheless, he explained that the post office within the Imperial Hotel did not only cater to hotel guests.

Yamazaki said, "After breaking up with me, I think Sugita went a little crazy."

That may be true, Tanno thought to himself. He had believed that Torii Masuko would be like a ray of light warming Sugita's soul, but the fact that she was taken from him by Yamazaki, his dearest friend, must have convinced him that everyone had betrayed him. This realization made Tanno very sad. He wanted to see Sugita one more time to tell him that getting worked up about this petty affair wasn't doing him any good. He needed to cast off his current way of life and get himself a factory job.

Yamazaki said, "But the thing is, Sugita already moved out this morning. He hasn't told me or anyone else where he is going."

So, this is the end, Tanno thought.

Yamazaki lived with the woman, and for a while they were comfortable. The woman still worked at the transportation service, and he had a job painting celluloid toys. As time passed, they lost their jobs in succession. As expected, they were very poor. Just as their supply of rice was about to run out, he found another job. He became a writer for a small yellow gossip paper[5] that was published in the town. This newspaper hired writers endlessly. This meant that there was no need to pay the writers a salary. In contrast, they worked under a system where the

---

5. This refers to yellow journalism, which is characterized by sensationalist and exaggerated stories, and often ill-researched topics.

journalist merely submitted a portion of the money that they "earned"
to the newspaper company.

Yamazaki's wife's uncle worked in an office, so from him Yamazaki
got old, shapeless hand-me downs. He wore those and rubber shoes,
and all he had to do was walk around with business cards labeled "xx
Newspaper Columnist." He would ask about things like some market
owner's concubine, or a hostess who had a younger man—scandals
of that sort. He would take his business cards and visit the homes of
people with bruised egos. When he visited some of them, they would
place in front of him something wrapped in paper. This was his "cut of
the money he earned."

Over time, his beard grew. A sparse goatee grew on the jawline of
the pale twenty-year-old boy. There was a particularly fearless colleague from Sawayama in the company. But in terms of fearlessness, he
wouldn't lose to any of his colleagues. And if he lost, he and his wife
would starve.

"Sensei, this business is profitable. The other day I saw an old fart
in a pub in Asakusa. *I have an ambition to run for district assemblyman
so if you put anything in the papers I'd be in trouble.* When I got ready
to leave, he wordlessly gave me an envelope with twenty yen! Sensei,
twenty yen!"

Yamazaki went to Tanno's place now and then, and in his high-
pitched voice talked about his profitable new business. But the rarity of
his success in this sort of business could be seen from his rubber shoes,
jacket, and pants, each a different color.

However, a woman like Masuko was never depressed. Poverty, dis-
grace, nothing brought her down; she sang her songs and held her dolls.
The kimonos she brought from her brother's home were almost all
gone. Things she had never experienced before at her home in Tosa, or
her brother's home in Tokyo—alleyway pawnshops, dinners consisting
solely of potatoes, and sometimes even fasting—none of this affected
her tanned, healthy skin. No matter what the situation, she happily
kept on singing her songs. Probably, there was no woman in the entire
world who could give life to the songs she learned in school as she did.

"Hey, what made you decide to be with a man like me?" Yamazaki
would ask. Every time, the same anticipated answer would flow from
her mouth,

"Well, you are poor now, but I expect you'll be rich soon enough!"
She was not saying this to make him happy. They were sincere words

that rang with strength and fearlessness. Yamazaki would be beside himself with delight.

He would say, "I also think I have more of a chance than Sugita. And that's why you didn't fall for Sugita and fell for me—I'm so lucky."

"We are lucky."

Her brother, who opposed them moving in together, now dropped his protests and allowed them to frequent his home in Ikebukuro. And yes, they were fortunate. She sang even through times when they did not have money for rice the next day. He was encouraged and went out. Desperately, he walked around town. I must become a bad man, he thought, an infamous man. Day by day, he became an infamous man in the yellow journalism business. In this way, he punished the dishonest households and the unpatriotic citizens.

Almost every day the topic of conversation between the two was something related to Sugita, but he had disappeared, hiding himself. The budding love between Yamazaki and the woman could not have been possible without him. It was unsatisfying that Sugita was not there to watch over their happiness. To them, Sugita evoked endless nostalgia.

Finally, after a month, a crisply dressed Sugita visited their dirty room. On seeing Yamazaki, he shouted, "Good heavens, what happened to your face!?"

Yamazaki was startled and rubbed his cheek.

"It's because we're poor." Masuko answered, laughing.

When Yamazaki mentioned his current work, Sugita warned him repeatedly, telling him not to put too much strain on his body. He himself lived on the second floor of a bakery in the sixth district, manning a stall that sold rayon sashes and undershirts.

When he was asked if he was still working on his novels, he replied sadly that he wasn't thinking too much about that sort of thing.

"One day when Tanno came by, I told him, if he could use my work then to please use it. I gave him all the writing I had saved up. At that moment, I made the decision to give up. You know, throw away my manuscripts, throw away my ambitions, I just couldn't do it anymore. I felt relieved," he said.

He looked rather dejected afterward. "Oh, well, let's not talk about such things." The lighthearted words did not match his bitter smile.

Then Masuko went downstairs to tend to a task, and it became just the two men.

Sugita seemed to hesitate, but said, "Today, I came because I had to see you. I couldn't help it."

Yamazaki said nothing.

"Hey, I'm swallowing my pride. I'm laying myself out in front of you and begging. One more time, just one more time is enough, come to my place, and become . . ."

When Sugita whispered these words into his ear, Yamazaki felt his companion's nervous sweat and shuddered.

Yamazaki stroked his goatee and laughed. "Sugita, look at this. I'm already growing a beard. It's different than before."

"Is that so?"

Sugita laughed helplessly.

Three or four days later Sugita once again came to Yamazaki's place. Aiming for times when Masuko was not present, he begged repeatedly, "Come back to me again."

"I'm already growing a beard." Yamazaki would reply.

In the end he got angry. "Who would ever accept your kindness?" He flushed.

Sugita sat in silence with his face filled with sorrow. To show him how angry he was, Yamazaki stopped eating the red bean pastries and snacks that Sugita brought. No matter how much his companion begged him, Yamazaki adamantly refused to eat, although he wanted to so desperately, he could taste the food in his mouth.

Despite this struggle, the two told funny anecdotes the way they used to, and sometimes excitedly suggested that they should start a new street stall. Yamazaki figured out that when Yamazaki and Masuko's love first formed, the reason Sugita became irritable and angry was not because Yamazaki stole Masuko away from him, but because he couldn't *stand* that Masuko was stealing away Yamazaki.

Yamazaki gradually became thinner, and the gauntness was more pronounced in his pale face. "I can't take it, watching you become this way." Sugita said relentlessly. "Just as I thought, without me, you won't make it." There seemed to be a hint of animosity toward Masuko behind his words. Yamazaki would retort, "Idiot, I'm strong. My body's not weak at all." Finally, after the passing of summer, he collapsed. He continued to cough lightly under the one blanket they owned and was so emaciated he could not even walk to the doctor's house. Masuko powdered her tan face white and worked at a fraudulent gambling café in the slums, but what she earned was hardly enough for the two of them to feed themselves, or even to have a sip of rice gruel.

"See, I told you." Sugita said, thinking this was the result of him overworking himself to live with the woman, and felt sorry for the young and stubborn Yamazaki.

"Oh, this is nothing. This measly cold is nothing. I'll be able to get up tomorrow." Yamazaki would say heartily. Sugita thought that he must be in pain, and overwhelmed with pity, turned his face away from the sick man. Eventually the fever subsided, and in ten days he felt better. Since he was so emaciated, he was unable to get up. His long face was pale like a flattened squid, and all around that goatee were patches of straggly hair.

One night, Sugita bought boiled eggs from a stall in Asakusa and brought them over. He sat by Yamazaki's bedside and said, "Hey, Yamazaki, they say it's very poisonous if you eat these boiled eggs face up. They say that people who eat them like that are going to die."

"That's a funny story."

"They say that in my hometown. Do you have the courage to eat lying down like that?"

"Yeah, I do."

"You're risking your life."

"Okay, then I'll show you how it's done," he said, taking an egg from Sugita, and shoved it into his mouth lying down.

"Nothing happened."

"Really. Well then, try eating one more."

Sugita watched him eat one more and then one more until in the end he ate all six. He went home satisfied. In reality, the first two were exceptionally delicious. Yamazaki was absorbed by the chewing and swallowing, but starting from the fourth one, he recalled Sugita's "you're going to die if you eat" fable. This was Sugita's childish trick to make Yamazaki, who wouldn't eat anything he brought, eat the eggs. "Because I'm so miserably thin." When he realized this, he became so emotional, his throat closed, and the food spread in his mouth. He fought back the grateful tears threatening to spill out, and telling himself to eat one more, he shoved a fifth egg into his mouth. He was filled with emotion and had no desire to eat, but he forced himself to eat one more. He wouldn't be able to live with himself if he stopped. His mouth was so dry, it felt like it was being filled with a big ball of wax, but with extreme effort, he swallowed, and said in a raspy voice, "Ah, that was good." When Sugita left, Yamazaki closed his shining eyes, but his pale ghostlike face was instantly wet with tears. When night came and Masuko returned from the café, he told her of Sugita and the boiled eggs. Once again, he became overwhelmed with emotion and cried.

When two weeks passed, he rose from his sickbed, but he had lost the courage to return to his newspaper company. He had been telling himself while bedridden that he should visit his father's home in Osaka before his physical exam for the national military service, which was coming up soon. But the more he thought, the idea of washing his hands of Tokyo and permanently living with his father in Osaka became stronger in his mind. The woman was also in favor of this. His father, who was in the gravel business, was saying that it would be an inconvenience if he came home now. Nevertheless, it did not seem that he would be so inconvenienced that if his son came home, he would ruthlessly shoo him back to Tokyo. In any case, his father had a business, so if he helped, it would be beneficial to all. His father and mother were both close to sixty, and though they grumbled, if their son came back to help, their business would definitely grow. If he did this, the Yamazakis would be released from the darker days of having to worry about tomorrow's rice money, and their lives would become increasingly brighter. Oh, even thinking about this suddenly made the world seem a more cheerful place. With visions of a stable life in his head, he could not go back to the work of threatening other people by waving around a business card from a thuggish newspaper.

The woman also wholeheartedly favored the move to Osaka. If he told his family in Osaka, they would tell him to stay away, so they decided to keep silent and just appear at their doorstep.

Paying for the expenses of traveling to Osaka was too challenging with just the savings from the café. No matter how difficult their lives were, the woman had never asked for money from her brother in Ikebukuro, but there was nothing to do but ask him for the travel expenses. Her brother gave them just enough money for the train fare.

Telling Sugita about their plans was so agonizing, it physically hurt them to do so.

"This will make your life easier. I approve."

Sugita had the same sorrowful look on his face—the same as when Yamazaki revealed to him that he was going to live with the woman. It was apparent from his words that he had all but given up. Yamazaki felt as if he was committing a betrayal even graver than when he told him about the woman, at this very moment. This betrayal was leaving

Sugita alone in the harshness of Tokyo and running away, just the two of them, to the comfort of his parents' home.

"Now, let's sing 'The Lorelei,' all three of us."

They bought sake that they rarely drank and had a farewell party in Yamazaki's room. After just a little bit of sake, they all turned bright red and sang together. Back when Sugita and Yamazaki were living together in Kanda, the woman would teach a line of this song every time she visited. It was just like the old days with the three of them singing, just like the days when Masuko was nobody's lover. But tomorrow, they were going to leave Sugita alone in Tokyo—when Yamazaki thought about this, his heart became full of memories of the times when he wandered from Asakusa to Shimotani, stopping at cheap lodgings and park benches.

"Hey, don't cry, don't cry. I'll eventually come visit you in Osaka."

"Yeah, come. If the gravel business seems to be going well, I'll send a letter immediately."

"Truly, Sugita, please come to Osaka. The gravel business will definitely go well."

"Yes, let's sing one more time."

The next night, Sugita came to Tokyo Station to watch the last train to Osaka leave. The Yamazakis, in contrast to the previous night's solemnity, were giddy with excitement. Sugita also matched their excitement, speaking in a loud voice. Soon the bell rang, and the train started gliding along the tracks toward a brighter life. Standing in the stairwell of the train, the Yamazakis raised their hands. It was a night when people were already starting to wear their coats, but Sugita stood threadbare in his casual clothes, in a daze, trying to maneuver his plump cheeks into a smile. Before that shadow of a smile could turn into a real smile, the Yamazakis lost sight of him.

Part II

The summer of 1929, when Tanno Orizo was out of town at a conference in Osaka, there was a mass arrest of the core members of Leftist cultural groups in Tokyo. While Tanno Orizo was writing a novel in Osaka's Umeda Hotel, eight police officers unexpectedly barged in, and he was taken to the district police station.

In contrast to his other colleagues, he alone remained in detention indefinitely. The police decided after two months that he could reside at an apartment near the Hankyū Railway. He was released on the condition that he would live near Osaka.

The trial was pushed back to the spring. One day, Yamazaki suddenly arrived at his apartment.

"Wow, you've grown up so much." Tanno said, and indeed, Yamazaki had changed quite a bit in the span of two years.

"I had some hardships. Masuko has always supported me, so the difficulties didn't get to me that much, but I guess it still changed me." Yamazaki said, rubbing his cheek.

He had come to Osaka thinking his father was in the gravel business, but this came from misreading his father's postcard. His father had written the word "susa." Yamazaki did not know what "susa" was, so he thought it must be "sand or *suna*," which sounded like "susa." However, when he got to Osaka, his father was living in deeper poverty than he expected. He was cutting straw in a run-down tenement house. Yamazaki learned for the first time that the straw used when stuccoing walls was called "susa." Thus, the young couple rented an apartment and promptly started looking for work. He explained that a few months later Masuko found work at a café in the outskirts of the city, and Yamazaki was able to become a columnist for a small newspaper that preyed on the eateries and cafés of the Tennōji district.

"We call it a newspaper, but it's just the owner and me. But this time around, I'm prohibited from going out. Only the owner can leave, and he's doing something fishy." He laughed as he said this.

There was no set monthly wage, and the owner merely gave him spare change occasionally. Consequently, their living expenses were covered mainly by Masuko's work. As usual, sometimes they wouldn't have enough money for rice and would often come to Tanno and reluctantly request some money.

A postcard from Sugita also came to Tanno. "Wishing that you are in good health." It was a short sentence, but in it, one could feel the sincerity of a proletarian's greeting. This recent postcard was so out of the blue after the last one saying "You will forever be the target of my hatred"—a sentiment that had punched him in the soul. Tanno was overwhelmed with emotion. Even if he tried to reply, there was no return address on Sugita's postcard. While he considered asking Yamazaki about Sugita's whereabouts, he thought better of it. He decided it was better to respect Sugita's desire to keep his location a secret.

At the first hearing of the trial in April, Tanno went to court. A young man in Western clothes stood in the hallway and walked toward him, asking, "Are you Tanno? I am Yamazaki's friend. Yamazaki was supposed to be here, but he is sick and could not come, so I am here in his place," he said, stuttering a great deal. When Tanno told him that he should make his way out because the trial was probably closed to the public, the young man obediently departed.

The first trial concluded with a sentence of two years. For about half a year Tanno lived in Shukugawa until the appeal. In the fall, right around when his appeal was about to start, Yamazaki came to visit after a long disappearance. Suddenly he blurted out, "Sensei, Masuko dumped me and left," and started crying.

Tanno could not console him. The woman had been working at the café, but two or three days ago, she said she would go to the shop and did not return. No matter how long he waited she did not return. Yamazaki became worried, so late into the night he went to her shop and shook the owner awake but was told that the woman had not come into the shop that day. He waited until morning without sleeping a wink, then scoured the areas of town he thought she might be, but he could not find her anywhere.

"I searched for her like a madman. When I asked her coworkers at the café, they said that apparently, she had become friendly with a taxi driver. I think she may have run away with him. Damn it! What an awful driver to tempt such a good woman," he said in a voice loud enough to carry to the next room.

Tanno was also amazed. To think that there exists a man who would steal away that woman from another man! It made him ponder of how extensive the realm of mad love was in this world.

"That woman is definitely being deceived. To be tempted by that sort of man, she's certainly going to be doomed. I can already see it happening. I can't seem to accept that she stopped liking me. She still loved me even when she left me." Yamazaki kept on talking. Tanno objected, no, that's not true, she grew tired of being poor, she thought that if she got together with the driver, she'd have an easier life than if she stayed with you. He continued to explain that she ran away because she wanted to be with the driver more than with you, but Yamazaki did not accept this. He was naïve. If she stayed by his side, it would be his burden. Yamazaki adamantly stated that she disappeared only because she thought she would hinder Yamazaki's goal of success—success in the bourgeoisie sense.

"Somewhere, the woman is still thinking about me and regretting her decision. And mark my word, I'm going to search for her and bring her back no matter what it takes. If I tell her that I forgive her, of course she will happily come back to me." One moment he would say such things with firm conviction, but then the next moment, he would waver and break down into tears. According to Yamazaki, the woman's escape seemed to have been well planned, because when he checked, her cabinet was empty of all her clothes.

"And then, she left behind the doll—the doll that slept between us every night."

His poetic words of lamentation continued not unlike a popular ballad. He said that because she must surely be working as a hostess at some café despite getting together with the driver, he was determined to search shop by shop all throughout the outskirts of Osaka. He did not have the money to drink a cup of coffee at each place, so he was going to disguise himself as a fortune-teller and enter the cafés. He was very enthusiastic about this plan.

Three days later, Yamazaki visited Tanno again. One of the hostesses at the café the woman previously worked in opened her mouth, and with that as his guide, he disguised himself as a fortune-teller and headed out to the outskirts of Osaka toward Miyakojima. He explained that he had looked in every single café.

"And then I found her. When I went into that café, she hid in the cook's room. I yelled, you're a coward! I yelled at her alright." Yamazaki told his story, tearing up.

In the end, they had no choice but to separate. "I still love you the same as before," she would say. "But I don't want to get back together with you again."

Just as Yamazaki suspected, her reasoning was as follows: "I'm breaking up with you for your own good, you know."

Yamazaki said, "Sensei, she is an admirable woman. She was prepared to be unhappy and thought about my fortunes and left. The driver was just a tool she used to run away. She said she was living with him, but she still couldn't give herself to him. Are you telling me you can't believe this? Fine, but I will believe her. Because I know very well what kind of woman she is."

A few days later, however, Tanno was suddenly dragged to a detention cell from the trial courtroom, and all his connections with the world of human interactions were severed. He had retracted his earlier statement that he made during his second trial, in which he said that he abandoned his revolutionary proletarian perspective. The judge pointed out his disrespectful behavior to the court. Not only did he sentence him to two years in jail, but he revoked his bail.

After a year and a half, Tanno was released. Since he fought his case all the way to the Supreme Court and five months had passed without a judgment, it was two years later when he came back to the real world. News of his release was in the papers, so he received many letters and postcards from his friends. In that pile was also a postcard from Yamazaki. "The fight begins now," it said.

Because he had changed his views during his imprisonment, Tanno lost his ideological position and had no direction in his work. His soul had been weakened; he lived a quiet life with his parents in Okayama. It soon became the first New Year's after his release. In the mix of New Year's cards, there was one from Sugita. He again did not write an address, but looking at the postmark, it was from the naval port in his hometown. "Ah, Sugita has returned to his hometown," he thought. He wondered why Sugita would feel like sending a New Year's card to a proletariat class betrayer like himself. Perhaps Sugita did not get angry with people as easily as he used to. Tanno felt that Sugita had matured and imagined that he was probably working at a company in the naval port in his hometown.

That thought was correct. Suddenly one February night, Yamazaki visited him in his Okayama home, telling him that he had just come from Osaka. In the bitter cold of February, he wore just one layer of summer cloth, with no coat and no hat.

"What happened to the woman?" Tanno asked and received the reply that the woman had left the taxi driver and gone back to her home in Tosa. Yamazaki sent postcards to her in Tosa every day for a year. Although there was never an answer, he kept on sending the postcards with determination. In the end, a single postcard came from her parents. The card said that they had married off their daughter to another man, and no matter how long he might persevere in sending her postcards, he had no chance. The card continued saying that in the future he should please ease off. He said that after receiving that postcard, his interaction with her had come to an end.

While talking about such things, he could hear the Tanno family's merry voices from another room. Yamazaki asked, "I just realized this when looking at your nameplate, but are you living with your father?"

When Tanno answered yes, Yamazaki said, "Oh, Sensei, I really do apologize. Visiting you in this sorry state . . . Please forgive me. When I saw the nameplate, I did think, oh dear, that I should have cleaned myself up!"

When Tanno gave him money for the return train, he left, bowing and holding the money almost reverently above his head. Coming all the way from Osaka and having him return right back on the night train without staying even one night was cruel, so Tanno tried to convince him to stay many times, but Yamazaki said, "Your father is here," and forcibly left.

During their visit, Tanno learned that Sugita was, just as he'd suspected, working in a factory back in his hometown. On his way back to Kyushu from Tokyo, Sugita visited Yamazaki in Osaka, and Yamazaki showed him around the underworld in the deep end of Tennōji. It was here that a man named Chiyo-chan used some cheap lodging as his headquarters, and who despite being a man, made his living in white face powder.[6] Earlier there was a man named S. who had become a German man's lover; he became notorious after he committed a murder fueled by passion, dumped the body in someone else's care, and went on the run. They all called S. Hana-chan, and he was actually Chiyo-chan's best friend. Sugita established a particularly special relationship with this Chiyo-chan. "Don't go cheatin' on me in Kyushu," Sugita was told. "Apparently while working in the factory, Sugita still carries on him the pipe that Chiyo-chan gifted him." This was the story Yamazaki shared.

That Sugita was a man with such perversions was something Tanno was hearing for the first time. This surprising news occupied little space in his mind compared to the happiness he felt in learning that Sugita had become a factory worker. A perverted man or not, Sugita was a man endowed with very human, very beautiful emotions. He had found work in a big factory and would be trained to be a metal worker. He will eventually wash away the grime of those lumpen sensibilities that had permeated the very pores of his body. He will no doubt be forged into a laborer with an iron will. On the other side of the superficial weakness of his character was an enduring passion. Tanno knew very well that a passion for something noble, something meaningful, was hidden deep inside of him.

"I do not know when that day will come. Life will always be dif-

6. Making a living in white face powder alludes to prostitution as an occupation.

ficult. But the day will surely come when he will not regret that he failed to become a novelist in Tokyo. Yes, the day will surely come when Sugita will realize he grasped a life of higher significance because of this."

Tanno kept thinking of this long after Yamazaki left. One can only hope that these aren't simply the sweet sentiments of a fallen novelist named Tanno who has lost all higher purpose in his work.

EIGHT

"Worse for Love" (Ai no shokei)
by "Sakakiyama Tamotsu"
(Mishima Yukio) (1960)

Translated by Sam Bett

Biography and Introduction

"Worse for Love" (Ai no shokei) originally appeared in October 1960 in *Apollo*, a literary offshoot of the members-only gay-interest magazine *Adonis*. Told with an assured sense of ceremony and obsessive valuation of the male body, this throaty, crepuscular tale of flummoxed lust between a male gym teacher and his favorite male student was first credited to an otherwise unknown writer named Sakakiyama Tamotsu. Ever since, its authorship has been a source of controversy.

Rumors spread, or were sown, of the real author being Mishima Yukio. Readers familiar with his style will hear the author's signature voice from the insistent first line: "The night was painfully hot." Immediately we are being told what we should see and feel, and told that it will hurt, but not without the promise that this pain will lead to some version of ecstasy.

Born Hiraoka Kimitake, Mishima studied at the Peers School in Tokyo, where as a teenager he published his first story, "Forest in Full Bloom" (Hanazakari no mori). Famous for ending his life through ritual suicide after a failed coup against the Japan Self-Defense Forces, he produced reams of novels, stories, poems, criticism, and plays both modern and classical over the course of his short though prolific career, and he is known outside Japan primarily for his fervent modernist prose style and the controversial nationalist politics that characterized his celebrity. Early on, he enjoyed widespread popularity as a zealous and often jocular essayist, and as the writer of light fiction that he published primarily in women's magazines. His iconic works include *The Sailor Who Fell from Grace with the Sea* (Gogo no eikō); the *Sea of Fertility* (Hōjō no umi) quatrology, starting with *Spring Snow* (Haru no yuki); the queer bildungsroman *Confessions of a Mask* (Kamen no koku-haku); and the short story "Patriotism" (Yūkoku), which he later adapted for film and directed, casting himself as the star.

"Worse for Love" is especially noteworthy for its thematic and stylistic similarities to "Patriotism," which appeared only four months later, in January 1961, first in the journal *Chūō kōron* and subsequently, the same month, as part of the collection *Star* (Sutā). Mishima's collected works (published by Shinchosha) includes "Ai no shokei" as part of a supplemental volume of early or otherwise acanonical writings. An explanatory endnote, which I have translated below, offers an answer to the authorship question, in light of an alternative manuscript found in 2005, the same year that the supplemental volume was released:

> It had been unclear if the work was in fact Mishima's, until recently, when a notebook containing a version in Mishima's hand was discovered among the possessions of [poet and novelist] Nakai Hideo. The version included herein is based on the content of that notebook.
>
> In the notebook manuscript, the main character is named Ōtomo Shinji (thus sharing a given name with Lieutenant Takeyama Shinji, protagonist of "Patriotism"), whereas in the version of the story published in *Apollo*, the character's given name is Takayoshi.

The *Apollo* manuscript makes the curious error of introducing the protagonist as Takayoshi, only to refer to him a few lines later as Shinji. Thereafter, the narrator reverts to Takayoshi for two pages before letting another Shinji slip, and then uses Takayoshi in all subsequent instances. If Mishima did compose both "Worse for Love" and "Patriotism," it would seem he rushed a bit too much to hide his tracks.

One could posit "Worse for Love" as a queer, apolitical iteration on the retreat from life, through love, and into death that structures "Patriotism," but the temptation is strong to see "Worse for Love" as the precursor and "Patriotism" as its politicized, straightwashed derivative.

Yet a comparison based solely on narrative arcs would be misguided. These stories are explorations of what consensual sexuality might look like when complicated by power, pushed as close to death as life allows, and tipped over the brink. The difference is their different attitudes toward safety. In "Patriotism," Shinji comes home, riven by irreconcilable loyalties, to a caring though unexpressive partner, Reiko, who ardently joins him in a lover's suicide. They share a final hour of erotic ecstasy before she bears witness to his *seppuku* and ends her own life with a dagger. At the start of "Worse for Love," Shinji is home alone on a Friday night, addled by shame. His student, Toshio, arrives with a censorious demand and a short sword. Their arousal, however shared and astral, is asynchronous and fraught with taboo, age difference, and performance. They may reach a kind of climax, but it wobbles dangerously out of balance.

My translation is based on the *Apollo* text, though I have standardized the use of the name Shinji in every instance where the name of the gym teacher is mentioned.

Worse for Love

The night was painfully hot. Once the last bus from town had come and gone at half past five, a mantle of quiet from deep within the mountains fell over the hillside. If you climbed the stone staircase built into the slope behind the bus route, you would find a rustic country home, the sort of place that would have been abandoned long ago if not for its eccentric tenant.

Originally the outbuilding of a large estate, the house had last been occupied by an old man who spent years suffering from palsy. When he died, his relatives were disinclined to sell the property, opting instead to put it up for rent. Then along came Ōtomo Shinji, gym teacher at a middle school downtown. The school had a good reputation, and Mr. Ōtomo—notwithstanding the peculiarity of being a single man in his mid-thirties—was youthful, affable, and cut like an athlete.

His landlords, more than satisfied, not only rented him the house for next to nothing, but went as far as hiring an older woman to come out from the city to do his housekeeping. She arrived on the first bus in the morning, tended to his cleaning and his laundry, and fixed his dinner. Incomparably tidy, she kept the house so clean it always felt a bit too organized for a bachelor.

Once she rode off on the final bus at half past five, Shinji was alone, and he could finally relax. His stated reason for living this far out was a desire to break free from the city and connect with nature. Surrounded by cedars, and overlooking the vast fields, this house fit the bill.

Its two rooms were both tatami: a bedroom and a living room. The dirt floor at the entrance led around a corner to a long and narrow cooking area. In the old style, the bath and the latrine were housed separately out back. Even this modest property was too much space for Shinji, who had no personal effects to fill it with. Timeworn, burnished posts stood in the corners, and high ceilings gave the space a languor that was difficult to bear. It didn't help that a sick man had died here after a long struggle. But the rent was too cheap to pass up.

That night after dinner, Shinji sprawled out on the planking of his side porch in his thin cotton yukata. It used to be that he could put away two giant helpings, but lately he could barely stomach any food at all. Under the dim electric light, his bushy eyebrows made a frown. Every few minutes, he let out another sigh. The house was silent but for the paper fan he flapped to cool himself.

It's all over, Shinji thought. *I'm done for.* He saw no reason to go on living. School was out for summer, but it felt as if his passion for teaching physical education was gone for good. He rolled up his sleeves and touched his girthy, capable muscles. Even in his sullenness, his body had retained its pointless strength, gleaming and defined in a way that felt perverse. Now, in the final hour, this body he had spent years toning failed to do him any good. It was time for him to die. The police had taken sympathy on him and settled the investigation, and the school had convinced the Tadokoro family not to press charges, but none of that mattered. The sadness and frustration were too much. He wanted to tear himself apart.

A silhouette appeared at the entrance.

"Hello?" asked a young voice.

Shinji perked his ears. He was not expecting company. "Who's there?"

"It's Toshio. Imabayashi. From school."

"Toshio! What's going on, bud?"

Shinji shed his somber expression. His face, agile from a life of exercise, snapped back to its usual look of exuberance; he stroked his cheeks and jaw, thrilled to find his skin was cleanly shaven.

"How'd you make it out here this late?"

"I walked from town."

The boy's voice traveled through the blinds

"What a hike! Come on in."

"Thanks."

Shinji had Toshio in his homeroom class. As far as good looks were concerned, he killed the competition. Tonight he stepped inside in a white polo shirt and black slacks, carrying his school hat in his right hand and a gym bag in his left. He sat on his heels and bowed.

His complexion was fair, like a peasant boy who covered himself up out of doors. His face was trim and comely, with pretty little cherry lips. Something in his build suggested endless adolescence; and his bone-white, skinny arms, though delicate, were not without a thin layer of fat that made him soft and registered as sensual. When he was embarrassed, he went red in the cheeks and at the corners of his eyes. Shinji had seen him in the showers. The rosy, miniature nipples, the clean scoop of his navel. Unforgettable. Not a coarse hair on his body. Feet like polished ivory. Always shy, reserved, maybe even a bit forlorn. Though he was never one to laugh out loud, and often hard to read, he always made high marks.

The ranks of each incoming class of boys were overrun with gangly young men, who at fifteen or sixteen were practically adults. Toshio and his best friend, Tadokoro, were the last two boys with any softness left.

Thinking in extremes, Shinji saw this sudden visit from his favorite student as divine intervention.

"I wish I had some snacks to offer, but all I've got is a thermos of cold tea. Hold on a sec."

"That's okay. Thanks anyway, though."

Shinji plopped back down, cross-legged. Beaming. "That's quite a hike you made." His teeth shone white against his tan. Between his legs, you could see the white loincloth at his crotch, black pubic hair frizzling from the edges of the fabric.

Toshio was stunned.

This is it, he thought, *what all the guys were talking about. Sensei's pubes are so scraggly he can't even tuck them inside his loincloth. Man, he's hairy all over. But I can't get carried away. I have important things to say. Afterward, I can gawk at him as much as I want.*

"So, you and your folks heading to the beach this summer?" Shinji asked.

"I'm here to discuss something far more serious than that."

"Serious? Like what?"

The boy was not amused. His eyes, gathering an alien power, aimed straight at Shinji's face.

"What is it?"

"Tadokoro."

"I see."

Shinji felt his living rapture die. This was the one thing he was most keen on forgetting. Its mere mention awoke him to the triviality of his excitement about Toshio's visit.

"I have to know exactly how you feel about everything," said Toshio. "My thoughts have kept me up at night since it happened. After a while, I had no choice but to come out here and ask you. Please hear me out."

"Absolutely!"

Shinji had always sensed something otherworldly in the presence of Imabayashi Toshio, but never, until tonight, had he been able to explore the contours of the boy's beautiful face with such open reverence. As if answering to a sorceress, he felt obliged to do whatever the boy said.

"What are your thoughts on Tadokoro's death?"

"Well, I can't help but feel responsible."

"Responsible! People say you killed him."

"Some might see it that way, but at the time I had no choice but to do what I did. We were in the gymnasium for the day, on account of the weather, so the only way to punish him was to make him stand outside, in the rain, while the rest of us exercised. He was out there for a good half hour, which is how he caught pneumonia, but the doctor was slow to realize. By the time he did, it was too late to save him. You gotta figure the doctor is partially to blame."

"And here I thought you were a man."

Toshio's eyes heated with resentment. His gaze, however sharp, sent pleasant shivers through Shinji's body.

"You know how he was," Shinji said. "Tadokoro was a difficult student. Always acting up in class. He called me awful names. He never gave me the respect that a gym teacher deserves. On the day it happened, I heard what he was saying behind my back. 'Go back to the jungle, Tarzan!' I'm only human. Who wouldn't be angry?"

"Are you saying that you killed one of your students out of spite?"

"Too far, Toshio. Don't say things like that. Unruly boys must be taken in hand. Now, I'll be the first to admit, maybe I didn't go about things the best way."

For a time, they were quiet. Toshio's cheeks were flushed, complementing the moist sparkle of his eyes. The blinding whiteness of the skin surrounding the boy's belly button infiltrated Shinji's thoughts. He rid the image from his mind.

"Sensei, you're lying."

Shinji was silent. Toshio raised his voice.

"You're lying! Why not tell the truth? You were in love with Tadokoro."

A baffled Shinji stared down Toshio.

"I'm right, aren't I?" Toshio asked. "I knew it."

"Alright, that's enough. Listen, as your teacher, it's not appropriate for me to say this, but I'll be a man and spit it out. Yes, I loved Tadokoro. But I love you too. When I see a boy like either of you, something comes over me. You need to understand, though, I loved each of you in different ways. With him, it felt like all he gave me in return was scorn, but with you, it feels like something is scouring me clean. I know what you're thinking: I punished him because he didn't love me back. But I'm afraid that you're mistaken. You're deeply mistaken. When I saw him chattering his teeth out there in the rain, his face all pale, just standing there, staring back at me with those ferocious eyes, totally drenched, he was more beautiful to me than he had ever been before. I never loved him more than I did then . . . can't you see . . . can't you see?"

The strain made Shinji's voice unravel.

"Ever since Tadokoro died, I've felt like my life was over. I've lost any sense of motivation. To be honest, at this point, I just want to die. I'm just . . . I'm just . . . a shell of who I was."

"Oh, is that right?"

Toshio's response was stolid and severe. He had taken the tone of an unforgiving litigator, but he backed off the pressure and proceeded with his case.

"That gives me a sense of how you feel. I can tell that your confession is honest. The question now is whether you're willing to pay the price for what you've done."

"I've given this a lot of thought, and I'm prepared to accept as much of the responsibility as possible. I know that school's already out, but I've decided to put in for my resignation."

"Are you kidding me?"

The boy's voice pierced his very being.

"Sensei, if you really feel so bad about Tadokoro dying, are you ready to atone? I'm here tonight, as Tadokoro's best friend, to hear what you have to say to that, with my own ears."

"What are you getting at?" Shinji asked.

"Didn't you just say that you wanted to die?" Toshio's voice was strangely quiet.

"I did."

"Tadokoro is dead because of you. Shouldn't you atone for what you've done?"

Under the dim light, the air of the living room was still enough to terrify. The gym teacher and his pupil sat across from one another, eyes locked, bodies paused. An unspeakable mirth reddened Shinji's complexion. He uncrossed his legs and sat straight up on his heels, knees pressed to the tatami. Resolute, he spoke in a voice of aggrieved joy.

"Well said, Toshio. Well said. Your words have made my duty clear to me. Dying is the only way. I'll do it, Toshio."

Witnessing this declaration, the boy did not so much as twitch an eyebrow.

"Do what?" he asked, eyes askance. "How, exactly, do you plan to die?"

"Well, I haven't thought it through yet, but I can't exactly shoot myself, not owning a gun. If I wanted to poison myself, the best that I could do out here for poison would be pesticide. I could always hang myself, but it wouldn't be pretty."

"When are we talking?"

"The sooner the better, now that it's settled."

"Do it tonight. Right here, where I can see you. Otherwise I won't believe it."

"Nothing would please me more than for you to watch. But I'm not sure what to do."

"I'll tell you this much, it's not going to be fun."

The boy finally smiled. His cherry lips parted, only slightly, as if letting out a sigh.

"You murdered my best friend. You think a murderer like you should get off easy?"

"Alright, if that's the way it's gonna be, you take the lead. Tell me how you want to see me die."

"I want you to hold onto the pain. I want it to rip you to pieces. This needs to be the most painful suicide possible. Sensei. I want you to commit seppuku."

"You want me to do what?"

The boy unzipped his gym bag and pulled out a short sword in a wooden scabbard.

"Use this. It's a family heirloom. The edge is razor-sharp."

"I can't use your family's sword. What will your parents say?"

"Don't talk back. Are you ready to repent for the wrong you've done? You'd be good to do as I say."

Following orders, Shinji unsheathed the sword. The icy luster of the antique blade tempered the air of the gloomy, musty room.

"One more thing. When you stick it in, I want you to be wearing the same clothes you wore the day you made Tadokoro stand out in the rain. White running shirt, white track pants. Get on your knees and rip open your stomach, like a man."

"Alright."

Shinji fixated on the edge of the blade. In mere minutes, it would be swallowed by his flesh. The wonderment of being given orders by the boy, and dying in his presence, fortified his ecstasy. This frigid boy had given him the gift of death, bestowed his death upon him like a blessing. How could death be any more exciting? Even if he lived a hundred years, he would never have a chance to die like this again. It felt like his life, up until this moment, had been lived but in the service of this most fortunate end.

Alright, he told himself, *let's give this boy an epic, tragic suicide.*

Muscles, numb with lassitude only minutes prior, surged with virulent activity.

I'm going to show this boy how a man takes a sword. He'll get exactly what he wants.

Shinji smiled and patted Toshio's shoulder.

"Alright, shall we get started?"

The ensuing rush felt not so much like a prelude to death as like the preparations for a banquet. Toshio suggested that the bedroom would be a good space for the suicide. They folded Shinji's futon, flat and hard with use, and stowed it in the closet, at the back of which, shoved into a corner, Toshio was delighted to find a squat wooden offering stand of bare wood, left behind by the last tenant.

"Sensei, let's close all the doors."

Shinji watched Toshio slide shut the paper screens on three sides of the bedroom and remove the scroll hanging in the ornamental alcove on the fourth. The white walls closed around him, reducing the room to a zone of old tatami that pulled at his body with a strange downward compulsion. Toshio set the sword upon a sheet of opalescent paper and placed these in the alcove, on the wooden stand. A festering heat leavened the air.

"You'll rot quick in heat like this."

"Come again?"

"You dolt. I mean your corpse."

Shinji snuck his hand into his yukata and stroked the taut muscles of his pectorals. Toshio paused by the screen between them and the neighboring room.

"What do you think? Isn't it grand?"

"Where do I sit?"

"A few feet back from the fat post at the edge of the alcove."

It was strange to consider that this was the room where he would die. Never to leave this room again. His hair sticky with sweat, blood pounding through its veins. In a matter of hours, this body would be no more than a side of meat.

Sidling closer, Toshio poked his face into Shinji's armpit, just above his rolled-up sleeve.

"You stink. Your sweat smells kind of tangy, though."

"That's what happens when you get pit hair."

"I like it. It smells manly. I bet it'll stick around long after you're dead."

Toshio told Shinji to wash up before he died. They left the prepared room for the drinking well out back. The crazed moon lit the yard like it was daytime.

The gym teacher slipped off his yukata and undid the knotted loincloth to stand fully nude under the moonlight. He was skinny, really, but every inch of him was bulging with firm muscle. Toshio knew this would be hard to beat. Here was everything—the bushy eyebrows, the lunar sheen of his teacher's shaven cheeks, and his entire body in plain view, all the muscle and the hair. His brawny pecs were thick with chest hair, nearly blending, by the nipples, with the lushness bristling from his armpits. A dark trail ran down from his breastbone to his navel, where the whorls of his hairy belly led into the black forest of his privates. Pubes spread unkempt over his thighs, hair reaching to his shins. The puce knob of his stiff dick gleamed, and below it dangled ponderous, hairy testicles. Shinji dumped a pail of water over his head and blew through his teeth. Droplets glistened in the moonlight where they clung to him.

Toshio marveled at the sight.

Pretty soon his body will be smeared with blood and on the verge of death. His hairy stomach will gape open, in a big red slash. Finally, his

*body is all mine. No one can interrupt us. This hunk of a man is going to
die before my eyes, exactly as I say. I can't believe it.*

Rapturous, Toshio stared until his vision blurred with tears.

Back inside, Toshio tended to the details of Shinji's final dress. First he
set about tying the loincloth. Wrapping its length around and around,
he made a pass and grabbed Shinji by the cock and balls.

"Hey, hands off. You can't just get me riled up like that before I die.
If I'm hard, you won't be able to tie the knot."

But it was too late. Shinji's cock was igneous.

"Here's a little tug for you," Toshio said, jerking on the cloth, "to
keep the knot nice and low on your stomach. That way it's easier to stab
yourself! Uh-oh, Sensei, those pubes just can't hold back, can they."

Shinji put on his running shirt. Skintight, it made the muscles of
his chest articulate. The bleach white fabric was a handsome contrast to
his tanned skin. Once he had pulled on the white track pants, the outfit
was complete.

"There's something I want before I die."

"What?"

"Give me a kiss," said Shinji. "Just one."

When Toshio smiled and leaned in, his gym teacher saw an opening
and hugged the svelte boy hard against his chest. Squirming got him
nowhere, locked in the man's mighty arms. He felt Shinji breathe into
his ear.

"I love you. Hear me? I love you. I can die happy knowing this is
what you want from me. I'm going to finish strong, just for you. My
body is yours."

The kiss they shared was passionate, but the hour of death was nigh.
Toshio broke free, throwing Shinji's musky man arms off of him. Any
more of this and Toshio would be the one to succumb to temptation.

As instructed, Shinji sat himself down, cross-legged, by the wood post
at the corner of the alcove in the bedroom. He unsnapped the top
button of his pants, relaxed his belly, and adjusted the full pouch of his
loincloth. Toshio commenced to administer the ceremony.

"Ōtomo Shinji, thirty-five years of age, you will now take penance
for your trespasses through ritual disembowelment. First, to retain a
relic of your living body, I will shave strands of hair from your armpit
and your groin."

As if by magic, Toshio produced a fixed-blade razor. He beckoned

Shinji to lift his right arm and shaved off a dozen or so hairs, catching them on a sheet of calligraphy paper before moving on to the left arm. The edge of the blade nicked skin.

"Yow!" Shinji winced.

"You idiot. You're about to take a sword in the gut."

Blood dribbled from Shinji's underarm. A stark red ribbon scored the chest of his white running shirt and continued down his torso.

"I've never seen your blood before, Sensei. It's beautiful."

He went on to cut hairs from Shinji's crotch, at each side of the bulge.

Feeling Toshio's thin pale fingers graze the surface of his thigh skin, Shinji could not quell his arousal. His senses were anything but telling him he was about to die.

"Okay. The relics are secure."

Toshio tipped the hairs into an envelope of white paper and set it squarely in the alcove, from which he took the fated short sword, balanced on its wooden stand, and set it on the mat in front of Shinji. The sight of it made Shinji's heart pound with a madness he could not control.

"Sensei, it's time for the suicide. Show me how a manly, valiant hero takes his life. Finish strong. I want you to cut as deep as you can go. Wrap the blade in the paper, leaving just about three inches bare, and drive it in, up to where you wrapped it. I know your abs are really strong, and it might be difficult to cut through, but give it all you've got. Then pull the blade in a straight line, six inches across. I'll explain what comes next after that. Are you ready?"

"Ready."

Shinji unscabbarded the sword. He folded the parchment and wrapped it around the blade, to leave about three inches clear. Beside himself, he was troubled to see his hands were shaking. Using his left hand, he jerked his running shirt up over his ribs and past his nipples, holding the blade steady in his right.

"Well, Toshio, I guess this is goodbye. Time for me to die."

"Goodbye."

Toshio's speech was a murmur. He faced Shinji dead on, hands on his knees, his tension manifest. You could see him twitching. His eyes were locked on Shinji, and Shinji returned his gaze. Realizing that this boy would be watching, eyes wide with attention, over every moment of his death, a delectable tremor flushed his nerves.

Shinji closed his eyes. He worked the fingers of his left hand into the muscles of his abdomen. Predictably, his toned stomach was hard to the touch. As he touched his navel, his nails caught the wealth of hair. *A little lower*, he thought, *that's where to cut*. He yanked on the pouch of his loincloth, to make more room, and massaged the flat area above his pubes.

Opening his eyes, he saw Toshio before him, those gorgeous eyes agleam. It was time. He brought the point of the blade to the left side of his stomach, where there was less hair, and the flesh was softer. A good place to begin.

He gave the spot a stab, but the blade only pricked his skin; the tip didn't go in at all. He would have to hoist it up and follow through on the downswing. He checked Toshio's face and saw eyes bloodshot with anticipation.

Investing his right arm with all his strength, and reaching up as high as he could reach, Shinji stared at his own stomach as if consuming the visual.

He let the high sword fall.

The shining blade pierced flesh, entering the skin with a granular tearing. There was no pain, only profound exhilaration. *That's it!* he thought. *That's it!* He reaffirmed his grip. The blade went curiously deep, stopping at the folded paper. No blood yet. *So that's all there is to it*, he mused. A gnawing numbness of the stomach.

"Sensei!"

Toshio cupped Shinji's face in his hands. The frigid countenance of seconds earlier was gone, replaced by the face of a blushing boy, alive with passion. His features were above all juvenile.

"Sensei! Sensei! Does it hurt? How bad? What does it feel like?"

"Not so bad."

When Shinji replied, a colossal pain from deep inside of him was rising to the surface; his bushy brows, askew, betrayed his agony. Toshio touched Shinji's stomach and showed his teacher both his hands, soaked with blood.

"Look at this! Blood everywhere!"

Tears fell from Toshio's eyes, but Shinji could barely believe that this was happening.

This vicious boy is crying just for me. He's sad because I'm going to die.

Toshio threw his arms around Shinji's mighty shoulders and bawled into his ear.

"Sensei! I'm so sorry. I lied to you. I knew that if I didn't say you were to blame, you wouldn't kill yourself. I don't even care about Tadokoro dying. I just wanted to see you do it. I wanted to watch you in your running shirt and track pants, to see you cut your stomach open. I'm crazy for you. I idolize you. I needed to have your body. Forgive me, Sensei. Sensei, will you still die for me?"

In the throes of trauma, Shinji's joy at this confession wafted through his cortex like a dream. His face had gone clammy with cold sweat, but his words were confident and true.

"It's alright, Toshio. Because I've always loved you. So much more than Tadokoro. I could never get close to you. You were so cold. But hearing you talk this way, it brings me peace. Hold on . . . oh, boy . . . Look, I've already cut up this hairy belly. If it makes you happy, then I'm happy to die."

"Oh Sensei! Sensei! I'm so happy."

Ecstatic, Toshio squeezed Shinji's face in his hands. But the mounting pain screwed up Shinji's eyebrows and his face, pulling his upper lip tight to his gums, revealing white front teeth. His breath was savage through his nostrils; his face was bright with sweat.

"I love it. The pain makes you look amazing. This is what I wanted to see."

Toshio kissed Shinji's clenched lips and all around his face. He dragged his tongue across the stubble of his jaw.

"To—Toshio! I'm . . . I . . ."

Blood trickled from his mouth. Toshio slurped it off his cheeks and swallowed.

"It's okay, Sensei. Go ahead and finish."

Toshio stood lithely and looked down on the moaning figure of his teacher. Taking a step back, to give himself full view of the performance.

Shinji jutted out his blood-sodden pecs, in a doomed attempt to maintain his composure. He tightened his grip on the paper. Having penetrated the intestines, the blade had snagged, and the chest muscles clamped down like a bear trap on the pain. Continuing the cut would demand awesome strength from Shinji. The swell of his pythonic biceps made the desperation of his effort evident. But the blade maintained its sure path through his flesh.

Shinji's wails turned into shrieks, and the muscles of his shoulders shined with perspiration. The blade advanced into the skin below his navel. The white pouch of the loincloth was incarnadine, and spurts of blood had made their mark on his white track pants. The bright white running shirt, hiked up past his nipples, had been dyed a gorgeous red by the blood spraying from the wound and dripping off his face. The volume of the blood was harrowing. Blood climbing up the blade caused his closed fist to slip, while his pubes floated like cordgrass in his lap. Blood disemboguing from his sodden crotch puddled in the seat of his pants. His face was getting paler by the minute; but through the pain, his eyes, under his bushy brows, were keen and valorous.

This is what I wanted to see, the boy told himself, eyes lit, heart pounding. *Just look at him. Blood soaking his shirt, soaking his pants, soaking his chest. That's the stuff. I sure am lucky. But I can't let this luck go to waste. I need to enjoy every minute of it.*

When you've cut your way across your stomach, the agony will be so intense you're liable to try and cut your jugular, to end the pain. But I won't let you die so easily. Just when you've pulled out the sword, I'll jerk it free, and use it to snip the running shirt and the track pants and the loincloth from your body, leaving you as naked as the day you were born.

I can see it now. The pain will make you tear at your own skin. Holding back your guts from spilling out, flailing in a sea of blood, you'll be screaming through your tears for me to take pity on you.

"Please, please kill me, Toshio! Do it, do it, let me die! I can't take it anymore."

"You cleansed yourself with water," I'll say. *"Now cleanse yourself with blood."*

Then I'll run this rope behind your neck and over your chest and tie your hands behind your back. This is the part I'm really looking forward to. You see, this is a special kind of seppuku, where the punishment really begins just when you thought it was all over. That's when I'll start the torture. Poking around your body with the sword, I'll make little cuts in all your muscles. I'll play with your hairy body like a toy, doing whatever I can to extend the pain. Your body will be mine, all mine, for me to savor to my heart's content.

Eventually you'll near the final spasm. Twitching, but less and less. When you let out your last breath, I'll kiss your bloody lips for a really, really, really long time. Then I'll just sit back and gaze upon your chiseled man face, wallowing with you, like your faithful squire, in the sea of blood, until rigor mortis finally sets in.

At dawn, I'll take cyanide and lay across your corpse. When they find us we'll make quite the story. As rare a double suicide as they come.

But listen, Sensei. It's all because I love you. I really do. I love you so, so, so, so much!

Tears fell in a constant stream from the boy's eyes as he watched the progress of the sword through flesh. Squealing like a lower animal, the dying man squeezed his eyes shut from the pain. Tears streaked his face. The blade passed the point below his navel, creeping rightward, as the hole torn in his stomach gaped afresh. Gray intestines nosed through the gap.

A cloying stench of viscera, like spoiled fish, filled the room. It was so hot. Only the white screens, illumined from outside by moonlight, retained any sense of coolness, but blood had sprayed as far as their thin paper. On the surface of the old sagging tatami, a rivulet of blood trickled from the body of the suicide, wetting the toes of the boy standing beside him.

NINE

"I Am Not Going on Sunday" (Nichiyōbi ni wa boku wa ikanai) by Mori Mari (1961)

Translated by Robert Tierney

Biography and Introduction

Mori Mari (1903–1987) was the elder daughter of Mori Ōgai (Rintarō, 1862–1922) and his second wife Shige. Her father was both a military doctor and a literary giant of the Meiji period who played a key role in introducing European literature to Japan. She was nineteen years old and in Europe when her famous father died in 1922. Although she began to publish her own work from 1929, she first gained a reputation for her literary reminiscences about her father, notably *Chichi no bōshi* (My Father's Hat, 1958), which was awarded the fifth Japan Essayist Prize. In a brilliant essay on her work, Keith Vincent speaks of Mari's "Elektra complex"[1] and her refusal to grow up, a theme that later found expression in her gay-themed fictions. While still a very young woman, she married twice but quickly divorced both times, and she spent a great deal of time in Europe, especially in Paris. After her early disillusionment with these experiences, she did not marry again and seems to have found marriage and heteronormative adulthood harsh and oppressive. Her later art-for-art's-sake (*tanbiha*) style owes much to French fin de siècle literature, and she often refers to obscure French or Belgian symbolists and decadent writers in her works, and even adopts their style of writing.[2]

---

1. A term coined by Carl Jung to describe a girl's competition with her mother for possession of her father (a female version of Freud's much-better-known Oedipus complex). Keith Vincent, "A Japanese Elektra and Her Queer Progeny," *Mechademia* 2 (2007), 64–79.

2. Tatsukichi, the fictional writer in the story, is extremely knowledgeable about French literature, and particularly writers from this period.

In her late fifties, she dedicated herself to fiction, publishing a small number of full-length novels and novellas, as well as several collections of essays (*zuihitsu*), before her death in 1987. One of her most famous and critically acclaimed prose works is *Amai mitsu no heya* (A Room Sweet as Honey, 1975), which depicts an extremely close emotional relationship between a father and daughter. Mari won the Izumi Kyoka Literary Prize for this work in 1975.

"I Am Not Going on Sunday," the work here translated, appeared first in a collection of Mari's short fiction titled *Koibitotachi no mori* (A Lovers' Forest),[3] which was published in 1961, when she was 57. This genre of fiction about male homosexual passion was known as *tanbi shōsetsu* (literally, "esthetic novel"). Like "Kareha no nedoko" (The Bed of Withered Leaves), and the title piece of the volume, "Koibitotachi no mori" (The Lovers' Forest), it depicts a passionate but tragic same-sex relationship between a sophisticated middle-aged man and a capricious but beautiful younger man. In these stories, the young men often use their sexual power and beauty to exploit the older man, thereby undermining his authority. The young Hansu in "I Am Not Going on Sunday" is one variation of this pattern. He is described as androgynous but also as resembling a non-Japanese, with double-lidded eyes and brown hair, just like his counterparts in other works in the collection, who also have Western names such as Leo and Paolo.

This work is emphatically not an example of "gay" writing in Japan, but it was one of the earliest and most interesting works by a female author to treat explicitly and sensitively the topic of male-male relationships. Mishima Yukio, an early champion of Mari's fiction, had a high opinion of her style. Her gay-themed works and their exotic heroes also inspired the vast genre of BL manga (*yaoi*) and popular novels about male-male love that started to appear in Japan in the 1970s.[4] The intended audience for these works was largely heterosexual women who probably had no interest in gay sexuality or identity at all. These works often represent escapist fantasies of women projected onto male bodies rather than plausible representations of gay relationships. The relationship between Tatsukichi and Hansu in the story, idealized as it may be, still follows a heteronormative imaginary in which Tatsukichi is marked as the older male and Hansu as younger and more female. The

---

3. The title of course plays on the writer's family name.

4. *Yaoi* manga artists and writers have frequently acknowledged that their narratives were inspired by Mori Mari's male homosexual trilogy. Such *yaoi* manga and novels (especially) are sometimes labeled *tanbi mono* (aesthetic writing) precisely because these artists have been so much influenced by Mori's writing style.

difference of age and gender between the two men also reflects the dynamics of the Edo tradition of *nanshoku*.

While "I Am Not Going on Sunday" may be thought of as a literary fantasy, it nevertheless is written in a more realistic style than other works in *Koibitotachi no mori*. The work offers the reader glimpses of homophobia in Japanese society in the early 1960s when it portrays the reaction of other characters to the relationship of the two lovers. It also offers a revealing portrait of the closet in which gay men existed at that time.

I Am Not Going on Sunday

A cameraman from the magazine *Tōnichi Graphic*[5] who had come to the prerelease screening of Heinrich Kahaane's film *The Virgin* took a few shots of the writer Sugimura Tatsukichi, but then latched onto Itō Hansu,[6] his beloved disciple, who had just entered the room. Arriving late, Hansu hurried down the aisle but he suddenly stopped and lowered his long eyelashes over his eyes as though he were afraid of the camera pointed in his direction. As a general rule, he struck one as a young man immune from fear.

His eyes were his most conspicuous feature, light brown except for the pupils. As if made of glass, they would reflect your image perfectly. They seemed half-closed and nearly hidden under the luxuriant awning of his eyelashes. His face was so small it could easily fit in the palm of your hand. It had a sculpted beauty, but if you looked at him in profile, you noticed that the gap between his eyes and eyelashes was just a little too wide. The tip of his slender nose was a bit crooked. The lips had a slightly pointy shape. His hair was brown. A light down covered his sideburns and forehead almost to the edge of his eyelids, as though soot had fallen and collected there. The sideburns grew abundantly, and his forehead had an angular look to it. His ear lobes, behind his sideburns, had a soft and fleshy feel like those of a woman. His jaw was small.

When you gazed at his clear, brown eyes in profile under the dome of his broad forehead, you felt as if you were watching a bird metamorphose into a young man. His skin was white and pretty in a feminine

---

5. This is an older name for a Mainichi publication, a kind of Japanese *Life Magazine*.

6. This is a foreign-sounding name that resembles Hans, but it is written in kanji meaning "half-red." The character *shu* (read *su* here) denotes cinnabar red, a reddish color with just a tinge of yellow.

way, but it had a coarser grain than a woman's and was even bristly to the touch.

As Hansu lowered his gaze, he put his loosely clasped right hand under his chin, as though he were pressing it against his own throat. He wore a tight-fitting black shirt that hugged his neck and had on a light gray summer coat; an engagement ring glittered on his little finger. Fear could be read in his lowered, drowsy eyes and his lips; there were even traces of tears from the sideburns to the cheeks, and on the slopes of his nose. The previous afternoon, he had fallen prey to anxiety and fear because of the shock that he received from the hands of Sugimura Tatsukichi. There was something immature and boyish in his fearful face. For some time, Tatsukichi, seated a row ahead of Hansu, had been observing this face, in which one could almost sense the vibration of smothered sobs.

"Turn this way," said the photographer as he contorted himself into an unnatural posture, the upper part of his body twisted to the left and his opposite elbow lifted high in the air. When Hansu looked up, he could see Tatsukichi's face right under the photographer's raised elbow, and the latter shot him a sharp glance. The light flashed, and then the image of this terrified youth was burned onto film.

For at least the past two years, wherever Sugimura Tatsukichi went, Itō Hansu, his disciple who wrote such bad novels but had such good looks, was sure to go as well, like his faithful shadow. To be sure, this custom had been practiced in the breach over the previous half year, but it remained so well known that even the photographer had not forgotten. Indeed, the photographer's "mistake" proved to be no mistake at all, since Sugimura Tatsukichi and Itō Hansu had, after an interruption of six months, resumed their relationship the previous afternoon.

Noticing that Tatsukichi motioned toward him, Hansu moved his hand from his chin to behind his ear and made a movement as if to smooth out his loose hairs. Then he dropped his eyes and hurried to occupy the seat beside Tatsukichi. Just at that moment, another photographer took a picture of two people seated near Hansu, turning the whole room into a blaze of light. Hansu looked up to avoid the glare and turned toward Tatsukichi, whose face took on a darkened, erotic air of a man whose lover is leaning against his shoulder as, facing the camera, he lifted his chin slightly and gazed expressively at the camera. There was something odd about this photo that captured the well-known novelist Sugimura Tatsukichi and Itō Hansu, his so-called disciple, but for ordinary people, whose minds are such prisoners of convention that they ignore realities staring them right in the face, such signs of the singular and unusual might as well be invisible. In this respect, journalists were hardly more perceptive than their peers. In Europe, where an assumed nonchalance is de rigueur, people understand such matters and deal with them with a light touch. Provided no jealous rival is present at the scene, such open secrets will retreat to a distant realm in which people's psychological radar seems to have no access.

Men like Tatsukichi tended to act boldly in public settings, made no effort to conceal their words or gestures of love, and fearlessly mocked the conventional views of society. Their arrogance was bred by a conviction that they lived in a world utterly impenetrable to prying eyes. This was a despicable character trait in the eyes of people who dislike everything outside the run of the mill.

"What's the matter?" Tatsukichi queried in a hushed voice.

Hansu could feel his side-glance pressing on his face.

"Were you able to sleep last night?"

"Yes . . . but just a little bit. . . ."

"I was up all night. It serves me right, I guess."

"Well, I am in the same boat . . ."

"I am impressed how well you understand me."

Pretending he felt tired, Tatsukichi threw his arm around the back of Hansu's seat and leaned slightly in the direction of his friend.

He said, "You will do exactly as I say then."

"Yes."

His voice was barely audible.

Suddenly, the chatter in the theater ceased and the lights dimmed. Just like at the start of a religious ceremony, the spectators held in their breaths and—as people tend to do in such rituals—they fiercely repressed every rebellious impulse of their bodies. Like a beautiful line of beetles advancing in formation, German subtitles marched meaningfully across the dark screen.

• • •

The day before, Hansu had spoken to Tatsukichi at Bel Ami for the first time in six months. From the time they met until their separation six months earlier, they always got together at the coffee shop Bel Ami on Hongō Avenue. Hansu thought of his relationship with Tatsukichi as that between a younger and older brother, but he sensed something more convoluted in the background. Without paying further attention to the matter, he became the object of Yatsuka Yoshiko's love and was now engaged to her in his usual careless way, without even suspecting that Tatsukichi might feel betrayed.

Yatsuka Yoshiko was a young, petite woman eighteen years old. She had a small face framed by reddish-brown hair and sensual lips that, for the past few days, seemed to overflow with nectar. The corners of her eyes sagged a bit, as though she had had a bit too much to drink. The bangs that fell lightly on both sides of her sallow face had a slightly gold tint, if you examined them closely. While she looked immature, there was already something of the woman about her. Hansu was most powerfully drawn to her maternal nature. He discovered in Yoshiko something that he had never found in the other young women that he had been involved with previously. Not one of them resembled her. He thought, "Apart from Yoshiko, I guess I have never been in love with anyone. I must never do anything to cause her pain." Reasoning in this fashion, Hansu was now engaged.

Yoshiko would never forget the only time Hansu had confessed his love for her. She made up her mind that she would never make him unhappy, even for an instant. Hansu had a sinking feeling when he thought, "she is offering up her whole heart to me, dripping with blood." Hansu had lost both parents when he was still a boy, and his elder sister Sami, his only sibling, had married and moved far away to Kyūshū. He was particularly susceptible to the charm of family life because he had been deprived of it up until then. He bathed in the warm atmosphere of the Yatsuka's home thanks to the hospitality of Yoshiko's parents and the cordiality of the old maid who had taken care of both Yoshiko and her older brother Kiichi (now living with his wife in London) ever since they were born. Although his sister Sami was twenty-four, two years older than Hansu, she was still a slender, lovely girl with a boyish look. Hansu, who was vaguely aware of the nature of Tatsukichi's real feelings toward him, did not want to have his sister meet Tatsukichi. He felt a faint stirring of jealousy, but he was otherwise heedless of Tatsukichi's feelings. He was no different from a little boy that hoards an entire plate of sweet pastries for himself. He never gave so much as a thought to the happiness of either Tatsukichi or Yoshiko. How could it have been otherwise? He was not one prone to introspection.

After he met Yoshiko, Hansu grew estranged from Tatsukichi. He used to act almost as though he was his lover, but now he felt awkward when they were together, almost as though he had offended him, and he visited him less often than before. While he used to see Tatsukichi three times a week, now they met only once, if at all. And this included times when they ran into each other by accident. Tatsukichi never mentioned Yoshiko's name and made no attempt to invite Hansu out.

Perhaps their relationship had become chilly through Tatsukichi's fault, but Hansu could not help but feel a sense of complicity. This very feeling of complicity was the actual cause of their estrangement. In the end, two weeks would go by without their even meeting once.

When Hansu returned from Yoshiko's house in Yayoichō to Morikawachō where he lived, he sometimes cut through Tokyo University, just as he used to do in the past. With his wedding to Yoshiko less than three weeks away, he might have taken this shortcut on a whim, from old habit, and for no special reason. Up until then, he had tended to avoid places where he might run into Tatsukichi, and the path that ran from the back gate to the Red Gate of Tokyo University was especially freighted with memories. He always felt guilty when he avoided the places that he and Tatsukichi had once frequented.

Hearing the sound of footsteps on the gravel, he looked up and saw the huge, dark shadow of Tatsukichi barring his path. When the latter stared directly at him, he looked as though he was carrying the weight of the world on his shoulders. When the two men drew closer, Tatsukichi casually suggested, "How about a cup of coffee?" His tone of voice was unchanged from the days when they had been like brothers. Because of the circumstances of their meeting, Hansu felt his old feelings awaken in his heart. He had once read an article about the heady smell of the Durian fruit, and he immediately associated it with Tatsukichi and the pungent odor of his beloved Kiriaji cigarettes. The dark, dense shadow of Tatsukichi seemed to enfold him anew, and it sometimes cast a cloud over his face even when he was with Yoshiko.

Hansu read Tatsukichi's latest stories, which were published every month either in *Bungei* or *Kaen* literary journals,[7] or even in both in the same month. Some of these stories, such as "Paolo" and "Sade's Descendants," portrayed a sadistic male protagonist. Hansu was frightened

---

7. *Bungei* is the real title of a literary magazine but—so far as I have been able to determine—*Kaen* is a fictional name.

when he realized that they always featured a character like the author and a young man like himself. He felt even more nervous when he came across recent photos of Tatsukichi appearing occasionally in these periodicals. One showed Tatsukichi in the middle of a group of friends, who were all smiling, while he alone looked somber. His unsmiling eyes made Hansu feel uneasy. Tatsukichi always opened his eyes wide when he smiled, but he wore a different look in these photos. In one photo of a few writers all facing the camera, he had such a frightening look that Hansu was startled. Tatsukichi was handsome, but like a Frenchman, he had strikingly individual features that could make his face seem distorted and ugly. Hansu knew from experience that Tatsukichi's eyes could sometimes take on an intimidating look, but he had never seen anything quite this disturbing. He even wondered whether this truly was the same person, and he blinked his eyes and then took a second look. This time, he felt as if these eyes could see right through him, boring right through his soul; he could hardly breathe. He ended up stuffing the periodical under a stack of magazines to the side of his bookshelf. The same issue carried another picture that showed Tatsukichi in profile at a banquet, with slouching shoulders and lonely, not himself at all.

Both his recent fictional works and these dubious photos inflicted an emotional wound in Hansu's heart. However, even as he felt anguish, he found it easy to rid his mind of this type of impression. He had a flair for forgetting things and he sometimes carelessly consigned to oblivion the very memories he strove to treasure.

People were puzzled that Tatsukichi and Hansu appeared alone in separate venues and asked them questions, but Tatsukichi dismissed them with an ironic smile, saying "That guy is a traitor" and changed the subject. When Hansu was asked, he looked flustered and mumbled something like "these days we hardly ever seem to meet . . . I . . ." Those more familiar with his situation would rib him, "I guess you are too busy now with your romance, right?" If they kept on his case, he turned aside, running his fingers through his freshly shampooed hair, and a youthful blush spread over his face.

Hansu sometimes bumped into Tatsukichi at social functions in the publishing world, and the latter would come up to him and behave exactly as before, engaging in small talk and laughing. The two caught the same taxi to go home, and Tatsukichi dropped him off at his apartment. Inside the car, Tatsukichi sometimes asked a few curt questions about the Yatsuka family, but he otherwise avoided eye contact and kept silent. At such moments, he did not appear moody, let alone frightening. He behaved in a natural way, without a trace of coldness or unkindness. The difference was that Tatsukichi, who had always turned toward Hansu in the past, turned away from him now, though not in a conspicuous way; in other respects, he behaved exactly the same.

However, on this particular day, he spoke just as he used to before they broke up, and he completely dropped his reserved manner of the previous six months. And Hansu felt it was perfectly natural and proper for him to do so.

"Okay." Hansu replied, just as he had before, and he started to walk side by side with Tatsukichi.

They passed in front the university library and then left the campus through the Red Gate. In the afternoon light of late summer, the brick buildings of Tokyo University and the dusty pavement looked parched. After crossing the Train Street, they headed toward Sakanamachi. The coffee shop Bel Ami was only three blocks away, close to the Agricultural College.

Tatsukichi didn't ask Hansu whether he was on his way back from the Yatsukas' home. Hansu shot him a side look, but then he looked down and kept walking. Deep in his heart, he had the uncanny sense that the reel of fate had rewound to the exact place it had stood a half year earlier.

Suddenly, Tatsukichi asked, "So when will the wedding take place?"

"On the fifth day of next month . . ."

"Hmm."

That was all, and he fell silent again.

When they arrived at the entrance to Bel Ami, Tatsukichi walked in first, just as he had always done in the past.

The interior was dark and empty, but it was like that most of the time. On that day, there was a student who sat at a table by the entrance and drank a cup of coffee. He was soon finished and got up to leave. Tatsukichi ordered for the two of them, "Please bring us two iced coffees." The waiter, a young man with a short, pointed chin and a carefree manner, disappeared behind the shop's partition. After a short interval, he poured the freshly brewed coffee into a shaker, and you could hear the noise it made as it blended with ice. Everything was exactly as it had been six months ago. Tatsukichi was fond of iced coffee without sugar, served freezing cold. Hansu added as much sugar as he liked to his coffee from the sugar bowl on the table. Hansu found it both strange and utterly natural that everything was exactly the way it used to be.

Hansu wore a wine-red, monogrammed tie and gray chalk-stripe summer suit made by a tailor at a Ginza department store where Yoshiko and her mother, Yatsuka Sugako, had taken him. His cream-white shirt, which had rounded collar ends, was the only part of his outfit that reflected Tatsukichi's taste. Everything else—the beige pigskin wallet he carried in an inner pocket of his coat, a present from Yoshiko, a shoehorn made of the same material hidden in a secret pouch in his trousers, a white linen handkerchief, monogrammed in white, hidden in his breast pocket—attested to the influence of his new environment, but when he rejoined Tatsukichi and reentered the milieu that he used to frequent, these new additions tended to adjust effort-lessly to Tatsukichi's style.

The waiter brought them their coffees and Tatsukichi sent him out on an errand to buy cigarettes. Tatsukichi always carried Kiriaji[8] around with him wherever he went, but he never actually bought them himself. He sent the waiter to a shop on the corner of Sanchōme, which carried foreign brands of tobacco.

Hansu sat slightly turned to the side and with his legs crossed. He wore tight-fitting, tailored trousers, resembling those popular among members of the beat generation. With his pale hand on his knees, he looked as though he was troubled by an obscure premonition. When he sat down at first, he quickly looked up to meet Tatsukichi's glance, but then he looked away. Tatsukichi threw his right hand over the back of the chair and looked down at Hansu with an aggressive look, just like a wild animal facing his prey, but his look also suggested the utter desola-tion and loneliness that pervaded his soul.

Hansu noticed that Tatsukichi was looking at him with his strangely large, "demonic" eyes—Hansu had given them that label when he started to get used to Tatsukichi.

"So the wedding ceremony takes place on the fifth. I guess all the arrangements have already been finalized."

Surprised, Hansu glanced up at him.

"So you're going to stab me in the back . . . You know exactly what you're doing, don't you?"

---

8. A popular brand of Camel cigarettes in the 1960s.

Tatsukichi paused for a long time before answering.

"If you were to chop my heart up into little pieces and serve it up to your in-laws, it would be the perfect wedding present . . . That's how I honestly feel now."

Hansu hid his face and bit his lips furiously, but he kept silent.

After a short pause, Tatsukichi continued: "You heard what I just said, didn't you?" Hansu bit his lips and turned away. Tears welled up under his long eyelashes, which made his eyes look shut. Tatsukichi asked Hansu what was the matter, and then continued, "You realize you've betrayed me."

Tears flowed in two zigzags down his cheeks. His red lips trembled as though he were feverish, but he chewed them frantically to hide his distress. The wings of his nose looked tense and his earlobes burned bright red.

The river of silence flowed on.

Tatsukichi gazed intently at Hansu, but then he turned away.

"Well, I don't really care. Do whatever you like."

Tatsukichi spoke in a totally different, much warmer tone of voice. Hansu heard him lift a coffee cup and then, after taking a sip, place it back down on the table. Tatsukichi leaned back in his seat and turned his half-closed eyes toward the ceiling. He had also wept, and his eyes were dry like those of someone who has run out of tears.

Hansu stood up.

"Hey."

When Hansu turned around, the whiteness of Tatsukichi's handkerchief flashed painfully in his slightly bloodshot eyes. He took the proffered handkerchief and walked quickly to the washroom at the back of the café.

The door opened, and the waiter walked in and brought Tatsukichi his can of Camel tobacco and his change.

"Thanks for all your trouble."

After receiving his change and the cigarette container from the waiter, Tatsukichi settled the bill by leaving a few coins right on top of the bill. Hansu came back just as Tatsukichi reached for a book in a cellophane wrapper published by Hakusuisha[9] that was on the side shelf. Behind him, the lights switched on. Hansu raised his eyes to look at Tatsukichi but then lowered them immediately, but Tatsukichi felt

---

9. A publisher of translations of foreign literature in Japan.

pity when he saw his reddened face, from which traces of tears had been washed away. Examining him as though to read what lay behind this pathetic expression, Tatsukichi picked up the can and the package and stood up ready to leave.

Hansu darted a glance at Tatsukichi, loosened his tightly knotted necktie with his finger, as he was wont to do, and then followed him out of the shop.

"I left the check on the table."

"Thank you very much."

They could hear the waiter answering them from behind their backs.

Although Hongō Avenue was already dark, the dried pavement glowed faintly white, and seemed to narrow as it stretched in front of them like a belt. Tatsukichi's face was slightly pale. For the two men, everything now looked different than before: the yellow sign of the bus stop, the dusty foliage of the gingko trees, the red bricks, the dark gray shadows cast by other pedestrians, a red dog wagging its tail as it walked alongside two people.

When they were walking side by side, Tatsukichi stood five centimeters taller than Hansu. They walked in silence, like two brothers who had reconciled after a quarrel. By force of habit, they headed toward Sanchōme.

On some days, Tatsukichi, who lived in a house in Asakachō, would stop by Hansu's apartment in Morikawachō, or else Hansu would invite him over. At times, they would pick up a bag of fruit and spend the day chatting over a cup of coffee at Bel Ami. Generally, however, after they cut through Sanchōme to Yamashita, they went to the Eden Bar in Ikenohata to have beer. At night, they took a taxi home, or if it was still daylight and the weather were nice, they climbed the hill to Yayoichō, cut through Tokyo University, and Tatsukichi brought Hansu back to his apartment. That was their regular course for two years.

"Please let me see your face. Your eyes still look funny," Tatsukichi said with a lightly humorous inflection to his voice.

Hansu looked up at him, but he then hid his eyes in the deep shadow cast by his eyelashes.

He wrapped a white scarf around his neck, which was slender for a man. His earlobes, still red and not yet returned to their normal color, suggested that he was still upset. It was a mental state peculiar to Hansu, in which joy blended with pain and fear in a volatile mixture, a condition common among women. He hardly ever engaged in introspection and he had an uncommon talent for taking things easy. He could betray someone without giving the matter a second thought, and afterward he could play the innocent. When Tatsukichi thought about his character, he felt a surge of violent hatred well up inside. He would not breathe easily until he had managed to drag him back to his side, no matter what the cost.

While Tatsukichi was separated from Hansu, he had once caught sight of him strolling on the Ginza. Hansu played with panache his new role as the son-in-law about to enter the family of a business mogul. As he walked along the street, he eyed his surroundings complacently, his eyes wide open and his eyebrows lifted; he wore a necktie that perfectly matched his handkerchief, and he looked as if Tatsukichi no longer existed for him. After this chance encounter, Tatsukichi felt as if he were on fire; he wanted to grab hold of Hansu and tell him off. But even if he did so, he realized that he would be behaving no differently than a jealous woman and he was overcome with a desolate sadness. Then he began to pity himself and realized he had to do something, but his sad mood darkened the light of his reason. Again, Tatsukichi felt a senseless, pointless impulse to tell Hansu off. Then, like someone who sits in a warm bath after a long walk in the cold and feels the blood rush back to the tips of his fingertips, he could not prevent himself from falling into a sweet dreamlike state. Tatsukichi needed to exercise considerable self-discipline to curb his impulses.

The easy path would be for Tatsukichi to punish Hansu and to divulge the way he really felt. However, after he had spent six months without a single pleasant meeting with Hansu, Tatsukichi began to despair about the success of his plan. He felt that his heart was directly exposed to the cold winds of the world. Even before he opened his mouth, he felt a stir of anxiety in his breast, vague but nonetheless real. When he considered how unreliable and capricious Hansu was, he lost any confidence in his ability to gauge whether Hansu had already assimilated to his new environment.

He thought, "Just the same, this little bird is mine. I must not loosen the net and let him fly away. I have no doubt that Yoshiko is completely infatuated with him. And there is something likeable and easygoing about him after all."

When they reached Sanchōme, Tatsukichi said, "Let's walk all the way to Yamashita."

"Sure . . ."

He could still detect some hesitation in the boy's voice, which still vibrated with suppressed sobs and hiccoughs.

The road up the hill was dark.

"I won't tease you any more. Or do you still plan to betray me?"

Hansu looked at Tatsukichi sadly, and then he looked down again. Tatsukichi put his hand on his shoulder.

"I give up. Let's go to Eden. They have sandwiches there. I need a drink."

They turned back in the direction of the Sanchōme where the neon street lamps flickered, and walked down the hill.

From that day, the two men returned to their old relationship. When Tatsukichi reached into his wallet to pay the bill at Eden, he handed Hansu a ticket for the prerelease screening of *The Virgin*.

• • •

When Hansu entered his apartment, he lay face up on his bed without removing his rumpled sports coat. Under the light cast by the stand lamp that he switched on before collapsing onto the bed, you could see the slight shadow that his small chin cast over his neck, which appeared to be twisted to one side under the glaring light. He placed his white hand on his chest. His heart was still pounding. His hand dropped off his chest, and his supple, slim body undulated gently like that of a snake, but then he returned to his previous posture. He put his hand over his heart again and kept it there. After the swelling receded, his eyes were filled with an erotic, feminine charm and his pupils seemed to hide behind the curtain of his upper eyelid.

Suddenly, he dropped his hand wearily to the bed and fixed his sparkling eyes on one spot. He thought, "I don't think that we are in a carnal relationship, like the little Greek slut and the aristocratic woman that Tatsukichi spoke about in *Dorian Gray*. When Tatsukichi talks about flirting, he always means that flirting is seductive and demonical. I never imagined that I would experience something like today. I felt suffocated, as if I could not breathe. It was so painful. . . . If I had known we would meet, I would not have gone there. I could have easily escaped into the crowd. Still, I had a feeling that something like this would happen. For a long time, I had a sort of premonition. Perhaps . . ."

Hansu pressed his throat and pushed one side of his face into the pillow, but his dark eyes remained fixed on the light of the lamp, which shone like a flame. He thought: "Will I go and visit Yoshiko two more times? Tatsukichi told me he will wait at Bel Ami and that I could meet him there afterward. Once that is over, all I need to do is to send her a letter and Tatsukichi promised he would write it for me. After that, we will be together and go away on a trip. . . ."

When he bent one of his legs, which felt numb, he saw that the things he had distractedly taken out of his pocket and thrown on the bed—his wallet, his fountain pen—were tangled in his white linen handkerchief, which was just a short distance from his foot in its deep-red nylon stocking with a black design. As a drowning man whose legs are caught in seaweed wriggles and thrashes to free himself, Hansu used his foot to kick the handkerchief under the bed, but it remained stuck at the edge of the bed cover and would not budge.

"Tatsukichi will stay by my side. What do I have to fear? He will be my strong accomplice." Hansu whispered these words to himself, as though to convince himself of their truth.

He tossed and turned and finally pulled the blanket over his head. Even then, he continued to wriggle under the covers most of the night as though he were in agony.

• • •

The next morning, Tatsukichi, dark circles under his eyes from lack of sleep, propped the upper part of his body against the bed, leaning his elbows on his pillow, and puffed away at a cigarette.

Noticing that the ashes were about to fall from the cigarette, he bent over to one side and put the cigarette out in the ashtray on a side table, and lit a new one. He had not shut the French windows, so they swung open and shut when the wind blew, making a sound like that of an oar hitting the side of a boat. Along with the smell of the match he had struck, the strong odor of gin rose over the smoldering ashtray. The bottle of gin that he had brought back from Eden, half empty, shone crystal clear in the morning light. A fountain pen and a box of matches lay on top of a pile of manuscript papers, while two completed articles, seven or eight pages in length, fastened with a metal clasp, lay on the back of the bed. There were two light brown, dried laurel leaves in a dark green glass jar by the side of the window, and they stirred and then fell back in the wind. Tatsukichi kicked off his blanket, which was checkered with large brown and dark-green squares, and ran his hand through his thick, jet-black hair, then, after looking down at the table with his bloodshot eyes, he jumped up and went into the bathroom. After showering and putting on a shirt, he returned to the room and closed the window, and poured himself another cup of gin as he leaned against the back of the bed.

He suddenly imagined he could see Hansu in his room. It was as though he was watching him as he slept, with his necktie and jacket scattered untidily on the bed.

"He must be sleeping like a baby now."

Then Tatsukichi felt as if a bolt of electricity had gone through his body. When he pulled his lips away from the cup of gin, a dark flame of ecstasy seemed to glow in his eyes. Tatsukichi, who had drunk gin and whiskey almost nonstop the previous night at Eden, nearly collapsed against Han's shoulder as they had stumbled toward the exit of the bar. Though Hansu had slender shoulders, he was much more solidly built, resilient, and powerful than his slight body might lead one to think. At that moment, Tatsukichi could not help but think of a chef who peels off the shell of a live prawn and uses a knife to remove the sinews in preparation for cooking.

They went outside and he hailed a taxi. Tatsukichi let Hansu get in first and climbed in after him and shut the door, but he then realized that he was much drunker than usual. He stretched out his arm behind Hansu's back and hid his face in his arm. His head bobbed up when the taxi hit a bump so that he almost rubbed Hansu' forehead with his own.

Hansu had not yet recovered from the shock he had received from Tatsukichi. On top of that, they had laid their secret plans to deal with the Yatsuka family. Tatsukichi promised him, "I'll wait for you at Bel Ami while you are at the Yatsuka house," but he felt crushed by an overpowering fear. Once, at Eden, when he was slow responding to Tatsukichi's question, the latter pushed him away cruelly, saying, "Let's forget all about it since you are still frightened in spite of my willingness to help. You might as well just go on as before." Hansu collapsed onto the divan and put his frail hand near Tatsukichi's knee. Tatsukichi placed Hansu's hand on top of his own knee and fondled it playfully. "You'd better pluck up courage. Don't think I don't care about what happens. I am pretty nervous since you are involved," Tatsukichi said; he used his left hand to fill his cup to the rim, even as he continued to hold Hansu's hand.

Nestling in the refuge formed by Tatsukichi's arm and his chest,

Hansu calmed down and grew mawkish, as though he had found a place of refuge. All of a sudden, the car made a violent jerk, pushing Hansu even deeper into Tatsukichi's chest, but he made no effort to pull himself up. Tatsukichi let Hansu nestle against his chest, while he dropped his head against the back of the seat; his pale forehead took on a hazy, ecstatic look but his bright eyes looked sad. As the car moved forward through the city, passing neon lights would light up his eyes or the shadow of some dark object would cast thick, wavering stripes over his face.

The car began to climb the steep road up the hill. Tatsukichi looked up and buried his fingers in Hansu's hair, pretending he was nursing a sick man. His head remained nestled in Tatsukichi's chest as though he had passed out. Groping his way in the dark, Tatsukichi placed one hand under Hansu's chin and turned him around so that he was facing up right under his gaze. He looked like an ailing child, with his eyes enfolded by double lids that looked deep, as though carved. He looked straight at Tatsukichi, whom he both trusted and feared to the very marrow of his bones. Like a child in a primitive tribe, who watches apprehensively as a doctor rubs an ointment into a wound caused by a poisoned arrow, Hansu kept lowering and raising his eyelids over his light brown, transparent eyes. He looked as if he wanted to ask a question. Perhaps because he was tired of looking, he turned his expressionless eyes downward. His half-open lips had lost their natural gloss.

Tatsukichi felt his whole body melt in his compassion for Hansu and encircled his cheeks with his hands. He touched him with his fingertips as a little girl might caress a cherished but fragile pet that a careless movement of her hand might crush to death. His gaze softened and his lips relaxed into a smile. When he looked down again, he could sense the well-being and emotional dependence in the boy's eyes.

Apart from a small puppy that Tatsukichi had loved and lost when he was very young, he had never seen anything so adorable in his entire life. He thought, "I want to put all my passion and all the thoughts of my lifetime into this kiss so that I will dissolve and disappear in selfless love. As long as I possess Hansu I don't need anything else in life. I would be willing to die for him. Hansu was born with a woman's soul and he probably has a feminine nature. For that reason, he is sometimes prone to hysteria like just now." Suddenly Tatsukichi smiled ironically. "The big question is whether I can free myself from all the other spiritual entanglements that bind me when the time comes. Before I die,

I want to write many more novels in which I can play with the fate of human beings like a puppeteer with his puppets. But nothing separates Hansu from me now," he thought. There are no longer any days or months. There is no public opinion to pay heed to. We are just two individuals, joined in a relationship that unites fellow human beings. At last, my endless solitude is over. Tatsukichi was roused by spiritual exaltation and sexual excitation at the same time. Now the boy's mouth was half open, and the cavity formed by his lips cast a small shadow. Until a moment ago, they looked like the innocent lips of a baby sucking at his mother's breast, but now they were already imprinted with the fear and pain of the past twelve hours. Besides being worried about what the driver might think, Tatsukichi was afraid to do anything that would traumatize Hansu.

Tatsukichi leaned forward over Hansu, placed the palm of his hand on his forehead to see if he was feverish, and in the shadow cast by his hand, imprinted a kiss on Hansu's forehead. He moved Hansu back to his former position leaning against his chest, and then he told the driver that his friend was feeling sick and told him to slow down. He dropped Hansu off at his apartment.

• • •

Hansu sat down softly on the bed and tried the new gloves on his white hands—they were moss green with a slight hint of yellow, and made of goatskin.

A week had passed since the dreamlike experience he had the day before the film screening. After the screening, Tatsukichi took him to a tailor shop in the Ginza to be measured for a loose-fitting, chestnut overcoat with raglan sleeves, and he had picked out gloves to match the day before also in the Ginza, right after his first visit to the Yatsuka's house. Hansu stood in front of the mirror wearing the moss-green stitched gloves on his two slender hands and he looked at his reflection, gently clenching and unclenching his hands. Because of his recent distress, he was pale, but his face was as handsome as usual with the slightly wide gap between his eyes. His lips were a light shade of pink. He smiled complacently when he pictured how he would look in his expensive chestnut overcoat and wondered if it would match his gloves and face. A touch of color spread to the area around his ears as well.

After taking off his gloves, he tousled his freshly washed hair with his white fingers and scratched the back of his ear with his left hand after he sat down on the bed. When he looked up, his eyes wore a seductive expression, and slight folds appeared at the corners of his lips. Letting himself fall back on the bed, he whispered to himself with brightly shining eyes: "Tatsukichi says that he will buy a new bed for me. People might think it strange if we sleep in the same bed."

Before he had gone to the Yatsukas' house the night before, he met Tatsukichi at Bel Ami and they sat side by side in a booth. While the waiter was working in the back of the shop, Tatsukichi gave Hansu a passionate, burning kiss that pinned him back against the seat. More than feeling merely surprised, Hansu had the sense of being overwhelmed by a staggering force. Like a good Burgundy, the kiss was at once astringent and sweet. He felt at first as if he were being bitten, leaving him no leisure to reflect on the weirdness or abnormality of the moment. Hansu felt his heart pound when he noticed the intrepid look in Tatsukichi's eyes, the fire of love in his lips, and the half-smiling expression he wore when he pulled back. After seeing the face of his yearned-for lover, he looked at the objects on the white tablecloth of the table, which was dim even in daylight—the translucent pale-green of the half-finished bottle of ginger ale, the plates with nothing but parsley sprigs and a few wedges of sandwiches left, the glass with a few remaining ice cubes, the used matches, the can of Kiriaji cigarettes. Everything looked different to his eyes after that passionate moment. He inhabited a welcoming and wistful world, filled with the familiar fragrance of Kiriaji, and utterly trustworthy.

"Today, you have to be unfaithful to me, but we will pass the night together, okay?" Tatsukichi said as he pressed his hand firmly, as if to encourage him to carry out what he had promised, and Hansu left the shop. Hansu felt a furtive chill of terror run up his spine when Tatsukichi continued to hold his hand firmly in his grip even after he tried to pull his own hand away. He blushed and furrowed his brows, while he gazed at Tatsukichi with a look of supplication.

"You want to get it over with quickly, don't you?" Tatsukichi smiled as he loosened his grip.

That night, the weather grew chilly and the glass entrance to Bel Ami was fogged up. At ten past nine o'clock, just ten minutes later than they had agreed, Hansu opened the door of Bel Ami with an anxious expression in his eyes.

"She has no idea what's going on but she definitely senses that something is wrong."

"It's fine just like that," Tatsukichi said, and then he turned his head to the waiter and said, "Two hot coffees, please." He looked back at Hansu.

"It's fine that she is beginning to catch on. Even if she does, there's no reason to think that anything is going to happen. You understand, don't you? How many times have I explained this to you?"

"Umm."

"She has nothing left to do but resign herself to fate."

When Hansu finished the hot coffee, he seemed to have calmed down, and the two men finally left Bel Ami, drove to the Ginza to buy a pair of gloves, and then stopped at the Silver Spoon, a restaurant that Tatsukichi frequented and that was famous for its soups, where they had a light dinner before going home. Hansu forgot all about his anxiety in the middle of the warm atmosphere of the room in the Silver Spoon, in which the unmoving flame of a candle cast its light on the thick, tan cups, the Russian-style meat soup in a silver bowl on a wooden tray, and the big silver spoon.

Sitting at their table in the corner of the room with a pot of white flowers, a heavy silver fork, and a spirit lamp set on a silver plate, he watched as Tatsukichi laughed and cut the bread and listened to Tatsukichi talk about the first half of *Bruges La Mort*. ("The second half is really boring, you know," he added.)[10]

Tatsukichi was well versed in French literature, but now he wrote mainly fiction. The novel in question was about a man who cuts off the beautiful, almost flaxen hair of his deceased lover and preserves it in a decorated glass box. When he started to talk about the description of the beautiful girl, he was carried away with enthusiasm and he cast a voracious gaze at Hansu's face.

"Are you really interested in this?"

"Sure . . . French writers—or was he Belgian? They really wrote some amazing things."

"Yes, there are some really great lines in the work. Things such as 'A kiss that does not forget to be cunning even in the midst of danger.' I can understand exactly what they mean. How about you?"

After saying this, he smiled.

---

10. *Bruges-la-Morte* is a short novel by the Belgian writer Georges Rodenbach, first published in 1892. It is still remembered as a famous novel of the Symbolist school and for its innovative use of photography, with thirty-five photos of Bruges inserted in the text.

When they got into the car to go back home, Hansu was seized by another anxiety attack, and Tatsukichi said, "Cheer up, Hansu. You only need to meet her one more time. The end result will be the same whether you worry or not. You realize that, don't you? Even if things end badly, I'll be there with you. And it's not your fault if something bad happens. Nor is it mine, either. This is just the natural course of events. You understand me, don't you? . . ."

Hansu moved his shoulder closer to Tatsukichi's breast. As he watched the city lights recede behind them through the back window, he felt like a small bird nestled under the wing of a much larger one. The sense of being sheltered under a large wing persisted throughout the entire night, as Tatsukichi assaulted him and kept him warm. By dawn, Hansu, who had fallen asleep, wore a sweet and peaceful expression on his face as though stroked by feathers in a gentle caress.

Hansu recollected the sweet but disturbing dreams that had continued the previous day until the night, put his moss-green gloves on the side of the lamp on the bookshelf, and began to get ready to go out for his promised dinner with Tatsukichi.

• • •

On the day of his final visit, Tatsukichi borrowed a car from his friend and, at nine sharp, he was parked just outside the wall that surrounded the Yatsuka residence. Hansu asked him to accompany him, and in fact Tatsukichi was impatient to snatch him away from the Yatsuka family forever.

Fifteen minutes after the agreed time, Hansu and Yoshiko walked outdoors, their bodies intertwined, and Tatsukichi lowered the visor of his hunting cap over his eyes.

Hansu said, "Why do you talk like that? You know I'll come again . . ."

"I'm sorry. But, to be honest, you looked as though you were bidding farewell forever."

"Well . . . People always feel they may be meeting for the last time when they say goodbye. But I will definitely be there on Sunday . . . In fact, I can hardly wait to see you."

"But Hansu . . . I do feel that we are parting for the last time . . ."

Hansu noticed the parked car, as he reached for Yoshiko's shoulder. He drew her toward him and looked around. Paying attention to nothing else, Yoshiko yielded herself to Hansu and held onto his raincoat with her small hands. Hansu put one arm around her back, and with the other, he patted her head buried in his chest. She made no effort to lift her head, and Hansu coaxingly placed his hand under her chin and helped her up. Tears shone on her eyes and cheeks right under Hansu's eyes.

Pretending to be surprised, he said, "What's the matter, Yoshiko? You know I will be back on Sunday." Soothed by his words, Yoshiko managed a faint smile with her lips, and Hansu, in desperation, covered her face with hot, passionate kisses. He felt as though he was locked in the embrace of a frightening force from behind his back.

When she pulled away from his kiss, Yoshiko hid her face again in Hansu's chest, as though embarrassed, and he looked furtively in the direction of the car. He could see two men walking toward them from behind the car.

"Some people are coming this way . . ."

They pulled apart, but still held hands and looked into each other's eyes. At that instant, Yoshiko first noticed the parked car and, to escape being seen, she hurried back to the gate. From there, she looked into Hansu's eyes as she made a gesture to rearrange her hair.

"For sure," she said, and then she turned on her heels and walked through the gate.

After looking at the car, Hansu watched until he could no longer see Yoshiko's retreating figure. She never turned back once.

Hansu hesitated for a moment but then walked toward the car.

He got in through the front door that Tatsukichi had opened, took out his handkerchief, and vigorously wiped his lips.

"I was afraid . . . I felt as if something frightening was embracing me from behind, just when I kissed her." After Hansu said this, he leaned against Tatsukichi's shoulder as though he had lost courage. Tatsukichi pushed him away and said, "What you really mean to say is you were afraid of me, right?"

"Not at all. You know better than that."

Checking his watch, Tatsukichi said, "She might become suspicious if I start the car too soon."

"Not at all."

The car drove past the front of the Yatsuka residence, turned at an intersection a little way ahead, and then passed by Tokyo University.

After he started the car, Tatsukichi said, "We're going to my place tonight, right?"

Hansu said, "Sure," then twisted his body around and looked at the road behind them. He wore a dark-blue gabardine raincoat that enveloped him up to his chin, and you could see his pale cheeks, his slightly crooked, slender nose, and his pointed lips peeking out above the collar. Even though Tatsukichi was busy driving the car, he twisted his neck to the side, looked down, almost grazing Han's cheeks, and said. "Keep still now. It's still not safe."

As he turned his head back, Hansu felt burned by the dark sparks that Tatsukichi's eyes seem to give off. Tatsukichi had observed them kissing without so much as flinching, but his eyes seemed to shoot flames when he looked at Hansu wrapped in his thick raincoat.

Hansu returned to his former position and leaned against Tatsukichi's shoulder. He touched his white hand softly to Tatsukichi's thigh while his hair, plastered against his face, rubbed against Tatsukichi's cheeks like the fur of a puppy. The car went up Dangozaka and veered onto Sakanamachi. As he was about to turn the corner at a bank located near his own house, Tatsukichi said, "You have really made up your mind, come what may," just as the car took the curve. Hansu stiffened his body and hid his face against Tatsukichi's shoulder.

• • •

On Saturday afternoon, Hansu was in Tatsukichi's room. The next day was Sunday, the day he had promised to meet Yoshiko. Wearing a sweater with an ivory-colored collar and grayish jeans, Hansu was trying out the key to the new suitcase Tatsukichi had bought and was engrossed with his other presents as well: a new blanket and towel, pajamas made of white terrycloth, and a travel brush. From time to time, a look of anxiety passed over his face and his hand was frozen.

On Friday morning, after he moved into the house, he wrote a letter to Yoshiko at Tatsukichi's dictation. It was terribly short. He jotted down the words, but Tatsukichi actually composed the letter, which was not at all in Hansu's style.

"I am not going this Sunday. I have decided to put an end to our engagement. Over the past month, I have changed my mind about our relationship. I still feel the same friendship for you. Please don't think badly of me. Things have just turned out badly."

Hansu was sent to pick up stationery at his apartment in Morikawachō. He wrote at the same table where they had just had breakfast. The instant he saw Tatsukichi's draft, he felt an irresistible curiosity about what was going to happen next and wrote the words effortlessly.

After he was done, he threw away the pen, as though he had been holding a disgusting insect by his fingertips. Then he walked away from the table and lay down on the bed. He watched anxiously as Tatsukichi put the letter in an envelope and sealed it.

Tatsukichi dipped his pen into the ink and brought it to him, but when Hansu wrote out Yoshiko's address on the envelope, he was trembling so hard that he had to rewrite it twice. Then they went out for a morning walk, entered Bel Ami, and entrusted to the waiter the task of dropping the letter in a mailbox.

Delighted by the touch of his soft white pajamas, Hansu lifted his arms to rub its fine material against his cheeks, but then, letting his arms drop, he returned to the bedroom, and lay back down on the bed. He looked up at Tatsukichi with a troubled look.

"It must have arrived there by now."

"They probably got it this morning."

Hansu heaved a sigh and then lay on his back.

"What's wrong?"

Sitting down beside him, Tatsukichi loosened the front buttons of his pajama top, stuck his hand inside, and put it just above Hansu's heart. When Hansu lay on his back, his small chin made a delicate shadow, but he soon turned to face the wall and his neck moved to the side. He twisted his body slightly.

"Don't put your hand there. It makes my heart pound."

Tatsukichi pulled away, and instead he quietly pressed his ear against Hansu's heart.

"My darling Hansu is alive," he thought.

He was gripped by a feeling of joy but also by sorrow; his own heart began to race with anxiety.

He stretched out on the bed beside Hansu and placed his hand back on his chest. Hansu covered Tatsukichi's hand with his own and time slowly flowed by as they lay there peacefully.

Then, after running his fingers through Hansu's hair, Tatsukichi pulled his hand away and sat up.

Looking up at him, Hansu said, "I'll be fine no matter what happens."

"Awfully brave, aren't you?"

Tatsukichi picked up his watch from the edge of the bed, stood up, and began to walk toward the door. "It's three o'clock now. How would you like to have cornichon à la Tatsukichi? I have some ham and cheese, too."

The doorbell rang just as Tatsukichi walked into the hall. He frowned. He could tell from the muffled sound the bell made that the visitor had to be an older bourgeois woman, the type of person who hardly ever visited his home.

The visitor turned out to be Yatsuka Sukako. She wore a white turtle-neck sweater and black slacks, and a casual overcoat with double black stripes on a dark gray ground. Sukako looked straight at Tatsukichi, who stood with his hands in his pockets, as she made a deep bow and introduced herself: "My name is Yatsuka Sukako. I am the mother of Yoshiko who—you may be aware—is engaged to marry Itō Hansu. Actually, I have come here because I would like to talk with you . . . regarding Hansu. I apologize for my rudeness in visiting you when you are no doubt busy . . ."

"Oh, please come in." Tatsukichi led her into his study, where he escorted her to an armchair and sat down on the bed. Hansu stood up as if he wanted to leave the room, but as soon as he recognized Sukako, he was frozen to the spot. From the entrance, you could see a door in the back that led to the bathroom on the left and the bedroom on the right. Hansu was just about to pass though the back door when Tatsukichi ordered: "Stay where you are. She came here because of you."

His tone brooked no resistance.

He looked at Tatsukichi, as if to beg his permission to leave, but then stood where he was, with downcast eyes and one hand lying on the back of the bed. After glaring at Hansu, Sukako turned to Tatsukichi and began to speak as she folded her hands over her knee.

"This morning, we received a letter from Hansu . . . We had already made arrangements to hold the wedding ceremony a few days from today, but his sudden letter announced that he had decided to call off the engagement. Why did he suddenly change his mind? Just a few days ago—I was not at home during his last visit—he left our home as though nothing whatsoever had changed, or so I am told . . . My daughter is past the point of tears, she is utterly speechless, and has gone into retreat. (Just then, she clasped her slender hands, from which an emerald ring shone.) I speak as a mother who has known her daughter for many years . . . Before my daughter first met Hansu, I understand that you were his mentor. Since you probably know more about the situation, I would like to ask you to explain it to me, if not to my daughter."

At her wit's end, the woman clenched her pale hands and rubbed them over her knee, then she tightened her grip again and lapsed into silence, as though she had reached an impasse. On the pretext of preparing tea for a guest, Hansu started to walk away from the scene through the back door. However, he remained pinned to the spot when Tatsukichi looked him straight in the eyes, and held on to the back of bed in desperation. The woman turned away from him.

"Did you send a letter to Miss Yatsuka?" asked Tatsukichi, adopting the tone of a person totally uninvolved in the whole affair. Hansu made no reply.

"Is that so? In that case, I understand you must be worried. There is really nothing new that I can tell you. He came here yesterday and said he planned to go on a trip. I must say I found the whole thing rather odd." At that moment, the woman noticed the luxurious suitcase flung down at the foot of the bed, a brand-new, brown-checkered blanket, looking a bit wrinkled, that lay on a table in the back of the room, a white terrycloth pajama that protruded from the suitcase, and scattered around these items, department-store wrapping paper, ribbons, and a small tortoise-shell comb. She looked at Hansu first, and then at Tatsukichi. She had been raised in a wealthy, very strict family, and she was now the wife of the businessman Yatsuka Kiyokichi; she had no other experiences in life to guide her. With the intuition of a woman almost fifty years of age, she sensed there was more than met the eye in the relationship between Tatsukichi and Hansu, even if it were not necessarily shocking and depraved . . . But, otherwise, how could such a thing have happened? She knew there was not a shred of sincerity in Tatsukichi's words. When he asked whether Hansu had sent a letter, he sounded very clever, but looked at from a different angle, the whole affair was highly dubious. After watching the behavior of the two men, she suspected that they had to be accomplices. She felt a chill run down her spine. At the same time, she felt nearly suffocated by the overwhelming spiritual power emanating from Tatsukichi, whom she knew at a glance to be no ordinary man.

She bowed her head deeply and continued to squeeze and massage her hands over and over. At the joint where the fingers joined the palms of her white hand, you could see a red threadlike line that appeared and disappeared. After a while, she looked up at Tatsukichi.

"But there must be some reason why Hansu . . . perhaps there is another woman in his life . . . Of course, Yoshiko had no idea of this person's existence, so I need hardly say that we knew absolutely nothing . . . Please tell me if there is something of this nature . . ."

Wearing a white sweater, Tatsukichi reached out his hand to pick up a Kiriaji cigarette and lit it. On his rough-hewn face, Tatsukichi pursed his lips tightly in a frown. After puffing at his cigarette, he went on without a glance in her direction. "In that case, let me try to find out what is going on. He looks as though he is at a loss what to do, but I bet that there is something behind this. He tends to talk a lot, but he always leaves out the most important part. Of course, he never discusses his private life with me. Our relationship is strictly work-related."

She realized Tatsukichi was an impregnable fortress. She lowered her gaze. The line between her neck and her chest seemed to tighten as she twisted her face slightly toward the entrance and her shoulders narrowed. Her beautiful hair, in which a few stray white hairs could be seen, was done up in a swirl, and it trembled slightly.

Tatsukichi looked at the woman as if to size her up, and then he turned away. He felt overwhelmed by the same desolation he had felt in the dark interior of Bel Ami, when he had put the screws on Hansu. The women's face wore a scowl like a Noh mask, and her shoulders grew narrower. She put her hand to her sleeve as though looking for something. When she had left her house, she had prayed that she would return with good news, and carefully selected clothing likely to bring her good luck. She had worn the same outfit on the betrothal day of her elder son, Kiichi, who now lived with his wife in London. Although the season was a little off, she was pleased to be dressed in the same fashion for this visit. As she touched her hand to the sleeve of her undergarment, she suddenly remembered this and bit her lips. After a few moments lost in thought, she pulled out a handkerchief.

"In that case, I will take my leave. I am so sorry to have disturbed you." The woman placed her indoor slippers neatly side by side, just as people do with Japanese *tabi*, and stood up, covering her face with a handkerchief.

"I am sorry not to have been of any help to you." With one hand in his pocket, Tatsukichi stood up from the bed holding a short cigarette stub in his other hand, and looked at her. She walked toward the entrance without looking back. When she gripped the doorknob with her white hand, she stopped and turned toward him.

Tatsukichi stood there with an invincible expression on his face. A faint note of mockery and impertinence shone in the depth of his dark eyes, so earnest and wide open. His ironical expression also expressed an unshakable pride and self-confidence. People like Tatsukichi suffered from one fatal flaw that inevitably showed on their faces: he could not help but gloat when his friends were victorious and his enemies in a pitiable state. This unfortunate habit in a man of this type was a weakness like the underbelly of the turtle. Although the triumphant look disappeared almost immediately, it nevertheless left a deep sting on her mind. Her eyes blazed like those of a wolf.

She looked straight in his eyes and said: "I cannot tell what people in your set really think. You imagine you live in your own world, a world apart from the normal one that we live in, and assume you are far superior to us. There's no point in your trying to deny it, since I can see it plainly written on your face. Just as you perhaps suppose, we do live in the normal, commonsensical world. But that does not give you the right to treat us like fools. Isn't it rather people like you that deserve to be treated with contempt?"

Tatsukichi tilted his head to one side and looked at her disdainfully. "I have no idea what you are talking about, but you should be more careful in your choice of words when you imply that Hansu and I are living abnormally. Leaving my case aside for the moment, I would remind you that Hansu is still a young man about to make his way in society. He does not have what it takes to be a man of letters, but he is gifted in mathematics, and so I am thinking to steer him in that direction from now on. I ask you, out of common courtesy, to refrain from using language that may injure his future prospects in the world." As he said these words, he noticed ashes hanging from his cigarette and quickly stubbed the cigarette out in an ashtray.

Biting her lips, she looked at Tatsukichi sharply without uttering a word, and then marched out of the room with a firm stride. Tatsukichi made a signal to Hansu and they both saw her to the door. She took some time putting on her gray Japanese sandals (*zōri*), but, as soon as she was ready to leave, she buried her face in her handkerchief and walked toward the gate slowly, even though she was in a great hurry. Eventually, she passed through the gate and her retreating figure disappeared from view.

When she could no longer be seen, Tatsukichi looked back at the place where Hansu was hiding himself and led him back to the room.

"Well, I am glad that's all over." Hansu looked down as Tatsukichi spoke, his youthful lips tightly pursed. Then he passed by the chair where she had sat and stood holding on to the back of the bed.

"Everything went fine. I bet nothing will happen from now on. You have driven a spike right through that girl's heart." Understanding what these horrible words meant, Hansu looked thunderstruck, and he said, "You really do frighten me." "I am so frightening that you probably hate me, right?" Tatsukichi sat on the bed and spoke in a totally different, warm tone of voice, as he looked directly at Hansu. Then he stood up, reached for the bottle of gin in the bookshelf, and poured himself a cup. He turned to Hansu, who gazed fixedly at his big, brawny hands with an expression of fear on his face.

"I will make you some good medicine to bring you around."

His nervous tension somehow relieved, Hansu turned the chair where the woman had sat toward the wall, parked himself on the bed, and pressed his lips to the cup of gin that Tatsukichi had poured and swallowed a mouthful. With the sound of ice cubes rattling, Tatsukichi came into the room carrying a tray with a bottle of Médoc, sugar, and a cup of freshly squeezed lemon, and he put the tray down on the table. Hansu moved out of his way to make room, and Tatsukichi started to make a punch.

"What's wrong? Hansu, what will ever happen to you if I go away?" As before, Hansu just stared off into space, without blinking, like a night bird in a cage covered with a cloth. Tatsukichi handed him a cup filled with punch, but Hansu just shook his head in silence. "Then, would you like some gin?" Hansu nodded and looked up with his dark, coquettish eyes. Drawing closer in silence, he touched Tatsukichi's arm and folded himself in his embrace, hiding his cheek on his arm.

"The pitiful bird of the night that knocks its beak against the windowpane." Tatsukichi suddenly recalled this phrase from Alphonse Daudet's *La Doulou*.[11] He gently released Hansu's hand, and then he placed his own hands on his sides, and pulled him toward his chest. Hansu leaned forward onto Tatsukichi, his body bent over at the waist,

---

11. Alphonse Daudet, 1840–1897, is the author of *La Petite Chose*, *Lettres de mon Moulin*, and many other novels. The line comes from his journal about his long battle with syphilis, *La Doulou* (*doulou* is a word in langue d'oc that means "pain"). This journal, written from 1885 to 1895, was not published until 1930, thirty-three years after Daudet's death. "*Pauvres oiseaux de nuit, battant les murs, les yeux ouverts sans voir . . .* [Poor birds of night, eyes open without seeing, striking the walls . . .]."

and he hid his face in Tatsukichi's chest and edged his hands up his
torso. He softly caressed the back of his neck with both hands. Tatsukichi threw his arms around Han's slender body and he buried his lips
softly in his hair.

After the visit by Mrs. Yatsuka, Hansu stayed inside Tatsukichi's
house and hardly ever went back to his apartment in Morikawachō.
When he went outside, Tatsukichi almost always accompanied him.
He was afraid to leave the house alone, even simply to go the corner
fruit store, because he might run into someone from the Yatsuka family.
Once a week, a maid visited the house and stocked their refrigerator
with sufficient provisions to last until her next visit, but often they
would run out of fresh fruit or other things in the course of the week,
or else go out to buy some seasonal treat. At such times, Tatsukichi
tried to send him out on an errand, but Hansu dared not step outside
the house unless Tatsukichi came with him, and he took advantage of
their daily strolls to shop at the grocery store or even post a letter.

Tatsukichi took Hansu to a movie and dinner on Wednesday, October 5, the day planned for the wedding ceremony between Hansu and
Yoshiko. At about noon, the sky grew dark, but they went out together
in matching navy-blue raincoats under Tatsukichi's umbrella. Hansu
had on a light blue silk necktie, and Tatsukichi wore a tie with diagonal
stripes of dark blue and blood red that peered out through the opening
of his coat. Tatsukichi struck others as a mature man in his forties by
his way of thinking and attitude, but he looked closer to his real age of
thirty-seven thanks to his neckties. The two could pass for brothers or
companions not so far apart in age.

On the main street, they hailed a taxi and got off at Tawarachō
in Asakusa to see the movie. On their way back, they stopped at Fuji
Kitchen,[12] on an alley off the main street between Tawarachō and
Nakamise, and had coffee. Tatsukichi suggested that they stop at Okada
for chicken, but Hansu said that he was not hungry, so they decided to
relax for a while at Fuji Kitchen. An orange lamp lit their way up the
stairs to the second floor, where there were bouquets of fresh flowers on
the tables in this European-style restaurant with patterned wallpaper. At
the table decorated with half-opened roses, Hansu listened as Tatsukichi
talked about a French novel.

---

12. Fuji Kitchen (Fujikichin) is one of the oldest *yōshoku* (Western-style) restaurants in
Tokyo.

After leaving Fuji Kitchen, they decided to go to the Jerusalem Bar in the Ginza, and they walked all the way to Tawarachō to catch a cab. By the time they passed under the overpass at Ueno Station, Hansu said that he did not feel well and leaned against Tatsukichi's shoulder as though he were seriously ill. His face grew pale and cold sweat oozed from his forehead.

"Are you feeling okay? Do you want to get out of the car?"

Hansu just gestured ambiguously in reply. When they reached the entrance to the Keisei Railroad station, Tatsukichi asked the driver to stop and helped Hansu get out and to his feet. When the taxi sped away, heavy rain poured down on them as though a cloud had burst right over their heads. Unfortunately, the only restaurants in the vicinity were stuffy shops that served every imaginable type of food besides coffee and that gave off a stench that turned one's stomach. When they reached Yamashita, the blustery but fine rain covered the entire park district of Ueno in a fine gray spray, including the wide stone staircases, while the hills that surrounded the park seemed to recede and shrink behind the curtain of gray haze. Tatsukichi had his arm wrapped around Hansu's side, but in this weather, one umbrella was about as useful as none at all. Tatsukichi helped him to climb the stone stairs to the Seiyōken restaurant[13] and they finally reached the entrance. He explained the situation to the waiter and they took off their coats and shoes in an anteroom, put on indoor slippers, and borrowed a towel to dry themselves and their clothing. Perhaps Hansu felt revived after being pelted by the cold rain. After a short rest, they entered the dining room.

As Tatsukichi looked over the menu, Hansu whispered to him, "Let's get up and leave now." When he looked up, Hansu gave him a meaningful glance and began to stand up. Turning around, he noticed a short, square man in his early fifties, most likely a successful businessman, who was having dinner at a nearby table. The man was accompanied by colleagues of about the same age, and by one younger man, most likely a secretary, who looked extremely pale. It was Yatsuka Kiyokichi. Though he felt sorry for Hansu, Tatsukichi refused to flee from the scene.

---

13. This restaurant is also the setting of the well-known story "Under Reconstruction" by Mori Ōgai, about a meeting between an older Japanese writer and a middle-aged German woman, presumably a former lover, who visits him.

"We can change places," he said to mollify Hansu, and they switched seats. Kiyokichi recognized Hansu immediately, but he struck an easygoing, comfortable pose and paid no further attention to him. As he cut his bread into smaller pieces and manipulated his fork, he was engrossed in conversation with his companions. Tatsukichi looked at Kiyokichi and realized at once that he must have heard everything about his wife's visit to his home.

Tatsukichi called the waiter and ordered consommé soup, chilled beef with a small salad, raisin pudding, fruit, and coffee. He then took out his notebook and began to jot something down quickly with a serious expression on his face, just as if he were planning a banquet menu or making a list of manuscript deadlines. Then he handed Hansu a message saying that Kiyokichi seemed ignorant of what had happened. Hansu looked distraught, but, fortunately, he noticed that the other party was now having coffee.

At last, after settling the bill, Kiyokichi strode confidently across the room, as a man of his position might walk across his own living room, toward the table where the two were seated near the entrance. He passed their table, then bowed slightly toward Hansu from a distance, and looked straight at him.

"Oh, it's you, Hansu. Please be sure to stop by our house when you have time."

Then he bowed to Tatsukichi and walked out of the room. He seemed to be a man who normally walked with a stoop, but there were other factors at play, too. Since the affair with Hansu, he had probably aged by several years, judging by the expression on his face and his overall demeanor. As Tatsukichi returned his bow, Hansu felt as though something irreparable had happened. He could grasp the full extent of Kiyokichi's sorrow, which seemed deeper than that of Sukako, who had found some outlet for her grief in her hysteria.

After Kiyokichi left the restaurant, Hansu heaved a sigh of relief and looked at Tatsukichi:

"Today I wish we had never come here."

"Yes, it has been one thing after another, hasn't it."

"Shut up. Don't say another word about her . . ."

Hansu spoke in a thin, sharp, and hysterical tone.

"I wasn't going to mention that. You're just not feeling well. Don't you have any appetite?"

"I'm sorry. I'm just not myself today."

"You haven't been yourself for a long time. You can relax and calm down now. Do you find me so untrustworthy?"

"Mmm. That has nothing to do with it. Please don't get angry."

Hansu ate more than he usually did and ended up polishing off most of the meal, with the exception of a few slices of the cold meat, and he really loved the pudding dessert. As Tatsukichi lifted the uneaten slices of beef with his fork from Hansu's plate, he looked at Hansu and said, laughing, "Recently, you haven't been this hungry in quite a while."

A solidly built semidouble bed, with carvings on the bedposts, was delivered to Tatsukichi's house in Asakachō from a store located near the Main Gate to Tokyo University that dealt in used furniture from the US Occupation Army. The bed was for Hansu. It was put in a Western-style room, previously used as a storage closet, directly across from Tatsukichi's study, after the maid had cleaned and aired the room.

After that, Hansu would sometimes become depressed for no special reason, but at other times, he would be in high spirits like a young woman. Moreover, Tatsukichi decided to cancel their upcoming trip because, as he put it, "it was no longer necessary," and instead he suggested they travel sometime in early November when he would have a breather from his work deadlines. Hansu resented the postponement and began to carp at Tatsukichi, which eventually got on the writer's nerves.

From the first time that Hansu had visited him, Tatsukichi had thought of him as one of the angels in Raphael's paintings, with his childish beauty, his pallid skin so quick to blush, and his solid but not excessively muscular build, which could be felt even when he wore a shirt. As delighted as he was with these physical traits, he felt even more drawn to his feminine character. Hansu in turn felt a superficial yearning for Tatsukichi's fairy-tale existence in the literary world, but he didn't even bother himself to read his works. He had possessed a shrewd grasp of his own interests that could not help but strike a perceptive observer, but he was still a child in his lack of self-understanding. There was something refreshing, almost comical in this childish side to his character, which he made no effort to hide. While he would sometimes behave like a grown-up man, the next moment he became a little boy, utterly engrossed in some foreign illustrated book that Tatsukichi had given him. With his half-opened lips, he looked like a baby craving for his mother's breast. Tatsukichi found him powerfully seductive when he looked up suddenly with his birdlike eyes, as though unaware that he was being observed carefully and intensely. Fully conscious of his beauty and charm, he sometimes looked up at Tatsukichi with a kind of rapt expression in his long-lashed eyes, a gentle smile playing on the edges of his lips. In his facial expression one could descry the characteristic egotism and coldness of the beautiful boy, but these traits were tempered by a kind of innocence and lack of malice. The first time that he paid Tatsukichi a visit, the latter could not sleep all night. Hansu left him a manuscript, and after reading the first line of this autobiographical and confessional work, Tatsukichi could not put it down. The book had a fresh and charming style, but it had little else to recommend it as a work of literature. Reading between the lines, he sensed that Han's feminine nature permeated every page. While he had planned to spend the evening perusing Henri Pieron's *Psychology of Suffering*,[14] he ended up leaving that work on his desk unopened. Both in his physical appearance and his inner character, he was exactly the type that Tatsukichi found most attractive and seductive. From their first encounter, he resolved that, come what may, he would make Hansu his own, and no matter what happened, he would never let go of him.

Tatsukichi lived like a helpless small bird or a drowning man, the slave of Han's coquetry, except when he devoted himself to work. The young man was endowed with a limitless, but also artless, coquetry. He had merely to express a desire for something and Tatsukichi would rush out and purchase whatever he wanted. He constantly craved new possessions to distract himself from fear and anxiety. These demands were also a series of tests by which he gained confidence in the extent of Tatsukichi's infatuation with him. When he noticed this aspect of Hansu, Tatsukichi was not angry, but it made him dizzy as if blood were rushing to his head. Sometimes, he refused to cater to Hansu's whims and treated him with severity, but with each passing day, he fell ever more deeply under the spell of his infatuation with the boy.

* * *

At last, the day of wedding ceremony had receded into the past, and at least a fortnight had passed since Mrs. Yatsuka's visit. Hansu had

---

14. Louis Charles Henri Piéron, 1881–1964, was one of the founders of scientific psychology in France.

regained his calm, and he began to put his notebooks from high school and his two years at the university in order under Tatsukichi's direction. After he reviewed the textbooks he had used in school, Tatsukichi told him to study more advanced mathematics, first on his own and later under the guidance of a teacher.

A firm where Tatsukichi had connections published Hansu's autobiographical work, but, other than being credited with a certain freshness, it flopped with the critics. Hansu had already advanced to the ranks of up-and-coming writer considered promising. He knew perfectly well that he owed the limited celebrity he enjoyed entirely to his good looks and to the fact that he was Tatsukichi's disciple. As his photographs appeared in popular magazines, he came to be treated like a movie star whose main claim to fame is his handsome face. When Tatsukichi asked the university math teacher what he thought of him, he gazed at Hansu like a proud parent. "What a child he is," he thought as he looked at the smile on the boy's face, a smile that was troubled and even pained, like that of a man who frowns when he looks into something excessively bright.

Finding him irresistible, Tatsukichi said to himself, "What's the point of making him waste his time writing bad novels?" One morning, while he was in bed, Hansu buried his head in the opening of Tatsukichi's white shirt with vertical blue stripes, and touched his lips to his chest, but Tatsukichi placed his hand on his chin and raised his head, holding it with both hands, and looked deeply into his eyes.

"I don't want you to be simply my wife. You have a mathematical mind in this forehead of yours." He pressed his fingertips strongly against the boy's forehead. Hansu smiled like a little girl and touched his lips to Tatsukichi's fingertips.

• • •

On a clear day, Tatsukichi accompanied Hansu to his former apartment in Morikawachō, settled his back rent, disposed of most of his furniture, and had a few items—a bookshelf, school notebooks, a clock, an armchair that they had bought from a store in front of Akamon, a lamp stand—sent to Asakachō. The two men were no longer only brothers,[15] but had become lovers as well.

---

15. *Anikibun* in Japanese, literally "elder brother," but implying a deeper emotional relationship.

Although Tatsukichi couldn't help but think of the Yatsuka girl, he tended to be reckless when they went out together. By contrast, Hansu was terrified of running into her one moment, but the very next he would forget about her altogether.

One day, they went to the Ginza to have lunch at the Silver Spoon and later walked to the Tōei Theater in Yurakuchō, where they lined up in front of the ticket office. Hansu had on a pale blue coat and a black turtleneck sweater, while Tatsukichi wore a dark-blue and red-striped necktie and a loose-fitting dark blue Inverness coat.

Tatsukichi had suggested they watch a French detective movie that was playing in the movie theater downstairs. He stood right in front of the ticket booth, his elbows resting on the counter, and was just about to take his wallet from his pocket to pay, when he heard an inhuman shriek from Hansu's mouth. When he turned around, he noticed that Hansu was gaping at the streetcar tracks with the eyes of an idiot, his lips wide open as though they had been wrenched apart. A girl of slight build had stepped off the streetcar onto the road and stood there oblivious to the commotion of the city, her small, expressionless face surrounded by auburn hair. But then, as the driver on the right side of the road slammed on his brakes, her sudden piercing cry merged with the ear-splitting screech of the car. Seeing what had happened, Hansu tried to run to the place of the accident, but Tatsukichi held him back by grabbing hold of his chest. Hansu felt his arms go numb and he collapsed against Tatsukichi's shoulder.

The next instant, Yoshiko was propelled into the air from the impact of the collision and then crushed like an insect under the front wheel of the car. She lay there with her small, gloved hands thrown outward, palms facing up, and the strap of her shoulder bag was wrapped around her neck. Her skirt was rolled up and her legs, exposed from the white underwear to her dark silk stockings, were covered with scratches from being dragged along the ground, while the heels of her black shoes were lifted in the air.

Looking terrified, Tatsukichi stared down at the corpse—it was obvious that she was dead—as though to verify beyond a shadow of a doubt this living sacrifice to his infatuation. He felt as if his mind had partially shut down. His eyes burned with a sharp light and he whispered to Han.

"Be careful. You'll draw public attention to yourself."

Tatsukichi supported Hansu, as if he were carrying him, and helped him to walk along the pavement from the Tōei building to the Tōnichi Newspaper building just around the corner, where he hailed a taxi in front of the distribution office of the newspaper. Behind them, they could hear, above the meaningless and indistinct din of the crowd, the loud voice of a policeman ordering people to disperse. He practically pushed Hansu into the taxi that stopped in front of them, and then got in himself and shut the door.

"Please hurry. To the street in front of Tokyo University."

When the driver circled around the dense crowd of onlookers that had gathered to see the accident and sped away toward Owarichō, Tatsukichi turned around and looked back through the rear window. A woman pushed her way through the crowd and crouched down besides the dead girl. She appeared to be a young woman about the same age as Yoshiko. Tatsukichi thought she might have been passing by the scene of the accident by chance.

The young woman rose to her feet and made a brief, whispered report to a police officer, but then she touched her hand against her forehead and started to collapse against the shoulder of an unknown man standing beside her. The work of lifting the front wheel of the car was already underway.

Yoshiko had come to the Tōei cinema at the invitation of a friend. She wore a light beige overcoat and a dark red silk dress that Sukako had picked out especially for her honeymoon. Ever since the affair with Hansu, Yoshiko had felt too sad to wear red; that day, she had intended to go out with a white blouse and an old dress under that coat, but her mother Sukako suggested that she wear bright colors to cheer her up. Around the collar of her blouse Yoshiko had on a blue, iridescent brooch with just a tinge of gold, and she carried a bag slightly darker than her overcoat when she went out. Because she had arrived late, she had hurried across the tracks, and just as she stepped down onto the street, she had noticed Hansu observing her from the entrance of the movie theater, with a cheerful and nonchalant look on his face. The skin on her face felt hard, as though it was being pulled in different directions, and her expression vanished. Her arms and legs stopped moving, as though paralyzed. Terror mixed with astonishment blocked her throat from calling out the name, "Hansu." Her lips were too dry and no sound issued from her mouth. She noticed that Hansu's expression changed and sensed that he was going to run toward her; but she stood there stiffly, like a stone statue, and was run over by the car. The young woman who flew out from the crowd had arranged to meet Yoshiko at the Tōei Theater and had also arrived late. A close friend, Asagada Tsuruko knew all about the situation with Hansu.

• • •

Hansu was like a man who has lost his consciousness. Tatsukichi lifted him up with his arms and laid him down over his knees as he leaned back against the seat. The taxi sped past Muromachi and then passed under the overpass near Kanda Station. He placed his hand on Hansu's forehead and felt cold drops of sweat on his hand.

"Are you all right, Hansu?"

Hansu looked up at Tatsukichi with his half-shut eyes, but seemed as if he were in a dream.

"Ah!"

Hansu merely groaned and fell back; he looked at Tatsukichi as if to appeal for help, but then he shut his eyes in silence. The air outside the car was very bright. The fact of Yoshiko's sudden death, which had happened in broad daylight, began to sink into Tatsukichi's consciousness. He felt that he would never be free of it for the rest of his life. Hansu might manage to forget it in the end, since he was still so young. Besides, he would find it easier to free himself from the throbbing pain because he was beautiful and he was loved. Tatsukichi looked directly at his eyes, which seemed closed under the luxuriant growth of his eyelashes.

When they arrived home, Tatsukichi nearly carried Hansu through the gate and noticed his maid, Nagatsuka Hana, standing in front of the entrance. This was the day she was scheduled to come.

"Oh, excuse me. I had completely forgotten," Tatsukichi said to her.

"Oh dear, what's wrong with Mr. Itō?" As she uttered these words Nagatsuka Hana switched from her peeved look to her suspicious one.

"He suffered an attack of anemia. I'll pay you extra since you came today. Are you free tomorrow?"

"I'm afraid not. But you needn't go to any trouble for my sake."

Nagatsuka was quite aware of Tatsukichi's way of doing business, so she made a pro forma show of declining his offer of extra pay, then added, "I am booked solid for the next few days, but I can came next Monday."

"Ok, let's make it Monday then."

Tatsukichi lowered Hansu onto the bed in the study and told Hana to make lemonade for him.

Hana mixed lemon juice with ice and sugar, brought it to Hansu, and placed it on the table. Then with profuse thanks she took the 500-yen note that Tatsukichi handed her. After looking at Hansu, she went out the wooden door of the kitchen and walked along the brick path that connected the main entrance to the front gate. There she stood and looked back with sunken eyes.

"Those two act just like a newlywed couple. I am sure something fishy is going on," she mumbled to herself. Hana commuted to various households for cleaning jobs and she was always curious about the circumstances of her clients. Tatsukichi paid her generously, but he was difficult to deal with. He had an aversion to engaging in small talk not directly related to her job. For that reason, Hana had no choice but to leave.

Tatsukichi came back from the bathroom with a towel and some hot water to wipe away the sweat from the boy's body. Hansu pushed the pillow aside and lay with his face to one side, and he kicked away the blanket that Tatsukichi spread over him as though it annoyed him. Tatsukichi removed his coat and unbuttoned his shirt so that he could breathe more easily. He dabbed his forehead with a moistened towel, and then, after wringing it out again, he wiped down his neck and chest. He threw the towel to the side of the sink and placed his hand on Hansu's heart. The heartbeat was slow and weak. Tatsukichi placed his hand on a lock of Hansu's hair that fell over his forehead, and then took a handkerchief from his back pocket to wipe his hair dry.

Hansu's throat seemed to move as if he had swallowed something, but he rolled over as if to brush away Tatsukichi's hand and burst into tears.

"I am the one who killed her . . ."

In the intervals between sobs, he spoke in broken phrases.

His eyes shining with a deep light, Tatsukichi gazed fixedly at Hansu and thrust his white hand and the handkerchief he had used to wipe Hansu's hair into his pocket. Hansu lay on the bed moaning, but then he lifted himself up and looked around for Tatsukichi. He grabbed at Tatsukichi's chest and tried to peer into his face, still holding his breath. He continued to sob but the tears no longer flowed from his wide-open eyes, and he fell back onto his side. When he lay on his back, his chin looked smaller and thinner than it had before; he started to weep for different reasons than before. His face was uncovered, his tears dried, and his throat was shaken by spasms. Tatsukichi lay down beside him and pressed their bodies together. With both hands, he gently tried to compress Hansu's throat and looked deeply into his eyes. Under the pressure of Tatsukichi's fingers, his throat continued to quiver intermittently. His eyes, the upper eyelids drawn down to the pupil leaving only the white part visible, were motionless and wore an expression that might have been either pain or weariness. His dry heaving would sometimes turn into a convulsive sob. Hansu placed his hand on Tatsukichi's wrist. Tatsukichi's hand softened and became a soft caress. Hansu touched Tatsukichi's wrist with his hand and then inched his way up his arm and gently supported it. Drawing in his chin, he bent down and touched his lips to Tatsukichi's hands.

By this time, he was no longer surprised by anything Hansu did. Sometimes, Hansu pulled away and held his breath, in a state of shock, perhaps to banish the hysterical terror he felt at Yoshiko's death; at others, like a clock that has been reset, he plunged into agony because Tatsukichi treated him coldly, with all thought of Yoshiko forgotten, and he again began to heave dry sobs like a child. Although he thought that he knew everything about the boy's unwitting coquettishness, he felt a new infatuation grow. Like water heated to a low boil, his blood started to simmer and then flow briskly to every part of his body. Tatsukichi gazed at Hansu's small face and at his eyelids, which hid in their shadows a moist love. His lips, like a certain kind of Noh mask, revealed a low row of teeth under the loosened lower lip. Perhaps roused by Tatsukichi's gentle attitude, Hansu began to sob again. His own suffering was visible in the vertical wrinkle that formed between his eyebrows, which also marked his utter exhaustion.

Tatsukichi stood up and went to the work desk by the window on the right side of the entrance, directly opposite the door to the bath. He took out an ampoule of sleeping medication and a syringe from the drawer, sterilized his hands and the point of the needle, and then gave Hansu an injection in his upper arm.

Hansu looked as though he had returned from a distant country when he glanced at Tatsukichi, but he immediately turned over to the side.

"For sure, I was the one that killed her."

Tatsukichi replied, "It wasn't you, Hansu. I'm the one to blame."

"I am more terrified of her now than I was when she was alive."

"Hmm . . . you'll be able to sleep after the shot. Do you feel thirsty?"

"I just want some water."

"Your voice sounds pretty hoarse. You cried a lot."

Tatsukichi went into the bathroom, rinsed out a cup used for gargling, filled it with water, and then put a few ice cubes from the tray on the table into the cup. Hansu made a purring sound as he quenched his thirst, then he fell back, and stretched his hand out to Tatsukichi. When Tatsukichi sat on the edge of the bed and held his hand gently in both hands, Hansu wore a smile on his pale lips, and he looked at Tatsukichi with droopy eyelids.

"For sure I was the one that killed her . . . But as long you stay with me . . . I don't care."

Tatsukichi smiled wryly, without any malice. "Well, it works out to something like that."

Hansu half closed his eyes and wearily faced toward the wall. Tatsukichi walked around the bed to put the hypodermic syringe away, and he noticed that Han kept his birdlike eyes open when he passed by his body. He stowed the syringe in a drawer, then he lifted Hansu's head so that he was facing up and imprinted a long kiss on his lips, as though he would suck the very life from him. He seemed to dissolve deeper and deeper into Hansu, as though he were entering a dark subterranean cave, and Hansu, though half-asleep, responded with his own lips. His hand rested on Tatsukichi's shoulder as though inert, and then it fell off. Twilight gathered in the corners of the room, and it was darkest in the space behind the bed, cut off from the window light. Nevertheless, Tatsukichi's face shone like that of a man utterly inebriated on the whiskey of love. He had deep folds in his forehead, and he clenched his eyes shut as though he were suffering from a sudden chill. Sometimes, he turned his neck to look at Hansu from a different angle and his face and lips looked different.

Hours crawled by, and the darkness deepened. Time was made up of an endless chain of events, but all of them were connected. Tatsukichi was prone to such musings in his ordinary state, but now his mind was a complete blank. However, he knew that the kiss exchanged by Tatsukichi and Hansu belonged to eternal time. It had entered the cycle of nature. Then Tatsukichi raised his head to kiss Hansu's sleeping brow, placed his hand under the top cover, and stood up.

He closed both windows and sank into the swivel chair by his desk on the other side of the bed, took a Kiriaji cigarette from the can, and struck a match to light it. As he leaned against the back of the chair, he gazed at the reflection of the sky in the window. The embers of love still smoldered on his lips. As he puffed at his cigarette, thick smoke billowed from his lips and flowed out over the desk. He picked up another cigarette with his right hand but then dropped it on the arm of the chair.

His face was still lit up by love that might prove ephemeral, but he had conquered and quelled the loneliness and pain that were its obverse side, its dark clinging shadow.

TEN

"Sacred Headland"
(Seinaru misaki) by Takahashi Mutsuo (1972)

Translated by Paul McCarthy

Biography and Introduction

The poet, memoirist, novelist, and playwright Takahashi Mutsuo (1937–) was born into a poor, working-class family in the coal country of northern Kyushu. His father having died soon after Mutsuo's birth, and his mother forced by circumstance to work elsewhere, he was raised by his grandmother and other relatives. The absence of "a real family" is one of the themes of his memoirs.

He graduated from high school and college in Fukuoka, despite poverty and tuberculosis of the lungs, and found his way to Tokyo in his twenties, where he supported himself for close to twenty years as a copywriter for an advertising agency. All the while he was writing poetry, at first self-published and then with established publishers. His early work drew the attention of the great novelist Mishima Yukio, whose friend and disciple Takahashi became from the mid-1960s until Mishima's ritual suicide in 1970. Others who recognized his work early on included the critic Etō Jun, the poet Tada Chimako, and the writer Washisu Shigeo. He shared with Mishima a fascination with homoeroticism; with Tada, an eagerness to explore the possibilities of modern free verse; and with Washisu, an interest in the Western classics and in Christianity, especially Eastern Orthodoxy and Roman Catholicism, which appear often in his early works.

Takahashi has been a very prolific writer, but I will mention here only some major works that have appeared in whole or in part in English translation (Takahashi has been well served by translator/scholars Satō Hiroaki and Jeffrey Angles, in particular): *Rose Tree, Fake Lovers* (1964), *Poems of a Penisist* (1975), and *Sleeping, Sinning, Falling* (1992) among poetry collections; and *Holy Triangle* (1972), *Twelve Views from the Distance* (1970), and *Zen's Pilgrimage* (1974) among many prose works in various genres.

Takahashi has received numerous prizes and awards, including the Yomiuri Literary and Takami Jun Prizes, the Grand Prize for Modern Haiku, and a decoration from the Japanese government for his contributions to modern Japanese literature.

"Sacred Headland" is an autobiographical novella describing the boy Mutsuo's social, psychological, and spiritual development from around the age of three until the end of middle school, when he was in his midteens. The setting is northern Kyushu: the small coal-mining towns in which his relatives worked and he was raised, and the port town of Moji where he attended primary and middle school, with a significant excursion to Shimonoseki, across the straits in Yamaguchi prefecture.

His family was very poor, and one of the shocks of his boyhood is the realization that he will not be able to enter an elite middle school despite having done brilliantly on the entrance exam because his mother could not pay the fee. "That's the way the world is," says the teacher who breaks the news to him.

His father is dead and his mother often absent, so he is raised mainly by his grandmother, who is depicted as an uneducated working-class woman. He longs for "a real family" and imagines it as existing always "Beyond." A handsome if severe young uncle inhabits that Beyond, having been sent to Burma in the Imperial Army, where he dies of illness.

Messengers from the Beyond appear—the postman who brings the uncle's letters and finally news of his death, as well as anonymous soldiers glimpsed on trains. Like Mishima Yukio, whose disciple he was before that writer's death in 1970, men in uniform play a great part in the boy's inner life. Looking back on that time, the mature Takahashi speaks of these visions and encounters in Christian religious terms—the Word made flesh, the angel of the Annunciation, the Vessel chosen to carry the Son of God (i.e., the Virgin). These do not of course reflect the thoughts and feelings of the boy as he underwent the experiences described, but are the mature writer's way of conceptualizing and coming to terms with them. The use of religious, and especially Catholic, imagery to convey deeply formative, usually erotic experiences is characteristic of much of Takahashi's poetry and prose.

"Angels" appear from time to time: a radiant classmate from the Beyond that is Tokyo, a handsome, aggressively friendly high-school student met in a park during young Mutsuo's trip to Shimonoseki—all of them reminiscent of the now-dead uncle, who loved Mutsuo and expressed that, in part, with blows. But Mutsuo had "gotten too used to waiting" over the years, and he detaches himself or runs away whenever happiness looms.

Near the end of the novella, there are two distressing encounters, one with an apparently pederastic schoolteacher who uses a poetry magazine to approach young students. Nothing happens, but the mood created clouds much that follows. At the very end, there is a creepy old lighthouse keeper, a master manipulator who molests both Mutsuo and a friend on the day of their graduation from middle school. No angels from Beyond, these, but very near and real evidence of the darker side of sexuality.

Takahashi is, in addition to being a fantasist, a realist. He knows that molestation occurs; he apparently experienced it himself at a tender age, and was traumatized by it. The inability of the two boys to even look at one another after the double molestation speaks volumes to the sensitive reader, as does their return home without even visiting the lighthouse, which was the original goal of their trip. They look back at the lighthouse-keeper's dwelling, where they were abused, and find it "looked very small." A more explicitly didactic writer than Takahashi might have added "and exceedingly ugly." It is a clearly painful end to the novella, anticipated ironically by the title of the work as a whole: "Sacred Headland."

Sacred Headland

Even now I can vividly recall the scene when the Word first revealed itself to me.

At the core of my memories is a red-copper potbellied stove. From the gaps in the rusty iron door through which the stove was fed I could see the pieces of still fresh, just-dug-up coal crackling as they burned. By the glow of the red-hot coals, six or seven faces floated up, surrounding the stove there in the dimness. A head wearing an old army forage-cap, a grizzled, hatless head, a head with a dirty towel wound around it—all the faces were expressionless, and between fifty and sixty years old.

Expressionless, yet with mouths energetically moving. As my eyes grew accustomed to the dimness, I could see that these aging men and women were sitting on four campstools set around the stove, eating their bento meals. From the tin lunchboxes, which had lost their shape and become porous from the acidity of the pickled plums and scallions they contained, the group lifted mouthfuls of rice and chewed them, their sets of false teeth clacking. Some of them indulged in clammy, suggestive gossip as well. Water was boiling away in the big iron kettle atop the stove, and the air was filled with the oddly raw smell of the rubberized work shoes they wore on their feet, extended toward the heat of the stove. The burning light emerging from the gaps in the stove's metal door stretched up through the cold dimness of the room, illuminating the inside of the gabled roof, with its wooden ribbing clearly showing high above them. Looking up, you could see that someone had just placed planking over the ridgepole and then nailed tin over that. At one spot they had used an old window frame just as it was in place of the tin, to form a skylight. The windowpanes must have shattered at some point, and more tin had been nailed on top as an obvious emergency measure. Three of the four nails used to keep the tin sheet in place were gone, and every time the wind blew, the piece of tin would lift up, striking against the window frame, making a deeply chilling sound.

Speaking of sounds: from the many gaps between the roughly nailed boards of the hut came a sound like a child's bamboo-grass flute as the wind blew in. These gaps between the boards served as a source of light in the windowless hut, letting in a kind of dim twilight glow. Straining your eyes through the gloom, you could see that, far beneath the great empty space created by the high roof, there was an uneven earthen floor, swept and swept again with a bamboo broom. On this earthen floor were piled in disorder, here a mound of gravel, there a sack of cement, as well as pieces of wood and stacked boxes of nails.

The stove was in the center of the room, where the earthen floor was plainly visible, free from the things everywhere else. As the gossip moved around the circle, with the nasty stories accompanied by grains of rice flying from eagerly moving mouths, sometimes it would be my grandmother's turn. In her *mompei*-trousers and a tunic with narrow sleeves, all made from large-patterned *kasuri* cotton, and with a hand towel wrapped around her head, she began: "That Maruya-san who lived in Urantan? He was a man-woman, you know, and he fell for Shinno-san from Kamōda in a big way. Then just when they were getting on so nice, there was talk of Shinno-san getting married. Now Maruya-san couldn't get over that, so he took a kitchen knife and stabbed himself in the throat, he did!"

Then, suddenly, glass appeared in the window frame onto which the old tin sheet had been nailed, and the glass seemed to radiate rainbow colors that blazed in the rays of light flooding into the building. The sheaf of light rays was the words themselves. Those words, which must have slipped from my grandmother's mouth, had become a sheaf of rays continuously pouring in through the window frame. Even the bad smell of the old people's rubberized work shoes roasting in the heat of the stove seemed changed into a fine fragrance that filled my nostrils and my brain with ecstasy.

My grandmother completely ignored the presence of her three-year-old grandson, who stood across from her as she spoke, behind the others, wearing worn-down women's geta clogs. Despite his grandmother's ignoring him—or rather, because of it—her words had the aspect of a visitation from invisible Heaven. Even as they turned into an abundant radiant waterfall, these words projected, in the petty form of "a sickness of the spirit," the Beyond from which the sacred thing comes, that soul-trembling, hitherto unknown, dazzling thing called "love," which exists in the distant sacred realm Beyond.

"That Maruya-san who lived in Urantan? He was a man-woman, you know, and he fell for Shinno-san, who lives in Kamōda, in a big way. Then, just when they were getting on so nice, there was talk of Shinno-san getting married. Now Maruya-san couldn't get over that, so he took a kitchen knife and stabbed himself in the throat, he did!"

"Maruya-san from Urantan," who was derided as a "man-woman," in my grandmother's words, was actually, on the contrary, sanctified by that derision, becoming the symbol of the chosen vessel who receives the One who comes from Beyond. And "Shinno-san from Kamōda" became the Archangel who came from Beyond in the form of a beautiful youth; he became the Word that the Archangel held in his well-formed fingertips; he became the Son of God as the radiant incarnation of the Word. The business about "there was talk of Shinno-san getting married . . .—so Maruya-san took a kitchen knife and stabbed himself in the throat" showed the terrible rupture that occurs when human beings become involved with the sacred. I could not have realized it as a child, but that nasty gossip that came from my grandmother's mouth had exactly the same value as the words "Hail, full of grace!"

Having served as the place where the nasty words of that ignorant old woman could be consecrated so as to become the Word, that storage house gradually came to resemble the blessed carpenter's shop, or the holy stable; and the Word became a sheaf of light that shone in upon the holy stable. My young soul was moved by the terror of this drama of "love" that the Word secretly holds; and I crept backward to the door of the storage house and silently went outside.

The building where the old folks gathered served as a storage place and office called "Eizen" (my grandmother pronounced it "Eijen" in Chikugo dialect). It was on the outskirts of the town of Nōgata, one of the centers of coal mining in the northern part of Kyushu. Within the extensive grounds of the Mitsubishi Mining Company, which was located in the Shinnyū area, offices, a cooperative store, an electric substation, public bathing facilities, company housing, an exercise ground, a coal-dressing plant, and the like were scattered here and there. "Eizen" was one of these.

The elderly men and women who were unable to become either unskilled miners, who would go down into the dark depths of the mine to hack out the burnable rock, or miners' helpers, who would load that rock onto handcars and trundle them up into the daylight above, were always gathered around that stove. When orders came to repair office roofs damaged by rain, or to rebuild walls around company housing—walls that had been blown down in strong winds—the old folks would drag themselves to their feet, collect boxes of nails and plasterer's tools, and then set off, as slowly as possible.

Since I had left the heat of the blazing stove when I went outside, it must have been wintertime. Yet for some reason, in my memory, it was summer outside the Eizen building. From just outside the door, gleaming steel-blue rails stretched off into the distance; around the rails grew dark summer grasses, knotweed, goosefoot, wild chrysanthemums, millet grass. In the green clumps of millet grass, grasshoppers chirped in seeming irritation.

The rails and rail ties and gravel beneath them blazed in the sun, giving off a shimmering haze. Distorted by the haze, the rails ascended a slope with a gentle gradient, seeming almost not to do so. Having come to the top of the hill, they appeared to descend gently on the other side, until finally disappearing.

Ahead of the now invisible rails would have been the entrance to the Number Six mine shaft, its black mouth wide open beneath Inari Hill in Yamantan. But the rails seemed to me to be heading toward "Kamōda," and "Shinno-san," whom my grandmother had spoken of. At that point I had never been to Kamōda. It was to me an entirely unknown land.

"Shinno-san" lived there, in Kamōda. For some reason, I imagined him as a not-too-tall, somewhat dark-complexioned, strong-looking youth, dark-eyed, with thick eyebrows and full sideburns, dressed in a small-patterned cotton kimono. "Maruya-san," on the other hand, who'd fallen in love with "Shinno-san," lived in Urantan. My mother's birth family used to live there, so I had often been to Urantan and was familiar with it.

Wandering along the maze of paths that wound from known Urantan to unknown Kamōda, then injuring his leg in some thicket in Yahata, "Maruya-san" could never have made it all the way to Kamōda, I thought.

And now, for some reason, I imagined Maruya-san as being tall, fair-complexioned as a woman, and wearing a slim-looking, striped kimono.

But what had Grandma meant by the words "Maruya-san was a man-woman"? And what was implied by "He fell for Shinno-san in a big way, and they were getting on so nice"? As I stood among the luxuriant summer grasses there and gazed in the direction that the rails, bent by the haze, moved toward, I felt inside myself, child that I was, the dark presence of a budding, uncertain lust that made my head start to spin.

In creating an image of "Shinno-san," whom I had never seen, I must have been influenced by the image of Shintan, whom Grandma had often spoken of. She used to tell me about Shintan as a kind of bedtime story when she wanted me to fall asleep. The look of "Shinno-san's" kimono may have been suggested to me by the *kasuri* pattern of my quilt as it rubbed against the tender tip of my nose while I listened to Grandma's stories.

Shintan had been Grandma's younger brother. He didn't like farm work, so he joined a gang of gamblers when he was still very young. It was early spring, and he was eighteen: there was talk of buying some land in the mountains, and he was sent off as the boss's representative. He never returned. A search team went out, and they discovered Shintan's body in the remaining snow on a bamboo-covered hill. Apparently he had been ambushed: his chest and thighs had been hacked away at with hand scythes and improvised bamboo spears, and his abdomen still showed the marks of a snowshoe. His blood had dyed the surrounding snow red and had hardened on the snow's surface.

The robbers who had ambushed him died a dog's death one after the other, with blackish blood oozing from their ears and nostrils. From inside the waistband of the young man whom they had tortured to death, the gang leader had stolen thirty blood-soaked yen notes, and certainly planned on making good his escape, But he and his men were all arrested at the Nagasaki ferry wharf, then tried, and sentenced to death. Grandma explained it as the dead boy's curse, but was it not, rather, a sign of the consecration of the boy who had died so young? Actually, from the point of view of farmers stuck for life in the soil, this boy who had chosen to become a gambler might seem to have found a home in a far easier, more comfortable heaven than they themselves ever would.

Why did Grandma so often pour into her little grandchild's ears this story of the cruel death of a young blood relative? Whispered so often into my ears, directly connected with the rich storehouse of memory, Shintan's story finally became the kernel of the Word that was to come to me. Loving this kernel with all my heart, I waited for the Word to come—this waiting indeed became, of necessity, my essential nature.

Shintan, however, seemed no more than the forerunner of the One who was truly to come, and at whose feet he would "bow, unworthy even to untie the straps of his sandals." That One was no other than Uncle Ken, born from my benighted grandmother's womb, a young man joined to me by close ties of kinship. He was at that time in his late teens, and I called him "Uncle Ken-chan," in the Chikugo way.

At the time the consecration took place around that potbellied stove, Uncle Ken was absent, attending a railway workers' training center in Moji. When, a few months later, he appeared before me, he became a god incarnate, prepared for by the kernel and the Word. One noon, he stood in his brand-new railway worker's uniform, shouldering the light that shone from the doorway onto the uneven earthen floor of my grandmother's house; and at that time, he was born from within me.

Uncle Ken already possessed, from the circumstances of his birth, possibilities toward Beyond. He was not my grandfather's son, but the seed of some man or other whom my "loose" grandmother had had sex with in Sasayama. Standing just outside the circle of our women neighbors as they gossiped, I had heard that any number of times. The strongest evidence that Uncle Ken wasn't a legitimate son of the Taka-hashi family was the fact that "he doesn't look like Asakichi or like Tsui, either," as the women said, nodding knowingly to each other.

And, certainly, handsome youth that he was, Uncle Ken bore no resemblance to anyone in the Takahashi clan. Though at the head of his class throughout primary school, he gave up on the idea of going on to middle school and got a job with the National Railway. On the way back from shopping in Nōgata, my mother (who was still living at Grandma's house at that point) and I would pass the charred wooden fence by the railway yard and catch sight of Uncle Ken in his working clothes, jumping down from a baggage car he had just coupled to the train, his hands in their white working gloves raised high.

Having finished his training at the center in Moji, Uncle Ken, now in his late teens, matched my image of "Shinno-san"—tanned and very muscular. Due in part to his having learned judo and karate in his free time, he had, like some ascetic, dammed up the drive toward sexual license typical of a youth of his age; but just because it was so suppressed, there was an intensely sexual atmosphere about him. In fact, I sniffed out the odor of a certain incident that had occurred while he was at the training center—the same sort of thing that Grandma had been talking about regarding "Maruya-san" and "Shinno-san," I believe.

After Uncle Ken came home from work in the evening, he'd go into his room, throw off his work clothes, smelling of steel and oil and a young man's sweat, and emerge wearing only a *fundoshi* loincloth. He would descend the steps to the ground in his bare feet, and go outside. Soon from the nearby bathhouse came the sound of water being splashed energetically about. The splashing continued at short intervals until finally Uncle Ken would return, his strong muscles resilient and with many quicksilver-colored drops of water beading his tight young skin.

With one swipe of a rough hand towel, the drops of water on his firm skin were wiped away. He dried his face, his arms, his chest, and his back; then, deftly tying the hand towel with which he had wiped the area from his shins to his thighs around his hips, Uncle Ken took off the *fundoshi* beneath. Using it to brush the dirt from the soles of his feet, he climbed up the steps. The now-soiled *fundoshi* he rolled up and put by the side of the steps; yet, strangely, there seemed nothing dirty about this most private piece of cloth. Even Grandma, so prone to scolding, had nothing to say against her son's daily rites of cleansing; she just silently removed the *fundoshi* from where he had left it. It may have been because she sensed that her young son would, in the not-too-distant future, have to travel Beyond as a soldier of the emperor; and this was her way of showing her care for him.

Having doused himself with cold water and gone into his room, Uncle Ken would firmly close the *fusuma* sliding doors and not emerge for quite a while. Even Grandma and my mother hesitated to go into his room in order to clean, and it was completely forbidden territory to me, his young nephew. I was in awe of my uncle's odor, which emanated from the gaps between the closed *fusuma*. What was he doing in there? I couldn't hear even a cough from beyond the sliding doors. But if I started to fuss, the *fusuma* would open a few inches and Uncle Ken, with his hair in a crew cut and his *kasuri* kimono pulled tight over his chest, would peer out at me.

"Mutsuo." His voice was stern but also gentle, to the same degree. For it was a voice from Beyond, and over and above the sounds "Mutsuo," it was calling out "O beloved child!"

One time, sitting on the veranda in the rays of the setting sun, I was playing with myself when Uncle Ken opened the *fusuma* and caught me at it. He grabbed one tender earlobe with a hot hand and dragged me over the tatami mats, pulling me into the forbidden territory of his room inside the *fusuma*. My buttocks, the back of my knees, and my ankles were chaffed by the edges of the tatami mats, and felt hot. I had bumped hard against the wooden threshold, and, jolted into the air, I fell into the intense physical odor of my uncle.

Leaving me curled up there, Uncle Ken took his judo black belt from a lintel nail and readied himself. I could probably have escaped if I'd tried, but I didn't. My uncle had had, since birth, a nature that tended toward the Beyond, and had now become a perfect adult by passing through an "initiation" in a place I knew nothing of. He had the right to pass judgment on a dirty-minded little kid. . . . Could I perhaps have realized that, even as a child? Yet what kept me from moving was, more than anything else, the intense odor that filled the room. I suspect that Uncle Ken, as he passed judgment on me, was also passing judgment on something that had occurred during the period of his own company "initiation." As he beat me, my uncle's handsome face was beautifully flushed with fierce emotion.

I lay curled up on the tatami under the blows of the black belt raining continuously down on me. My eyes were wide open, and gradually the whole of the dimly lit room that surrounded my uncle grew clearer. Hanging from nails in the lintel above the *fusuma* through which I had just been dragged were, alongside the judo clothes now minus their belt, work clothes and a railway-man's cap, and, further on, a *kasuri*-patterned *haori* coat. Beneath that was a small low desk, just near my head as I lay there on the tatami. Looking up, I could see an inkstone box and part of a stack of writing paper. The smell of fresh ink and the sight of used paper, crumpled up and tossed onto the tatami by the desk, showed that my uncle had been practicing calligraphy until moments ago.

Apart from that, there was only a bookcase with glass doors set at a right angle to the desk. The whole space that my uncle governed was filled with ink and books and dust, plus work clothes and judo gear that gave off a strong male odor. And my uncle was there, at the very center of that odor. The lower part of the skirt of his *kasuri* kimono was torn, giving a glimpse of his shins, which were light brown, to be sure, but also lithe and unexpectedly white by contrast with the dark blue in his kimono.

In the fragrant depths of this asceticism and damned up sexuality, my young uncle and his little nephew shared, just the two of us, a single space. One may say, paradoxically, that the victimizer who did the whipping without making a sound and the victim who endured it without making a sound were in an intense relationship that could be likened to "love." I ruminated upon the harshness of the word—or, better, fleshly sound—"Mutsuo," so rarely spoken by my taciturn uncle, and the gentleness hidden within that harshness each time the belt became a whip and descended on my body.

The following year, Uncle Ken went off to the war. There on the railway platform where he himself had worked, he was endlessly raised on the shoulders of his friends, until at last he boarded the troop train in the midst of hosanna-like shouts of "Banzai!" Off he went into the distance where the rails disappeared, those rails that carried this consecrated man Beyond.

Three months later, I went to see him off again, to Moji in Kita Kyushu, together with Grandma and my mother, who had come back home for a while. Now the direction of the rails that would carry my uncle Beyond was determined. He was sent to Niigata and then, by freighter, to Burma.

Having gone Beyond, Uncle entrusted his words to an angel of a lower rank than himself—that is, to a mailman in the service of the post office of the Empire of Great Japan. There was a pond in front of Grandma's house, and the road in front of the house curved, following the pond's outline, and then disappeared behind a hill when it had not quite completed a half circle.

The lower-ranked angel who brought my uncle's words from Beyond appeared from behind that hill, riding a bicycle. I stood waiting in front of the house. The angel on the bicycle, clothed in light, grew bigger and bigger. He disappeared behind a row of houses for a while, then reappeared, pushing his bicycle with one hand, and with an envelope or postcard in the other. This balding angel wiped the sweat from the top of his head and asked,

"This is Takahashi Asakichi-san and Tsui-san's house, right?"

Nodding, I took the sacred message. It was my job to read Uncle's words to my grandfather, whose eyesight had suddenly weakened, and my grandmother, who had never learned to read. Ever since we had shared that experience of punishment with the judo belt, Uncle and I had grown especially close, so I felt it was of course *my* duty to transmit his words to the others.

The message was short and written in a simple script that even I could read, though I would not enter primary school for another couple of years:

"Are you all well? I'm fine, so please don't worry."

Wasn't this Uncle's version of Christ's words to the disciples of John the Baptist, "Go and tell John what you have seen me do"?

There were no more messages for a while, and when the angel appeared again, he had a moustache and was wearing an army uniform. This uniformed angel said in a very quiet voice that my uncle had died of illness in Burma, thus announcing his perfect sanctification.

Nōgata was a small town that had sprung up along the banks of the Ongagawa, the largest river in northern Kyushu. The Ongagawa flowed through the center of a narrow plain; the railway's Chikuhō Line ran parallel to the river to the west. West of the Chikuhō Line was Shinnyū, with its coal mines and villages. The area between the railway and the river was where the town of Nōgata was located, while to the east of the river were more villages. After I saw my uncle off to the war, my universe had extended this far. It couldn't grow any wider, sandwiched as it was between Mt. Fukuchi, towering in the east, and Mt. Mutsugadake, blocking the west. But this narrow universe of mine lost all significance after Uncle had gone over the mountains, to the Beyond. The god to whom I ought to direct my love had gone. This meant that the love that was the only thing that had bound the god and me together had vanished.

Of the two walls that formed the extreme limits of my world, I felt closer to Mt. Mutsugadake, which was near the Shinnyū area. At the base of the mountain, hidden in a grove of cedars, was the Tsurugi, or Sword, Shrine. The shrine floats, which were assembled and paraded every other year, were borrowed from Hakata beyond the mountains, and the liveliness of our festival was famous in the surrounding area. All this stopped, however, in 1937, the year I was born.

It must have been in the winter when I was two that there was a ceremony to mark the rebuilding of the main shrine by the group of supporters of the village youth who had gone off to war. They were going to throw festive red and white mochi rice cakes to the crowd, we'd heard, so adults and children came running from everywhere nearby, despite the hail that was falling. Soon the rather cramped grounds of the shrine were packed with people. I had been hoisted onto someone's shoulders and my hands were gripping his forehead. Who was it? Might it not have been Hiroaki, then a sixth grader? I vaguely remember the feel of short bristly hair brushing against my arms as I held on to that forehead.

Hiroaki was the grandson of Granny Teshima, who lived one down from my grandmother's house and acted as a village healer. Usually there were just Granny and her husband, who suffered from diabetes, living there; but Hiroaki came from Kurosaki beyond the mountains whenever there were holidays. I thought he looked a lot like the stone statue of the Buddhist deity Jizō, which stood, carrying his trademark monk's staff, near the well in Granny's yard.

Strange sounds echoed inside the square building that stood in the center of the shrine precincts, open on three sides. A monstrous creature with a bright red face was dancing and cavorting. The person carrying me on his shoulders twisted his head to explain: "They're doing sacred *kagura* dances!"

The monstrous being turned toward us and came rushing to the very edge of the stage, and then retreated with sliding steps, moving sideways. Its nose stuck straight out, as thick at the tip as at the base. My carrier turned again and announced "It's a *tengu* monster!"

I started to cry, which flummoxed the person carrying me.

"I'm scared! I want to go back to Grandma's!" I bawled there atop his shoulders. He had to lug me all the way back to my grandmother's, without us getting even a single piece of *mochi* to eat.

Another reason I think it was Hiroaki is because it was he who took me to Tsurugi Shrine shortly after Uncle Ken went off to war. This time he didn't carry me on his shoulders; we walked along together—Hiroaki in the second year of middle school, and I four years of age. On the way back, Hiroaki picked a Y-shaped yam from a vine that had twined itself around a kumquat tree by the roadside, and stuck it onto the tip of his nose with some spittle.

"Look—I'm a *tengu*!"

He had stuck two ends of the Y-shaped yam to his nose, and the last one rose a little into the air, in an I-shape.

"You try it too!"

Another Y-shaped yam, much smaller than Hiroaki's, was stuck to the tip of my pug nose with more of Hiroaki's spittle. The dried-up yam must have risen in an I-shape from the tip of my nose as well.

"It was a long time ago, but you remember the *tengu* you saw at Tsurugi Shrine, when they were tossing *mochi* to everybody? Well, *tengu* steal kids just like you and take them way over there, deep inside Mt. Hiko!"

He pointed south as he said the words "way over there." We were standing at the top of a slope that had risen very gently and now fell away just as gently. From the top we could see the mountains in all directions around us. But the south was where the mountain ranges to the east and west approached each other, almost joining. It was hard to get a clear view of what was south—it was an area of uncertainty.

"If you go like this, it's easier to see," said Hiroaki, standing with his behind to the south, then bending over and looking in that direction from between his trouser-clad thighs. Imitating him, I looked in what seemed to be the direction of Mt. Hiko from between *my* thighs, hitching up my short flannel kimono to do so.

There, beyond the *torii* formed by my thighs, was a scene clearer than any I had ever experienced—perfectly still, and upside down. There were great trees, straw-thatched roofs, distant mountains, and above them all a clear blue sky. Through a sky so clear, surely *tengu* might fly, and far in the distance, there might be a *tengu* mountain. Mt. Hiko, "way over there," was in the opposite direction from that of the rails that carried my uncle away; but I had been looking from between my thighs at an upside-down scene, and so the directions too might have been reversed, I thought. Well then, the *tengu* could also be my uncle! I longed to be abducted by the *tengu* and carried off to Mt. Hiko.

We went down the gentle slope and started to cross the wooden bridge over the Innaki River, a branch of the large Onga River. I was in front. Suddenly Hiroaki's footsteps came to a stop just behind me. I looked back to see Hiroaki laughing as he pulled out his erect penis from the slit at the front of his pants.

"Hey, look—it's a *tengu!*"

His erection rose up, slanting toward the heavens, the naked tip a shocking pink. Hiroaki guided my small hand with his own and made me hold his odd, throbbing thing in my hand.

"This is what the *tengu* do on Mt. Hiko!" Laughing, he then put his hand into the front of my kimono. When that big hand of his moved around, I couldn't help turning bright red.

Someone was coming, so we separated and began walking as before. We passed beside rice paddies full of stacks of rice straw, passed the outer walls of a school, deserted during the winter break, passed below a graveyard. I was hoping that Hiroaki would start the *"tengu* game" again, but in fact he never did; and when the winter vacation ended, he went back to Kurosaki, beyond the mountains.

I suspect Hiroaki too was a *tengu*—he who showed me the upside-down scenery I could view from between my thighs, and who gave me a glimpse of the dazzling stuff of love, and who then disappeared beyond the mountains. *Tengu* are, despite their devilish looks, very angelic creatures. One evidence of that is the fact that Hiroaki looked so much like the Jizō statue that stood beside Granny Teshima's well. In a different sense from the angel on the bicycle and the one in the military uniform, Hiroaki too was an angel.

This bristly-haired angel in the second year of junior high introduced into my infant soul the desire to be carried off far, far away. Traveling medicine-salesmen and entertainers and mediums came to our village from time to time. The village adults would threaten the children, saying that these medicine-salesmen, entertainers, and mediums would steal us away; but I *wanted* to be stolen away by the medicine man, with his thick sideburns and the huge cloth bag he carried on his back; by the entertainer, the line of whose nose was accented with a single streak of white face paint, and who danced in time to clanging cymbals; and by the mendicant, who asked for alms after chanting an invocation in a deep, frightening voice. They were all angels who had taken the form of a traveling medicine-salesman, an entertainer, or a mendicant.

And the most impressive of all these abducting angels were the troupe of circus performers.

Leaving the southern outskirts of Nōgata and crossing a bridge over the railway tracks, you came to Taga Shrine, behind its soot-blackened stone torii. If Tsurugi Shrine was the center of devotion for the villagers of Shinnyū, Taga Shrine was the one that towered up in the hearts of Nōgata people. It enshrined the parental deities of Amaterasu Ōmikami, the sun goddess and ancestress of the imperial family. As such, it far outranked a village shrine like Tsurugi and was much more splendidly built.

You would pass beneath the *torii* and walk along a gravel path between low, soot-colored privet hedges until you came to a gallery guarded by images of Takeuchi Sukune no Mikoto and one other minor deity. The gallery extended around the shrine's main hall in all four directions. Entering the passageway between the two guardian deities, you followed a stone-paved path up to the main hall itself. Inside the main hall were plain wooden stands bearing white china bottles for ritual sake and white paper pendants marking the sacredness of the place, and beyond these was enshrined a well-polished metal mirror, the symbol of the deity.

Though it was already included as part of my universe, I had only occasionally been taken to Nōgata by adults, and it seemed to me a foreign place. Taga Shrine, therefore, was the home of a foreign deity. The only attractions at a Tsurugi Shrine festival would be things like "savory pancakes, Western-style," "Tokyo pound cake," balloon vendors, and peepshows. But during festivals at Taga Shrine, the path to the main hall was lined with tents: an ox-girl, a snake-girl, a "human cistern," a haunted house, a circus—painted advertisements and banners for all of them fluttered in the breeze to the sound of accordions and cymbals. The rasping voices of the barkers for the various shows coming through old-fashioned microphones; the tents much weathered by wind and rain; the smell of cheap face-paint—they were all colors and sounds and smells from a strange land.

It wasn't just that the town of Nōgata was a strange country that I could see. Nōgata and Taga Shrine were only temporarily strange lands; but the objects of worship carried on the floats and the shows in the various tents at the festival were things that came from the real, invisible foreign land beyond the mountains. But why did that unknown foreign land fill me with such nostalgia? I think it was probably because

I had belonged to it from the very beginning, and believed that I would someday be spirited away there, in keeping with my true nature. When I thought of that "foreign land," I meant my uncle, who had left me behind when I was very little, and Mt. Hiko, where he might well have turned into a *tengu*.

Among all the tent shows, the one that most attracted my attention, that made me stop, as if rooted to the ground, was the circus tent. Elephants and giraffes were shown running across a savannah where tall palm trees and banana plants grew. From the rear came a lion and from in front a tiger in hot pursuit. In the distance a man dressed explorer-style in pith helmet, short-sleeved shirt, and short pants stood firing his gun straight at me. In front of such a canvas as it swayed in the breeze, a bald man in a clown suit was shouting to the passersby, holding in one hand a microphone that provided sudden interludes of violent static now and then: "Come one, come all to the amazing Yamashita Circus, heir to the famous Kinoshita Circus, loved not only in Tokyo but throughout the world! Acrobats swinging through the air and diving through rings of fire, a lovely young lady who tames wild animals, children, big and little, riding on an elephant—all here for your entertainment!"

Then the canvas curtain with its exotic tropical scene was raised, and to the accompaniment of ever-louder band music, an elephant approached, brushing against the raised curtain. On its strange-looking, nearly hairless back, two lads, one about seven and the other about three years of age, sat side-saddle. They wore light-blue trousers covered with gold and silver star-shaped spangles and purple vests to match, and sent big smiles out to the people standing outside the tent. They left a vivid impression with their almost sorrowfully large eyes, outlined in mascara, and their charming noses, highlighted with single lines of white face paint as they and their elephant mount vanished behind the quickly lowered curtain. During a short interval, you could hear the sound of a whip being cracked against the floor to make things more exciting.

"Hear that? The kidnappers are cracking their whip!"

Who was it who supplied that explanation to me, as I sat piggyback there? Hearing it, and aided by my active imagination, I formed a clear image of the head of the circus, whom I had been hearing about for some time. He would stand with his legs apart, wearing tall leather boots like an army officer's. His trousers would fit perfectly into the tops of his boots, and the shoulders of his leather jacket would be hand-somely squared. With the fingertips of one of his leather-gloved hands, he would hold a whip. After having struck the floor, the whip should just be hanging limply from the fingertips of his now-relaxed hand, yet it undulated like a snake fleeing the sunlight.

Above the square shoulders of the leather jacket, I set the handsome face of my uncle. I thought about the intimate time I had shared with him in the dimness of his room at dusk that day. Then, too, his black belt had descended on me as a whip.

I raised a ruckus there on my carrier's shoulders, demanding to go into the tent, but he ignored me completely. When, on my perch, I started kicking at the air, he said angrily, "You want to be like those kids just now? They don't feed them right, and they lock them up at night so they can't get away!"

And in fact, I did want to become one of those boys on the back of the elephant. The adults said they were unlucky, but I saw them as spangled with stars, a white line of makeup drawn on their noses—the sign of their election. Who cared if they weren't fed properly? Worldly things like food were not needed by the chosen ones. And as for that prison where they were held captive each night—wasn't it filled with dark, secret joys, like the dim room I remembered so well?

So I raised a ruckus. I did so because I wanted to go into the tent of the "abductors." But the adults thought that I was acting that way because I was afraid of the abductors, and so they took me back home. All that evening, I cried, screaming "I want to see the circus!" Not knowing how to handle me, the adults gave in and took me to Taga Shrine the next morning. But the festival was over, and the road through the shrine showed no signs of the tents; only scraps of paper were blowing about in the morning breeze. I was sure that the head of the troupe in his square-shouldered leather jacket had taken each of the spangled princes in his well-muscled arms and flown through the air beyond the mountains, like a *tengu*. The elephant and the clown-barker and the tent would have flown through the air as well, following them. I didn't cry anymore.

"Can you see Tokyo? Can you see Tokyo?" An adult would press his hands to my temples and lift me up almost as far as heaven. In the midst of the pain from my temples and a feeling of insecurity as I swung in the air, it seemed to me that I saw for a moment something dazzling in the distant sky.

I kicked my feet as I shouted in a shrill voice, "Yeah, I see it! I can see Tokyo!" I wanted to be free as soon as possible from the pain in my temples and the feeling of swinging in the air. Yet once I was let down, I wanted to see the dazzling thing again, even in the midst of pain.

It wasn't my father's hands that held me up. He had died on the 105th day after my birth. Nor were they my mother's. She had left me behind when she went away to find work, and she seldom came back to our town. I was left in the care of my grandmother, but she and the others went off to work all day, and were not at home much at all. From the age of three, I had to make a cold lunch and slurp down cold soup all by myself. The person who lifted me up to show me "Tokyo" must have been some other adult, who felt sorry for me.

Or perhaps that adult intended to show me the place beyond the mountains where the parents of this orphaned child lived. And, certainly, that lonely little boy could feel the presence of a family to which he belonged, there beyond the mountains. It couldn't be that he alone should be this lonely, this unhappy. He ought to be surrounded by a much larger family, and be much happier.

I did not, however, include my father and mother among that family. My father had left me while the first light of consciousness had yet to penetrate the darkness of my soul: it was as if he had never existed. And then my mother—she who abandoned me any number of times and went away—how could she be a part of that family for which I felt such nostalgia? The only one of my relatives who could be part of that family was my uncle, who had "gone for a soldier."

Around that time, my mother went to Tianjin in northern China in pursuit of a lover. The place she had gone to was a distant, dazzling one, beyond the sea that I had never seen, which was beyond the mountains; but still, my mother could not be grouped together with my uncle. On the other hand, the picture books and toy gliders and paper parachutes that my mother sent from time to time could certainly be gifts from my uncle's side.

Whether at my grandmother's or at one of the families I was sent to for foster care, I eagerly opened up these gifts sent me from that dazzling place.

The picture books, the toy gliders, and the paper parachutes were all part and parcel of the soldiers who formed my family in that dazzling place. Just as the letters from my uncle had been, so too the picture books, toy gliders, and paper parachutes were letters giving me news from the other side, to which I had originally belonged. And yet the picture book dealing with "The Three Heroic Soldiers Who Became Human Bombs" got lost on the veranda of my grandmother's house. The toy glider carrying an invisible kamikaze pilot got dropped into the muck behind a factory on the outskirts of Nōgata, where I had been sent as a foster child, and became all muddy. The paper parachute with a lead reconnoitering-party soldier dangling from it got caught on the tallest branch of a persimmon tree that grew behind my aunt's house, and grew shabby-looking as it swayed there.

At last my mother returned from China. I had entered primary school by then, and we moved to Moji, beyond the mountains. Moji served as a port for many freighters, and it was filled with soldiers about to be sent overseas.

Once, as I stood holding fast to my mother on the Western Railways train, a private second-class in a brown overcoat was standing in front of me. I could smell the familiar military odor of the overcoat, close enough to brush against my tender nose; I looked at the flat gold buttons one by one, going from bottom to top; and finally I peered into the face shadowed by a field cap pulled down low. The soldier became aware of the young child looking up at him, took from his pocket something in a paper wrapper, and put it in my hand. After getting off the train, I opened it and found several pieces of sugar candy, which was reserved for soldiers. When I brought it to my nose, I could smell the faint odor of the soldier's overcoat; and I kept that treasure in my desk drawer for a good long time.

Another time, my mother and I were on our way home from seeing a motion picture. We stood at a rail crossing, blown by strong winds from the ocean, and waited a long time for a locomotive engine to be replaced. A solder came from behind and stood next to us and suddenly put a slip of paper into my hand. I looked up in surprise, and he said, "Take it home and then look at it. It's something real nice." The barrier at last was lifted, and we crossed together. I looked up any number of times at the soldier walking alongside me, but his face was covered in shadows. My mother, who was walking on the other side of me, thanked him repeatedly.

After we crossed the tram tracks, the road divided into three. Giving us a military salute, the soldier took the road that went alongside the tracks; we took the road that led toward the ocean, at a right angle to the tracks.

Unable to wait until I got home, I stopped beneath the naked bulb

of the first street light we came to, opened my tightly closed fist, and
looked. The slip of paper in my hand was a used Western Railways
ticket for Orio. "Imagine making fun of an innocent child like that!"
exclaimed my mother angrily; but I carefully put the used ticket away
in my breast pocket. Children love tickets, even if they're of no use.
Besides which, although the ticket's visible destination was Orio, to me
it was a ticket to that dazzling place I longed for. It had lost its power, I
thought, because I had broken my promise to "look" only "after returning home."

I had gone beyond the mountains, in terms of Nōgata; in other words,
I had come to the Beyond. I'd boarded a train together with my mother
and arrived in Moji. The day I entered our new house, near the sea,
everything was new: the horse-drawn baggage carts that continually
went by, rattling our glass front door; the sea, which was right at the
end of the lane next to our house; the castle-like red-brick brewery
that rose up in the western part of the town. Yet the freshness of these
things faded almost at once. I had to learn that when my foot trod
there, or my fingers touched them, or my eyes saw them, those new
scenes instantaneously became "here." The Beyond had fled to a place
still further in the direction that the roads the horse carts were running
along pointed to; a place still ahead of the destinations of those ocean-
borne ships.

On the one hand, this meant that I was someone who had come
from the Beyond, since the first grade, group 1 students at the school
I had transferred to knew nothing of Nōgata, beyond the mountains.
Even now I can recall the excitement in the classroom when, accompanied by Miss Fujikawa and Miss Yoshida Hana, our homeroom teachers, I stood on the teaching platform at the front of the class.

"I want to introduce our new friend, Takahashi Mutsuo, who's come
to us from Nōgata."

When Miss Yoshida said those words, I felt myself captured by 100
glittering eyes. The substance of all that bright radiance was curiosity. Just as the eyes of the crowd, including me, had captured the two
princes spangled with stars beyond the raised circus curtain, so too did
everyone's eyes capture me at that moment. Those many eyes were as
one in believing that I had come from the Beyond. I was bewildered,
never before having been the radiant center of such attention.

I was given the second seat from the rear in the second row, counting from the corridor, placed between two girls surnamed Kume and Ogino. I read aloud from our Japanese textbook as one of fifty voices; along with everyone else, I drank one-fiftieth of the miso bean-paste soup provided by the school; and by noon recess, I had somehow blended in nicely with the other pupils. They welcomed me into the circle of blindman's bluff, and inside the charcoal lines drawn for the master cat game. It looked as if the transfer student from beyond the mountains was to become just another inconspicuous member of the first grade, group 1 class.

After about a month had passed, there was a storytelling session. Students climbed onto the teaching platform one by one, starting from the first child in the row nearest the corridor. Each talked about whatever he or she wanted to, and then sat down. Then it was the next student's turn. I was the second from the rear in the second row. The talks by the first-grade elementary-school pupils lasted three minutes at most; some pupils told riddles that took less than thirty seconds. Soon it would be my turn. My heart was ticking away like the second hand on some clock whose inner mechanism has gone crazy. I was hoping that the recess bell would ring right away. As Kume from the seat in front of me was finishing her rather affected version of Aesop's fable of "The Fox's Sour Grapes," the bell signaling the end of classes could be heard from the playground beyond the corridor. My relief, however, lasted only for a second, as Miss Yoshida announced that there would be no recess that day, and that the storytelling would continue into the next hour.

"Takahashi Mutsuo is next."

It was my turn! The clock that was my heart seemed suddenly to stop. I stood up and walked between the rows of classmates, who turned to look at me, heading for the teacher's platform. I seemed to be treading empty space. The faces I looked down at from the platform were out of focus, as if viewed through too strong a lens—I couldn't distinguish among eyes, noses, and mouths. I could tell, however, that those flat, wavering faces were all gazing at me.

I felt dizzy. Yet despite that, my mouth opened automatically and began to spew forth funny stories about Mokubei, which I remembered having heard from someone or other when I was in Nōgata: Mokubei was sitting by the edge of a pond plucking crab-lice from his testicles. A crow cawed at him, "Ko-kaa, Ko-kaa," those sounds the same as the words for, "Is that your kid?" And Mokubei answered, "It's not my kid, as it happens." Actually it was hard to know whether he was saying "as it happens" or "It's my balls!" since the sounds for those words were also the same.

When someone praised the rapid growth of the scallions in his garden, Mokubei complained, "They grow quickly enough, all right, but the thing is, they're all hollow inside!"

Mokubei's wife was illiterate and mispronounced common words, creating spoonerisms, and thus providing fodder for her husband's humor.

And there were specific words that tickled Mokubei's fancy: "Pot lid! Step on that and this pops up!" And, "Oh shit—the reason for a thing and your asshole—there's only ever one!"

By the time I finished, I was so tired I wanted to hunker down right there on the teaching platform. I couldn't do that, though, because these stories about Mokubei that spewed from my mouth in a kind of desperation, country-hick jokes though they were, had delighted the whole class, which responded by offering to me, as one who had come from Beyond, their thanks in the form of a wave of applause. In addition, a completely unexpected change was occurring inside my schoolboy's short pants. I needed to be determined and resolute, in order both to be worthy of their thanks, and to hide what was going on inside my shorts.

I had once again become the radiant center of everyone's curiosity. I knew all about matters beyond the mountains, of which they knew nothing. When, during study period, Miss Yoshida Hana came to replace Miss Fujikawa, all the pupils demanded "another story from Takahashi!"

My shining status was not limited to the first grade, number 1 group, either. Rumors that "Takahashi's a good storyteller" spread throughout the school, and the fifth- and sixth-grade classes sent messengers asking if they could borrow me. Miss Fujikawa would urge me to go right in the middle of reading and arithmetic lessons, and my classmates watched me leave with envious eyes. On the teaching platform of the fifth-grade number 1 group, and on the teaching platform of the sixth-grade number 3 group, I secretly worked changes inside my shorts, thinking of my distant uncle.

In the town beside the coast, where my new house was, I was again a chosen one, in a different sense from at school. I was a much fought-over prize among the rowdy kids who ran around the backstreets of that town.

At that point, we had scads of cookies and candies sent by my mother's lover in Tianjin. It was a time of scarcity in Japan; and naturally the pockets of my shorts, always bulging with sweets, must have won the hearts of the other kids, starved for anything sweet as they were.

Yet it would be truer to say, I think, that it was not so much the sweets themselves as the brightly colored cellophane wrappers printed with English words in gold letters, in which the sweets were wrapped, and also my shorts and shirts themselves, inseparable from the sweet smell of candy—it was these things, rather, that aroused the children's longing for the unknown. They didn't necessarily long for the candy itself. There were some who just wanted the small pieces of cellophane around the sweets. They had discovered a new game: putting those pieces of cellophane to their mouths and making a blowing sound— poo, poo! Some of my friends were eager to touch my shorts and shirts. In contrast to their patched and dirty clothes, the things my mother had brought me from China looked neat and always smelled of soap.

They all called me "China Boy," from the children's play song of that name. Children used to face the one who was chosen to be "It" and sing, "Let's play, China Boy!" The one who was "It" would answer, "I'm eating my meal just now." Everyone would ask, "What're you having?" "It" would answer, "Pickled plums and radishes." But those "Pickled plums and radishes" would often change to "Snake!" which made everyone run away as fast as they could. They always picked me to be "It." I would answer "Cookies!" or "Candy!" instead of the expected "Snake!" though.

The children related to this boy from beyond the mountains in two ways simultaneously: with longing and with repulsion. It was their longing for the place beyond the mountains that made them pass me from one group to another. Their means of passing me on was repulsion. The point was that these rowdy kids dragged me into their groups by violence so that they could make me part of their "sex games."

There were three groups of young rowdies in the area by the sea. They were centered on Ei, the son of the local council chairman; on Kiyo, the head of the student group in the elementary school; and on the son of the boss of the Ando group of street-stall keepers, who controlled a nearby neighborhood. Ando was a bit of an outsider, a fence-sitter who attached himself to Ei's group for a while but then shifted to Kiyo's. So there were really only two groups that mattered.

Partly because our mothers were good friends, I was in Ei's group at first. It consisted of Ei, in third grade, and "Onion," his little brother, who was in first grade; Ishida, a third grader who was the son of a postal worker; Teraura Yoshiaki, the son of a factory worker, and a first grader; and me. While in this group, I received instruction in the "sex game" from Yoshiaki, known as a weakling; then from stubborn-as-a-rock Ishida; and lastly from Ei and his little brother, who liked to put on a show of strength. As a sign of loyalty, I visited the council chairman's house every evening. Ei, Onion, and I could hear his parents chatting in the next room as we stripped from the waist down and played with the things we found between each other's thighs, taking them into our mouths there in the dark, with only a little light seeping in from the cheerful family scene taking place right next to us.

Ei taught me the ins-and-outs of "sex play," but he didn't train me how to fight. He himself hardly ever used violence against the members of his group. His body was brown, tight, and agile-looking, but it seemed he had only the authority of his father, the local committee chief, to rely on, as the tag line given him by Kiyo indicated: "Eigorō, always trying to seem stronger than he is." I was dissatisfied with his lack of forcefulness. After all, hadn't love been inextricably tied to violence in the rite of love between my uncle and me, which had been very much like the secret exchange of friendly courtesies among Ei, his younger brother, and myself?

Just around that time, I was summoned by Kiyo's group. The summons came from Okino Tetsu, a third grader who had recently come to the fore in that group:

"You've been getting cheeky lately, so I'm gonna beat you up good! Wait for me at the funnel." "Funnel" was a mistake for "tunnel," and referred to an underpass where puddles tended to form, below the rail crossing on the way home from school. I had no duty to wait just because I was told to do so, but I *did* wait by a puddle in the deserted underpass. What sort of expression did I wear, I wonder, as I waited in terror for the coming of that fierce radiance. As foretold, Tetsu drowned me in an oceanic nosebleed. His painful blows, however, filled me with a strangely keen pleasure. On the way home, I vacantly remembered the dimness of my uncle's room. At home, my mother tried persistently to get the name of my assailant out of me, but I never revealed it.

Two or three days later as I stood on the seacoast, a classmate named Shiokawa Tamotsu came to get me. This small, dark-complexioned first grader was quick to fight, and was a powerful member of Kiyo's group. I followed Tamotsu to the area behind the beer company's warehouse. He brought out his penis to show me, and I followed his lead. He came closer and rubbed his penis against mine. Then he pulled his foreskin forward and placed it around the tip of *my* penis.

"When we do this, it feels great, like fucking a girl—right?"

I didn't have any sensation of pleasure, but I nodded and answered, "Yeah, it feels good." I wouldn't be accepted in their group, I thought, unless I agreed with Tamotsu. And indeed, this intimate act was a test for admission to the group. I knew that it was so because, on the very next day, I was permitted to join the group in their excursion to the boat-builder's shack.

The boat-builder's shack. . . . It was a crude hut that blocked the view of the sea at the very end of a back street reeking of urine that ran next to my house. The old man had gathered driftwood washed ashore by the sea on a stormy day and thoroughly gnawed at by insects, had roughly clamped the pieces together to form walls on three sides, and then, on the side facing the sea, had hinged together two old doors from somewhere or other. A large piece of rusty tin formed the roof. The master of this shack blown by harsh sea winds was a small old man known to all as "the old boat-builder."

In the daytime his compact body, red-copper color from the top of his bald head to the soles of his bare feet, was covered only with a short coat, grubby from constant use, and a loincloth that looked as if it had been boiled in low-grade salt, and that served for both summer and winter.

"He can tell tomorrow's weather from that loincloth," the adults would say, "and that's why he never washes it, no matter how dirty it gets."

There was another resident of the shack—a young girl. She always wore a plain kimono of common silk, faded from frequent washings. With her hair hanging down in two braids, schoolgirl fashion, she would bring a bucket to get water to do her laundry from the pump located midway down the urine-smelling back street. That spot was always lively, with women drawing water and doing laundry, and children playing. The women would try to talk to the girl from the boat-builder's hut, but she just answered "Yes" or "No" and showed no inclination to talk. Sitting in front of her bucket filled with water and busily moving her hands over the washboard, however, stray locks of hair would fall on her rosy cheeks, like any young girl's, and her bosom looked ample beneath the kimono, drawn neatly around her.

Rumor had it that she was the old boat-builder's only child.

"Her mother had a lover and ran off with him, and the old man raised his daughter all by himself. He's afraid some man'll take her away from him, and that's why he doesn't let her dress like a woman should." That's what the adults said; and there were some who added: "The old man and his daughter sleep together on a single futon, they say . . ."

"Yeah, but I hear she's got a man, even so," offered another adult.

"Yeah, he's a young railway worker. The old man's afraid that they'll get up to something on the sly, so he makes them meet at the shack."

"Well, they can't do anything right in front of the old man, can they, the poor things!" The adults smiled suggestively.

We kids were crazy to see the inside of the boat-builder's shack. It was surrounded by scorching hot sand, beyond which the sea gave off a flame-like light. To the left of the hut, the old man would be at work on a small boat, removing the nails he held between his lips and pounding them into the side of the boat one by one. At times like that, we would slip out of our *geta*, sneak up to the hut from the right side, and peek in through the half-rotten planks, as the sea lice scurried away. It was hard for our eyes, used to intense sunlight, to see anything in the gloom of the hut. We would press our eyes to the holes in the wood in an effort to see better, and then a stone would come flying in our direction. Looking to see where the stone had come from, we discovered the old man standing on the shoreline, screaming at us. His narrow eyes and the white hair on either side of his bald head and around his ears were gleaming.

But children are good at evading adults' attention. We learned from a report by Kitahara Yoshinori, who was not yet even in primary school, that on a given day the residents of the shack were both away. The daughter had gone to draw water while it was still dark, and was not back yet, and the old man had gone to look for her. Our band of six, led by Okino Tetsu, raced over the sand, heading for the hut. I was among them, by permission of Tetsu.

The wooden door that faced the sea was only held in place by bricks piled outside. Excited, we tugged at the door—it was like the moment you open a chest full of treasures that you had been longing to see.

Together with the daylight, we danced in and saw at once a grimy futon folded near the wall facing us, and on a nail above that, a kimono with a bright flower pattern that was completely at odds with the atmosphere of the shack itself. As our eyes got used to the darkness of the hut, so different from the dazzling sandy beach we had just left, we could see near the entrance a small clay cooking stove with a pot and kettle, a chopping board and cleaver, a water jug, and a tub of pickles and the like. On the walls on either side were hung a carpenter's plane and adze, a hammer, and other tools. Several large empty sake bottles lay about the floor.

At Tetsu's direction, we closed the entrance door from inside. We unfolded the futon on the floor, which was gritty with sand, took off our trousers, and began rolling around on the futon. Tamotsu grabbed the flowery kimono from its nail, pulled it over his head, and began to play the part of a woman coming on to Tetsu. It was a wild scene! These rowdy boys, from five to eight years of age, made their little "horns of flesh" stand erect and gave themselves endlessly to their play.

As a sign of acceptance, I was "mounted" by all the members of the group (including even five-year-old Yoshinori) one after the other. Through it all I kept my eyes wide open. Countless rays of light poured in from the gaps in the walls on all sides. I remembered the dimness of the Eizen shack where I had heard the story about Shinno long before, and the dimness of Uncle Ken's room.

Next day in the evening, I heard cries of "Murder! Murder!" and rushed to the boat-builder's hut. I thought that yesterday's ravages had been discovered and that Tetsu had been killed by the old man. The shack was surrounded by a great crowd of people. I squirmed my way through the ranks of adults and came out in the middle of it all. The old man, his carpenter's adze in hand, was panting, held back by two men of the neighborhood.

"Lemme go! Take your damn hands off me! A daughter who won't obey her father—Why, I'll kill her with my own hands."

It wasn't Tetsu after all. The old man had brought his daughter home, quarreled with her, and then run out onto the beach, intending to kill her.

Two passing fishermen had restrained him. His dirty coat was slipping from his shoulders, and his mouth was drooling messily. He smelled of sake. Probably he had been drinking, and that was the lead-in to the quarrel with his daughter.

As usual, the adults were whispering among themselves.

"It seems she ran off with the railway worker, and Gramps discovered them wandering around in front of Kokura Station."

"And they say the daughter had the railway worker's baby in her belly—about five months, it was!"

"The old man watched her like a hawk! I wonder when she managed to get pregnant . . ."

"He may intend to watch her like a hawk, but he's an old man. He's in his second childhood!"

"He controlled himself till he got her home, and then couldn't stand it anymore and started to drink. And this is the way it ends up."

I listened, rapt, as if I were hearing a fragment of some holy legend. The girl ran away from the old man once again, and never came back. It was rumored that she was living in Hakata with the railway worker. The old man became still more taciturn and spent all day hard at work on his boats.

"He's a real master," the adults said. "People come from Ōshima in Suwa and Innoshima, even, to order boats from him."

When evening came, the old man would bring out his fishing nets and cast them wide, as if to catch distant Hikoshima, dyed in twilight colors on the opposite shore. Did he do that time after time, hoping in his heart to catch his now absent daughter and the railway worker who had run off with her, I wonder? With feet planted firmly on the shoreline where slivers of twilight burst among the waves, silhouetted there against the failing light, this lonely old man casting his net seemed like a holy Apostle of old.

We rowdy kids could hardly be expected not to take advantage of the weakened state of the old man, now that he had lost his daughter. When the sun went down and the stars appeared, the children would surround the boat the old man had been working on, there beside his hut. The central figure at such times was Kiyo. He was now a sixth grader, and left the management of the group to Tetsu. But though he had "retired," he was still at the center of things whenever "dirty jokes" were on.

As a sixth grader, he wore long trousers and had a hand towel smartly at his waist. Goggle-eyed and pimply, Kiyo would settle himself on top of the boat. On either side of him were Tetsu and the "guest" Ando, with everyone else surrounding the three. When everyone was in place, Kiyo would at last begin: "You lot—Do you know what you call doing it standing up?"

"Nope," Tetsu would say.

"Nope," Ando would say.

Then everyone would say "Nope," one after the other.

"You don't know either?" Kiyo would ask each one, until he came to me.

"Hey, the China Boy's here too! This kind of dirty joke's not for you, China Boy. Go on home."

Everybody roared with laughter. I got beet-red in the darkness. I was no longer a radiant person who had come from a dazzling place; I had received a sentence of banishment, deemed unworthy even to receive news of that dazzling place. "Boy." "Boy." "China Boy." Now, if asked "What are you eating for your meal?" I answered "Snake!" nobody would run away. And if I shouted "Sweets!" no one would look in my direction. Because Kiyo's "dirty jokes" were full of mystery, and far more appealing than anything I could say.

Kiyo would continue: "You don't know? Dummies! You do it standing up, so it's called 'a standing fuck.'" Kiyo laughed suggestively. After a little while, everyone else did too.

"If you do it sitting down, it's called 'a sitting fuck.' If you do it diving into the water, it's called 'a water fuck.' But you gotta be careful not to let water into the woman's beaver, or she'll die. If you do it on a boat, it's called 'a boat fuck.' When the boat rolls and you roll with it, it feels super-good! And then there's this one: A young sailor on a fishing expedition catches an octopus, brings it back, and then does it with the octopus. He makes the octopus's suckers suck on him! That's called 'an octopus fuck.'"

The words that came from Kiyo's mouth, full of decaying teeth and foul breath, were obscene, but at the same time wrapped in an unknown radiance. So far as I knew, such things as women did not exist in that dazzling place beyond the rails that had carried Uncle Ken away. Nonetheless, I was pained to hear what Kiyo said. My pain resulted from the fear that I might be exiled forever from the profound secret involving my uncle. I thought of women as horrifying things, like the suckers on an octopus.

"Come here, Boy!" When I went forward, Kiyo pointed to the place between his thighs that was already showing an obvious change.

"Gimme a hand job!"

Within thirty seconds, before everyone's anxious gaze, the motion of my hands made Kiyo cry out, as a rich, thick substance flew onto the ship's planks. At almost the same moment, the door of the old man's hut flew open: "You little bastards! What the hell are you up to now?"

"It's Gramps!" someone shouted, and we all jumped down from the boat and ran off as fast as our legs would carry us.

We soon learned what it was that had made the old man so angry. Once the planing of the surface of the boat that we had been sitting on was finished, tar was applied to the sides, and the name *Abe-maru* was scrawled there in red paint. "Ohh, so it was Gramps's own boat . . ." We understood now, for Abe was the old man's family name.

One day in early winter, when I was getting ready to go to school, Tamotsu came running, all out of breath. "The old boat-builder's disappeared!" We ran to the beach but there was no sign of the *Abe-maru*. We pulled aside the door of the shack and found it completely empty. Soon there was a crowd of children there. We gazed at the offing, forgetting that our geta were being wetted by the tide, which had just begun to shift from full to low there on the beach.

A man wearing sunglasses came toward us, his boots creaking in the sand. He was a boat owner, the only one on the beach to have a motorboat—"Motorboat Nishikawa," we called him. He would know everything there was to know about the sea. . . . We stared up at him.

"The old boat-builder? Why, he got into the boat he'd made for himself and went off somewhere before dawn today." Motorboat Nishikawa laughed loudly.

"But where? Where did he go?" we asked; but whether it was to Hikoshima, visible just over there, or to Ura Moji, hidden beyond Mt. Tonoue, or to the old man's hometown of Innoshima, or to someplace else entirely—even this adult who knew all there was to know about the sea could not say.

"Women caused Gramps a lot of trouble, so maybe he went to an island where there aren't any women!" Motorboat Nishikawa laughed again, but his laughter didn't have the force or energy it had had earlier. The words "an island where there aren't any women," however, echoed in my heart. "An island where there aren't any women"—wasn't this another name for that dazzling place to which my uncle, in the guise of a soldier, had departed forever?

I looked again at the offing. In its deep green, I saw a sea railway, the white wake left behind by a boat that has passed by. I had no way of knowing what boat in fact had made that wake, but it seemed to me a path left by the old man's boat, *Abe-maru*.

The distant view to the west from the town of Moji in northern Kyushu is blocked by the Hobashira mountains near Yahata. The flocks of steel birds that roared through the air in my childhood at first flew over our heads and disappeared beyond the Hobashiras, but later came from beyond those mountains and flew over our heads going in the opposite direction.

Clearly, the war was going badly. The airplanes that disappeared beyond the Hobashiras had been those of our Japanese Air Force, while those that came from beyond were American.

When a black formation of planes appeared from that direction, sirens and fire alarms would echo across our town, and we schoolchildren would rush from the gate of the primary school, satchels strapped to our backs. As I ran, breathing hard, I would often look up into the sky. Those steel birds seemed to me to be signals sent by "the real but distant family" that I so missed.

At night, too, the sirens and fire alarms would sound when I was fast asleep. I'd put a protective cap on my head, wear a wadded cotton jacket, and rush to the air-raid shelter by the beach. Looking from the beach, I could see the western side of the river-like straits dividing Moji from Shimonoseki—the Yahata coastline—entirely ablaze, while the fires burning at many points along the Shimonoseki coastline on the opposite bank came to form a continuous line even as I watched. I gazed at the scene almost in wonder. For me, there was no distinction to be made between my uncle's army and the enemy's. There was only here and over there, Beyond.

Next day in drawing class I drew a picture of the war, and was praised by my teacher, Mr. Sugino. In the foreground, there were two large U.S. Grumman fighters falling through the air in flames. In the distance, another two Grummans were caught in the intersecting beams of searchlights. Below, towns were beautifully burning. My picture was in praise of the Grummans, though Mr. Sugino didn't seem to be aware of that. Even now I wonder if there is anything so beautiful as the moment a plane goes down in flames. The Holy Spirit descended in the form of tongues of fire. The earth that awaited that fiery descent was also burning.

In Moji, too, American planes often fell from the sky. The destination of these planes that fell spouting flames was usually mountainous areas like Jinai or Nagakuro or Okuda. Classmates who came from the mountain areas would pick up fragments of bulletproof glass that were scattered around the wreckage and show them to us. When we rubbed those fragments against the tops of our desks, they gave off a sweet, pleasant smell. Hashimoto Tora and Matsumoto Katsu kept these fragrant pieces of glass in their pockets, and, to me, the insides of their pockets seemed radiant.

One day, hearing that an enemy plane had fallen in a grove of trees near Nagakuro, I ran to see it, along with Tamotsu and Onion. When, panting heavily, we arrived at the site of the wreckage, we found that a rope was stretched from scorched tree to scorched tree, and a soldier with an armband was walking around the area. There was a strong scorched smell.

On the way home, Onion said, "There was an American soldier all charred black and everything! I saw it, but I was afraid of the military policeman, so I didn't say anything."

"Liar!" said Tamotsu angrily, giving him a punch. Onion started to cry. But I also thought I'd seen a charred American back there. The soldier from that dazzling place was charred black all right, but he left us those pieces of sweetly fragrant glass. I regretted more than anything that I had been unable to pick up any of that fragrant glass.

Okinawa fell, and the number of enemy flights from beyond the Hobashira mountains increased more and more. The enemy planes dropped many mines in the ocean as well, and ships blew up in the offing virtually every day. It was rumored that the red and blue devils from America would be landing any day now. In the schoolyard, members of the Women's Patriotic Association, dressed in white aprons with white cloth bands to secure their sleeves, practiced using bamboo spears.

The end of the war came suddenly. I was flying paper planes in the back street where Tamotsu's house was when he came out and said quietly,

"The war's over."

Did this mean the end to communications from "my family"? In a few days, however, a continuous stream of odd-looking vehicles with flat roofs snaked their way along the Western Railway's rail lines from the direction of Kokura, beyond the mountains. The vehicles were jeeps belonging to the occupation army. From the jeeps, soldiers wearing dark-green uniforms with rectangular caps of the same color on their heads were waving and shouting. They were not the red and blue American devils we had feared, but rather messengers from that dazzling place, and we sent back to them a password that had magic power: "Hello! Hello!"

Then from the line of jeeps flew brightly colored presents. The adults looked unhappy, and muttered "Acting like beggars, you are . . ." But, like the fragrant glass from before, the cheese and chocolates and cubes of sugar were brilliant fragments bringing news from Beyond. Our group gathered in the boat-builder's hut that had now become our right and proper domain and showed each other what we'd harvested, sharing equally in the sacrament of sacred manna.

With the war's end and the end to lighting restrictions and curfews, we found that there were all sorts of empty places in the town of Moji. "Old Moji," on the eastern outskirts, was almost entirely burnt out. In Dairi to the west, where my house was, roughly twenty percent of the land had been turned into empty lots by the wartime policy of forced evacuation. In Hiroishi, Shirakizaki, Kuzuha, and Komorie, between those two areas, there were ruins of burned buildings here and there. These nail marks of the war seemed to me to be hidden escape routes leading "over there." I thought that the people who had lived there had gone, via those empty lots, to a place that the rest of us could not touch.

A strangely large number of murders took place in those empty spaces. Every time I saw an article about such a homicide on the front page of the newspaper (now shrunk to tabloid size), I thought that the ones who had been killed were the victors in the struggle, while the killers were the losers who had failed to make it to "the other side."

Through the burned-out districts strutted the American soldiers who had come in the long line of jeeps from beyond the mountains. Between "Old Moji" and Dairi there was a bare mountain called Mt. Kazashi, with a height of nearly 500 meters. During the war, the army had had fortifications along its long ridge, which ran almost parallel to the straits. Mt. Kazashi was virtually in the center of Moji, but entrance to it was forbidden; it was a foreign land in the midst of the town. The fortifications had been taken over by the army of occupation and turned into radar stations. Mt. Kazashi remained a foreign land to me, now wearing the aspect of a branch office of that dazzling place on "the other side." The American soldiers who swaggered through town had come down from the "branch office" atop the mountain, I was sure.

Very soon the soldiers found partners in the town. Girls with frizzed hair and thick lipstick wearing bright-colored blouses walked hand in hand with the soldiers. Where had the girls come from? The adults would point to the railway lines that entered the Moji-Shimonoseki tunnel just to the east of our rail crossing, and explained that "they were burned out of their homes way over there." And indeed, the women had about them something of the smell of burned-out ruins.

They walked around holding hands like lovers, the tall soldiers and the midget-like women. Watching them, the married women of the town muttered, "Ugh. Just like animals. . . ." Though both parties came from far away, they were certainly odd, ill-matched couples.

Nevertheless, the soldiers walked with the women. Moreover, both sides of the tramway were lined with bars that catered to these couples. Their glass doors displayed depictions of soldiers and women embracing in silhouette, with the English word WELCOME written diagonally from the lower left to the upper right of the doors.

Once, at night, I was hurrying along the tramway street with my mother and a woman friend of hers. The door of a bar some ten meters ahead of us opened, and a big, tall soldier emerged with a woman who seemed as small as a child. They had taken two or three steps together when the soldier turned toward the woman, bent over, and suddenly started to kiss her on the face, which would have been about chest height were he standing upright. Bending over so quickly seemed to make him lose his balance, and he tottered a bit as he said something to the woman. "Wonder what he's saying," said my mother.

"'Gimme more,' probably . . ." answered her friend, and they both laughed.

After class the next day I stayed in our classroom to draw fire-prevention posters. My homeroom teacher, Miss Sugino, and the teacher of the homeroom next door, Miss Kitadai, were there too, doing knitting. Out of the blue, I said: "Say, do you know what an American soldier said to his whore?" The two teachers shook their heads, No. I proceeded to repeat what my mother's friend had said: "He said, 'Gimme more.'"

Miss Kitadai looked amazed and asked Miss Sugino, "Does his family run a bar or something?"

"No, but his mother's quite the sophisticate," said Miss Sugino, and the two of them exchanged glances. They didn't grasp the criticism that I was directing at the American soldier. To my way of thinking, the soldier, coming as he did from the same place as my uncle, should not have bothered to bend over for that woman, with her odor of burned-out ruins, in the first place.

The women with frizzy hair and red lipstick were not necessarily all from far away. Mitsu, Shiokawa Tamotsu's older sister, abruptly turned into a frizzy-haired woman. One of the neighborhood women went to Kokura to do some shopping and saw Mitsu, "with her hair as frizzy as wood shavings and her lips as red as if she'd just eaten someone for dinner. . . . Walking arm-in-arm with an American, like some whore!"

"Why, she's just turned fifteen!"

"Oh, but you know those Shiokawas—born with loose morals, all of 'em."

On and on the adults gossiped. Tamotsu's mother was a professional on-call barber and an attractive widow of the sort men are naturally drawn to. Perhaps the other women were envious of her.

But could Tamotsu's older sister Mitsu really have turned into a "frizzy-haired woman"? She was eight years older than we were, but still she had joined in our games. If we said "Beaver!" she made a face and answered "Prick!" Could she have become an adult woman now, who'd walk around arm-in-arm with an American soldier? Incredible. Yet the rumors seemed to be true. When we saw her on the street, she looked as childlike and immature as ever; but sure enough, her hair was frizzy, she had on twice as much lipstick as her lips warranted, and she never deigned to look at us.

I could tell she was trying to act as adult as possible. I thought of a stray dog from the beach. It still looked like a puppy, but it was pregnant and walked through the rain with the timid eyes of a bitch with pups.

Mitsu's American G.I. partner was from Camp Jōno, beyond Kokura.

Apparently they usually met in Kokura, but in time the soldier started coming to the Shiokawa home. When the G.I. and Mitsu came down the street, people stood lined up at the doors of the houses on both sides, nudging and whispering to each other. The tall blond soldier, whose arm the childlike Mitsu held firmly, seemed, despite his impressive looks, to be her captive.

After the soldier began visiting, the Shiokawa family's fortunes took a clear turn for the better. Tamotsu, who had at first disliked any talk of his elder sister, now used such topics as the army of occupation's tanks and Lockheed planes and bazookas as pretexts for talking with pride about his sister's lover.

One day on the way home from school, Tamotsu suddenly said, "Last night, I took a bath with Robert."

I nodded silently.

"He's big! He got in first, and the hot water spilled out all over the floor. I couldn't take my bath!"

I nodded. I was waiting for Tamotsu to say something else, something more important. At last he started to talk about it.

"His prick's super-big, too! It's about as big as one of those gray mullets you see jumping out of the ocean. The hair there's the same color as on his head—blond. It's all crinkly-like. . . ."

Tamotsu promised to let me touch that part of the G.I. next time. When I thought of touching that part, surrounded by the shining hair of this soldier who'd come from the place where my uncle was, I blushed.

In time, I stopped catching sight of Mitsu at all. The G.I. came by often.

"Mitsu's had a half-caste kid," the adults said. As for the soldier who scurried past the door of our house each Saturday—he was a person who no longer had any connection whatsoever with my distant uncle.

Postwar educational reform led to the reorganization of the elementary school I attended. I had been a second grader when the war ended during our summer vacation, but was now a fourth grader. Entering our classroom a few days after the opening ceremony, I found that the room was dead quiet, even though the morning class had not yet begun. A boy I had never seen before was standing on the teaching platform with Mr. Tomosada, our homeroom teacher, beside him.

"This is Kondō Yorio, who has just come to us from Tokyo. He's going to be in our number 1 group of fourth graders. I want you to make friends with him."

It was as if my own experience of that morning three years before was being reenacted. The boy atop the teaching platform looked just like me when I was a new first grader—from his freshly cropped head, fragrant with baby powder, to his neat, Sunday-best shirt and trousers.

But I had been blushing and trembling from nervousness, while this boy was relaxed and smiling. He had come, not from Nōgata right nearby, but from distant "Tokyo" itself. Was that what made him appear so self-confident?

Starting from the first-hour recess, the boy climbed on the jungle gym and did broad jumps in the sand with the rest of us. Before you knew it, this "Tokyo Boy" became one of the most popular kids in the class. Everyone completely forgot about the "China Boy" who had come from beyond the mountains three years before. Just as then every-one had been eager to hear my country-hick tales of Mokubei and to get their hands on the cellophane wrappers of the candies from Tian-jin, so now they were eager to hear Kondo's petrol-smelling stories of Tokyo and wanted the illustrated English vocabulary cards he had in his pocket. They would do anything to win "the Tokyo Boy's" admiration.

I made a point of keeping my distance from Kondō. He had robbed me of my former position as the center of attention in the class, though in fact most of the shine was already gone from that. If I approached him, it would mean acknowledging my own defeat. And yet the usurper showed goodwill toward me. One Saturday after class had let out, I was sitting by myself on the jungle gym when Kondō came over and sat alongside me.

"How about coming over to my house tomorrow?" The words that were now directed toward me were fancifully clear and pure, the same as the words in our standard textbooks. I never expected that Kondō would direct his Tokyo speech at me; and it took me a while to recover sufficiently to ask "Whereabouts do you live?" Kondo jumped off the jungle gym, crouched on the ground, and started to draw a map in the dirt with a piece of wood. I crouched down across from him and gazed at the map, which he drew in strong, careful lines, as an adult would.

"Got it?" Kondō said, raising his head. As he did so, his forehead brushed against mine. He maintained that position for a while, looking into my eyes and smiling. I never dreamed that such a gentle way of expressing goodwill existed, and was already growing to like this frank transfer student.

I could hardly sleep that night from worrying about what the weather would be like the next day. I felt that the weather on the day of my first invitation from Kondo would be a direct omen of our future relationship.

When I woke up next morning, I could hear the distant sounds from the kitchen of my mother chopping vegetables and getting water ready to boil, but I burrowed further into my futon, head and all, for quite a while. When, roused by my mother's voice, I finally stuck my head out of the quilts, I kept my eyes shut tight, turning in the direc-tion of the glass door of the veranda that faced onto the street. Then slowly I relaxed the area around my eyes and gingerly opened them a little. The very slight gap between my eyelids functioned like the gaps in a wall made of planks: the narrow rays of light that entered from there struck the sensitive crystalline lens of my eyes. The weather was fine! At last I opened my eyes wide.

Kondō's home occupied one corner of a wooden apartment building owned by the beer brewery, and was in the center of town not far from our school. It was much more spacious than the apartments of the other residents of the building, and was an indication of the high status of Kondō's father within the company. Unlike all the other apartments, Kondo's had an entrance area built on outside the front door, and standing there, I called out the greeting I had been practicing along the way: "Kondōoo!"

The glass window beside the entrance way opened, and there was Kondō, visible from the waist up, smiling at me in his pajama tops. I myself slept every night in the pajamas my mother had brought back from China for me, yet I felt that Kondō's pajamas were the garments of a prince from some distant land.

We played together the whole day in that sunlit room behind the glass window. Wooden blocks and playing cards and books—Kondō brought out these treasures redolent of Tokyo one after the other, tossing them onto the tatami mats. He was not a prince because he had treasures. Rather, they were treasures precisely because they belonged to Kondō, the prince. As proof of that, Kondō generously offered to give them all to me.

I wanted these rare gifts not because of the treasures themselves but because Kondō's fragrance clung to them. I refused to accept them, however. If he had offered them to me again, I would have taken them for sure; but this utterly frank young prince just nodded, saying "Oh, really?" and did not offer them again.

It was drawing on toward dusk when, by chance, Kondō made the same expression of goodwill toward me that he had by the jungle gym the day before. And not only that: with the delicate skin of his forehead pressed against mine, the prince from "Tokyo" said in his characteristically innocent way, "I like you better than anybody else in the fourth grade, number 1 class. Who do you like best?"

Bewildered by this completely unexpected upsurge of friendliness, for a while I could say nothing. When, blushing, I managed to say something, it was not "I like *you* best," but rather "I really dislike Tajima." I regretted it as soon as I had said it. Why couldn't I have said, honestly, "I like *you*"? Why did I have to intrude a third person like Tajima into the "private" relationship I was developing with Kondō?

Nevertheless, I felt happy at Kondō's easygoing expression of good-will. Still, the sun of my happiness was darkened by the misfortune that might come about due to my perverse response to his question. My happiness and the sharp anxiety that lay within it made me want to be by myself as soon as I could. I left Kondō's house hurriedly. He was amazed, yet he saw me off as far as the wooden gate of the apartment house.

Soon a rumor spread throughout the class: "Takahashi's trying to get in good with the boy from Tokyo." The source of the rumor was Tajima, who stood at the top of the class hierarchy. This class tough guy, with a permanent scowl on his face, wanted to be best friends with "the Tokyo Boy."

Kondō was completely unaware of this, and was always smiling at me and talking to me, whether in the classroom or on the playground. And each time, Tajima and his underlings would give me dirty looks. I started to make an effort to ignore Kondō, and he was, again, amazed at my reaction.

In fifth grade, Kondō was put into the number 3 group, with Mr. Kuratomi as his homeroom teacher. Soon he found a friend—Wakaizumi, who had transferred from Hokkaido and was put into the same number 3 group. Wakaizumi's father was the manager of the beer company's brewery, and their spacious house was located right behind Kondō's apartment building. As they went out of the school gate together, I watched them, half-dazed, from five or six paces behind, remembering how Kondō had expressed his friendliness toward me a year earlier. Now that he was gone from me, I felt all the more clearly the weight of his existence.

I had only been able to respond to his straightforward expression of friendship in a warped way, and now I was being punished for it. I thought that I must at least repay him in a straightforward way. Drumming up my courage, I stood in the entranceway of Kondō's apartment carrying two or three books under my arm. When I called out, the glass window opened, but the person who peered out at me was not Kondō but his mother, her hair drawn back into a matronly bun.

"Yorio is over at the Wakaizumis'."

I walked home through twilit streets, feeling that I alone was excluded from the charmed circle of happiness. I tried visiting Kondō four or five more times, but he was always at the Wakaizumis'. Finally, on my sixth or seventh try, I saw Kondō himself rather than his mother.

Realizing that at last I had been able to see the person I had been hoping to, I blushed and, standing there rigidly, offered him the books I'd been carrying under my arm.

"Here, I'll lend you these . . ."

For an instant, Kondō looked flummoxed by the situation. Then, after a while, he gave me his familiar smile and took the books. "Thanks," he said, and closed the window.

One day when classes were over, shortly after I had entered sixth grade, Mr. Tomosada, my homeroom teacher, stopped me as I joined the line of students noisily hurrying through the corridor on their way home. Broad-shouldered Mr. Tomosada walked in silence in the opposite direction to the flow of students, and I followed behind.

Entering the classroom, he passed in front of the teaching platform and seated himself on the teacher's seat next to it. I stood in front of his desk, and across the one meter space between us, teacher and pupil looked into each other's eyes. After what seemed a long time, Mr. Tomosada's rather thick lips opened, as did his white teeth.

"How about taking the exam for the 'Fuzok,' Takahashi?"

When they fell from between his parted teeth, the two syllables "Fuzok" emitted a dazzling light, as certain ornamental letters are drawn with ray-shaped "whiskers." All I could do to keep from being blinded by that light was to repeat to myself those two syllables beginning with "F."

I was stunned at the suddenness of it all, but Mr. Tomosada seemed to think that I had not understood him, and so supplied a commentary. He explained that "Fuzok," short for *fuzoku*—affiliated—referred to the entrance exam for the middle school affiliated with the Kokura Teacher's College.

"You've heard of it, right? So how about it? Will you take the exam? I think you could pass it."

The Kokura Teacher's College Affiliated Middle School was the best in northern Kyushu. Its uniform cap had a white line running around the headband and a badge with the characters for "Affiliated Middle" written in special script. To the primary-school students of northern Kyushu, it seemed a precious crown that could be worn only by the chosen few. That crown gave off a light from its radiant insignia, and that light was inviting me to come. This totally unexpected thing was actually happening!

At one time I, too, seemed to be someone worthy of this radiant invitation. I was often chosen to ascend the teaching platform, and the arrows of everyone's admiring eyes seemed to make me shine brightly. Gradually, however, my ascents to the heights grew fewer, and with the appearance of Kondō, I definitively lost my "shine": I became a boy of clay, standing out from the others not at all. Why should someone like that receive a summons from the light?

The teacher went on: "I hear that Kondō will also be taking the test, from the number 3 class."

Now the situation was clear to me: Kondō, the child of light, was lifting me, made of mere clay, up, so I could become worthy of the light. I was being drawn up from the thick mire, and might just be able to make the lightness of light my own. I agreed to Mr. Tomosada's suggestion.

My class's extracurricular lessons began at the end of the week. Apart from me and Tajima, who were going for the Affiliated Middle School, there were over ten students intending to take the exams for the Tokiwa Middle School and Seinan Academy. The sunlight striking the sycamores outside our classroom windows gradually diminished, and in time, the evening sun began to dye both sycamores and windows. Then the evening sun weakened and disappeared, and leek-colored dusk enclosed the playing field outside. The teacher walked over to the door that led to the corridor and turned the switch on. The classroom blazed with electric light.

Throughout the long extracurricular lessons, I listened to the teacher's explanations halfheartedly, my mind focused on Kondō, who was attending Mr. Kuratomi's class two rooms down the corridor. The thought that I was moving toward the same goal as he was enough to make me want to jump for joy.

By the time we finished and went outside, the sky above was filled with stars. I went out the school gate, laughing and joking with my classmates, but my consciousness was fixed on Kondō, there in the middle of a bunch of students from the number 3 class. We belonged to different classes, to be sure, but I felt that we had surmounted that barrier, and were as one. I wanted to run up to him, put my arm around his shoulder, and announce, "I'm going for Fuzok, too, Kondō!" But I held back.

The exams for the Affiliated Middle School were held in the early part of February. The day before, Tajima and I went to see the test site, accompanied by Mr. Tomosada. We got on the Western Railway tram in front of Moji Station and got off at Tomino in Kokura City. Then we went straight along the road that runs by the Tomino stop, heading up toward Adachi Hill.

When we reached the top of that gentle slope, Mr. Tomosada pointed out the school. It was a two-story building no different from our primary school; the glass in all the windows gleamed with a dull light from the cloudy sky. Because I was seeing it for the first time, however, and because I yearned for it to be so, the building seemed to me like a sacred hall facing toward a dazzling world.

The actual day of the exam, too, was cloudy and slightly cold. We examinees, from the five cities and two counties of northern Kyushu, gathered in the cavernous gymnasium. As I listened to the instructions of the teacher who was to proctor the exam, I kept my eyes fixed on Kondō in the next row. The exam consisted of four subjects: Japanese, mathematics, natural science, and social studies, and each subject was tested in a different classroom. Even so, the position of the desks was almost exactly the same, and Kondō was generally in the next row, a few desks ahead of me. I would always watch for him to begin writing on his answer sheet before I began writing on my own. And I always left the test site after he did.

We would go back to the gymnasium after each test to look at the correct answers marked in red on an answer sheet posted on the blackboard. I would push my way through the crowd of examinees gathered in a knot in front of the answer sheet and quickly run my eyes over it. It seemed to me sometimes that all of my answers had been correct, and sometimes that all had been wrong. Kondō was indifferent to the answer sheet, and spent his time bantering with the students from his own class.

How did I spend the one month between the day of the exam and the announcement of results? The thirty cloudy days were devoted to one thing—waiting. Had the summons from the light been counterfeit, or a real invitation? I would know the answer only when the notice of having passed the exams, that formal invitation, had come. Kondō, however, when I saw him in the school hallways or the athletic field, continued to smile as usual, completely carefree.

On the day before the announcement, as I was about to leave the classroom and go home, I was stopped by Mr. Tomosada. As before, I stood in front of his desk. After everyone else had left the classroom, he finally began to speak.

"Takahashi, you got ninety-eight points in the exams—the highest of all the examinees."

I remained silent, waiting for his next words.

"But it turns out that to enter Fuzok you need to pay a matriculation fee of 5,000 yen. One of their teachers called me and asked if your family could pay the 5,000 or not. . . ."

I understood what would follow, but let Mr. Tomosada continue.

"Five thousand yen is a lot of money. I gave it some thought and decided it would be unkind to ask your mother to pay such a large amount. So, though I felt really bad for you, I went ahead and declined your acceptance."

I had understood what he would say, but even so, hot tears welled up, and Mr. Tomosada's face and his desk and the classroom became a blur.

Through the blur, he continued: "But you know, that's the way the world is. You've got to remember that."

I left the classroom and walked across the athletic field toward the school gate. More and more hot tears came. The tear-filled lenses of my eyes blurred the playing field and school building, but I could clearly see Kondō in the middle of the playing field, laughing and talking with some students from number 3 class as they played dodge ball. His happy face meant that he, without doubt, had received a formal invitation from the light. Kondō was now, clearly, a person of "the other side."

That night as I lay in bed, I used my hand to abuse myself all the way, for the first time. I was miserable. I had now been definitely cast aside by my shining family there Beyond.

In my second semester in middle school, there was a transfer student, this time from Kobe. Accompanied by his mother and Mr. Kawano, our homeroom teacher, he stood on the teaching platform: slightly dark skin, clear, near-black eyes, a well-formed nose, tight lips—in short, a handsome first-year middle-school boy.

"My name is Kyōgoku Tetsuo, from Kobe. Nice to meet you all!" The transfer student gave a proper bow to the class.

"Kyōgoku's father is a department head in the customs office. Kyōgoku was always at the top of his class at his school in Kobe, so let his presence here spur you on to do your best! All right, everyone?"

When Mr. Kawano added this last comment, I saw in my mind's eye the wharves of Moji harbor, which, though they were in the city where

I lived, I saw at most once a year: the ships at anchor there, and the gray customs building, located at one end of the concrete wharf, glaring out at the ships. I thought that the boy now standing on the teaching platform had boarded one of those ships and come straight from distant Kobe to the gray-colored customhouse. I wanted to make friends with Kyōgoku.

Clearly, as I looked at Kyōgoku, I was associating him in my mind with Kondō, from fourth grade in primary school. This time I mustn't make the same mistake that I had with Kondō! Then, Kondō had spoken to me, but this time I needed to speak to the new boy first. Tajima, whom I "really disliked," had entered the same middle school in Kokura as Kondō, so he wasn't around. But there was a guy named Fujita who was showing friendly interest in Kyōgoku. This rival was hard to deal with precisely because Fujita and I were on good terms. When, at the end of gym class or on going out the school gate after classes were over, I managed to be alongside Kyōgoku, Fujita was always there too. Patiently I waited for a time when I could be alone with Kyōgoku.

Was it at the end of October? The sky visible between the trees at the edge of the playing field, whose leaves were already turning red, was as clear as water. We'd finished exercising, and everyone was heading toward the taps to wash their feet. At the edge of the playing field, Kyōgoku and I were at last alone. I followed him as he walked toward the horizontal bar. "Now! . . . Now!" I told myself over and over. Kyōgoku kept his back turned to me and jumped up to catch hold of the bar. There was a little mud on the seat of his training pants, but that made them, presented there a little above eye level, look much cleaner by contrast.

Kyōgoku did a full swing on the bar, and in the next instant sandwiched it between his thighs and stomach and hung there head down. His face, which was closer to the ground than any other part of him, was looking at me. The "Now!" inside me was about to become a shout. Kyōgoku's eyes, in his upside-down state, were perhaps gazing at the realm of *tengu* now, I thought. His face was bright red from the blood flooding down into it. At last I said "Kyōgoku," and probably followed it with "Let's be friends," though I can't be sure. I felt that my whole body was on fire.

Kyōgoku executed another turn and stood with his feet on the ground. He looked at me, smiled, and said "Okay!"

How happy I was to be walking alone with Kyōgoku through the now empty playing field. To extend that happiness, I tried to imitate him. He often allowed his shirttail to show over his trousers. When he walked, he leaned forward and looked at the ground. Instead of the standard phrase "while walking," he would say "with walking." So I deliberately let my shirttail show over my trousers, walked leaning forward and looking at the ground, and used the phrase "with walking."

This time the friendship seemed likely to last! But when I was confronted with that fact, my happiness became an unbearable burden. We had promised that I, who lived far from school, would drop by Kyōgoku's house, which was nearer, and we would walk to school together. One day I was dillydallying at home until there were only fifteen minutes until the start of classes. Then I heard a voice from in front of my house: "Takahashi!"

It was Kyōgoku. I suppressed the urge to run out to him, and stood in the house, holding my breath. He called out a few more times, and then there was the sound of his footsteps walking away. When the sound of his footsteps could no longer be heard, I left the house and started to walk, kicking at stones along the way. "I'm alone . . . I'm alone," I told myself. By the time I entered the classroom, class had already started. Kyōgoku looked at me and sent me a signal, but I pretended not to notice. Even when class was over, I avoided him.

It pained me to keep avoiding him. But the pain was easier to endure than perfect happiness. Since I was small, for much too long a time, I had gotten too used to waiting. And when the longed-for object appeared, I couldn't bear it—was that the explanation? As had been the case with Kondō, I was once again alone.

My being "good at telling stories," mentioned earlier, at some point turned into the writing of poems. By the end of my first year in middle school, my relation to the outside world would have been very difficult without the habit of poetry. Writing poetry could have been called my ship. Boarding this ship of words, I set sail endless times to the further shore that was the outside world. One could say that the failure of my relationships with the actual Kondō and Kyōgoku was due to my excessive clinging to this ship of words.

The further shore of my writing poetry was ultimately invisible poesy. The visible further shore was the city of Shimonoseki. It could be seen at a distance of around three thousand meters from the customhouse where Kyōgoku's father would have been bringing a pair of binoculars to his eyes.

After my relationship with Kyōgoku ceased to go smoothly, I often took the ten-minute train ride to Moji Harbor, the last station on the line, in order to view the customhouse and the ships and Shimonoseki on the opposite shore.

Soon I got tired of just looking at the opposite shore.

When you emerge from the underpass inside Moji Harbor Station, going in the direction of the sea, you come to the wharves, from which a double-decker ferry plies back and forth between Moji and Shimono-seki. The one-way fare was only twenty yen, and I often took the trip, exulting in the voyage of only fifteen minutes. It was fun watching the opposite shore come steadily closer and closer as the prow of the ferry plowed through the crests of the waves ahead. In time the bell that signaled landing would noisily clang, and the ferry's stern would vomit forth a great stream of salt water. The ship's movements steadied, and a rope was thrown from the first-level deck onto the Shimonoseki wharf, which had come right next to us.

Though it had been only a fifteen-minute crossing of the straits, how strange and wonderful everything seemed on this "opposite shore." The hills jutted out toward the sea, and the town that huddled between sea and hills was almost totally burned over from the war; but all that was the same, as between Shimonoseki and Moji. So the strangeness and wonder depended simply on the fact that it was "the opposite shore." Even though it differed hardly at all from the Moji side, I walked along Seashore Avenue, which seemed new to me each time I came, cut through the crowds in the market, and always, finally, climbed up to Hiyoriyama Park.

The park was on top, not so much of a mountain, as of a small hill that jutted out toward the sea. You climbed a long, long flight of stone stairs rising at a sharp angle from Seashore Avenue until you entered a grove of cherry trees. From there the long narrow town of Shimonoseki and beyond it the sea with its many ships could be seen at a glance. And beyond the sea and ships was Moji, which had now become "the opposite shore."

My second year of middle school had drawn to a close, and it was the third day of the New Year when I crossed to Shimonoseki by myself and, as always, climbed the stone stairs to Hiyori Hill. At the top was the grove of cherry trees, with a plaza and a narrow lane in the center. There was no one in the park on that cloudy, chilly day in New Year's week. No—actually, there was one other person: A tall high-school student wearing a tan raincoat over a black serge uniform with a stand-up collar stood about ten paces ahead of me on the path that wound its way diagonally through the grove of trees. He was looking back at me, but I ignored him. I wanted to be the only person who was looking at "this shore" that had now become "the opposite shore," from "the opposite shore" that had now become "this shore." I turned my back, erasing his presence, and gazed from between the cherry trees at the cold-looking straits beneath the coiled winter clouds, and at the town and mountains of Moji huddled on the opposite shore.

At the same time, I was aware of someone approaching me from behind.

My heart beat like a clock gone wild. I tried, however, to appear calm and continued to gaze at the further shore. Suddenly the person behind me became a pair of hands in black leather gloves that came from either side of my face and covered my eyes. Everything went black, and the blood from every part of my body rushed toward my eyes, now blinded. Still, I pretended to be calm, and did not move.

The hands removed themselves as suddenly as they had appeared, and light flooded into my eyes, which saw standing before me a tall, radiant figure. The winter clouds above had parted, and the brightness of high noon was pouring down like a waterfall. Dazzled, I closed my eyes, and when I opened them again, the person standing before me was smiling at me, his long, narrow eyes clear beneath thick black eyebrows.

"Where'd you come from?"

I silently pointed to the other side of the straits.

"From Moji? By yourself?"

I nodded, without saying anything.

"By yourself? Let's go someplace together. . . ."

I looked into his eyes. Then I turned from him and ran through the cherry-tree grove without looking back, and then down the long stone stairs. I thought I heard a voice shouting from behind me. My heart, too, was shouting in a loud voice.

I submitted the "poems" I wrote to the West Japan edition of the *Middle School News*. Since I did so almost every week, naturally a lot were accepted, and I received over ten letters a month about them from other middle-school students. One day, among these immature scrawls, there was a postcard written in a skillful hand. It said that the sender was a primary-school teacher from Hagi; that, reading my poems in the

Middle School News, he had been impressed by them; that he aimed to gather middle- and high-school students from western Japan with literary gifts and create a small group magazine; that he hoped I would join them; and that he often traveled between Hiroshima in Honshu and Kagoshima in southern Kyushu to meet such middle- and high-school students, and so he wanted to meet me as well.

All this detailed information was entrusted to a single postcard.

Somehow this brought to mind the person with the leather gloves whom I'd encountered at Hiyoriyama Park. His action in covering my eyes, his smile, and his questions had all been seductive invitations directed at me.

If so, then the author of this postcard, who signed his name "Yanai Seiichi," might possibly be the same dazzling person who had stood before me then. Hagi was on the same, opposite side of the straits as Shimonoseki. The only considerable distance between here and there was that between the two shores of the straits: there was almost no real distance between the two cities on the opposite side. I gradually superimposed my impressions of the high-school student whom I'd encountered at Hiyoriyama Park onto this person who sedulously kept sending me letters once or twice every week.

It must have been the evening of a long day in spring just after I had entered the third year of middle school. I was "sword-fighting" with a neighborhood friend on an artificial hillock in his garden when I heard his mother call out "Mutsuo—you have a visitor!" I went out as I was, with my sweater sleeves tied back with a cord, a stick in my right hand, and bare feet to find, standing in front of my house, a man who said, with a slight Yamaguchi Prefecture accent, "Are you Takahashi Mutsuo? My name is Yanai."

I imagine the look on my face was the same as Kondō's when he had opened the glass window near the entrance to his house some years before. I needed several seconds, perhaps more than ten, to grasp the situation. The "Yanai" I had been imagining was a handsome youth in a tunic with a stand-up collar, bathed in a flood of light from the sky. But the person standing in front of me now was a man of uncertain age with a sickly complexion. Though it was springtime, he wore a grayish overcoat and, with his head bent slightly forward, revealing white hairs among the black, was looking at me timidly.

I was, after all, just a third-year middle-school student, so I simply nodded and said with a blank look, "Yes, well . . . ," My mother wasn't at home, but I invited him in. He followed me with a weak smile. I, the barefooted swordsman, could do nothing but sit on the short stairs that led up to the entranceway, and the man in the overcoat followed suit.

I remained silent. The man, seeming not to know what to do, opened the briefcase he was holding in both hands and took out several photographs:

"This is Satō from Chikugo, who writes tanka classical poetry. This is Yahiro—he writes haiku, and is in middle school in Karatsu. This is Ueda, who writes modern verse, and this is Kawakami, an essayist."

I knew all the names from the *Middle School News*, and so the photos certainly should have meant something to me, yet I felt only a kind of awful darkness, looking at them. Handled by that strangely timid, sickly looking man, the photographs seemed to be his captives. I muttered the word "abductor" quietly to myself. This "abductor," however was very different from the abductor I had yearned after when I was at my grandmother's house in Nōgata.

"You're a third-year boy? You'll be going on a school group trip soon."

But I said, "Yes, but I won't be going. I don't have the money to." Then the man shoved his hand into the inner pocket of his overcoat and brought out two 1,000-yen bills and one 500-yen one, all very crumpled, and pressed them into my hand.

"My mother'll be mad at me if I take this," I said. The man cupped my hand in his unpleasantly damp ones and said "Don't worry. I'll write your mother to explain." Then he held both of my cheeks in those same hands.

I ran outside.

Thanks to Mr. Yanai Seiichi, I was able to go on the May school trip. The places visited were Unzen and Nagasaki. Whether at the hotel in the mountains of Unzen or at the inn in the city of Nagasaki, we boys splashed hot water at each other in the large public baths, ran along the corridors, had pillow-fights—and always, we ended by "playing sex." Five or six boys would hold another down and pull off his trousers and underpants as he kicked and struggled. Even if you were now among the attackers, you could never tell when and how you might become a victim. Breathlessly, you would run away, then pursue, then run away again. When I suddenly found myself alone at the turn of a corridor or in the corner of a room, Mr. Yanai's weak, uncertain smile flashed before me, and my pleasure would at once be covered by a damp darkness. I felt bad about doing so, but I couldn't help trying to shake off all memory of that smile.

Mr. Yanai's letters continued to come regularly. I rarely sent back proper replies. The more I felt I should respond, the harder it was to write. In time, the letters from him stopped coming.

I was close to graduation from middle school when the notice of Mr. Yanai Seiichi's death arrived. Apparently he suffered from a heavy neurosis, and his sudden death was virtually a suicide. When the death notice came, I was in front of my house, playing "Ride the Wild Horse" in the sun with a group of friends. I called for a time-out and read the notice to the end; the bright sunlight seemed suddenly to darken. I stuffed the postcard into my trouser pocket and resumed playing with my friends.

The day after graduation was fine and clear.

That day, Kyōgoku and I had plans to go on a final picnic together to the lighthouse at Hesaki, since he was going to be attending high school in Yokohama from that same spring, his father having been transferred again.

The Hesaki lighthouse was almost at the very tip of the Kiku Headland, which jutted out into the straits between Shimonoseki and Moji and the Inland Sea. To get there, we had to leave Moji behind, going through Saruhami Pass, coming out at Ikawa, and passing through coves and inlets like Hishakuda, Kitaku, Ōtsumi, Shiranoe, and Aohama.

We left at a little after ten in the morning and first went through the narrow defile of Saruhami Pass. After emerging from the pass, we saw a scene that was completely unexpected. It was a pleasant experience, just right for us who had left behind our time in middle school and were about to enter the new world of high school. The refreshing sight that impressed itself on our wide-open eyes filled us with hope for the high-school life we would begin in April. At the same time, it made us expect that something special had to happen today.

Kyōgoku and I were alone together for the first time in a long time. And tomorrow, Kyōgoku would cease to be a resident of Moji. I wanted to discuss so many things with him, but was unable to say anything much. We hurried along the road doing our best not to look into each other's faces.

Beyond the defile was the settlement of Saruhami, with the village of Ikawa visible across spreading wheat fields, now at last a rich, dark color. Through sparse stands of pine in the distance, we could see the chill, clear sea of early spring. It was the same sea as the one we had seen so often in the straits between Shimonoseki and Moji, but it seemed still more essentially "the sea." Beyond the straits were the island of Hikoshima and Shimonoseki, but in the sea at Ura Moji that we were now looking at, there was nothing at all in our field of vision.

Ikawa, Hishakuda, Kitaku, Ōsumi, Shiranoe, Aohama—all of these coves were surrounded by sandy hills. In order to get to the next cove, you had to go over the hill or make a detour around it. To go over the hill and encounter the new scenery of each cove was to enter upon a new experience. At Hishakuda octopus pots were lined up on the beach to dry. The smell of fish mingled with that of the sunlight, and in mid-sky a group of hawks were flying. At Kitaku, where there was not a single house, a dugout was being tossed about by the incoming waves. At Shiranoe, on the beach where a seamen's training center was blown by chilly winds, students were practicing signaling with flags.

There were no more human dwellings after Aohama. From there, we went along the seacoast road where spider lilies and Japanese laurels grew luxuriantly, arriving at Hesaki after two in the afternoon. A two-story white chalk observation hut clung to a spot beneath a cliff, where the road came to an end. At the top of the cliff, reached by a winding path, rose another white chalk but far more imposing structure—the Hesaki lighthouse.

As we crossed in front of the observation hut to access the path to the lighthouse, the door of the hut opened, and a man came out— the old man from the boat-builder's hut! Actually, the old man who emerged there was wearing, not a grubby coat and a loincloth that looked as if it had been boiled in low-grade salt, but a pair of neat, clean white trousers and a shirt with an open collar. But his bald head, his small size, the appearance of age, and his way of walking were not a bit different from those of the old man who had disappeared so suddenly from the boat-builder's hut on our beach. So then, had the old man sailed in the *Abe-maru* he had worked so hard to build, not for Hikoshima, visible from Moji on the opposite shore, nor for distant Innoshima, but simply for Ura Moji, quite near our beach?

"Going to see the lighthouse, are you, boys? Why not come in for a while before you climb on up?"

When the voice emerged from the old man's mouth, however, it was clear that that voice, warmer and somehow wetter than seemed natural for an old man, was not the old boat-builder's. *His* voice had been more exposed to the salt winds, more cracked. Then too, more than ten years had passed since the boat-builder had sailed away. He would be still more bald, still more bent with age, still more the stumbling old codger than he had been the last time we saw him.

"You lads must be tired. . . . I'll just make some tea for us."

Kyōgoku and I exchanged glances. Today was our last chance to be on our own together. Also, we wanted to climb up to the lighthouse as soon as possible. But the old man went on into the hut, unconcerned with what we might have been wanting to do. We had no choice but to follow suit. Just inside the door there was a tiny bare cement area, and then a wooden floor.

Right beyond the wooden floor was a door that opened onto a steam-filled room—apparently the bathroom. Next to it was a staircase leading to the second floor. There the old man stood waiting, with his back to us. Forced by the sight of that back, we gave in, taking off our rucksacks and walking onto the wooden floor.

Having made sure he heard our footsteps on the wooden floor, the old man proceeded to climb the stairs. Once again we exchanged glances. The old man stopped halfway up the stairs. We did, after all, have to go up those stairs as well.

The second floor consisted of a tatami room with two glass doors at the farther end, from which you had a direct, unobstructed view of the sea. The old man brought out two *zabuton* sitting cushions, which had been piled in a corner of the room, turned them over and offered them to us. What could we do but sit down?

"You've got a nice view of the sea from here—a Liberian ship'll be passing soon." His words sounded kind, but they forced us, in effect, not to move from where we'd been placed. We went over to the glass doors and looked out at the deep blue of the March ocean.

The old man came back upstairs bringing a tea tray and a flat, wooden sweets box. He turned the teacups right side up and poured the tea, then urged us to have some hard candies from an empty powdered milk tin. When we declined, he took one of the candies himself and popped it into his nearly toothless mouth. His lower right cheek, which was unpleasantly shiny in appearance, bulged out, and then the bulge shifted to his left cheek. We also took one hard candy each.

"'Those who are shy will get no pie,' as the saying goes." Laughing, he opened the flat wooden box. Inside it was a notebook of the sort college students use. When he lifted that from the box, we could see an inkstone and two writing brushes with worn-down bristles.

"I just *love* young, energetic lads. I have the ones who visit the lighthouse come up here and write down their names for me!"

Opening the notebook, he showed us a list of names and addresses written in thick black ink: Moji, Kokura, Shimonoseki, Chikujō County, Hakata, and even Hiroshima and Osaka. We felt a bit more relaxed. I and then Kyōgoku signed our names. Then, "Oh yes, the bath's well heated up by now!" the old man said emphatically. He scurried down the staircase, and when he came back up, we told him we were leaving.

"What do you mean? Here I am, doing my best to entertain you lads, even heating up the bath for you. Now, if you're worried about getting into the lighthouse, don't. I telephoned them just now to say you'd be coming a little later . . ."

The old man's manner did not give us any choice in the matter.

"Now then, you go first," he said, urging me down the stairs.

I took off my clothing and shut the bathroom door. I was soaking in the hot water when I heard him call, "How's the temperature?"

"It's fine," I said, but the old man came right into the bathroom. His trousers were rolled up to the knee, and his sleeves tucked up as well.

"So, get out for a moment, and I'll give you a good scrub down."

I refused at first, but the old man brought out a small wooden seat and kept urging me to sit there. I finally sat down and placed my washcloth over my loins. Neck, back, underarms, chest, belly, arms, legs—he soaped all of them down and then rubbed them with a towel. His touch was strangely gentle.

"Shall I give your groin a wash, too?" He reached for the washcloth, but I hurriedly fended off his hand.

But the old man just said, "You don't have to be shy—us men have all got 'em, you know." He reached his soapsuds-covered hand toward my groin. Under his caresses, delivered on the pretext of "washing," I felt the organ between my thighs undergo a change. There was nothing for me to do but keep my eyes shut tight. I felt that I had been sure this would happen from the instant I met this strange old man. In my brain flashed an image of my Uncle Ken's room, and of the light and darkness in the Eizen shack at the instant the consecration had occurred due to what my grandmother had been saying.

Hot water was poured over the area between my thighs any number of times. The hands that poured the water next made me stand on the tiled bathroom floor. I kept my eyes closed and did as the old man said. Feeling something unexpected, I opened my eyes to see the old man's bald head stuck to my abdomen as I stood there, legs wide apart. That head, which was making slight, jerky movements, was bald and shiny; but, looked at closely, it was also wrinkled and spotted with age, and had many patches of fine, grubby-looking hairs on it as well. All of the hairs were sweaty.

Looking at each one of those sweaty fine hairs from so close up, I almost retched. I stood with both feet planted on the floor of the bathroom amid a strange mix of disgust and pleasure, and felt myself changing into a massive, erect statue moment by moment. The blue-painted ceiling of the bathroom, bending inward and beginning to lose its paint, and the wood-plank walls, painted the same blue, which was beginning to flake off here and there, were all covered in sweat, each bead of which glittered like a treasure-jewel. The steam that filled the three-mat-sized room was dazzlingly radiant. Finally, the ceiling seemed to disappear, to be replaced by brilliantly shining glass. That bathroom became the Eizen shack at the time the Sacred Word descended upon it; it became my uncle's room at the time that "Love" was there. This time, however, I was not looking up at the ceiling from a dark earthen floor or from tatami mats, but on the contrary, was looking down from the ceiling on the earthen floor and the tatami. And I certainly heard that voice:

"That Maruya-san who lived in Urantan? He was a man-woman, you know, and he fell for Shinno-san, who lives in Kamōda, in a big way. Then, just as they were getting on so nice, there was talk of Shinno-san getting married. Now Maruya-san couldn't get over that, so he took a kitchen knife and stabbed himself in the throat, he did!"

The bathroom seemed about to burst due to the dazzling light. Perhaps that explosive light was radiating from my massive body as I stood there, feet planted, on the bathroom tiles. As I waited for the Holy Word, went on waiting for the Second Coming of the divine Son, could the Son have come to fruition within me? Could I, finally, have become the Son, or become my very uncle? Certainly the old man who knelt at my feet, who buried his face in my abdomen, had the appearance of someone who was waiting for the Holy Word. I superimposed the image of Mr. Yanai onto the old man.

Was "the Beyond" the reverse side of things, and did re-encountering the Holy Word mean that I myself was to be transformed into the Holy Word? I remembered what my mother had often said of late: "You look more and more like your uncle Ken. . . ."

But the dizzying height was soon past, and the cold descent began. I got smaller and smaller moment by moment, and soon I was alone again. I soaked in the bathtub. Submerged to my neck, I looked up at the ceiling and the walls, and found that they were once again just dirty painted boards.

I put on my clothes and climbed the stairs: Kyōgoku had a suspicious look on his face. The sun was already darkening over the sea beyond the glass doors.

Next it was Kyōgoku's turn. It took an incredibly long time. At last Kyōgoku came up the stairs. Neither of us tried to look the other in the face.

Silently, we went down the stairs and left the hut. From the lighthouse, a whitish light was sent out toward the twilit sea. Though we climbed the path to the lighthouse, we didn't enter it.

We turned to look back. Beneath the cliff, at the very edge of the coast washed by the waves, the shabby hut stood, utterly cast aside by even the whitish light from the lighthouse. It looked very small.

ELEVEN

"Red Palm Leaves" (Akai yashi no ha) by Medoruma Shun (1992)

Translated by Davinder L. Bhowmik

Biography and Introduction

Medoruma Shun (1960–) is an Okinawa-born writer-activist who was not known nationally until 1997, when he won the prestigious Akutagawa Prize for "Droplets" (*Suiteki*), though he had been receiving regional literary prizes since the early 1980s. He hails from Nakijin, a northern Okinawan castle town located on Motobu Peninsula. Verdant Nakijin abounds in various crops such as sugarcane, watermelon, leaf tobacco, greens, and pineapple, and is part of Yanbaru, the largest surviving parcel of subtropical forest in Okinawa. The remains of Nakijin Castle, awash every January in Japan's earliest-blooming cherry blossoms, mark what was once the hub of cultural and economic activity in northern Okinawa during the Ryūkyū Kingdom. Yanbaru, whose forests are home to endangered species of flora and fauna, lies at the heart of Medoruma's fiction.

Nakijin was a world apart from the life Medoruma would go on to live in Shuri, where he attended the University of the Ryukyus. There, Medoruma had to forgo use of his native Nakijin speech and use standard Japanese. He studied Japanese literature with Professors Nakahodo Masanori and Oka-moto Keitoku, two of Okinawa's foremost literary critics. For a decade after graduating Medoruma took a number of jobs throughout Japan in order to gain experience as a writer. The author's keen attention to the language his characters speak arises from the gulf he experienced not only between his own speech and that in the southern city of Shuri, but also from the foreign standard Japanese he would go on to teach.

At age thirty-four, a year shy of the deadline to do so, Medoruma applied for teaching credentials, after which he taught Japanese in various high schools in Okinawa while continuing to write fiction. In spite of a self-imposed seclusion from local literary circles and public events, the Futenma Replacement Base controversy, which erupted in the late 1990s due to impending construction of a military base in Henoko, just south of the author's beloved Yanbaru National Forest, forced Medoruma out of obscurity. Thereafter, the author immersed himself in local politics, writing weekly essays on Henoko for several national magazines. Medoruma continues to write a daily blog, "From a Roiling Island" (*Uminari no shima kara*), in which he describes his everyday activities as part of a canoe brigade that monitors and attempts to intervene in base construction.

Medoruma's literary style might be described as earthy, given its rootedness in Okinawan terrain. Surreal, and sometimes magical realist, the stories for which he is best known center on the ongoing effects of wartime trauma, specifically that incurred in the Battle of Okinawa, which raged for eighty-two days, decimating the island and killing nearly half its population. Medoruma did not experience the war firsthand, but several close family members had. The resonance of their stories together with detailed descriptions gained from the author's geographic proximity to war relics and memorials make Medoruma's fiction eerily like that of a wartime participant. "Droplets" (1997), "Spirit Stuffing" (1999), and "Tree of Butterflies" (2000) form a loose trilogy of the author's most critically acclaimed fiction. Also of note are three novels, *Sound of the Wind* (*Fūon*, 2004), *Rainbow Bird* (*Niji no tori*, 2006), and *In the Woods of Memory* (*Me no oku no mori*, 2009).

Red Palm Leaves

That winter day, I was sitting in front of the TV with my younger brother. It was early afternoon, and slightly cloudy. Our parents were at work. When the man we had been waiting to see finally appeared on the black-and-white TV screen, we burst out laughing. He looked comical in his baggy white shorts.

We had first heard the name Cassius Clay a few days earlier. His match against Joe Frazier was coming up, and my father couldn't stop telling me what an incredible boxer he was. I was in sixth grade at the time. "He floats like a butterfly, and stings like a bee," my father said, describing Clay's light footwork and sharp punches. He added that Clay took the odd name, "A Mouth that Roars," for his bravado, and he was the youngest heavyweight champion in the history of boxing. But when he refused to be drafted for the war in Vietnam, he was stripped of his title. My father talked about Clay like he was a hero among heroes.

After hearing my father praise the man to no end, I was sure the match would be terrific. My brother and I gazed at the TV screen in eager anticipation. But when the bell rang, one round followed the next, and our anticipation turned to disappointment. The boxer's movements lacked animation. We saw nothing of his famed elegant footwork and sharp punches. That Clay went down in the fourteenth round, ending the match, confirmed to us that our father was wrong.

Back then, Okinawa was still occupied by the U.S. military. Like the teeth of a saw, the black tails of B-52s preparing to go bomb Vietnam were lined up on the other side of the barbed wire fence surrounding Kadena Air Base.

The day after watching the match on TV, I told my friends at school about it, making clear my disappointment. S must have overheard, because he approached me suddenly, as everyone was preparing to go home. S was one of the shy, reticent boys you see one or two of in every class. He had transferred to our school the previous summer and had no real friends. We'd never spoken one on one before.

"Do you like boxing?" S asked, flashing me a bashful smile. I nodded ever so slightly, and he drew close, looking happy.

"Do you want to see a match?"

"A boxing match?" I asked.

S nodded and told me he knew of a place where we could see one. I didn't know of any boxing gyms in the area. As I gave him a suspicious look, S timidly took hold of my hand and led me to the bus stop.

He encouraged me to get on the bus, and after passing several stops, we got off at a town that had been built in front of the gate of a U.S. base. Roads jutted off from the government highway running along the fence, and sloped gently downhill toward the coastline. The narrow sidewalks were lined with short palm trees and bars with faded signs written in foreign lettering. S led me down one of those roads. It was early afternoon so not many people were out. Peering into the barber shops and pawn shops along the road, I saw that most of them were still closed. Narrow alleys branched off here and there, many of them extending barely 300 feet before turning into vacant areas overgrown with grass and weeds. Beyond a forest of pines, I could see the ocean, faintly glittering as it reflected the sun that slightly cloudy afternoon. The wind smelled of rust as it coursed through the street, gently swaying the reddish leaves of the malnourished palm trees. The leaves swayed languidly in the breeze. S walked ahead of me, occasionally turning his head to give me a bashful smile. He stopped suddenly, pointed to a narrow alley lined with gas cylinders, and then walked toward it.

It was more a narrow space between two buildings than an alley. When we slipped through the cool shade of the passageway we could hear the faint echoes of people cheering, even though we were outside. We had reached a square space formed out of the walls of surrounding buildings. Arranged on the concrete ground were a worn-out sofa and wooden boxes on which sat men whose backs shook whenever they shouted and whistled. A blond young man wearing a dark-green jacket raised a brown bottle up high and yelled something, then turned around and looked at us. I was petrified. The cramped courtyard was filled with about twenty men, most of whom were American soldiers from the military base. S grabbed my hand more boldly than before, leading us behind the soldiers, and then climbed on top of some wooden boxes stacked against a wall. I climbed on top of the wobbly, empty boxes to sit beside S. Beyond the heads of the American soldiers, I saw two men facing each other in the middle of the courtyard.

It was a true boxing match. The soldiers had put on black gloves and, on top, wore only an undershirt. The two breathed heavily as they pitched forward, glaring at each other. It seemed they'd been at it for a while already, since one had blood dripping from his nose. The other men egged them on loudly, but neither attempted to throw a punch. A man who appeared to be the referee said something to the two boxers, and one of them finally threw a reckless punch at the other, and they wound up tangled in an embrace. When they staggered to the sides the men watching pushed the boxers back into the center. Finally, they threw three or four more sloppy punches before taking off their gloves and collapsing onto the sofa, exhausted. The other men laughed derisively at the two who just sat, so worn out they couldn't even bring to their lips the beers they were offered. Some of the soldiers eyed the boxers with what seemed like contempt, but I was enormously excited to see with my own eyes, for the first time in my life, not just two men exchanging blows, but two American soldiers nearly twice the size of the average Okinawan man.

The circle of boisterous men quieted down for a while. Then, the next two boxers took off their jackets and put on gloves. One was a frighteningly tall black man. It looked like the Okinawan man going around to collect money from the soldiers could have strode through his legs. The boxer bent his overly long arms, sinewy like an insect's legs, and used his teeth to tie the glove strings. His opponent had a big build, too. Sporting curly blond hair, long enough to cover his back, he was chewing gum at an astonishing pace. At the referee's signal the two faced off. The man collecting money hit the oxygen cylinder-cum-bell, and the match began. Clearly, this was a different level than the previous match. The black soldier circled with light steps, extending his long arms to throw sharp jabs at his approaching opponent, and then retreated. For his size he moved with unbelievable speed. If it had been a real boxing ring, he'd probably have easily won, but the uneven circle made by the American soldiers in the tiny courtyard was too small. What's more, what they were hoping for was a flashy brawl. Instead of a rope, the fighters were surrounded by the other men's hands pushing them back into the center of the courtyard. The instant the black soldier lost his balance from being pushed by the surrounding men, his opponent jumped on him and began throwing continuous punches at his body and face. A fierce battle began. The sound of the fighters hitting flesh reverberated through the excited cheers of the men, vibrating deep in my chest, making it hard to breathe. I didn't know which punch was the winning one. Several men stood up, shouting, and raised their arms up. The black soldier appeared to have a look of fear in his eyes as he gazed down at his opponent, who had fallen between two chairs. His opponent couldn't get up. At that moment, the black soldier seemed to me like the Cassius Clay my father spoke of. I looked over at S from on top of the dangerously tottering wooden boxes. His face flushed, S stared at the black soldier, who was talking loudly to the men next to him as he removed his gloves.

I told S my thoughts about the fight after the excitement following the match had settled, and before the next match began. S smiled as he listened, and the short responses he worked in to our conversation, which revealed the depth of his knowledge about boxing, surprised me.

Match after match followed. All ended quickly, but none of the fighters came anywhere close to that amazing black soldier. Gradually I got so I could view the matches calmly, but then became aware of something going on in the courtyard. I couldn't tell if the courtyard had always been a vacant lot, or if a building had been demolished leaving the space empty, but it was a communal courtyard for the four build-ings, the backs of which joined together. Sometimes, the back door of a building would open, and American soldiers endlessly came in and out, replacing both fighters and spectators.

The number of American soldiers kept increasing, until it reached around forty. When it grew dark, two streetlights in the corners of the courtyard flickered on. Knowing I should head home, I became con-cerned, but I also felt like I wanted to watch more fights. I stayed seated there, even though my mind was unsettled. Just then I spied a woman looking across the courtyard from the shadow of an open back door. It looked like she was wearing thick makeup, as her face was strangely pale. She seemed young, and when her eyes met mine, her face broke into a smile. Inadvertently, my heartbeat raced and I averted my eyes, then all of a sudden the wooden boxes shifted as S jumped down and walked over to her. She put her arm around S as if to protect him from the rowdy crowd, and drew her ear to his lips to hear what he was say-ing. She smiled with the same exact bashful smile as S, then beckoned for me to join them. Despite being flustered and feeling self-conscious, driven by curiosity, I made my way through the crowd of American sol-diers and went to stand behind S. The woman bent down slightly and said something, but I couldn't hear her over the raucous cheers of the soldiers. When I saw her close up, she was older than I had thought. Even so, when I thought about my dark, stout mother who everyday briskly set off for work at the pineapple factory bearing no trace of makeup, this woman was incomparably beautiful. She beckoned me to come closer and opened the paper packet she was holding. She took out a piece of candy that looked like a deep-red ruby and handed it to me. Then she removed another piece of the same candy from her own mouth and placed it between S's slightly opened lips. I swallowed as I watched a fine string of saliva attached to the candy extend from the woman's mouth, and then disappear into S's mouth.

"Go on home before it gets dark," she said.

The woman looked back and forth from S to me, smiling. Then she disappeared into the building. The two of us came out into the alleyway and walked to the bus stop. The street glowed with neon signs, making it unrecognizable as the same street we had walked down that after-noon. Suddenly my interest in the boxing matches cooled.

"Was that your mother?" I asked.

"Yeah," said S, nodding slightly. I hesitated to question him further.

"Aren't you going to eat it?" he asked.

S's question made me realize I'd been clutching the candy in my right fist. It had melted a bit and made my hand sticky. I wanted to say something, but no words came to me, so I just put the candy into my mouth silently. I rubbed my red-smeared hand on the trunk of one of the palm trees along the road. A strong mint flavor filled the air.

Standing next to each other, we waited for the bus. One after the next, American soldiers came through the base gate, crossed the highway, and strode into town. When the bus came, I got on first, and waited for S to follow me, but he didn't get on. I sat down and looked out the window. As the bus took off, S kept waving to me, and smiled that same bashful smile.

Remembering images from the courtyard got me so excited I couldn't sleep that night. The loud cheers of the drunk American soldiers. The scent emanating from their muscular torsos. The frightened look in the black boxer's eyes. The color of the blood dripping from the soldiers' faces onto the ground as they bent down. What captured my eyes most was S's mother, who had opened the back door and beckoned me. I recalled again and again how her vaguely pale face became young like a girl's and how she took the candy from her mouth and put it into S's. My heartbeat quickened and it became hard to breathe. Before I knew it I stopped imagining her putting candy into S's mouth and started imagining she was putting candy into my mouth.

When I saw S the next day, he broke into a smile like we were close friends. I had barely even noticed him until the day before, so seeing him smile like that felt like the first time. I couldn't concentrate in any of my classes that day. I felt like S wouldn't stop staring at me from the seat behind me, and time and again I wanted to turn around and check. But when it was time for recess, I lost my nerve and couldn't talk to him, so I went outside and ran around the schoolyard with other boys in my class. The whole time I couldn't get S out of my mind. He'd probably been waiting all day. After we finished cleaning the classroom and school wrapped up for the day, even though people started leaving the classroom, S, alone, remained seated, flipping open a book and peering inside his backpack now and then. I had stayed in the classroom to talk with my friends, but I still couldn't approach him. It was time to go but no one talked to S. Eventually, S and a few girls were the only ones left in the classroom. One of the girls made fun of S on her way out the door, and everyone laughed, mocking him, but S just smiled timidly in return.

On my way back home, I was filled with remorse for not talking to S. Halfway home, I told my friends a lie, saying I had forgotten something at school, then ran back to the classroom. No one was in the room. I was frustrated and angry, but at the same time I felt like I had been betrayed. I shouldn't have come back. As I headed in the direction of the school gate muttering to myself, I saw S standing under a bare cherry tree. The instant I caught sight of that bashful smile of his, my anger went away, and my heart raced. I felt kind of embarrassed. Without saying a word, S just started to walk beside me. All along I'd been wanting to take S to my very own secret spot. I thought that the place he had taken me to the day before was a special place S hadn't shown anyone else, and I wanted to return the favor.

We turned away from the road that led to school, a new road that had been cleared by the U.S. military after the war, and headed down an old road that cut right through the woods. The old road had stone steps leading down to it here and there, and since it was a shortcut that led to the village's northern coast, it was well travelled but neatly maintained. The forests that encircled the village were 150 feet high, and the road wended its way through the trees, sometimes cutting through stone or dirt walls; the road continued to the northern coast. Along the way, the road passed through a small basin in which rice paddies still remained. Nearly all the rice paddies in the village had been converted into sugarcane fields. But only in that one area, a small amount of rice was cultivated by installing narrow irrigation canals that used water seeping from beneath the forest. It was our favorite place to play back then. My friends' and my favorite pastime was catching the tilapia and betta fish that swam in the mouth of the spring and the canals. S and I made our way down a path that glittered with specks of limestone, then crouched at the edge of the spring and used both our hands to scoop and drink the cold water spurting from behind the rocks. As it gushed forth, the water shook the roots of white trees. S squealed when he saw freshwater prawns and betta fish, which would vanish if a person got too close. Happily, he said it was his first time seeing these kinds of fish. His words surprised me. There were always a few betta fish swimming in the big mayo jar I had on my desk. S also said it was his first time drinking water from a spring. He gazed longingly at the spring and the irrigation canal, so I promised him we'd come fishing together on Saturday, then hurried him along. The place I wanted to show him was further ahead.

We cut across the old road to enter the village and made our way to a sacred garden on the southern edge of the castle forest. Religious ceremonies were held in one corner of the garden, where a prayer house stood. S came to a standstill and gazed at that prayer house, clueless. Six stone pillars built from rock cut and brought from the coast held up a thatched roof so low that even a child would have to bend over to get below it. The low roof smelled of dried trees and kept the space within cool. During festivals, *kaminchu*, women who served as conduits to the spirit world would come dressed in white, sit in a row, and pray here. S said he knew absolutely nothing of such things. While I told him about the festivals, I wondered where he'd been born. We left the garden and took a path that went downhill through a lush verdant area, before reaching the river that separated opposite sides of the village. Then we walked along the river toward the ocean. Once we got to the village S abruptly turned silent. Even when I spoke to him, he just showed me that bashful smile of his and gave only a brief response before ending the conversation. It was quiet but I didn't feel like it was an awkward silence. I don't think S found it awkward either. But as we walked along side by side, he would sometimes turn to check behind us, or look around nervously, as though he felt uneasy.

The water that flowed from the paddies settled in one spot and then coursed from south to east of the castle forest, before pouring into the river. After crossing a suspension bridge that hung where the channel flowed into the river, we came to a narrow dirt road with strips of grass growing between the ruts. Overhead, the branches of the forest lining the left side of the path mingled with the branches of the mangroves lining the river, forming a dim tunnel. Feeling the cool from the shade of the trees, we walked briskly toward the mouth of the river. Dug into a rocky crag at the edge of the forest was a row of graves. Here and there, the stones covering the entrances of the graves had crumbled, and we could see burial urns and bones inside some. Suddenly, S reached for my hand. His was a small, soft, moist hand. While long-tailed bulbuls chirped overhead and black butterflies fluttered about us, we walked through the woods, hands joined. Blue bottleflies buzzed as they took off from around our feet. Strewn across the grass were the remains of a tilapia. Its scales had dried up and turned white, and a fly had burrowed into the fish's sunken eye socket, not even attempting to break free. The waste and raw sewage flowing from the sugar-processing plant and the pig farm located upstream had completely polluted the river. People had almost all stopped fishing there after starting to catch fish that were deformed, with sunken-in noses or twisted spines. The people who still fished did so for fun, releasing fish back into the water or throwing them into the grass. The blue bottleflies circling around alighted on the tilapia. S turned his face away, looking ill.

After walking a bit further, we emerged from the densely wooded area into a small vacant lot. There we saw a storage room for the sugar-processing plant's supply water pump. The place I wanted to show S was ahead of the lot. S hesitated, but I urged him on as I climbed over the barbed-wire fence and entered a grove of white lead trees. These densely grown trees, the trunks of which were enveloped in a milky-white bark, completely covered the sandbar at the mouth of the river. The trees made it too difficult to keep walking hand in hand. Sometimes, I would stop and wait for S, who was having difficulty finding a way through the trees. When he saw me watching him, he smiled like he was embarrassed, and grabbed the trunk of one of the white lead trees, freeing his leg of the vines that had entwined it. When I looked at his feet, I saw that one of his shoes was covered in mud. Had he stepped in a puddle? Since his shoes were pretty new I felt awful. "Just a little farther," I encouraged him. Finally, the raw smell of the delicate white lead tree leaves and the sound of the grass we trampled underfoot diminished, and the scent of the ocean, beyond the stand of tree trunks, began to waft.

"We're here!" I said.

I grabbed S's hand and we left the grove together. A loud sound of flapping wings filled the air as several dozen white herons, egrets, and plovers rose up in a boisterous flurry. We stopped and stood, watching the plovers screech as they skimmed the water's surface, and the flock of white herons recede into the distant, darkening sky. When the herons stopped in a cluster of pine and acacia trees on the opposite shore, it looked as though Korean morning glories had bloomed. My heart wouldn't stop racing.

"Surprised?" I asked.

S looked at me, face flushed, and nodded. We sat down on the dry sandy ground. Before our eyes, the river opened up and flowed into the inland sea. Mangroves grew thickly in the muddy water of the shallows. Below the cape that jutted out on either side of us, two large rocks with curved bases stood in the distance like pillars. There was a story about how traders would moor their ships to those rocks back in the days when there was brisk trade with *Yamatu* and China. Now, though, there were no more ships. Now and then an old man who lived alone in the neighboring village would take out his small boat to fish, but that's about it.

"That fish is poisoned!" I had told the old man once, as he returned to shore, tilapia in hand.

The old man brushed aside my concern and said with a smile, "If I die of poisoning, I'll just move on to the afterworld."

The setting sun gave off a soft light from beyond the woods that reached all the way down to the end of the cape along the river. The silver light moved slowly across the pale blue sky. The sea was almost completely calm, and the gentle flow of the river created a swaying path of light across the water's surface. We barely spoke. When I asked where he was from, S replied he was from a fishing town in the central part of the island. He had transferred from school to school, and now lived with his mother in an apartment in the town adjoining the base. That was about all he said. S didn't seem to want to talk about himself. Nor did he ask about me, either. We just sat there, shoulder to shoulder, leaning against each other and gazing at the scene at the mouth of the river, which grew quieter. There were many things I wanted to ask him, but when I saw S squint his eyes at the flickering light reflecting off the sea, I refrained from asking anything else.

"Look!" S suddenly pointed up at the sky.

"What?"

"Up there!" I looked in the direction S was pointing. The wind rustled the fine leaves of the *mokumaō*, and a slender thread of light flickered, then disappeared. A strand of spider silk was floating in the pale blue sky, which had started to take on a tinge of purple. The strand seemed to shimmer first green, then gold, and extended out from a tree branch and gently undulated out toward the sea. It was impossibly long and thin. Dispersing a clear fleeting light, the strand hovered between the ocean and the horizon, appearing and disappearing as it swayed in the breeze. We gazed at it, mesmerized. I felt S's shoulder move. His arm reached behind me to embrace my side, and then reached for my chest.

"Don't move." S rested his cheek behind my ear and whispered into it. My chest trembled beneath his soft palm, and the heat of his body pressed against mine made it hard for me to breathe. S's right hand traveled slowly from my chest down to below my abdomen. Finally his hand started to move in rhythm, and a sensation I had never felt before budded forth. My whole body became warm, and something began to flow forcefully inside me and then take form. Instinctively, I tried to stop S's hand. But he paid no attention and continued to move it around. Something close to fear or anxiety welled up and I wanted to run away, but I couldn't move. The sensation of S's hand movement made me at once afraid and consumed by desire. I closed my eyes and let my body lean against his, inhaling the scent emanating from S's neck and underarms.

My reverie broke abruptly when S began to reach for my belt buckle. I wrested myself from him reflexively, pushing him as I jumped up. He caught himself from behind by thrusting out his hands, and stared up at me with that bashful look in his eyes. A serene smile even played upon his lips. I raced back into the grove of white lead trees. S ran after me, but I kept running without looking back. Inside the forest it had already started to become dark, and the sweat of my body made me cold in no time. The sound of branches being swept aside further heightened the turmoil in my chest. My pants had become too tight, making it difficult to walk.

S finally caught up to me when I reached the suspension bridge. I ran across, ignoring him, but as I headed down the road to the village, he grabbed my hand from behind. I shook him off. When I looked back, I could barely see his pale face in the dusky light. I couldn't make out his expression, but I thought he was afraid. Unconcerned, I pressed on. I was definitely not mad at S. I was just confused. I couldn't make sense of the unexpected change in my body, or my feelings toward S. I walked slowly through the path, which had become completely dark. S stayed a few steps behind me, no longer attempting to catch up. There was a girl in class whom I had previously liked. But I felt a different sort of affection for S. Neither of us spoke as we walked to the bus stop on the prefectural highway, nor while we waited for the bus. Unlike the other day, when the bus came it was my turn to see S off.

"Tomorrow . . ." I said to S's back as he got on. He turned and gave me his bashful smile, nodding. Then he got on the bus and sat at the very front. As the bus departed he gave me a small wave.

I was exhausted that night and went to bed earlier than usual. I awoke just as dawn broke. A hazy light poured into the room, and I lay in bed half-awake, mulling over the dream I had just had. I was in a deserted town, wandering around, lost in a maze of alleyways. No matter how many corners I turned, there was no end to the concrete buildings. Their faded pink and blue walls had English graffiti scrawled on them. Every time I turned another corner, the alleys grew narrower. Not knowing where I'd end up made me so anxious that I wanted to scream. Suddenly, a door opened. S's mother was beckoning me. In spite of my shyness I approached her and she took a piece of bright red candy out of her mouth. A string of pale red saliva stretched from her lips to the candy. When I closed my eyes and opened my mouth, waiting for her to put the candy into it, someone grabbed me from behind and pushed me to the ground. I was lying face down with S on top of me, holding me tightly and whispering something in my ear. His faint breath caressed my neck, and his right hand moved slowly from my chest down to my stomach. Just as his fingers touched me, something shot from my groin down to the tips of my toes. All the strength left my body, and a soft, sweet sensation drifted through my lower abdomen. I closed my eyes and luxuriated in that sensation. My younger brother, who was sleeping next to me, made a quiet noise. I quickly looked over, but he seemed to be asleep still. My wet underpants started to feel unpleasant. I wasn't sure what to do with my right palm, which was all sticky. As I brought it out from under the covers, I smelled something raw and organic. Suddenly overwhelmed by a sense of anxiety and shame, I realized I had done something I shouldn't have. Just lying there became intolerable, so I slipped out of bed and headed toward the bathroom as quietly as I could. The chill of my wet underpants that stuck to the skin of my lower abdomen and shrunken penis made me feel even guiltier. I knew I couldn't let anyone in my family discover what had happened. When I reached the bathroom, I took off my underpants and threw them down to the very bottom of the pit toilet.

When I had returned to my room and was about to reach for a pair of clean underpants, my mother caught sight of me.

"What are you doing?" she asked, peering at me from the hallway, about to go in to the door of our bedroom.

"Nothing!" My voice came out louder than I had expected. My mother looked taken aback.

"What's with this kid," she said, and headed to the kitchen. My brother had woken up, and looked at me from the bed, his eyes crusty with sleep.

"Go back to sleep, it's too early!" I snapped, and he quickly hid his face under the covers. I got back into bed and slipped on the clean pair of underpants, then turned onto on my side and closed my eyes, but

I couldn't fall back asleep. Light was streaming in through the shutters and the knotholes in the walls. Dust swirled in the beams of light. Something else was fluttering silently in my chest. I couldn't lie still, so I got up and washed my face. My mother saw me and gave me an odd look.

"It's my turn to be class leader today," I said. It was a feeble excuse for a lie, but my mother didn't say anything. By the time my younger brothers were washing their faces, I had already finished my breakfast and left the house.

There were only two girls in the classroom when I got there. I was never late to school, but I usually got there just in the nick of time, so my two classmates looked surprised to see me. I had never paid the slightest attention to those two girls before, but now, when they looked at me, I suddenly felt a subtle power in their gaze, as though they could see right through my secret. I threw my backpack on my desk and went out into the schoolyard.

The morning light had filled the partly cloudy sky. Reddish-brown dried needles were scattered over the ground, falling from the old pines that encircled the schoolyard. The shadows cast by the trees' narrow branches swayed on the schoolyard. I avoided the eyes of the teachers and students who were sweeping the schoolyard, and climbed over the low concrete wall on the eastern side of the school, entering a small wooded area. Filled with acacia and elaeocarpus trees, this area was one of my favorite places to play with my friends. Dried leaves were piled on the ground, making it springy underfoot. I pushed my way through a patch of dense shrubbery, and arrived at a clearing where about ten of us could fit if we sat knees hugged to our chests. That was where we held our secret meetings. I stood in the middle of the parcel of well-trodden grass and looked up. The sky was hidden by the layers of tree branches that stretched overhead from all sides. The noises of the schoolyard sounded very far away. I closed my eyes, and could feel the plants all around me start to move silently, reaching their branches out to envelop me softly. Their lively tips entered me from the slightest opening in my body before spreading white roots. The branch tips pressed my soft flesh, making a hard bud emerge. The sensations of earlier that morning revived in me. I was tormented by strong feelings of guilt, but I couldn't fight against what had so vigorously started to bud in my body. I suddenly felt someone watching me. My eyes darted to an opening in the surrounding shrubbery, and I sensed something run away. Flustered, I quickly adjusted my clothes and leaped into the thicket, but no one was there. The ground was untrodden, but somehow, I knew I had been seen.

The bell that rang five minutes before homeroom sounded. I ran back toward the school, feeling more and more certain that I had been seen. My growing embarrassment and bitter anger made it hard to breathe. I jumped over the concrete wall and ran through the schoolyard, which by now was nearly empty. When I entered my classroom, I felt the eyes of all my classmates, who had been conversing animatedly, rest on me. Someone called my name. It was S. Everyone looked at the two of us with raised eyebrows. S got up from his seat and headed toward me, clutching something to his chest as though it were very dear to him. He had the same bashful smile on his face. When I saw that smile, and his gestures, which looked somehow girlish, I felt something akin to anger or revulsion well up inside of me. I suddenly remembered the movement of his fingers from the day before, and recalling the way my body had responded on its own, my face got hot. S knew what had happened that morning. In fact, it was he who had just been watching me through the trees. He could see right through me. He knew everything that I had done from the day before until right now, and he knew how I was feeling, too. That's what I thought right then.

"Here. . . ." S said in a low voice, handing me the notebook he had been holding. I knocked it out of his hand, and then, without thinking, struck S in the chest. The sensation of his small, bony chest remained in my palm. S fell, toppling over the desk of a girl in the front row. Somebody screamed. S hit his back on the corner of the desk as he fell over backward. Bent over, he groaned in pain. Some boys cheered and gathered around us. They looked at me with anticipation, egging me on in hopes of getting to see a real fight. As soon as I felt their eyes on me, my anger toward S dissipated. The notebook he had been holding had fallen open at my feet. It was a fat scrapbook full of articles cut from newspapers and magazines. From the pictures, I could tell they were articles he had collected about boxing. S grimaced as he leaned forward to pick up the notebook, then stood and tried to return the toppled desk to its upright position. Two girls jumped up to help S, gathering together fallen books and pencils from the floor. When S returned to his desk, he put the notebook back inside it without looking up. He wasn't crying. He was trying hard to remain expressionless, suppressing his pain and sadness. I suddenly realized what a terrible thing I had done, and was filled with remorse, but I couldn't apologize. I went to my seat and quietly emptied the contents of my backpack into my desk. The boys who had gathered around returned to their seats looking disappointed. Soon after, our homeroom teacher arrived. He could tell from the atmosphere of the classroom that something had happened, and asked about it, but no one answered.

I didn't talk to anyone that day. During our recesses, I ducked out of the classroom without saying a word and passed the time in the empty landings of the staircase or at the edge of the pond. My friends kept coming over to ask me what had happened with S, but I just glared at them and said nothing, and they gave up. I couldn't stop thinking about apologizing to S. Even during class, it was all I could think about. But all day long, I wasn't able to apologize, and eventually it was time to go home.

The next day, S wasn't at school. He didn't come the following day, or the day after that, either. Our teacher said that he had a bad cold, but all I could think of is that he wasn't coming to school because he was hurt by what I had done. After he had been absent for four days straight, I decided to go visit him after school.

It was my first time going to the entertainment district in front of the base gate by myself. Just like the last time, there were hardly any people around when I arrived. Walking along the road lined with malnourished palm trees, I immediately found the side road lined with gas cylinders. It took courage to make my way down the narrow alley, dark from the shadows cast by the surrounding buildings. When I reached the concrete courtyard, it was so quiet I couldn't believe it had been the location of such a rowdy scene just days before. Looking around, I finally realized the courtyard was not surrounded by the backs of apartments, but rather by the backs of small bars packed tightly together. Flowerpots containing twisted aloe plants and scrawny bonsai trees lined the walls, next to piles of beer and whisky cases. Unlike the front of the bars, which may have been faded but were at least painted pink and blue, in the back, the concrete-block walls were exposed, and just looking at them gave me a desolate feeling. I walked over to the wooden boxes that S and I had sat on the last time. Looking around from there, the courtyard looked so small it was hard to believe that it had been filled with so many American soldiers. In the corner was a well, and a white cloth tied to the pump faucet was soiled. Next to the well, on top of a pile of blocks, was a washbasin. The half-used bar of soap on it glistened coldly. The back doors of all the bars were covered by slabs of corrugated metal, which were full of English graffiti scribbled in magic marker. I knocked on the door that S's mother had come out of the last time. I heard the door being unlocked from the inside, and when it opened, a very fat young woman peered out at me. I said S's last name and asked if a woman by that name was there. The young woman looked at me listlessly and, without saying anything, closed the door. I didn't know if I should wait there or go home. I felt like I had waited a long time before the door opened a crack and S's mother peered out. I was startled for a moment by how different she looked from when I had seen her in the twilight a few days before. The afternoon sun mercilessly revealed every strand of disheveled hair and every wrinkle on her un-made-up face.

"You were here the other day, right?" she asked me.

I nodded, and her suspicious look disappeared as her face relaxed. Her slightly bashful smile looked just like S's.

"Is his cold very bad?" I asked. S's mother looked like she wasn't sure how to answer.

"Hmm, he might be able to go back to school again soon, I suppose . . ." She looked down. I didn't know what to say.

"Where do you live?" She asked me.

I looked up and told her the name of the village I was from. She just said, "Oh," and gazed at me.

"Wait here a second, okay?" I felt her soft hand on my shoulder, and then she disappeared behind the closing door. When the door opened again, S's mother smiled and handed me a paper parcel.

"Eat it on your way home," she said.

I thanked her and took the paper parcel, then went back down the dark, narrow alley toward the bus stop. I could feel something hard inside, which I had put inside my pocket. I knew it must be another one of those red candies. I recalled the harsh taste and scent of mint. As I waited for the bus I stroked the paper softly. I couldn't bring myself to eat the candy. When I got home, I put the parcel in my desk drawer.

At the end of the next week, S still hadn't come back to school. Every time I went into the classroom, it was unbearably painful to see S's empty seat. At one point, our teacher and class representative went to pay S a visit, but they came back saying they hadn't been able to see him. Suddenly, everyone was talking about S. Nobody said anything to my face, but I had a feeling they were criticizing me behind my back for pushing him, and I started to spend most of my time alone during recess. A few of my friends made fun of S and praised me, saying they were glad I had hit him. I said nothing, but the irritation showed on my face. Eventually people stopped talking to me. I didn't really mind being alone. What hurt the most was the guilt I felt toward S, together with another sort of guilt. I had gotten to a point where I couldn't stop masturbating in bed at night before going to sleep and in the morning after waking up. My fantasies changed from images of S and his mother to thoughts of a certain girl in my class. When I saw her at school, I felt guilt along with a fear that I had somehow defiled her, and I couldn't bear to make eye contact. I felt like she was also angry at me for hitting S, which made me feel terrible, but also resentful toward S. That in turn made me hate myself even more. I wanted desperately to escape from all the pain.

I went back to the town by the base. It was a Saturday afternoon. I hadn't been able to ask our teacher for the address of S's apartment. I didn't think I could answer if he asked me why I wanted to know. Anyway, for some reason, I felt like I would be more likely to find S if I went back to that courtyard than if I went to his apartment. When I got off the bus, I raced down the gently sloping hill. I hesitated for a moment when I got to the alley lined with gas cylinders, but cut between the buildings, taking care not to lose my footing on the wet concrete. The courtyard was deserted just like the previous time. My hopes of seeing S sitting on top of the pile of wooden boxes, swinging his feet and smiling his bashful smile at me, were dashed, and I stood in the middle of the courtyard looking around, not knowing what to do. The twisted aloe plants and the soap next to the water pump hadn't moved. I stood in the center of that quiet space and looked up at the sky. A few clouds floated lazily across the pale blue sky, and the telephone wires running diagonally across the courtyard hummed softly. I knocked on the back door of the bar where S's mother worked. The corrugated metal over the door felt cold against my knuckles. I waited a minute, then knocked a second, and a third time, but nobody answered. I tried turning the doorknob, but the door was locked from the inside. Just as I was wondering what to do, I sensed someone coming out from between the buildings. It was a tall, skinny American soldier. His long arms stretching out from under a gray T-shirt were covered in tattoos. He reeked of alcohol. He stroked his red freckled face, then pressed his fingers against his eyes and muttered something.

He looked only about twenty years old. He watched as I backed away, then raised his right arm, and stared at me with his gray eyes and said something. There was no way out except for the alleyway behind him. The young man kept muttering something as he approached me. I saw a gap and tried to run behind him and escape. His long spidery arms grabbed me by the scruff of my neck and drew me toward him. He was much too strong for me to resist. He grabbed me from behind and drew me close, wrapping his long fingers around my neck. When I writhed and struggled to break free, the fingers of his right hand dug harder into my throat, and his left hand punched me in the pit of my stomach. My voice lost its way in my strangled throat, disappearing in a gasp. Everything started to vanish as though it were being sucked deep down into my eyes. Darkness spread before me. The American soldier's hands started stroking my motionless body roughly, and he touched my genitals from over my pants.

Just then, a piercing yell came from behind me. The young man's fingers relaxed for a second, and I pushed away his arms, which were covered in blond hair. Slipping out of his grasp, I tumbled down onto the concrete ground. A door on the opposite side of the courtyard had opened and a hunched-over old lady shouted loudly, batting her arms in front of her face like a cat trying to intimidate a predator. The young man's figure looked warped as he strode away. The woman kept waving her arms and shouting curses after him. I held back my tears and tried to make my way toward her, but she started to scold me loudly.

"This is no place for a child! Get on home right now!" she yelled.

The woman kept repeating the same thing over and over, her eyes glittering in her dark, wrinkled face. Before I could make it to my feet, she had slammed the door, and I heard the lock click. I didn't even have the energy to wipe the blood off my scraped knees and hands. I just stared at the metal-covered door. I stood for a moment, imagining S and his mother standing there smiling at me. I knew it wasn't true, but I stood there for a while, just staring at their door. When I finally headed back toward the damp darkness of the narrow alley, I was hit with the fear that the young American soldier might be hiding in the shadows. I crossed my arms and hugged myself tightly as I slipped into the alley. My eyes darted around nervously, but there was no sign of the American soldier. I hurried toward the bus stop. The wind smelled of the ocean as it blew down the street lined with bars covered in faded paint. I quickened my pace as I passed behind a black soldier peering into the window display of a pawn shop, and tried to hide in the shade of the palm trees as I passed by four or five young American soldiers talking loudly to each other as they made their way down the street.

There was nobody sitting on the bench at the bus stop. Young soldiers made their way across the street, paying no heed to the stoplight. I turned my face away from them and fixed my gaze in the direction of my bus. I couldn't help shivering from the wind, which had become chilly. The light of the sun sinking toward the west was blocked by the buildings and didn't reach the bus stop. The bus still didn't come. I knew that I would never see S again. I didn't know if he had moved away, but I was sure that I would never see him again. I sat on the bench and rubbed my arms, covered in goosebumps. The leaves of the palm trees, reddish from malnutrition, shook in the breeze. I picked a leaf off one of the trees and held it to my lips, whispering S's name inside my head. I read the letters on the rusty bus-stop sign, listened to the sound of the palm leaves rustling in the wind, and waited for the bus to come.

TWELVE

Selected Tanka from *Rainstorm* (Haku'u) and *The Book of the Friend* by Kasugai Ken (1999)

Translated by Scott Mehl

Biography and Introduction

Depending on one's point of view, Kasugai Ken's (1938–2004) career as a poet began either auspiciously or inauspiciously, when his first collection of tanka,[1] *Miseinen* (Underage, 1960), was published with a fulsome appreciation by the novelist Mishima Yukio (1925–1970). Mishima's foreword to the collection concluded with what was meant as high praise: "In many respects the present age bears comparison with the age of the *Shinkokinshū*, and"—Mishima added, as proof of this resemblance—"we have had our young Teika," in the person of Kasugai himself.[2] Fujiwara no Teika (1162–1241) had been one of the compilers of the eighth imperial *waka* anthology, the influential *Shinkokinshū* (1205), and sole compiler of the ninth imperial anthology, the *Shinchokusenshū* (ca. 1234); Teika also selected the poems for the *Hyakunin isshu* (One Hundred Poems by One Hundred Poets, early thirteenth century), which would become a cornerstone of *waka* culture for centuries.

By comparing Kasugai to Teika, Mishima was, to put it mildly, calling attention to what Kasugai had achieved in *Miseinen*. When Kasugai began publishing the poems that he would later gather in *Miseinen* he was nineteen years old; when the collection itself appeared, he was twenty-one. Kasugai's

---

1. Tanka are 31-syllable poems (5-7-5-7-7). In earlier eras, tanka were known as *waka*.
2. Kasugai Ken, *Miseinen* (Tokyo: Tanka Shinbunsha Bunko, [1960] 2000), 7.

precocity might be explained by the observation that both his parents were tanka poets; his father edited the Chūbu Tanka Society's journal *Tanka*, in which Kasugai published his first poems as an adolescent. Perhaps detecting in Kasugai's work a precociousness to match his own, Mishima—himself only thirty-five in 1960—extolled Kasugai, prophesying that Kasugai's importance and influence would equal Teika's.

It was a prophecy that few writers' careers could have fulfilled. After the early success of *Miseinen*, Kasugai seemed to lose interest in tanka, occasionally publishing verses in various outlets while working as a scriptwriter for television serials and radio shows. Ten years after the publication of *Miseinen*, in 1970 Kasugai published an anthology of his tanka to date, *Ikekaeru koto naku* (No Going Back). Another collection, *Yume no hōsoku* (The Laws of Dreams, 1974), was a gathering of verses written around the same time as the poetry of *Miseinen*; that 1974 collection aside, Kasugai ceased publishing tanka altogether until 1979.

Reflecting on why he stopped writing verse during these years, Kasugai wrote:

> It wasn't that I'd lost my words. It was just that I felt I'd had enough of tanka and wanted it to leave me alone. [. . .] I'd say it was like love. When I was younger I had a passion for tanka that burned intensely but briefly, then I put that passion aside.[3]

His reason for returning to tanka in 1979, he would later say, was the death of his father in that year.[4] Kasugai suffered another loss in 1983 in the death of his collaborator and friend Terayama Shūji, a dynamic artist whose many contributions to modern Japanese culture included important collections of tanka. In 1984, Kasugai wrote, in the afterword to his collection *Aoashi* (Green Reeds): "[Death] forced me to see life. I could not close my eyes. Writing was bound up with seeing."[5]

With those words, Kasugai positioned himself as a witness to the deaths of others, and the tanka that appear in the present anthology can be categorized, I would argue, as poetry of witness.[6] The principal theme that links

---

3. Quoted in Kita Akio, "Kasugai Ken nenpu," in *Gendaishi techō Kasugai Ken no sekai: "Miseinen" no ryōbun* (Tokyo: Shichōsha, 2004), 250.

4. Kasugai Ken, *Kasugai Ken zenkashū* (Tokyo: Sunagoya Shobō, 2010), 199.

5. Kasugai 2010, 199.

6. The phrase "poetry of witness" is brought into sharp focus by the work of Carolyn Forché, as in her edited anthology *Against Forgetting: Twentieth-Century Poetry of Witness* (1993),

the tanka here is illness—more narrowly, the complex of illnesses associated with HIV and AIDS. The poems hew—not always, but generally—to the 5-7-5-7-7 syllable pattern of the traditional tanka, but the archaizing style in which Kasugai's tanka are written belies their present-day concerns. Some of the poems are about celebrity AIDS deaths; others are about an unspecified, plague-like illness that afflicts an unidentified "friend" of the lyric persona. The AIDS-themed film *Philadelphia* is the inspiration for more than one poem; other poems refer to works of sculpture or literature that conjoin the themes of sensuality, illness, and death. The reason for Kasugai's interest in illness and death in these poems, all of which are drawn from the collections *Haku'u* (Rainstorm, September 1999) and *Tomo no sho* (The Book of the Friend, November 1999), is avowedly autobiographical: in March 1999, a lump was found in Kasugai's throat, and he began taking treatments for cancer soon thereafter.[7] As he later wrote, he assembled the tanka in *Haku'u* and *Tomo no sho* while lying in a hospital bed.[8] It might be observed, however, that the first published versions of all of the tanka that appear in the present anthology predate Kasugai's cancer diagnosis, some of them by as much as a decade.[9]

As for Kasugai's subsequent collections, the poems in *Mizu no kura* (The Water Storehouse, 2000) date to 1984–1987.[10] In 2002 he published *Seisen* (Wellspring). Kasugai's last collection, *Asa no mizu* (Water in the Morning), was published on May 15, 2004; seven days later, he died of the mesopharyngeal cancer that had been with him for the five preceding years.

The tanka poet Kurose Karan has written, "I think it likely that Kasugai is the only modern tanka poet who has taken up HIV as a literary subject."[11] It is certainly the case that Kasugai's tanka treat HIV and AIDS as occupy-

---

and in *Poetry of Witness: The Tradition in English, 1500–2001* (2001), edited by Carolyn Forché and Duncan Wu. The principal themes of Forché's anthologies are war and political unrest.

7. Kasugai 2010, 489.

8. Kasugai 2010, 249.

9. Generally, the later printings of the tanka are identical with the first versions, but when a revision is made that has influenced my interpretation, I mention the details in a footnote to the translation.

10. A note about publication sequence: because of the order in which the poems were originally composed, Kasugai has called *Mizu no kura* his fifth tanka collection, *Tomo no sho* his sixth, and *Haku'u* his seventh (Kasugai 2010, 249), even though the collections themselves were published in the reverse order (*Haku'u*, and then *Tomo no sho* in 1999, *Mizu no kura* in 2000).

11. Kurose Karan, "Inochi kiwamaru uta: Kasugai Ken 'Bāsu yuki' o megutte," *Tsubasa* 14 (August 2016), 113. I am unaware of exceptions to Kurose's generalization.

ing an intersection between illness as a broadly conceived diachronic social phenomenon—as see in the references in his tanka to plagues of earlier eras—and the particular experiences of individual human beings who were Kasugai's contemporaries and, in many cases, his friends.

From *Haku'u* (Rainstorm, 1999):

such youth in my friend
who comes to announce
the morning light on the deep snow
even though his body is so sickly
that it harbors death

*shi o yadoshi yamu tomo wakasa ōyuki no asa no hikari o tomo wa
tsuge kuru*

死を宿し病むとも若さ大雪の朝の光を友は告げくる
(March 1997)[12]

_____

12. I present the poems in triplicate: an English translation, followed by a transliteration, followed by the Japanese original. In the transliterations I have generally tried to reflect the received spellings of premodern Japanese (e.g., *yuku* instead of *iku*); in the case of one or two words that have not appeared in standard reference works, I have had to offer a conjectural transliteration. The translations are presented in five lines in recognition of the conventional division of tanka into 5-7-5-7-7, although I have not attempted to recreate the meter.

your immune system
is weakened
you should avoid chills
the cold that precedes
the apple aphids[13]

men'ekiryoku yowarite areba tōzakeyo yukimushi o sakidatete kitaru
samuke o

免疫力弱りてあれば遠ざけよ雪虫を先だてて来たる寒気を
(March 1997)

in one of the books
I have placed on the black leather
of the desk it says
one should make one's peace
with dying before age forty

kurokawa no kijō ni okeru sho no hitotsu shijū ni taranu shi o yoshi to
suru

黒皮の机上に置ける書のひとつ四十にたらぬ死をよしとする
(March 1997)

---

13. According to Mizuhara Shion, *yukimushi* (which I have translated here as "apple aphids") are insects found in the northern part of Japan in late autumn or early winter. Their presence is said to be a sign of imminent snow (*Kasugai Ken: "Wakai Teika" wa azayaka ni sono nochi o ikita* [Tokyo: Kasama Shoin, 2019], 69).

hope to have just
one more day
one more moment
but ready yourself
for the inevitable

sa are hitohi ikkoku nagaku arashimeyo sono toki no shitaku totonou to
   ie

さあれ一日一刻永く在らしめよそのときの支度整ふといへ
   (March 1997)

stoking the fire
when they burned the corpses
of those who died
in the plague:
Bassompierre's*[14] memoir
  * From a short story by Hofmannsthal.[15]

maki kubete eyami no hito no kabane mosu Passonpiēru* kaisō no sho
  * Hōfumansutāru no tanpen shōsetsu

薪くべて疫病みの人のかばね燃すパッソンピエール回想の書
＊ホーフマンスタールの短編小説
  (March 1997)

---

14. The asterisked explanatory notes are given by Kasugai.

15. The name is spelled as *Passonpiēru* in all Japanese versions of this poem that I have seen, including the first serialization (*Tanka kenkyū* vol. 54, no. 3 [March 1997], 113). Kasugai's source is the story "Erlebnis des Marschalls von Bassompierre" (1900), by the Austrian writer Hugo von Hofmannsthal (1874–1929). It is available in English as "An Episode in the Life of the Marshal de Bassompierre" (Hugo von Hofmannsthal, *Selected Prose*, translated by Mary Hottinger and Tania and James Stern [New York: Bollingen, 1952], 309–20).

across the ceiling
glide the shadows
of the plague-stricken lovers
illuminated by the fire
that their desire ignited[16]

*yokubō ni hanachishi hi tomo haimawaru eyami no hito no tenjō no
kage*

欲望に放ちし火とも這ひまはる疫病みのひとの天井の影
(March 1997)

there is still more
life in these veins
we will
see the darkness of the coming day
and the light

*seikon wa mada tsukihatezu tanjitsu no hiura hiomote warera
mirubeshi*

精根はまだ尽きはてず旦日の日裏日表われら見るべし
(March 1997)

---

16. This tanka, too, seems to refer to Hofmannsthal's story. See the previous tanka.

said to be a sacrament
that can cure a sick man
how sad
the sight of him buying
the water of Bath[17]

yamu mono o iyasu hiseki o tsutae koshi Bāsu no mizu o kaite sabishie

病む者を癒やす秘蹟を伝へこしバースの水を買ひてさびしゑ
   (June 1997)

the name of the disease
was announced
to the patient himself
on that evening
when the sunset was like water

byōmei wa kanja mizukara ni tsugerareki mizu no gotokarishi kano
   yūtsube ni

病名は患者みづからに告げられき水のごとかりしかの夕つ辺
に
   (June 1997)

17. The waters of the town of Bath, in southern England, are said to have curative properties. According to Shino Hiroshi, the subject of this tanka is Kasugai's brother-in-law ("Inochi e no katsubō," *Tanka* vol. 56, no. 4 [March 2008], 78). Kurose Karan proposes a more generalized interpretation, reading the "yamu mono" as "a friend afflicted with a certain illness" ("Inochi kiwamaru uta: Kasugai Ken 'Bāsu yuki' o megutte," *Tsubasa* 14 [August 2016], 113). I thank Kurose Karan for sharing with me his writings about Kasugai.

my friend knows
but does not tell his parents
is it for fear
or is it
because of the prejudice?

mizukara wa shiritsutsu oya ni tsugezaru wa okubyō to henken izure waga tomo

みづからは知りつつ親に告げざるは臆病と偏見いづれわが友
(June 1997)

if one were to line up their portraits
on the wall of a gallery
Clift[18]
Mercury[19]
Tina Lutz* and more
* Model, jewelry designer, a Japanese woman who was known as Aquamarine Tina.[20]

shōzō o naraberu naraba rō no kabe Kurifuto, Mākyurī, Tina Rattsu nado*
** Moderu, hōshoku dezainā, akuamarin no Tina to yobareta nihonjin josei.*

肖像を並べるならば廊の壁クリフト、マーキュリー、ティナ・ラッツ*など
＊モデル、宝飾デザイナー、アクアマリンのティナと呼ばれた日本人女性。
(December 1997)

18. I surmise that "Kurifuto" is Montgomery Clift (1920–1966), the American actor. Elisabetta Girelli has written a study titled *Montgomery Clift: Queer Star* (Detroit: Wayne State University Press, 2014).
19. Freddie Mercury (1946–1991), British singer, who died of AIDS.
20. Tina Chow (born Bettina Lutz, 1950–1992), who died of AIDS.

although I did not know
what the disease was called
at the time of Tina's death
the open sea was
the color of aquamarine

Tina no shi no koro wa michi narishi byōmei no sa wa are akuamarin no oki wa

ティナの死の頃は未知なりし病名のさはあれアクアマリンの沖
は
(December 1997)

staying at a hotel
on this island
when he died
on the beach, Aschenbach[21]
was younger than I am now

Asshenbahha ware yori wakaku kono shima ni todomaritariki shimabe no shi made

アッシェンバッハわれより若くこの島にとどまりたりき浜辺の死
まで
(December 1997)

---

21. Gustav von Aschenbach, a character in the German writer Thomas Mann's (1875–1955) novella *Der Tod in Venedig* (*Death in Venice*, 1912). Despite warnings of a plague outbreak, Aschenbach remains in Venice because of his attraction to a young man, and dies.

trying to brush off
the shadow of death
pushing and pushing it away
with rapid upward movements
of supple hands and feet[22]

shi no kage o harawan to shite takaku hayaku uchikaeshi shinau tewaza ashiwaza

死の影を払はむとして高く速く打ち返し撓ふ手わざ脚わざ
(January 1998)

somehow the beating
of Donn's* heart
came to an end
bringing comfort
on the day he died
* Jorge Donn, star of the Ballet of the Twentieth Century. Died
of AIDS.[23]

yukishi hi no Don* no kodō wa ika yō ni uchi todaetaru ian o etaru
*Joruju Don, "20-seiki Baree" no sutā. Eizu ni bosshita.

逝きし日のドンの鼓動はいかやうに打ち途絶えたる慰安を得
たる
＊ジョルジュ・ドン、「二十世紀バレエ」のスター。エイズに没
した。
(January 1998)

---

22. This tanka perhaps refers to Jorge Donn, the dancer who is the subject of the two following tanka; all three poems were originally serialized together and appear on consecutive pages in *Haku'u.*

23. The Argentine dancer Jorge Donn (1947–1992) was best known for his work with the Ballet of the Twentieth Century (Ballet du vingtième siècle).

with the single-minded
intensity
of the *homo faber*[24]
Jorge Donn gives form
to a beautiful stillness

homo faberu no ittosa o mote Joruju Don hashiki shijima o zōkei seshimu

<ruby>工作人<rt>ホモ・フアベル</rt></ruby>の一途さをもてジョルジュ・ドン美しきしじまを造型せし<ruby>む<rt>は</rt></ruby>

(January 1998)

the February
rain that fell
upon sorrow
on the quiet day
when I saw the film *Philadelphia*[25]

eiga "Firaderufia" o mishi hi no shizuka naru hiai o uchite kisaragi no ame

映画「フィラデルフィア」を観し日の静かなる悲哀を打ちてきさらぎの雨

(April 1998)

---

24. *Homo faber*: Latin for "man the maker," "human as craftsman," as the glossed ideographs suggest.

25. In *Philadelphia* (1993), directed by Jonathan Demme, a lawyer wins a wrongful termination suit against his employer, who has fired him because he has AIDS.

the disease affects the immune system
so when the intoxication ends
afterward your mind
will be more lucid yet
Hello, My Sickness[26]

men'eki no yamai ni areba ei hatete sara ni sae kuru Hello My Sick [yaa boku no . . . . . .]

<ruby>免疫の病にあれば酔ひ果ててさらに冴えくる<rt>やあ ぼくの ……</rt></ruby> Hello My Sick
   (April 1998)

the one who made him
tell his mother the news
was me
you were singing
Santa Maria

sono haha e no kokuchi o shiishi wa ware ni shite santa maria na ga utai iru

その母への告知を強ひしは吾にしてサンタ・マリーア汝が歌ひ
  ゐる
   (April 1998)

---

26. About this poem, Kurose Karan has written: "A crux: what kind of illness would this be? It is a disease of the immune system. Hence, it is probably an HIV infection" (Kurose 2016, 114). I interpret the original tanka's *sick* (because it is preceded by the possessive particle *no*) as a noun: hence my translation *sickness*. Another point in favor of rendering "sick" as "sickness": in the first published version of the poem, the last line reads "Hello Sickness" (*Tanka kenkyū* vol. 55, no. 4 [April 1998], 9).

incomprehensible
how Fate nods in greeting
then just passes by
and leaves oneself
unscathed

unmei wa eshaku shite soba o yokogireri taika nakarishi koto koso
fushigi

運命は会釈して傍を横切れり大過なかりしことこそ不思議
(April 1998)

on my way home
from a ceremony where I said
a final goodbye
I think of those who
were caregivers for so long

hito o okuru shiki yori kaeri kite omou nagaki kaigo o seshi dare kare o

人を送る式より帰りきて思ふ長き介護をせしだれかれを
(July 1998)

my friend
holding an unfolded map
of the cemetery
says he visited the grave
of Marguerite Duras[27]

*bosho no chizu hirakinu tomo wa Maruguritto Dyurasu no haka o
tazuneshi to iu*

墓所の地図ひらきぬ友はマルグリット・デュラスの墓を訪ねしと
いふ
(July 1998)

because she
was near
madness
Yann Andréa[28]
stayed by Duras's side

*mizukara ga kyōki ni chikaku arishi yue Dyurasu o sasaeshi Yan
Andorea*

みづからが狂気に近くありしゆゑデュラスを支へしヤン・アンド
レア
(July 1998)

---

27. Marguerite Duras (1914–1996), a French author, notable for (among other texts) the screenplay for Alain Resnais's film *Hiroshima, mon amour* (1959). See the note to the following tanka.

28. Yann Andréa (1952–2014), the homosexual man whose long-term relationship with Marguerite Duras, almost four decades his senior, was the inspiration for Duras's 1992 novel *Yann Andréa Steiner* and many other of her late writings. Yann Andréa, too, wrote about their relationship: see, for example, his *M.D.* (1983). For a biographical account see Laure Adler, *Marguerite Duras: A Life*, translated by Anne-Marie Glasheen (Chicago: University of Chicago Press, 2000), 323–44 and 364–69.

how alone he must feel
on learning that for a time
he will not want sex
the young man
a beast from the waist down

*seiyoku wa kono nochi to ie kahanshin kemono no shōnen sabishikarazu
ya*

性欲はこののちといへ下半身けものの少年淋しからずや
    (August 1998)

when I was thinking
of my ailing friend
in that early morning hour
I could feel the stirrings
of a phantom pain*
    * Feeling a pain that has no physiological basis.

*yamu tomo o omoi orishikaba hakugyō ni fantomu pein ware ni
    kizashitsu
    * jitsuzai shinai yami o kanjiru koto*

患む友を思ひをりしかば白暁にファントムペインわれに兆しつ
    ＊実在しない病みを感じること
    (August 1998)

the Peacock Revolution
the men who refused
to be sent
to the front lines
and put on makeup instead

pīkokku kakumei senchi e omomuku o kobamite keshō seshi otokotachi

ピーコック革命　戦地へ赴くを拒みて化粧せし男たち
    (October 1998)

I want to have my friend reside
somewhere so cold
that the virus
will not be found there
the rippling of clear water in early autumn

uirusu no naki kanreichi ni sumawasetaki tomo ari sensen to haya aki
  no mizu

ウイルスのなき寒冷地に住まわせたき友ありせんせんと早や秋
  の水[29]
    (October 1998)

---

29. The fact that this tanka explicitly mentions viral infection led the tanka poet Hishikawa Yoshio, writing about the theme of disease in Kasugai's collection *Haku'u*, to conclude the following: "By what disease, in the end, is [the young man who is written of in these verses] affected? Is it cancer or AIDS? Judging from [this tanka], we may consider the disease as one spread by a virus" ("Eien no hika: kutsū ga motarasu shigan no kani," in *Zoku Kasugai Ken kashū* [Tokyo: Kokubunsha, 2004], 149). The strong implication is that AIDS is the disease in question.

one more time viewing the film
Philadelphia
when I first saw it
I was so naïve
I had never heard of the disease

*hatsu ni mishi koro wa yamai o shirazariki eiga "Firaderufia" o
futatabi*

初に観しころは病を知らざりき映画「フィラデルフィア」を再び
(October 1998)

"Now, in come the strings
and it changes everything—
the music"
Maddalena's song
fills with a hope[30]

*"gen ga hairu to kyoku ga kawaru yo sō tsugi da" Maddarēna no uta ga
takanaru*

「弦が入ると曲が変るよ　さう次だ」マッダレーナの歌が高鳴
る
(October 1998)

---

30. In the film *Philadelphia*, one character describes to another a recorded aria to which they are listening; his description includes the lines, "Now, in come the strings and it changes everything. It's like the music—it fills with a hope. And that'll change again. Listen." The aria so described is "La Mamma morta," sung by the character Maddalena in the opera *Andrea Chénier* (1896) by Umberto Giordano (1867–1948). In the original version of Kasugai's tanka, the quotation braces enclosed the whole tanka (*Tanka kenkyū* vol. 55, no. 10 [October 1998], 9), but later revisions limited the quotation to the first three lines of the poem. I liberally incorporate the film's dialogue in my translation.

meeting again
the scene in which
the sadness of the music
is matched only by
the young man's ecstasy[31]

seinen ga takaburu hodo ni kanashikarishi ongaku no shīn ni saikai o
seri

青年が昂ぶるほどに悲しかりし音楽の場面に再会をせり
(October 1998)

even knowing that
there would be no talk of a cure
the young man
will not come again
to meet the doctor's indifferent smile

chiryō no hanashi idenu to shiredo seinen ishi no suzushiki bishō ni
mata aite konu

治療の話出でぬと知れど青年医師の涼しき微笑にまた会ひて
来ぬ
(October 1998)

31. This tanka may refer, as the preceding one does, to the film *Philadelphia*.

From *Tomo no sho* (1999):

the several days
following the death
of Freddie Mercury
We will rock you
I will rock you

Furedi Mākyurī shishite ikunichi We will rock you, I will rock you.

フレディ・マーキュリー死して幾日 We will rock you, I will rock you.[32]
(May 1989)

"The Sculpture"

(A sequence of tanka, originally published in May 1995.)

I sleep fitfully
wake up
when it is still dark
remembering again
my friend has the disease

asaki nemuri ni tsukite wa samuru hakumei ni mata omou tomo wa
yamai o etaru

浅き眠りに就きては醒むる薄明にまた思ふ友は病を得たる[33]

---

32. Kurose Karan describes this verse as Kasugai's first published tanka about HIV ("Zen'en ga kage to naru toki: Kasugai Ken ni okeru HIV no imēji 1," *Sai* 2 [2009 January], 44).

33. These eight tanka form the entirety of the section of *Tomo no sho* entitled "The Sculpture" (Chōkoku 彫刻), inspired by the classical sculpture known in English as "the Dying Gaul." (The original publication included only seven of these tanka; the May 1995 sequence did not include the tanka that begins "thinking now.") Kurose Karan has observed a remarkable coincidence: "The sculpture [the Dying Gaul], [which] figures in many anthologies of gay art, [. . .] is also used as a metaphor for the gay lover who dies of AIDS in the film *The Dying Gaul*, directed by Craig Lucas" (Kurose 2009, 49. n. 12). Kasugai, who died in 2004, could not have seen Lucas's film, which was released in January 2005. (The film itself was based on Lucas's play of the same title, performed in 1998; I have seen no evidence that Kasugai might have known of Lucas's play.)

it was an evening
in springtime
the deep blue color
the weight on my knees
as I held my fallen friend

taoretaru tomo o idakeru waga hiza no omosa konjō no shun'ya narikeri

倒れたる友をいだけるわが膝の重さ紺青の春夜なりけり

the young
suffer
as a rule
the agony of the Gaul
that was carved in stone

wakamono wa nabete kurushimu mono nagara ishi ni horareshi gōrujin no ku

若者はなべて苦しむものながら石に彫られしゴール人の苦

propping himself up
on his right arm
left hand
fallen on his thigh
he will stand no more

hanshin o sasaeru migite futomomo ni okeru hidarite mohaya tachi ezu

半身を支へる右手　太股に置ける左手　もはや立ち得ず

for years on end
always in
the same pose
the Gaul persists
ever on the point of dying

iku toshitsuki onaji shitai o jizoku shite hinshi no gōrujin wa tae iru

幾年月おなじ姿態を持続して瀕死のゴール人は耐へゐる

I have learned to love
the pitilessness
of him who gave form
to suffering
making it beautiful

kurushimi o hashiku katachi to seshi mono no hijō o aishi kitarinu
    ware wa

苦しみを美しく形とせしものの非情を愛しきたりぬわれは

thinking now
of what that Gaul suffered long ago
has made apparent
what one should expect
after the notification[34]

haruka naru gōrujin no ku o ima ni shite kokuchi no nochi o sumite
　aru beshi

はるかなるゴール人の苦を今にして告知ののちを澄みてある
　べし

the youth that one thinks
will last forever
is but a moment
marmoreal skin
knows nothing of aging

seishun wa ikkoku ni shite towa to omou dairiseki no hifu oyuru o
　shirazu

青春は一刻にして永遠と思ふ大理石の皮膚老ゆるを知らず

---

34. A difficult line. *Kokuchi* (notice, announcement, notification) appears here with-out evident relation to an agent or patient: to this reader, it is not clear who is making the announcement, nor who is hearing it. It might be observed that, in other of Kasugai's poems, *kokuchi* is readily interpretable as a public statement that someone has AIDS: see, for example, the tanka that begins "the one who made him / tell his mother." The related verb *tsugu* (writ-ten with the first ideograph of the word *kokuchi*) appears in several other tanka that I have translated here, and it too usually refers to an admission of illness. Is the lyric persona wait-ing to hear from his physician? Is the persona going to tell a lover? Is some other situation implied? Believing the matter undecidable, I have tried to translate neutrally.

THIRTEEN

Selections from *Gay Poems* (Gei poemuzu) by Tanaka Atsusuke (2014)

Translated by Jeffrey Angles

Biography and Introduction

Tanaka Atsusuke (1961–) was raised in Kyoto, where he still lives and works as a part-time high-school mathematics teacher. In 1991, the prominent poet Ōoka Makoto identified him in the journal *Yuriika* (Eureka) as one of the outstanding new poetic voices of his generation. Along with Takahashi Mutsuo, Ishii Tatsuhiko, and Aizawa Keizō, Tanaka is one of the small handful of well-received contemporary poets who has written in unflinching detail about his sexual feelings and history. Although those poems originally appeared scattered throughout his oeuvre, in 2014 he brought together many of his poems about same-sex relationships written over the years and published them in an anthology entitled *Gei poemuzu* (Gay Poems), which served as the source for all of the poems translated below.

Some of Tanaka's early poems, such as "Takano River" and "Like Fruit Floating on Water," first published in the early 1990s, are fairly straightforward examples of free verse, but since the mid-1990s, Tanaka has been writing in a more experimental, avant-garde vein. Many of his poems are in linguistic registers that more conservative poets would see as falling outside of the narrow confines of "poetic" language—the speech of teenagers, speech in dialect, erotic language, colloquial song lyrics, and even mathematical formulas. Many of his poems feature nontraditional punctuation and other flourishes to make his writing interesting on the page.

In some poems, he incorporates portions of real conversations verbatim, creating a record of personal exchanges that under more ordinary circumstances might easily be forgotten. "Marlboro," for instance, includes some of the conversation that took place before a fateful sexual encounter that Tanaka had in his youth. Similarly, "Under the Guava Tree Was the Name of the Hotel" describes the conversational lead-up to a visit to a love hotel. Like Francis Poulenc's experimental, modernist opera *La voix humaine,* which presents only one side of the conversation, it presents only Tanaka's side of the story, thus recording some of the silly, flirtatious, and heart-breaking statements an adolescent gay man might make as he opens up to an erotic encounter with a stranger. In these poems, one sees Tanaka's hallmark combination of youthful playfulness and adult sensitivity.

During Tanaka's youth, one of the boys whom he loved in school drowned during a visit to the sea. Tanaka describes him nostalgically in the poem "Memories of Summer." Not coincidentally, the sea becomes a symbol of lost opportunities and passions in later, more experimental poems, including a handful of poems to which he gave the identical title "Burying the Sun." One should note, however, that in those poems, the word that I have loosely translated as "sun" (*yō*) also means "yang," the masculine, active, positive principle in the yin-yang binary. In other words, the poems "Burying the Sun," when read together, form a requiem to an already absent masculinity, which some gay men eagerly seek to recover.

In 1999, Tanaka published a book with the English title *The Wasteless Land,* which contains a series of experimental, postmodern pastiches that draws inspiration and incorporates quotations from an astoundingly wide array of sources, including pop music and R&B, classic Western and Japanese literature, science fiction, and Tanaka's own conversations with friends late at night in bars. Since then, Tanaka has published seven volumes in *The Wasteless Land* series. The longish poem "An Average of Six Per Year," which presents a series of meandering and sentimental memories about a long-lost lover, comes from volume four. In this poem, Tanaka swings back and forth between more traditionally poetic language, colloquial speech in Kansai dialect, and the kinds of slangy writing one might find in emails or texts. Similarly, the poem "What's Going On" incorporates fragments of memories, voices, and song lyrics. (The title, which is in English, comes from the famous song by Marvin Gaye.) In this way, Tanaka expands the vocabulary of poetry in ways that might suit the postmodern lifestyles and eclectic culture of people living in the twenty-first century.

Takano River[1]

(1993)

The flow of clear water through its shallow bed
Is high and clouded due to yesterday's rain
I stand on the bank waiting for the bus
And watch the grass reflected on its surface
The reflection trembles as the water moves
An ochre canvas dyed black
Water strikes shallow stones and swells
Trailing like clouds in the sky
Dead branches rush between ripples
While withered grass sinks, rudderless

As I wait on the bus
Your nearby room
Feels far away
I think of many things
Of how the more I think of you
The more confidence I lose
Of how one day, all will go wrong

By the dam, the water stands stagnant
One eddy flows backward through
It captures my abandoned cigarette
Which dances in a circle for some time
Gradually comes undone and throws itself in
Leaving only the filter to go round and round
Like a fisherman's float, rising and sinking

---

1. The Takano River is located in northeastern Kyoto.

Like Fruit Floating in Water

(1993)

No matter how I try to draw you close
You, like fruit floating in water,
   Do not return at all
If anything, you float farther,
   Farther from me

Even though it was I who picked you
   It was I who threw you in the water

Memory of Summer

(1993)

summer
white summer
memory of summer
reflections of light
concrete
clubs
locker rooms
you were on the volleyball team
you shone
dazzling to the eyes
me lined up
sitting down
I was on the judo team
we were still freshmen
summer
white summer
memory of summer
reflections of light
overlapping
hands and
hands and
sweat and
light
white light
reflecting
concrete
dark shadows
no one was there
that day
that summer
that summer vacation
that time
was just our time
just you and me
you and me

(just you and me, right?)
you shone
summer
white summer
sun
that day
was my first time
I didn't know
that it was such a ticklish place
the lips
touching scanty whiskers
(just a few, no matter how you let them grow, right?)
lips and
sweat and
dazzling
it lasted
only
a moment
summer
a memory
of white summer
a first kiss
(you did taste of sweat, didn't you?)
but
that was all
that was all
that day
that time
that time anyone ever saw you
we didn't stay at the camp
the teams ended early
why
did you go
out for a swim
with her
in the sea?
summer
a summer
day

white memory of summer
forever shining
my
your
summer
day
the memory of that summer day
flipping through summers
flipping through
each time I come to it
it tears my heart
apart
tears my heart
to shreds
then scatters them
to the wind
summer
white summer
memory of summer
reflected light
concrete
clubs
locker rooms
overlapping
hands and
eyes and
lips and
sweat and
light and
shadow and
summer

Under the Umbrella

(1993)

under the umbrella
I hear your voice clearly

the rain filters away
everything unnecessary

all that reaches my ears
is the sound of your voice

Marlboro

(2001)

He had a tattoo.
Under his leather jacket, a solid, white T-shirt.
Don't look at me.
I thought I didn't make the cut.
There're lots of other young ones.
I'm nothing to look at.
But he chose me.
Want to grab a cup of coffee?
He didn't add any cream.
So, we're the same age.
He smoked a cigarette.
Only a week of no smoking.
The name of the love hotel was
Under the Guava Tree.
Rain had soaked our socks.
Should've bought some new shoes sooner.
I showered with him.
His dick was white and beautiful.
Why am I writing this down in a poem?
Once and that'll be all.
Just once and that's okay, someone once said.
I didn't go home right away.
That was true for both of us.
We both lingered on and on.
I was in Tokyo for seven years.
Dicks rained down.
Lots of them rained down.
It's good if there are natural enemies for people.
There was nothing in Tokyo.
His face said nothing was there
So he was here.
He was beautiful.
His back turned, he placed
His can of cola on the table
Half-consumed.

Under the Guava Tree Was the Name of the Hotel.

(2001)

Have you ever thought about doing something totally nuts
Like sneaking into a hospital in the morning
And writing *cancer, cancer, cancer*
On the foreheads of the sleeping patients?
Using an invisible marker, of course.
A weird little gift to take home.
But probably
I'd feel too sorry for them.
Ha-ha, look at your hair!
It's all curly, making swirls.
Look at those swirls!
Um, didn't you forget something?
Yeah, but, I . . .
Suddenly you're talking about a love hotel,
You surprised me, that's all.
Yeah.
So, I. . . .
You know the word *sugasugashii* (refreshing)
'Til just the other day, whenever I saw it in a book
I thought it was pronounced *kiyokiyoshii*.
The other day, I said it to a friend,
And he was like, huh? What'd you say?
He made fun of me,
That's how I figured it out.
Um, hey, you hungry?
Let's go to KFC or somewhere.
I'll show you where it is.
I like you.
Ha-ha, don't stare at me like that.
What'd you do if you stared a hole right through me?
Um, say there,
You like breasts or thighs better?
I like thighs.
They're easier to eat.
I'll give you the breasts, okay?

Just think about it, this bird's happiness
Came from being eaten by me.
Yeah.
Um, you're weird too.
It's not easy to eat the breast meat, is it?
Lots of teeny-tiny bones.
Look, my hand's shaking.
So, level with me,
Am I really your type?
Even though I'm chubby?
Oh, come on, cut it out.
People will see.
My nipples are super sensitive.
Especially the one on the left.
They're different sizes.
Maybe I've played with it too much.
Huh?
This is your phone number?
You're not married?
You know, I'm not smart,
But people say I've got a cute face.
A boyish face.
You know, people who like folks like me
Are called chubby chasers.
I'm cute?
Ha-ha.
I've been called fatso, fatso since I was a kid.
I totally hated it,
But now I'm glad
There's some like you
Who says I'm cute.
I also like chubby guys.
They look so sweet, don't you think?
Like you.
Ha-ha.
Sure.
I like you.
I really do.

Burying the Sun

(2001)

A single road appears before my eyes.

As I travel the road, I come to the sea.

Say, I can hear the faint sound of waves.

Now I see it.

The sea.

No one there.

An angel's ear has fallen.

It is broken even before I touch it.

The sea sinks with the weight of a plumb.

The angel's ear made the sea.

The sea's memories forgotten then remembered.

The unborn waves form a single road.

As I travel that road, once again I come to the sea.

Burying the Sun

(2001)

A moonlit night
I picked up an ear

A beautiful ear
Clad in moonlight

A moonlit beach
Waves lap at the water's edge

I walk and search, wondering
If an angel somewhere is missing its ear

Burying the Sun

(2001)

    ——Where'd you come from?
The sea.
    ——From the sea?
From the sea.
    ——Then let me return this to you.
The angel kept smiling.

Burying the Sun

(2001)

A moonlit shore,
An angel with folded wings leaned his ear toward the voice of the
　　waves.

A moonlit shore,
An angel leaned in with his lost ear to listen to the voice of the
　　waves.

A moonlit shore,
The voice of the waves whispered to the angel the whereabouts of
　　his lost ear.

A moonlit shore,
The angel murmured he needed the ear no more.

Burying the Sun

(2001)

　　　　——If you had wings, would you be an angel?
That's right.
But right now they're broken.
　　　　——You're holding wings in your arms right now.
That's right. Holding them to warm them up.
They're cold and starting to die.
　　　　——I like you better that way.
Like me better this way?
　　　　——Just a plain boy who looks kind.
With that, the angel spread his arms
To embrace his other self.

An Average of Six Per Year

(2009)

I suppose I was in my late twenties at the time
Hiro-kun was my lover and his father was a lawyer
Dealing with workplace accidents, he said that at one printing
    company
They lost an average of six per year
That was how many fingers were severed and smashed
When they cut the paper
And hands got caught in the machines
Hiro-kun
Was tubby like Winnie the Pooh
Was still in his twenties
But even though I was older
He called me by my first name
No standing on formality
When we were walking
He patted and pinched
My derriere
Later
When we parted in the subway underneath Vivre, the department
    store at Kita Ōji
He had no problem telling me to kiss him
Right there in front of everyone
To tell the truth
The station worker gave us a wide-eyed look
And I felt rather embarrassed
I remember these things
Hiro-kun
Had a part-time job
In a small movie theater in Umeda in Osaka[2]
Once when he got his paycheck
He told me he'd treat me to dinner
We ate yakiniku at a place he knew well

---

2. Umeda is a busy downtown area in Osaka where the pleasure district, including many
gay bars and saunas, is located.

In Umeda
So anyway
I was talking about fingers
I think it was after we broke up
Maybe there were four or five
I was grilling bratwurst in a skillet
Flavored with herbs inside
I added some ketchup
Was shaking the skillet
The severed fingers covered in blood
Rolled back and forth, back and forth
Totally grotesque
Try it and it'd taste good
But it looked disgusting
I felt sick
And let out a sound of disgust
So anyway
The first time I met Hiro-kun
We were at Hokuōkan, a gay sauna in Umeda
He was a super cute, tubby guy
It took me time to screw up my courage
By that
I mean to make my move
I didn't think I was good enough
I was nothing to look at
Compared to him
Still
He was so cute
I wanted to take a closer look
I crept closer
Suddenly he said
"Man, you've got guts"
This shocked me
I lost my cool, turned my back, and was about to leave
When he grabbed my arm from behind and spun me round
Frightened, I opened my eyes
So anyway
I'm nearly 180 cm tall
He was about the same height

His chest was thick, shoulders broad
He looked so much bigger than me
So anyway
With his forbidding frame
And Winnie the Pooh face
He was really cute
He gave me a big grin
Ah
I realized I was good enough
I was relieved
Then
I told him I wanted to be alone with him
So
We talked about going to a love hotel
So anyway
We left the sauna
Right away
And went to a local love hotel
A love hotel that would let in two men
It was named Apple
If I remember right
We fucked
Then went out to eat together
Ah
We had *okonomiyaki*
He gave me a big smile
"So Atsusuke-san
You can do it both ways, huh?"
I hadn't reciprocated yet
So I didn't know what he meant
"Do what both ways?" I asked
"I can't stand getting special treatment from older guys," he said
"Sure," I said
While I was resting my head on my arms
I had rubbed his head
But that made us both feel strange
So I made up my mind
I let him embrace me as if I was the one getting special treatment
He held me tight and I let him take the lead

For the rest of the evening
So anyway
A week later
"Atsusuke-san"
Had turned into just
"Atsusuke"
Much more affectionate (lol)
He was primarily a top
So anyway
That was a good thing
But I was young too
I'd fucked some nice guys
I'd even tried being a bit sadistic too (lol)
That reminds me
Hiro-kun
Had a pink plastic adult toy
The "Pink-rotar" I think it was called
The kind of thing you put in your ass and let vibrate
Once he brought it over and put it in me
When he flipped the switch
It hurt like crazy
I had him turn it off right away
His dick didn't hurt that much
He always wanted to put it in
So I became passive
But when we were going out
He really
Plowed it to me
I began to want to reciprocate
I was almost ten years older
But there were times I didn't really mind
So anyway
I only ever
Stuck it in him once
It seemed to hurt a lot
I felt bad
So we only ever did it
Just that once
He was always on top

I was always on the bottom
But he
Always lapped up my cum
When I asked why
He responded,
"A man's essence
A man's extract
Will make me more masculine"
I wondered if he was right
But it seemed like he did it out of love
Once in the bath
We switched off the lights making it pitch black
He made me take his dick in my mouth
I tried to spit out his cum without him knowing
He accosted me, "You just spit it out, didn't you?"
And got really angry
He once gave me a picture he'd drawn of a Buddhist statue
He drew it when he was waiting in my room
For me to come home from work
It was really good
Drawing statues was one of his hobbies
He drew lots and lots
There are still so many memories
Memories I treasure
Lots of memories of his smiling face
Lots of memories of his laughing voice
I wonder what he's doing now?
Ah
At the *okinomiyaki* shop
I asked about the marks on his arm
"Were you tied up earlier?"
In response, he asked
If I wanted to give it a try
So I did
The lover I'm seeing now
Looks entirely different than Hiro-kun
But he often reminds me of him
Yesterday
For the first time in ages

I spent half a day with the new guy
I kept on looking into his face
He kept asking
"What is it?"
Each time I answered
"Nothing"
But people are mysterious
Memories are mysterious
The lover I'm seeing now is dear
But memories of Hiro-kun are mixed in, making him even dearer
Sometimes in the face of one person
I see the face of another
Sometimes I take out
The photos I took with Hiro-kun
But I am dead
Hiro-kun is dead
I see us smiling in the photo
And wonder what's going on
I was in love
"You want to meet again?"
"Sure, sounds good."
I can still hear
The words from that first day
The voices
"Atsusuke"
Hiro-kun's voice always sounded slightly angry when he called my
    name
Come to think of it
Yesterday
My new lover said,
"You're being stupid"
"Why're you always moving at your own slow pace?"
"You're disgusting."
"You tick me off."
"What a bother."
The only ones who can call you
Stupid
Or
Disgusting

Are your lovers
But I suppose the fact I don't get upset
Is
Precisely
What's so disgusting
I was in love
I gave Hiro-kun
All of the issues of *Eureka* that had my poems in them
I also gave him all the books of Yoshimasu Gōzō's poetry I had[3]
He didn't write poetry
But enjoyed reading it
Ah
There was a guy who was chubbier than Hiro-kun
Who loved it when I recited poetry
Quietly in his ear
Hiro-kun did kendo
That other guy did some sport too but he gave it up and put on
     weight
That's what he told me anyway, but it seemed like he'd gone too far
He looked totally different than his high school picture (lol)
I hope I die soon
Ah
On the phone I told Jimmy-chan
I was writing about Hiro-kun now
"That guy from the movie theater in Osaka?
The Gemini with type A blood, right?"[4]
My goodness, I didn't know
The same as my lover now
Maybe that's why I'm remembering
When I said that
Jimmy-chan answered

---

3. Yoshimasu Gōzō (1939–) is one of Japan's most prominent and provocative avant-garde poets. His poems are typically long, meandering, and filled with strings of loosely related ideas and vocabulary that invite the reader into the world of the poem to try to make sense of it. Sometimes his poems even involve other languages, as if Yoshimasu is probing the boundaries of the Japanese language and even Japan itself. At the same time, he also fills his poems with lots of small, intensely personal autobiographical details, not unlike Tanaka's poetry.

4. In Japan, it is a common belief that blood type, like one's astrological sign, will help determine the compatibility of two romantic partners.

"Probably"
My goodness
Ah
Come to think of it
Tintin was also a Gemini with type AB blood
What's going on?

What's Going On.[5]

(2014)

I often drive around the Arashiyama area. I cross the Togetsu Bridge
and take two or three spins around each bank of the Katsura River.
Me: "What's so good about Arashiyama?" My friends: "Two mountains
press against the wind from each side, that's where Arashiyama's name
comes from—'The Stormy Mountains.' People like the beauty of the
mountains and the pleasant feel of the wind coming off the river." Me:
"Where does the truth reside?" My friends: "Are you saying the truth
you seek isn't there?" The words I'm about to say catch in my throat.
As I smile, they branch apart, a camel with two humps. One of the
words is itself, a single deep abyss. At what angle does a river become a
waterfall? Even a vertical river wouldn't be a waterfall if it falls slowly. If
a waterfall fell slowly, it would still be a river.

Love is not only an indispensable, but also a beautiful thing.
(Aristotle, *Nichomachean Ethics*, Book 8, Chapter 1)

Beautiful?
(J. G. Ballard, "Cry Hope, Cry Fury!")

Don't tell me there is anything more beautiful than being in love.
(Manuel Puig, *Heartbreak Tango*, Part 2, 13)

When I was living in Kitayama, there were lots of fields nearby.
There were tight rows of labels stuck into every field. I dreamed I was
asleep, curled up and buried in the ground like a dead body. There were

---

5. Throughout this work, Tanaka uses quotes from numerous sources written by various
international authors, but in each case, he cites a published Japanese translation of the text.
In the Japanese, the quotations flow together smoothly, as if the books are participating in
Tanaka's own inner dialogue. At first, as the translator of this piece, I attempted to locate the
original text or, in the case of a Spanish or French original, an already existing English translation; however, when those quotations were sutured together, the quotes seemed far more
disjointed and disconnected than in Tanaka's poem because they appear in a different context
than the original authors had envisioned. Rather than use the quotes directly, I decided to
treat Tanaka's Japanese as the "original" and back-translate all the quotations into English. The
information in Tanaka's text about where to find the original quotes has been retained in case
a dedicated reader would like to go back and view the source.

lots of other corpses sleeping parallel to me. Somewhere in my mind, I felt like I was following suit, imitating the other corpses. Perhaps I wasn't dreaming. A friend called me. As we were talking, I sank down into the soil with my friend. Perhaps that was because I was lying on my side as I was talking into the phone. My friend lives in a room on the fifth floor of a building, so he had much further to sink than me.

The person above us started pounding again.
(Julio Cortázar, *Hopscotch*, 28 pages from the end)

Two or three times.
(James P. Hogan, *Realtime Interrupt*, Prologue)

The next will be the fourth.
(David Brin, *Startide Rising*, Part 10)

What is the probability that a thing will become me? One out of how many? One out of how many tens? I walk down the street whispering these questions to myself. I see an electrical pole. And the electrical pole becomes me. I see a stoplight. And the stoplight becomes me. I see the white lines of a crosswalk. And the white lines of the crosswalk become me. I go into a bookstore. What is the probability that the books lined up on the shelf will become me? One out of how many? One out of how many tens? Metaphors are so vivid they torment. Torment is always vivid. That is one of torment's special characteristics. The other day, I saw the word "Order list" (発注リスト) and since the characters are so similar, I misread it as "Go crazy list" (発狂リスト).

Lovers and madmen have such seething brains, / Such shaping
    fantasies . . .
(William Shakespeare, *A Midsummer Night's Dream*, Act 5, Scene 1)

Love knows no limit.
(Marcel Proust, *In Search of Lost of Time*, Vol. 6: *The Fugitive*)

Do you understand what this means?
(Walter M. Miller Jr., *A Canticle for Leibowitz*, Part 3)

In Kyōgoku, there is a porno theater called the Yachiyokan, and in front of it is a small park where guys cruise for sex. The other day, there was a young man squatting on a bench, not wearing anything from the waist down. As I approached, he stuck out his bottom, looked over his shoulder at me, and said, "Take it." He was an attractive young man who reminded me of a junior league baseball player. There were still some traces of childhood about him. He was probably around twenty. As I got closer, I saw the tip of a ballpoint pen sticking out of the crack of his ass. As I stood there silently looking at him without doing a thing, he once again looked over his shoulder and said, "Take it." So I did. "Now, don't look," he said as a pile of shit came sliding out.

Madness and imagination are the same in that neither knows no limits.
(Jean des Cars, *Ludwig II of Bavaria or the Fallen King*, The Dove and the Eagle)

It seems that in your foolish head, you create relationships between people that don't actually exist.
(Marquis de Sade, *Justine*)

Even love must be stopped within certain limits.
(Marcel Proust, *In Search of Lost Time*, Vol. 4: *Sodom and Gomorrah*)

There is a kind of peppermint candy called "Frisk," which makes your mouth feel cool when you suck on it. I know this guy named Aki-chan who enjoys lying out along the banks of the Kamo River in the sun, wearing only a *fundoshi*. He's close-cropped, bearded, gay, and a nudist. One time he handed me something and told me to try using it the next time I had anal sex. He said it would make me tingle, that it would make even people who don't like getting penetrated eager to stick something up their ass. I haven't tried it yet, but I've nicknamed the stuff "the Frisk Effect." When one writes, it is the same as taking a good look at oneself. Expression is cognition. All self-knowledge is always too much or too little.

What's the problem?
(Janet Fox, *Faithful*)

As long as you're happy, it shouldn't matter at all.
(John Wyndham, *Trouble With Lichen*)

That's what love is, right?
(Philip K. Dick, "Frozen Journey")

    I missed the last train and was sitting on a bench in Aoi Park when a young man who appeared to be in his midtwenties sad down on the bench next to me. He began to rub my groin. As I looked at his hand on me, the thought crossed my mind that the only reason he was doing it was to give his hand some pleasure. Instantly, all my arousal, excitement, and curiosity vanished. I stood up and walked away, even though I knew that if I refused his affections, there wouldn't necessarily be any forthcoming from anyone else. Until that point, I used to think that I was the kind of person who loves intensely and hates intensely. But I was wrong. I merely love hastily and hate hastily.

You don't love me.
(E. M. Forster, *Maurice*, Part 2, Chapter 25)

Of course, you're right.
(Terry Bisson, *Get Me to the Church on Time*, Chapter 3)

Oh noooo!
(Richard Laymon, *The Woods are Dark*)

    I have no idea which of my feelings are real and which aren't. Same with my memories. There are strange places here and there in my memories. When I was in elementary school, my parents used to take me to the Daimaru department store near Kyoto Station. I remember that near the middle of the room, there was a place where the waitresses would inevitably trip. One of them rammed her face through some glass. I clearly remember her crying, her face covered in blood, as her sobs reverberated throughout the room. No one moved or did anything. When I talked about this with my mother, she said nothing like that ever happened.

Didn't you tell me you loved me?
(George R. R. Martin, *Fast Friend*)

And if so, so what?
(Stephen King, *Cujo*)

I was just surprised, that's all.
(Ernesto Sabato, *On Heroes and Tombs*, Part 1, Chapter 3)

    I had a phone call from my mother right as I get home from work. "I died today." "Huh?" "Today I—your mother—was in a car accident and died." I spit out my tea. "But I can still die again, any number of times." "Sure, Mom." "I'm sure I'll have another car accident and die again." "I wonder . . ." Silence settled between us for ten seconds or so before I put down the receiver. There was a letter in the mailbox which said, "There will be rain . . ." But the weather was completely clear. Earlier, all throughout the day, I had several distant memories of rainy days lined up in my head. In Japanese, there's an expression "When dealing with good, hurry," which means "strike while the iron is hot." There's another expression, "If you hurry, you'll get turned around" which means "slow and steady wins the race." Put these two proverbs together, and you'd get, "When dealing with good, you'll get turned around."

The person above us started pounding again.
(Julio Cortázar, *Hopscotch*, 28 pages from the end)

There is the fourth.
(Roger Zelazny, *For a Breath I Tarry*)

What are we going to do . . . ?
(A. A. Milne, *The House at Pooh Corner*, Chapter 8)

    I saw a white piece of paper the size of a person floating slowly down an empty staircase. As I passed by, I brushed it with my hand, but it was just an ordinary, thin piece of paper. On the platform where I change trains on my way to work, there are rows of lots of pieces of white paper about the size of a person, all swaying back and forth. I casually opened my hand. The entire day today I was a single sheet of white paper. Bringing my mouth to my hand, I breathed on it. A small, white sheet of paper danced upward from it, riding the breeze. Lots of white, trembling sheets of paper were flying through the sky, blocking the entire sky from view. On the platform, we were all shaking back and forth. The train would be arriving soon.

Are you going to scream?
(Hans Erich Nossack, "Clontz")

That's about it.
(Gerald Kersh, "Whatever Happened to Corporal Cuckoo?")

And then?
(W. B. Yeats, *A Vision*, "The Phases of the Moon")

FOURTEEN

"The Story of a Strange Belly" (Kifukutan) by Fukushima Jirō (2005)

Translated by Bruce Suttmeier

Biography and Introduction

Fukushima Jirō was a twenty-one-year-old college student in 1951 when he approached the home of the writer Mishima Yukio, clutching a note that asked where he could find the gay bar in *Forbidden Colors*, the novel Mishima was then serializing. A maid ushered him in to meet the famous writer, who then took him along on an afternoon of errands, promising to soon show him the bar described in the book. The brief relationship that followed looms large over much of Fukushima's career, most spectacularly in his 1998 best-selling memoir of their relationship, *Mishima Yukio: tsurugi to kanbeni* (Mishima Yukio: Sword and Cold Crimson), the object of a lawsuit by Mishima's children claiming infringement of copyright and of Mishima's "personality rights" (*jinkaku-ken*) for its use of several letters. They no doubt also objected to the candid descriptions of the sexual relationship between the two men. He fictionalized their encounters in several works, weaving his observations of intergenerational desire with an implied confession: he felt no desire for the older writer. Perhaps his most famous fictional work is *Basutaoru* (Bathtowel), a finalist for the 1996 Akutagawa Prize, depicting the relationship between a high-school teacher and his much-younger student.

In the story translated here, "Kifukutan" (The Story of a Strange Belly), published in the 2005 collection *Ingetsu* (Lurid Moon) just before his death, Fukushima further explores the asymmetry of desire between older and younger men, exploring attraction to bodies deemed unattractive within mainstream straight and gay aesthetics. As Fukushima puts it in the story, the "undesirable and deficient" become the "designated superstars of all such odd and endearing types" of eroticized bodies. Shingo, a sixty-six-year-old gay man working the overnight shift at a love hotel in the city of Hakata in Kyushu, struggles to make sense of what he has seen (or thinks he has seen) when two men rent a room for the night. The mysterious episode, with all its playful and sinister implications, features a complex erotics of queer male attraction, endowing the protruding male stomach with attributes both erogenous and therapeutic. As articulated to Shingo by the admiring young men he encounters, such a belly was "just magnificent, magnificent," embodying a significance of experience they themselves had not faced. "These young men would maintain that the stomach of a big, middle-aged man holds his very life, in all its immense gravity."

The Story of a Strange Belly

Shingo had married and had a daughter, but once his wife learned he was gay and divorced him, he fled his hometown of Hakata for the Osaka region. He got by through a mix of day laboring and company jobs until he found himself approaching fifty. For the next dozen or so years, he served as a manager at a gay bar in the Shinsekai neighborhood of the city, but then three years ago when he turned sixty-three, he returned to Hakata and took a job working at a love hotel run by an old acquaintance. One could be forgiven for wondering why at sixty-six he would want such a job, but Shingo had to save whatever money he could these days for his one real pleasure: visiting his daughter and grandchild in Kumamoto every other month. His ex-wife had long since passed away.

The hotel Hana where he worked was set behind Watanabe Avenue amid a narrow row of old houses, its three-story Western facade covered in black tile. It was here, flicking on the light above the price list in the lobby window, that Shingo would start his workday. The manager's mother and daughter would clean the entire building in the afternoon, and then Shingo's shift, from seven o'clock at night until ten the next morning, would begin.

A stifling nighttime heat always settles over Kyushu during the summer, as the television points out each year, but the nighttime heat and humidity this July were particularly oppressive. Even a quick trip to the end of the alley for cigarettes and ice cream left Shingo's undershirt drenched in sweat. He compared the condition of those poor saps in the back-alley tenement where he lived, in rooms without air conditioning, to his own pleasant overnights in the well-cooled air of the hotel, leading him to wonder what they did to get through nights like this. With an air of self-satisfaction, he'd sit in the reception room off the lobby and read magazines, watch TV, and wait for customers.

On that particular evening, by 10 p.m. there had been only one couple renting by the hour and two couples staying overnight. He figured he was in for a slow night, but just then he heard the sound of the front door echo through the lobby. He peeked through his small window. There were two men, one in his late fifties and the other about twenty. Several gay bars had set up shop in various spots around the neighborhood, and it wasn't unusual to get pairs of male customers drifting in. Having taken similar paths in his own turbulent past, Shingo hardly gave it a second thought.

In his first six months of employment when a man and woman arrived, he was all business, dutifully collecting payment and showing them to their rooms. But when two men arrived, by contrast, he was immediately struck that they had shown up at his window, unashamedly eager to enjoy a night together. As he stood with male couples in the lobby, Shingo had often been unable to stop himself from staring at their faces and bodies, his gaze prolonged and insistent. But now, with the passage of time, he felt no such inclination to stare.

He came out onto the floor, wearing a smile and rubbing his hands. "Would the gentlemen like a room for the night?" he asked. The older man wore a cream-colored alpine hat, its brim lowered over his eyes, with a dark-blue hemp jacket. To his side, he held a black attaché case. In the dim light of the hall fixtures, the man's hat concealed his eyes, but Shingo could see his puffed-up, heavy white cheeks and could see his chin nod twice in vigorous assent. "Well then, I would be happy to show you to your room." As Shingo spoke, the two men changed into slippers. The younger man wore navy shorts with a nautical-striped Breton T-shirt. Seeing the sweat-stained, frayed T-shirt, Shingo sensed that the young man had just thrown it on over his small sunburned, muscular frame, like a Japanese badger from an old tale who, needing to transform, finds a leaf for atop its head.

Shingo took the 6,000-yen charge for the two-person stay, and led the way up the stairs. The hotel Hana couldn't boast an elevator, but it took pride in its sole standout feature, its stairs with a glittering gold handrail and lush red carpet. He decided to head to the third floor, where he chose to put male couples when it wasn't crowded.

To help his two quiet guests feel at ease, he spoke as he reached the landing, "It is quite the heat wave we're having, isn't it? No end to these sweltering nights." He turned around and suddenly noticed that the older man, his upper body slightly swaying to the side, was clutching the handrail. He seemed a bit unsteady on his feet. The young man followed close behind, plodding forward like a stooped beggar, his hands stuffed into the pockets of his shorts.

Climbing the stairs to the third floor and opening the door to the "Pleiades" room, Shingo motioned the two men toward the room. "Here you are." The older man entered the room without a word, his head down, his alpine hat still on his head. The younger man, not to be left behind, hurriedly followed him in. It was clear that the older man, while of average height, was significantly overweight. Despite the heat, he was wearing a linen jacket and showed no signs of sweating. The younger man sported a crew cut and had large eyes set in a cute, round face, though one could see bits of grime around the bridge of his nose. Shingo headed back to the reception room, mulling over this couple. Were the two men lovers? Had they just met at a bar this evening? Was the young man perhaps just a trick the older man had picked up on the street? On reflection, though, the two seemed less like lovers and more like an owner with his pet dog, as if the younger man, a dearly departed canine companion reborn in human form, had followed the older man here. While the older man seemed hostile or a bit depressed, the younger man resembled nothing more than a squirming, irrepressibly cheerful puppy.

Around 8:00 the next morning, a signal light and buzzer in the reception room told Shingo that the door to the Pleiades room had opened. It was what Shingo had been waiting for, and the signal had finally come. He walked into the lobby as the older man slowly worked his way down the stairs, gripping the railing and leaning his heavy-set body to the side with each step. "We appreciate your business, sir," Shingo called out, heading to the shoe rack near the stairs to grab their dress shoes and sneakers, lining them up on the entry floor, then standing and turning to see that the man was, in fact, by himself. He was repeatedly running his hands over his stomach, turning his head to glance at the top of the stairs, as if remembering something.

"And your companion?" Shingo asked, to which the man waved his hands back and forth excitedly—"Down later . . . down later . . . ," he managed to mumble in a hushed tone. His alpine hat was pulled low, just as it had been the previous night, the expression of his eyes unclear beneath the brim. "He is still asleep in the room then. I understand, sir. These young people do tend to be late sleepers." His answer was an inadvertent acknowledgment that he understood the ways of the chicken hawk (those connoisseurs of male love who prefer only young partners), and Shingo, embarrassed that he had exposed himself as gay, hurriedly offered the man a shoehorn. But the man did not put on his shoes right away, instead milling about the narrow lobby as if waiting for the young boy to come down the stairs, his excited and irritated appearance a stark change from his composed, one might say sluggish, manner of the previous night, leading Shingo to wonder, as he again gazed at the man, what was wrong.

Even covered with a jacket, there was no hiding the man's rather prominent stomach, but this morning, with the front of his jacket unzipped, it was all the more evident how his stomach strained against his untucked white shirt. Complimenting him on his amazing belly was out of the question, so Shingo was left to marvel at it. One could sense that the front zipper was undone, not because he had forgotten to close it but because he was no longer *able* to pull the two sides together. Had his belly gotten bigger since last night? That's ridiculous, such a thing wasn't possible. Shingo stifled his childlike urge to stare and again offered the shoehorn to the man.

The man twisted around as he sought to grab the long handle, and as he did, the clasp on the attaché case, held in his other hand, came undone, the freed flap swinging downward and dangling toward the floor, like a clamshell popped wide open. Everything inside was sent tumbling onto the ground, spilling at the man's feet and scattering to the far edge of the entryway.

The man's anguished groan was dwarfed by the large, dramatic shout—"Oh my goodness"—emanating from Shingo. The man must be some PR liaison at a construction site, or a statistician, Shingo figured, given the predictable stash of documents tumbling with a thud and scattering on the floor, but along with the papers was a nautical-striped Breton T-shirt, shorts, even purple underwear, covered with what looked like lines and creases from being wadded up and stuffed into the briefcase. Flung out and exposed, their sad, shriveled state resembled the discarded shell of an insect. The man, flustered, scooped up his things and frantically shoved them back into his briefcase, slamming it shut once more. Shingo sat formally with both knees on the floor, his mouth open in amazement, his hands immobile in front of him as he stared at the man's actions. With a sidelong glance at the staring Shingo, the man quickly composed himself, threw back his shoulders, pushed open the glass entry door, and walked out.

Shingo sat there, without a word, lost in his thoughts, then he quickly stood up, put on sandals, and rushed out of the hotel onto the street, the summer sun blazing above, to check which way the man had headed. He appeared to be moving toward the main road, which given his current pace would take him some time to reach. Hurrying back inside, Shingo ran through the lobby and straight up to the third floor. He was breathing heavily and coughing as he reached the front of the Pleiades room, but he headed right into the room without hesitating and began to look around.

The bed had been slept in but was empty now. Still panting, Shingo examined every inch of the room, but nothing was out of the ordinary. He nervously pulled open the door to the bathroom. He peered in the large wardrobe. But there was no young boy's naked corpse or any such thing, as he had readily imagined. He even crawled under the bed and poked around, but found nothing.

What had come to mind, as soon as Shingo had seen the man off, was homicide. Perhaps it had happened after some strange dalliance, or perhaps during a quarrel as they were leaving. Maybe the man had seduced a straight boy and, when push came to shove and he defended himself against the youth's angry reaction, it had ended in tragedy. All kinds of scenarios ran through Shingo's head—the wealth of overheard stories from the gay world alone formed a rich source—so after making sure there was no corpse, he thought of calling the police.

Perhaps the youth had escaped in the middle of the night? Or had there even been trouble with the boy trying to rob the older man? Shingo opened up the window and peered outside. The wall of the adjoining building loomed immediately outside, its sheer surface offering not a single place to grab ahold. Nor was there even room in the narrow space between the two buildings for an individual to drop himself to the ground. And even if one did manage to get down there, posts at either end of the alley prevented access either in or out. Where in the world had the body of that boy disappeared to? With his breathing finally back to normal, Shingo sat down on the edge of the bed and shook his head several times, unable to see how he might make sense of these bewildering circumstances, until at last, dumbfounded, he went out to the hallway and headed straight for the stairs, slowly making his way down to the first floor where, on reaching the reception room, he collapsed, face down, on his still-unmade bedding.

As Shingo walked down the stairs and fell into bed that morning, wondering what had happened last night in the Pleiades room, he was at the mercy, as it were, of his own wildly eccentric imagination. But when the next customers arrived, a man and woman, and he showed them to their room, he had already begun to reject the core of his initial hunch. There was no way such a thing can happen. If I'm willing to entertain such fantasies, he thought, then on my sixty-sixth birthday next year I'll wish for a return to being a sprightly forty-six.

Two days passed, then three. He went to work at Hana as he had before. Though he sought to stay unruffled at work, he sensed himself on edge. He steered guests away from the Pleiades room. There were thankfully no nights at full occupancy. On the streets, the hot humid nights continued.

He figured it had been his eyes playing tricks on him. The young man, following behind like a loyal puppy, like a shadow trailing in his wake, had nestled himself right behind the older man's fat frame, and so had stayed out of Shingo's sight. But the memory of seeing the young man's three articles of clothing splayed in the entryway was indisputably vivid. How could he explain that?

Suddenly, the word "senility" popped into his head. He knew two classmates from elementary school who had grown senile in their early sixties. He vigorously shook his graying head from side to side. He couldn't be accused of that, not when he was still here working—there was no way he was going senile already.

For the next week, even as Shingo sought to steer clear of this unwelcome memory, he couldn't shake the sense that he wanted to dig deeper, wanted to confirm for himself the dark, perplexing reality he had glimpsed ever so briefly. He tried various ways to tie it all together, and after much thought, settled on a single conclusion, ultimately the same one that had struck him immediately after the scene unfolded. It was a theory no one would ever believe, even less credible than if he spoke of small figures getting in and out of spaceships. He couldn't say a word about it to anyone, since if he did, people would surely think he was going senile. If rumors to that effect got back to his daughter and grandchild, there would be serious repercussions.

At this point, I interrupt the story and beg your forgiveness as I turn my attention momentarily away from the matter at hand.

It's a mystery why the types of men that women fall for and adore are so utterly different from the types desired by men in the gay world. By the same token, the sort of "quality guys" that women prefer often share a common set of characteristics, while for gay men the preferred partner might come in a million different forms, including the least likely of love interests, those more often greeted with disbelief who have their admirers all the same.

In particular, we pay no attention to the opinions of those who adore "the homely, the teeny, and the chubby." The general public deems these three types undesirable and deficient, affixing to them sharp and stinging insults, while in the gay world they are the designated superstars of all such odd and endearing types. The term "homely" gets defined as an unattractive woman or an ugly man, but in the gay world it suggests plain, rustic, artless, rumpled, lumbering, and lacking polish. Men with "homely" faces in particular often possess a winning charm; they are outgoing, wild, larger than life, good-natured, rulers of their roost, radiating a strong sense of shared humanity. Being called "homely" simply sets one apart from the conventional handsomeness of a movie star. "Tiny" implies petite or small-statured, and a huge percentage of gay men are attracted to these shorter body types, while by contrast very few fall for the tall, striking figure of the fashion model.

I begin with a proposition: that a man's instinct to embrace another, whether or not he harbors a wish to be embraced himself, stems from a powerful fascination with the other person's body type. And I do so to offer the following view—that isn't "chubby," in fact, also an exceptionally popular type in the gay world? Though we roughly categorize gay bars into places for chicken hawks (those drawn to young men) and places for daddy-chasers (those drawn to much older men), aren't there bars for chubby-chasers everywhere? Aren't there monthly magazines dedicated to chubby enthusiasts? Aren't there undeniably vast numbers of men in the gay world—especially gay Asian guys—who adore obese men?

Of course, just because one prefers chubby men as sex objects does not mean that one wants to be fat oneself. At events like the chubby-chaser monthly magazine parties, most of the attendees are men of normal size or of slim build. Yet in this day and age, with the gradual spread of an elite American mindset on dieting, the singular cache of chubby men in the gay world only grows.

While I'm at it, self-indulgently offering wild hypotheses, let me add to this account: that there's a subset of those who love obese bodies who are drawn, with a ravenous longing, to the fat man's large, protruding pot belly itself.

Even Shingo, who had slimmed down to near-skinny after his diabetes had worsened, had been until his late fifties rather obese. His popularity as a big man in the gay world often led him to think fatness was akin to fair skin, which as the saying goes, "masks a multitude of sins," especially since Shingo's own face, he suspected, was nothing to write home about.

Shingo remembered too from his numerous experiences the many young men who showed an extraordinary attachment to his own protruding belly. At gay bars, he'd be aggressively cruised, urged by young men into sex, but once they got home and into bed, Shingo soon realized the boys were less smitten with him than they were with touching his large pot belly.

Even in the bar, young boys would ask if they could touch his stomach, stroking and patting the front of his shirt, such that when he'd actually take one to a hotel and strip off his shirt, the boy seemed about to burst, his face showing flickers of happiness, of longing, of admiration as he lovingly stroked Shingo's stomach again and again. Even at times after sex when Shingo would be sleeping, he'd suddenly notice the young man pressing his lips or rubbing his cheek against his stomach.

Some young men would clamber up the unclothed Shingo before sex, or would even put aside sex entirely to climb atop him, put their ear to his stomach, and murmur in a singsong voice, "I wonder what's inside here. What could it be?"

"It's my internal organs" Shingo would say, and the boy, playfully nipping at the fleshy stomach, would respond, "Don't say that, silly." When pressed, these young men would maintain that the stomach of a big, middle-aged man holds his very life, in all its immense gravity, a weight they themselves had not yet experienced. For some boys just touching such a stomach was enough to put them at ease.

One time a youth blurted out, "It's just magnificent, magnificent. My precious mountain," while another buried his face in Shingo's soft belly and just stayed there, finally raising his head to address Shingo in a serious tone, "What I wouldn't give to get inside this big belly." He remembers that same young man telling a story one night in bed. He didn't emerge from his mother's womb, he told Shingo, until several months past her due date. When his mother later revealed this to her now adult son, she recalled that "you sure didn't want to come on out into the world. I figured you just wanted to stay inside my stomach forever." He relayed this to Shingo, expressing his surprise at the accuracy of his mother's words, since he knew himself to be of a particular personality: overly shy, insufficiently sociable, lacking assertiveness, unable to love the world around him, even wishing to escape to some hole in the ground if he could.

"Do you want to go back to your mother's womb?" Shingo asked, "or would any old large woman's womb work just as well?" The boy shook his head and answered in a sweet voice, "I like older guys so if it's not inside the big belly of some daddy I like, then forget it." Liking his men young and muscular, Shingo had certainly had his fair share of experiences with such guys, but this young man's way of thinking, even now, made no sense to him.

Your mainstream gay man, among all those drawn to masculine charms, prefers a particular type of physique—a well-defined musculature, a symmetry drawn from Greek statuary, a suntanned masculinity that radiates health, and surely there's no shortage of such mainstream guys with similar tastes. Yet as Shingo saw it, this extreme abdominal attraction that is indifferent to conventional male beauty, that focuses its attentions so intently on corpulent frames, does not seek out the powerful, solid stomachs of pro wrestlers, sumo athletes and the like, but rather pursues bellies that possess a softness, a gentleness, an overflowing of life, bellies that are less sexual objects than they are nostalgia-filled sites for sad, lonely young boys who subconsciously wish they had never been born into this world.

Shingo had known, from his earliest impression, what had happened that night: the youth had burrowed inside the belly of the older man. When the man awoke from his deep sleep, the youth was gone, only his clothes remained. His own belly, oddly changed.

The man only half-grasped all this, and when he came down to the lobby, he was at his wit's end, completely perplexed. Or perhaps, just maybe, all this was just the start of Shingo's senility.

FIFTEEN

"Time Differences" (Jisa) by Tawada Yōko (2006)

Translated by Jeffrey Angles

Biography and Introduction

Tawada Yōko (1960–) is one of the best-known contemporary novelists from Japan. She has lived in Germany since 1982, where she relocated after finishing her university studies in Tokyo. She has completed an MA in German literature at the University of Hamburg, and a PhD from the University of Zurich. In 1993 she received the Akutagawa Prize for her experimental, fantasy narrative *Inu muko iri* (The Bridegroom Was a Dog). She also writes in German, and in 1996, she won the Adalbert von Chamisso Prize, a German award recognizing foreign writers for contributions to German culture. In 2005 she received the Goethe Medal, an official decoration of the Federal Republic of Germany. Translations into English from Japanese and German include *The Bridegroom Was a Dog* (Kodansha International, 1998), *Where Europe Begins* (New Directions, 2002), *Facing the Bridge* (New Directions, 2007), *The Naked Eye* (New Directions, 2009), and *Memoirs of a Polar Bear* (New Directions, 2016).

Inspired partly by her own experiences as an immigrant, Tawada has frequently used her work to explore the lives of people who have crossed geographical and linguistic boundaries, choosing to live and work among people who look, speak, and act differently than in one's birthplace. While past generations might have seen migrants as part of a small minority, Tawada's work reminds us that in the early twenty-first century, this kind of cultural, linguistic, and identity-related hybridization is a common feature of advanced capitalist societies. In fact, the cultural cross-pollination and hybridization that one sees embodied in the lives of migrants is related to a much broader phenomenon of border-crossing and cultural cross-pollination. As Tawada's story "Jisa" ("Time Differences") shows, it would not be especially unusual for a Japanese resident of Berlin to sit down with students from multiple nations to talk about North Korea while eating Pakistani food. Similarly, a German resident of New York might sit down with a Bulgarian student to talk about job prospects in mainland China, and an American resident of Tokyo might sip Russian vodka on the same evening he chats with someone in Japanese about creating his own manga. Tawada shows us that in the twenty-first century, there are more complex ways of engaging with the world than simply identifying oneself as belonging to the particular nation, language, or race of one's birth. If anything, those simplistic modes of identification are fictions that do not represent the complex realities of people coming together, mixing, and sharing ideas, languages, and DNA. The old, singular ways of identifying oneself as belonging to a particular nation or language no longer fit the realities of the increasingly globalizing world, where elements of various cultures come together in combinations that are not always predictable from the onset.

Considering that Tawada is so eager to show how traditional modes of self-identification such as race, national origin, and linguistic identification do not necessarily match the realities of the contemporary world, it should perhaps come as no surprise that she also presents us with characters who do not fit neatly into traditional categories of sexual identity. Many of her works feature characters who do not engage in entirely heteronormative behavior; for instance, the novel *Das nackte Auge* (The Naked Eye), which was first written in German, features a woman who engages in a sexual affair with both men and women. Sometimes her characters even feel strong amorous attractions to other species, as in *The Bridegroom Was a Dog* and *Yuki no renshūsei* (Memoirs of a Polar Bear). Tawada rarely, if ever, uses words like "gay," "lesbian," or "bisexual," which describe a particular, historically constructed paradigm of sexual behavior and identification; instead, she is more likely to show her characters in all their complexity, leaving labels aside. In this regard, one might call Tawada's writing "queer," in that she consistently avoids or even subverts delimiting categories of identity and prefers to show behavior and modes of identification that cannot be easily pigeonholed.

The story "Time Differences" was first published in the January 2006 issue of the literary journal *Shinchō* (New Tide) and appeared in the collection *Umi ni otoshita namae* (The Name Dropped into the Sea) published the same year. In private conversations with the translator, Tawada has commented that the story is among her personal favorites. It features a triad of three seemingly middle-class, male characters, Mamoru, Manfred, and Michael, all of whom live and work in a country other than the one where they were born. (In this regard, the story is typically Tawadaesque.) As the story unfolds, we find that the three characters know another and have even slept together, even though they themselves are not aware of all of the links among them. All three live in a busy but relatively flat world emotionally; none are especially enthusiastic about their work, but in sexuality, they have discovered a way to relate to each other, even though those feelings are not always reciprocated. The only real connections among the characters are a series of telephone calls that cross the world's oceans. These calls might bring the characters together temporarily, but when they hang up, they are left alone in their own individual worlds in different times zones scattered across the planet. As a result, the characters feel unsatisfied and increasingly aware of their own loneliness. On one hand, Tawada shows her awareness that sexuality—and perhaps gay male sexuality in particular—represents a way for individuals to forge emotionally charged connections with one another, but she also shows that those connections do not always necessarily translate into real-life community or lasting systems of social support. One might read Tawada's "Time Differences" as a cautionary tale suggesting to readers that one cannot assume that people of the same sexual orientation will always relate to one another, and that perhaps sexual identity, just like the old, simplistic notions of national or racial identity, does not always forge lasting links between people as they would like.

Time Differences

"Nine o'clock." The alarm on the radio switched on, and the low voice of a woman filled the room. Mamoru opened his eyes. "This is the news." He heard place names in Israel, numbers of casualties—then the announcer skipped to domestic German news as if there were no other countries in the world: growing problems with the insurance system, rising unemployment, goals scored on the soccer field. Then the weather report: cloudy today with occasional rain, possibility of showers. In the traffic updates, Mamoru heard the names of towns he had never heard of before. Until a few years ago, he'd wondered how there could possibly be congestion between such small towns—after all, most people never visited those places in their whole lives.

The dark bread with sunflower seeds had grown hard, five days' worth of dryness. The red currant jelly was covered with white, cottony mold; no preservatives, the label said. The refrigerator was empty—as always on a Monday—so no milk or coffee. Shopping on Sunday wasn't easy, but not shopping on Sunday led to headaches. He might have stopped at the store in the train station by the Berlin Zoo on his way home from the Delphi Theater. So what if the prices were a little high? Manfred had said, "If you've gotta pay three times the regular price for a cup of coffee, you're better off drinking tap water." If Manfred was still in Berlin, that might have started another argument, but right now, Manfred was probably sound asleep in his apartment in downtown New York. Maybe he was snoring his usual cat-purr snore. Mamoru wondered if Manhattan at 3 a.m. was still alive with wailing sirens and the laughter of people walking down the street. Manfred was the kind of guy who, once asleep, wouldn't wake just because of a little extraneous noise. Once, a parade blaring techno music had passed by their apartment, but even that wasn't enough to wake him. As he thought of Manfred, Mamoru's molars begin to throb, and he lost all interest in the hard bread. He opened the cupboard to see what else there was. Behind the brown sugar, which was hard as a rock, and a bag of old trail mix with the label "student fodder," he found some cereal Manfred must have bought.

Mamoru rattled the box. There was probably a quarter of the box left, but there wasn't any milk. He thought of the childish gestures Manfred would make, sliding his spoon into his bowl at a forty-five-degree angle and opening his mouth absurdly wide. His cheeks were round and full—it was the only part of him that retained the soft traces of youth. He wore only short-sleeved shirts, even in the dead of winter, which caused the muscles of his forearms to tense up. Once, while asleep, Mamoru had buried his nose in the curly, light brown hair on Manfred's arm, and the tickle inside his nostrils woke him. Manfred would sometimes flop over in bed in the middle of the night. At those moments, he might knock Mamoru on the cheek, and Mamoru would wake up with a groan. Half-asleep, Manfred would lift up a little and mutter, "What? Someone hit you?" Then, with eyes still closed, he'd lie on top of Mamoru. His weight seemed less like that of a human body than that of a mass of inorganic matter, like a sandbag. "You're crushing me," Mamoru would say, unable to get out from under him. His parts were feeling numb and distant, yet there was a flow of blood that made him hard. Was Manfred moving his hands in his sleep?

Mamoru stood motionless in the kitchen as these thoughts went through his mind. Suddenly looking at the clock on the wall, he kicked himself into gear. His appointment at the dentist was at nine-thirty. His Japanese class at the university was in the afternoon, so he hoped the anesthetic would wear off by then, allowing him to speak normally. He went down to the communal basement to retrieve his bike, which he'd parked there. Bicycle thefts were on the rise. As he repositioned his linen bag across his shoulder, he felt something poking him in his side. What was it? A sashimi knife, brand name "Nippon," although made in China. He had bought it at a department store last week and had obviously forgotten about it. There wasn't any time to go back into the apartment and leave it. He imagined falling while riding his bike and stabbing himself—the sort of thing you might see in a manga. But the knife was in a case, so he doubted that would happen. He stepped on the pedal and took off.

The wail of the siren trailed off into the distance, marking what, by coincidence, turned out to be nearly an hour of unbroken silence, but eventually the drunk lying on the side of the road woke up and resumed shouting his monologue, starting up where he had left off yesterday. Another hour, then a compact car drove by, then another, as if the cars were coming out of nowhere. A garbage truck made its way down the narrow downtown streets. Its gigantic metal claw grabbed the trash and tossed the rotten remnants into the huge, gaping mouth on its back. Sounds of breaking glass and crumpling plastic. In his dream, Manfred was lying face down, buck 'naked, on a wet floor, which seemed to be the deck of a ship. His wrists and ankles were tied up in a fishnet, and he couldn't move. The boatman approached. He leaned down and with his knife poked at the tensed muscles of Manfred's buttocks. He seemed to be checking if Manfred was dead or alive. If he realized Manfred was alive, he'd jam the knife up Manfred's rectum, killing him on the spot. Manfred pressed his abdomen against the damp deck, clenching his teeth, holding his breath; some little fish from the net, however, had found their way underneath him, and they wriggled under his weight trying to free themselves. They were ticklish. How could Manfred stay still with this going on under him? Damn it, hurry up and die. He wished he could crush them, but no such luck. The slightest movement and he'd be done for. The fear and ticklishness were getting unbearable. He was having to squeeze to hold back the contents of his bladder. If he pissed himself, he'd be punished. He'd be strung up in a public square and his ears lopped off with scissors. And then his nipples, and then . . .

Fortunately, the alarm clock went off. He always had it set for six. He jumped out of bed and, naked, went into the kitchen, where he splashed water over his face. The shower was so old it looked like it was out of the thirties. It hadn't given him any trouble when he first moved to New York, but recently, it had been on the fritz. It wouldn't spit out enough water to satisfy a cat's thirst. In Berlin, it had been his routine to take a cold shower each morning. He'd use so much water it was like standing under a waterfall. A cold shower helped tighten his drooping skin, and not being about to take one made him irritable. He went back to the bedroom and straightened the sheets and blanket. He found himself growing emotional as he remembered waking up with Michael there. It hadn't been that long ago. On the day they parted in the airport café, Manfred had cried. He had watched his own large tears fall into his cup of coffee. Michael had watched this too, amazed that such a big, muscular man would cry like that. Did Manfred not know the law governing the ratio between muscles and tears? Michael had been born on the East Coast of the U.S. and had spent his whole life there, but it was now time for him to leave it and Manfred behind. As Michael got up and made his way to the gate, he smiled. He had nothing more than one piece of red carry-on luggage in hand as he boarded the plane. He seemed as happy and carefree as if he were going to visit a cousin in Boston for the weekend.

Manfred had not intended to wait faithfully, but he had already developed the habit, every time he looked at the calendar, of calculating how many months it would be before Michael's homecoming. People invited Manfred to parties, but he had stopped putting in appearances. He couldn't stay in New York forever. He was a student and supported himself by teaching German, but it wouldn't be long before he'd lose his current position as a teaching associate, which put much-needed cash into his pockets. He had heard it was difficult to renew positions like his. If things didn't work out, he'd be forced to go back to Berlin at the same time that Michael finally got back to New York. He didn't want to go home anymore. He wanted to find a job in New York and get a green card. He wasn't sure if Michael wanted the same thing for himself in Tokyo, but what if he did? What if he didn't come back from Tokyo? Manfred wondered if there was such a thing as a green card in Japan.

That day he'd go "together" with Michael to the gym—or, more properly speaking, they would speak to each other on the phone and confirm that they were both going to the gym at the same time. Despite the distance, they would work out at the same moment—that was what Manfred meant by "together." If it was early in the morning in New York, it'd be nighttime in Tokyo where Michael was. If they went to the gym simultaneously, they could sweat at the same time. Manfred had trouble imagining what a gym would look like in Tokyo, so he asked Michael to send him a photo, but Michael hadn't bothered, saying that gyms are the same everywhere. Instead of a photo of the gym, Michael had sent a photo of himself in a light, bedtime kimono, sitting in a Japanese-style room. Manfred had heard of sliding doors made of paper and flooring made of something like woven straw, but was that what he was seeing in the photo? Manfred stuck the picture on the wall, but it only worsened his mood. Michael said he was going to the gym, but he was probably going somewhere like that room instead. Manfred imagined Michael dressed in a kimono with his head propped on his arm, nodding off to sleep in the second home of some low-level manager from a big company. He didn't like the way the kimono was half-open, half-closed. The thing ought to have a zipper or buttons or something. "You're supposed to be going to the gym. What were you up to just now?" Manfred was curt as he barked these words into the receiver. "Huh? Oh, it's you." "What were you doing? Is there someone in your room with you?" "There's no one here. I was drawing my dog manga." "All you do is draw. You're not there to learn how to draw manga." "It's fun. It's easy to get hooked." "Just put the drawing aside and go to the gym. If you don't go work out, it means we won't be doing it at the same time." "Doing it at the same time? You'd think we're having phone sex or something."

Michael begrudgingly closed his sketchbook. He could lie and say he had gone to the gym when he really hadn't. There wasn't much chance he'd be found out. Michael liked the ring of the Japanese word *bareru*, "to be found out." He used to go to the gym a lot in New York, but after being in Tokyo a while, he began to take more pleasure out of going to the public bath in the evening. There, he'd soak in the hot water and gaze abstractedly at the steam rising off the water. Michael had a part-time job teaching at a company so he only had time to go to the gym twice a week, but recently, even twice a week had come to seem like a hassle. He didn't really care if he and Manfred went to the gym "together" or not, but he couldn't bring himself him to say that to him. Going to the gym at the same time even when far apart—if they broke that tradition, they'd shatter the illusion they were living in the same moment in time. In reality, the only bond still tying him to Manfred was the telephone. Their bodies never touched. For a moment, Michael was unsure what to do, but in the end, he decided to go the gym after all. He slipped on his white shorts and red running shirt, then headed out from his apartment.

On the sidewalk, a fellow who looked like a businessman, briefcase clutched to his chest, was pushing open the door to a coffee shop when he suddenly stopped midway. It was obvious he was staring at Michael's thighs. Michael stopped, wondering what the man would say, but he didn't say a word. He simply looked at Michael as a thing, ignoring his subjectivity. He might as well have been gazing at a poster. Miffed, Michael spoke to him in a loud and absurdly formal tone, "What part of my lower extremities do you think is the most artistic?" The man turned away, clearly vexed.

There were the same three high school girls hanging out, as always, at the entrance to the gym, and when they caught sight of Michael, they quickly fell silent. Michael went to the gym every Monday and Wednesday evening, so it wasn't impossible that they were lying in wait for him. "Lying in wait," perhaps, but it wasn't as if they would attack or anything. He decided to say something. "If you think I'm a famous singer or something, you've got the wrong guy. I've got one of those faces, but I'm no celebrity." One of the girls, whose face was caked with makeup, burst into a big smile, showing all of her overlapping teeth. "Doesn't matter to me if I do have the wrong guy!" she said. At least this girl had a sense of humor, unlike the businessman.

Five minutes after finishing his workout, Michael had already forgotten which machines he had used. The instant he got on the machines, his body became part of the mechanism and his brain stopped working. He had set the timer on his wristwatch to go off in forty-five minutes, and when it beeped, he jumped off the machine and made for the locker room. Next door to the gym was a public bath. As he entered through the *noren* curtain in the vestibule, he was greeted by the smiling owner, who had already come to recognize him. In the changing room, Michael peeled off his clothes, damp with sweat. In the bathing area, the only other person was a young man, who was bending over, washing his legs. There were none of the usual chatty old men or cheerfully shouting young boys. Michael sat on the stool next to the young man and splashed a pail of water over himself. He had brought some soap that smelled of cypress, and rubbed it into his long, narrow washcloth before starting to scrub his midsection. He glanced furtively at the young man beside him and realized he didn't look entirely unlike Mamoru.

He had met Mamoru two weeks ago. It was late at night, and he decided on a whim to stop into a bar he had never been to before. There was a single customer in the place, a young man drinking a whisky-and-water quietly at the counter. Michael broke the ice with a lie, "Say, haven't I seen you somewhere before?" then asked his name. The young man explained that he lived in Berlin, but he had come back to Tokyo for his younger sister's wedding. Michael turned the conversation to dogs, but Mamoru grew fidgety and said it was time for him to get going. Michael followed him out the door. Thinking to grab a taxi, Mamoru headed to the main road, but the traffic there had ground to a halt. Mamoru didn't look over his shoulder, but he seemed to sense Michael behind him. He walked down a narrow street alongside a convenience store, coming to a dark parking lot surrounded by apartment buildings. Two cats were fighting there, raising a howl that split the night.

Michael remembered the crisp tan lines on Mamoru's buttocks. He wished he had asked Mamoru when he had gone swimming. And with whom? And was the Baltic Sea far from Berlin or not? Later, as Mamoru was leaving, Michael asked him for his email address. Michael had sent three messages but hadn't gotten any response. Maybe there was someone who kept Mamoru from writing back, or maybe he had gotten caught up in his work at the university and didn't have time to reply. For the first time in his life he thought he might like to visit Berlin. It wasn't as if Michael had no connection with Berlin whatsoever. When he was young, he had learned that his grandparents had owned a house in the Schönefeld neighborhood of Berlin, but it was confiscated when they fled to the States. After the war ended, Germany was divided into east and west, and the east took its time restoring property seized by the Nazis to the rightful owners. After the wall came down and east and west were reunited, Michael's parents often mentioned the possibility of reclaiming the house. Michael asked if they were planning to go to Berlin to see it, but his parents simply shook their heads, no. His mother did say she remembered going to the Berlin Zoo when she was three. She still remembered the exceptionally smart elephant there. Michael teased her, saying elephants were smart regardless of whether they were in Berlin or Washington, but she insisted that wasn't true; the elephant in Berlin had been very, very bright. The other day, when his mother called him, Michael had said, "I've been thinking maybe I'd like to take a trip to Berlin. I'd like to check out those elephants." His mother didn't ask the reason for his sudden interest, but she was clearly pleased. "Really? Well then, we'll buy you the airline ticket for your birthday." Michael found himself dreaming how much fun it would be to go to the zoo with Mamoru, then as closing time approached, sneaking off into the bushes so they could spend the whole night in the park. He pictured the wet hefty legs of the hippopotamus, the bright red penises of the baboons, the sharp antlers of the bucks, the sandpapery tongue of the lioness methodically cleaning the bums of her cubs, the sparkling eyes of the crocodiles that seemed so full of tears . . . These animal visions filled Michael's mind as he sat in the steaming-hot water of the bath. He felt a rush of blood to his head and he hurriedly got out of the tub. By the time he looked at the clock in the changing room, it was nearly ten.

At that moment, Mamoru was having a caffè latte with three students from his advanced Japanese class. The dentist had drilled a molar and had told him to stay away from any milk products that day, but by the time he thought of the dentist's advice, it was too late and the latte was almost gone. Oh well. Still, this brought on the memory of how indignant Manfred had gotten one day: "Some company has gone so far as to control our linguistic habits. The word *milk coffee* has disappeared from all the menus, and you hardly ever see *café au lait* anymore. Everywhere you go, all you ever see is *caffè latte*." Manfred was so ticked off he pulled out a pen and started scratching out "caffè latte" on the menu and writing "café au lait" instead. "You're going to America, right?" Mamoru had said to him. "Maybe you ought to go to France instead." There was sarcasm in Mamoru's tone, and Manfred stiffened at this affront. Mamoru thought of this exchange whenever he had a latte.

It was only two in the afternoon, but the café, which was close to the university, was buzzing with students tipping back beer mugs and arguing loudly about the new system of tuition. Mamoru turned to the three students with him and said to them in Japanese: "The students are on strike today." They responded with worried expressions and a barely audible "*hai.*" These students of his were not interested in anything in the world other than *kanji* and Japanese grammar. The new system of tuition didn't seem to trouble them at all. When they heard there was going to be a strike to protest the rise in tuition, all they were concerned about was whether the remaining Japanese classes of the summer term would be cancelled. Mamoru had wanted to honor the strike in some way, but he also didn't want to disappoint his conscientious students. In the end, he decided on a middle course: he'd meet his students in the café, and he'd talk in Japanese with them about the strike. That way he wouldn't be breaking the strike, and the students could still practice their Japanese. In the end, however, the students didn't want to talk about the strike at all. They wanted to talk about university life in Japan. "How much are the monthly fees at Waseda University?" they asked. "Can poor people go to university in Japan?" Mamoru answered their questions politely, but his mind kept wandering. Before meeting his students, he had stopped by the post office and bought some stamps with Schiller on them. They were in the display case, and Schiller's gaze seemed to fix on him like a guy wanting a date. Once, at the Marbach Literary Archive, he met someone who explained why the portraits of Schiller were always so handsome. It seems that Schiller had given detailed instructions to the artist on how he should be painted, then requested touch-ups to the parts of his face that he did not like. Mamoru supposed that this wasn't unlike pop singers who undergo plastic surgery to get the look they want. But Schiller's plastic surgery was on the canvas. No scalpel ever cut his face in real life.

On Sundays, Mamoru would write a letter to Manfred. This week, he'd send it using one of the Schiller stamps. And the letter would be something different. First, he put green paint on his lips, then pressed them onto a sheet of paper. That wasn't enough to satisfy him, so he painted his genitals green and pressed them onto a sheet of letter paper on his desk. He let everything dry before putting the sheets of paper in an envelope and sealing it with glue and Scotch tape.

That was the second letter Mamoru had sent that day. The other was to a woman named Sylvia who had been his student the year before. She had started learning Japanese because she wanted to study the *Kokinshū*, an early-tenth-century collection of verse. Eventually, she got a scholarship to study in Japan and had left three months ago. Since then, she had written to Mamoru almost every day. No doubt the postman thought she was Mamoru's lover, considering all the artsy, brushed calligraphy on the envelopes. The letters didn't contain any overt expression of love, but they seemed to imply a great deal with all their allusions to poems and metaphors. Any hidden meaning was lost on Mamoru, however, since he wasn't well versed in the Japanese classics. He worried that if he didn't pay attention, he might accidently make her some promise in response. Each time a letter arrived, a heavy feeling came over him, but he wasn't sure how to put an end to the correspondence. He had thought about telling Sylvia he had a lover and that his lover was growing jealous, so he didn't want her to write anymore. Still, she had never overtly expressed an interest in a physical relationship with Mamoru. If he were to come right out and be presumptuous enough to say something, it might make the situation even more awkward. It was like insisting you couldn't lend someone money when they'd never actually said they wanted a loan. Perhaps it'd be better if he simply described his daily life and just casually mentioned Manfred. Perhaps then she'd realize that Mamoru and she belonged to different worlds. It wasn't, however, an easy thing to casually work in details of his life with Manfred since Manfred wasn't there from day to day. As he sat to write to Sylvia, staring at his fingers and racking his brains, the sight of his hands brought Manfred's rugged knuckles to mind and Mamoru felt a sudden longing. He thought of how, when Manfred stuck his fingers into the entrance of his bowels and wiggled them, Mamoru would think small snakes were slithering inside him, each with a cruel smile on its face. He'd move his hips to make it easier to withstand their assault, but the snakes would move as he moved and exact an even more intense toll. Mamoru found himself wondering if, at that moment, Manfred's thickly jointed fingers were resting quietly on top of a textbook as he taught his morning class.

Manfred rinsed the sweat off his body in the gym shower. By half past seven, he had bought a coffee near the subway entrance and was sipping it as he rushed into his building at the university. By eight, he was standing in front of his German class. Ten students had enrolled, but only four were present. "You pay such high tuition. Don't you think it's a waste to come late?" There was sarcasm in his voice, but the students didn't seem to get it. "In Germany, the universities are still practically free, so it's no surprise if students are late, but here . . . ?" No one even cracked a smile. One student, a serious expression on his face, asked: "If they don't collect tuition, how on earth do they run the universities?" "They run it with taxes," Manfred snapped. "Taxes aren't supposed to be used for war. They're supposed to be used for education." The students sat there uncomfortably, saying nothing. "All right, what did you think of this?" Manfred waved the day's reading in the air. "I want you to express your opinions freely," he said, then fell silent. He wasn't going to open his mouth until one of the students spoke. I'm not a salesman, he thought. The students looked at him with the proper expression of upper-class folks pretending not to notice that a stranger was unaware of breaking the rules of decorum. They coughed and blinked their eyes. The reading for the day was a collection of interviews with a Jewish writer now living in Germany. After a few moments, a student with a Slavic accent chimed up. "When I read the first interview, I didn't expect there would be those sorts of questions. Here's why . . ." Thanks to this one student, it seemed like the class would get on track.

As he listened to the students talk, hunger began to gnaw at his stomach. He had office hours as soon as class ended. Students could drop in to talk about whatever they wanted. No appointments necessary. He'd have office hours until the department meeting later on. The meeting might turn into a long one. He was so hungry he felt like his stomach might cramp. Perhaps he could run over to the bagel shop and have them throw together a sandwich with salmon and alfalfa sprouts. But would he have that much time? There was always a line at this time of day. He'd be in real trouble if someone spied him at the bagel shop when a student was looking for him at his office. The students were like customers, and customers were to be feared. Then he remembered seeing advertisements for a new, takeout pizza joint. Maybe his only choice was to have a pizza delivered to his office and to eat it while he was talking to the students.

Right then, Michael was at an outdoor noodle stand eating a bowl of ramen. He slurped loudly as he sucked up the noodles, which were topped with a mound of thinly sliced, half-transparent scallions. He'd been on his way home from the public bath and couldn't resist stopping here. It was just after ten o'clock, still too early for the businessmen who'd stop by for a bowlful on their way home from the bars. Michael had a superstition that when he broke apart a pair of chopsticks, if the chopstick on the left came out bigger, the next day would be a good one. When he broke them apart today, however, the chopstick on the right ended up much bigger. "Ugh, a right-wing day," he sighed. He wondered if they had ramen with scallions in Berlin. It would be a little after two o'clock in the afternoon there. Was Mamoru still teaching his Japanese class? Perhaps he had finished and gone to eat somewhere. Michael wondered what he ate for lunch. Eisbein and sauerkraut? Surely not. Should he try calling to ask? But Mamoru didn't have a cellphone. Come to think of it, Manfred didn't use to have one either. He said he preferred the tinkling metal of the pay phones in New York. He walked around with four quarters in his pocket, and he'd stick them clumsily into the pay phones with his thick fingers whenever he needed to make a call. But Manfred had bought a cellphone recently. Michael didn't tell Manfred he'd also bought one because it'd be a hassle if Manfred started calling him all the time. The cook at the noodle stand looked at Michael through the steam and asked, "You want more scallions?" Michael cocked his head slightly and replied, "If I ate any more scallions, I might turn into a priest." Perplexed, the cook let out a "Huh?" "You know, 'cause the flower of a scallion is called a 'scal-lion priest,'" Michael explained. "Because both flower and the head of a priest are round." The cook laughed. "Michael-*san*, I sometimes don't know if your puns are funny or not!" This little give-and-take was just then interrupted by a woman in a brown suit, who called out, "Michael-*san*? Is that you?" Michael raised his face from the steamy bowl of ramen. There was something about her that reminded him of Astro Boy. "Do you remember me? My name is Kanagawa. I inter-viewed you about two years ago when I was writing an article for an English education magazine." Michael scooted to the left to make space for her. "I remember. It's been ages. Want some ramen with scallions? It's really good. By the way, do you know what the *kanji* for 'scallion' looks like?" The *kanji* was difficult enough that most people didn't know it. "You know, you talked a lot about *kanji* when I interviewed you. Since then, I quit the magazine and started my own manga maga-zine, if you can call what we do 'manga.' It's kind of offbeat." "What kind of manga are you making?"

At that moment, Mamoru was also talking about *kanji* and manga. His student Jan was denouncing a German scholar who had proposed getting rid of *kanji* completely. "A Eurocentric fool," Jan called him. Jan liked *kanji* so much that when he was ten years old, he had put fake tattoos of the *kanji* for "beauty" and "love" on his arms, then proudly explained their meaning to his classmates. Hearing that, Mamoru found himself at a bit of a loss. "But if we rely too much on *kanji*," he ventured, "then the Japanese language might grow weak." Jan expressed surprise. "'Rely on'? What do you mean?" "When people write difficult *kanji,* they feel like they've written something magnificent. However, when people say they can only express something by using *kanji,* maybe they don't really understand the thing they're talking about." Silke, a student who wasn't very good at *kanji,* leaned forward and asked for an example. "Okay, there's the word *rachi,* which means to take someone away, right? People use it when they're talking about North Koreans abducting Japanese citizens and taking them to North Korea. The word is difficult and isn't easy for people to digest. It isn't transparent and has ominous connotations. Because we use difficult words like that, people have a hard time understanding what's really going on." "But I think it's because you've got *kanji* that you developed the culture of manga," interjected Tobias, the third student. Tobias had originally started studying Japanese because he wanted to read more manga, but now for whatever reason, he found himself interested in *Konjaku monogatari,* the ancient Japanese collection of stories.

The mention of manga reminded Mamoru of Michael, the American who liked to draw manga about dogs. They had met each other in a bar a little while back when he was in Tokyo for his sister's wedding. Michael had leaned over and asked if he would like to model for a manga he was drawing. He then mischievously whispered into Mamoru's ear that he wanted him to behave like a dog, too. When Mamoru didn't seem to understand, Michael, enjoying himself even more, explained that he wanted Mamoru to lift a leg and do his business on a telephone pole. Not just act it out, do it for real. Mamoru felt himself blush as he remembered the way Michael's eyes brightened, flashing like the scales on the belly of a fish, and the way creases formed around the corner of his eyes as he laughed. To clear his mind, Mamoru abruptly said to the students, "I'm hungry. Shall we go get something to eat?" His Japanese sounded like it was right out of a textbook. He had no sooner spoken than Jan asked, "Would it be inappropriate to use the expression 'I'm starved'?" Mamoru replied, only half-sounding like a language teacher, "That sounds more macho," as he paid for the students' coffee.

Mamoru tended to eat at the same places: mostly it was the Afghani restaurant across from the Literature Faculty or the Pakistani restaurant beside that. Today it would be the Pakistani restaurant, where the waiters were in their twenties, had black wavy hair, long eyelashes, and slender waists, and wore black. Mamoru led the students inside and headed straight for the big table in the back. Jan, who was a bit behind, shouted to him, "*Sensei!*" The waiter looked up at Mamoru. Mamoru felt uncomfortable when people called him that, and here he experienced a moment of irritation, realizing the waiter would think *Sensei* was his name. "*Sensei!*" Jan shouted again before adding, "The pocket on the side of your backpack is open." Mamoru took his backpack off and zipped up the pocket. After ordering some tea, the students began talking about their research projects.

Jan said if he got the chance to go to Japan, he wanted to live in a town with a tradition of producing ceramics. Mamoru didn't know the first thing about pottery, so all he could do was quietly nod his head. His parents had liked ceramics, but if given his druthers, he'd have chosen plastic dishes with the logo of Leo the Lion instead. There was nothing simple or elegant about them—not the slightest whiff of the restrained elegance or rustic simplicity so highly prized in Japan.

Silke wanted to write her thesis on the history of the death penalty. "In Europe, it's possible for people to get sentenced to life in prison without the possibility of parole. In Japan, people can't be sentenced to life without parole. A life sentence would be a light sentence. A heavy sentence would be the death penalty. Japan can't get rid of the death penalty because it doesn't have anything in between. Japan really ought to create life sentences without parole. But if it does, then there won't be any advocates who do their best to save prisoners. The mafia in jail will stop respecting the people who sentence criminals to parole. And then . . ." Silke's impassioned soliloquy went on and on, spittle flying from her mouth. Mamoru and the other students listened meekly.

The food arrived at their table. They had barely gotten to the restaurant in time for the lunchtime special, which was salad, rice, and grilled lamb on a large plate. Tobias said if he went to Japan, he wanted to find a job as the assistant to a manga artist. Mamoru said, "That might be difficult, but I know a guy who is aspiring to be a manga artist." He promised Tobias he'd ask. Mamoru had finally found an excuse to write Michael an email. Their relationship had been purely sexual, but Mamoru was no good at writing erotic emails, so he had been trying to come up with something to write about.

When Mamoru paid the bill, he met the eyes of the waiter for several seconds. Mamoru wondered if the guy recognized him, since he came there so often. He wished the waiter didn't think his name was *Sensei*, and he racked his brains for a way to start a conversation. Had the guy seen the Pakistani film the theater behind the restaurant was showing? The waiter shook his head. Mamoru tried to keep the ball rolling, but when he noticed a man in his fifties with a broad face, his thick eyebrows knitted, watching them from the kitchen, he let the conversation drop.

After parting ways with the students, Mamoru made his way to the university library. Several students were making signs and putting up posters in the plaza in front of the building. Because German universities hadn't charged tuition until recently, Mamoru had been able to pay for his living expenses while getting his master's degree simply by working part-time. Now he was making a living by teaching Japanese, but over the last year, he had been nurturing the secret desire to write a book. That was Manfred's influence. If he succeeded in writing a book, Mamoru would feel like he had gotten something out of their love, even if Manfred never returned to Berlin. As a result, Mamoru was going to the library even more often than when he was a student. On his way up the stairs to the entrance, Mamoru stumbled and let out a cry of surprise, thinking he might fall.

Right then, Manfred was opening a grease-stained pizza box that had just been delivered. He looked intently at the grayish mushrooms and salami floating on top of the cheese. It was so oily that it looked like it had been coated in varnish. The salami reminded him of the cross-section of a human arm; but he nonetheless bit into a slice with gusto. At that moment, there was a knock at the door. It was Bogdan, who always spoke up in class and whose German vocabulary was also far greater than the other students'. Bogdan was from Bulgaria. Perhaps there were many people there who spoke German, but even so, Manfred couldn't help giving him a special smile each class. "Mind if I come in?" Bogdan asked politely. "Not at all, come in, come in." Manfred grimaced at his overly affable tone, which reminded him of a salesman. Bogdan looked at what Manfred was eating. "I see you're having pizza. Have you grown to like food in our country?" There didn't seem to be any sarcasm in his voice. In fact, he seemed to be in quite a pleasant mood. Manfred was surprised by the words "our country." Pizza wasn't Bulgarian food, and Bogdan hadn't been in the States for a decade. Could he really use the words "our country" to talk about American fast food? He mulled the question over but didn't say anything. He couldn't really be critical of others; after all it was he who had dug into this pizza. In Berlin, working-class teenagers were the main market for cheap pizza, so if a friend caught you eating one, you'd feel you needed to make up an excuse. Manfred hurriedly wiped his tomato-sauce-covered fingers on a napkin and took a swig of Coke. "How are you doing?" he asked in a friendly tone. "Well, to tell you the truth," Bogdan began, "I decided not to study in Vienna next year after all. You went to all the trouble to write me a letter of recommendation so I feel really bad." His tone of voice didn't indicate that he felt bad at all. "Why'd you change your mind?" "I got an opportunity to intern at the Beijing branch of my uncle's company during our summer vacation. He tells me I might be able to work there after I graduate." "What kind of company is it?" "They export and sell Chinese-made Christmas items in southeastern Europe." "Really? That sounds promising. If you knew about this earlier, you could have studied Chinese instead of German." Manfred could not entirely hide the jealousy that crept into his voice. Bogdan's response, however, showed a great deal of grace. "Chinese is so difficult, I doubt I could've done as well as I did with you. I've been studying German since high school, and it's really fun for me. Thank you for such a good class. Anyway, I don't want to disturb you while you are eating. . . ." He stood up politely and left.

The pizza had grown cold and unpalatable. As Manfred picked up another piece and bit into it, he glared at the phone on his desk. Manfred often cursed that telephone. It was the kind of phone you might expect to see at a poor university out in the sticks somewhere. To make matters worse, it could only be used for calls in the city. He'd have understood if it was only for calls in the country, but in the city? It made him feel like livestock fenced in a pasture. With no other choice, he had recently given in and bought a cellphone. If he used it to call Michael often, however, his bank account, which was low to begin with, would quickly dip into the negative numbers. When he was in Berlin, he had looked down on poor kids who spent all their money on the internet and phones, but now, he was in a similar situation. He wanted to hear Michael's voice, even if it was only for two minutes. Not bothering to wipe the grease from his fingers, he began pressing the buttons on his phone: zero one one eight one three . . . He knew that if Michael picked up, he had to keep it short. But no one was home. It was past midnight in Tokyo, but Michael wasn't back yet. Where could he have gone? And with whom? It didn't matter how much he'd tried to persuade him to get a cellphone; Michael said he was against them and refused to listen. If he had one now, Manfred could have called and asked where he was. Of course, it's easy to lie over the phone, but Manfred would have preferred a lie to not being able to reach him at all.

Out of the corner of his eye, Michael watched Kanagawa Sakurako eagerly gobbling down her scallion ramen. He poured himself some sake. After a bit, they decided to go somewhere to grab another drink. They walked down one of the busier streets, full of shops and restaurants, and happened onto a fight. Making their way to the front of the crowd of spectators, they saw two men yelling at each another for all they were worth. The onlookers, however, seemed to be enjoying themselves, and whenever the two drunkards said something, they'd laugh. It only made sense they'd laugh: The drunkard who'd picked the fight was a robot. The fellow getting picked on was apparently a street performer pretending to be another robot. The man was speaking in an overly dramatic fashion, as if he were on stage. "You! You wanna fight, eh?" The robot, which had been programmed to speak in a way that sounded like a machine, shot back, "You! You're the bozo who wanted to get into it!" Kanagawa said, "I've seen people act drunk before, but the robot's really got it down. I wonder if it's really responding to the guy or if it's just playing back a bunch of recorded lines." She tilted her head as she said this. Michael replied, with apparent interest, "Oh, it's hard enough to make a robot that walks on two legs, but a robot that can stumble on two legs is amazing. You know, I once tried drawing a manga with a robot as the main character, but it was too difficult. I couldn't figure out a way to make people feel emotionally involved." "Really? I remember once when Astro Boy got hurt. I felt so sorry for him that I cried. It was more than just emotional involvement for me. I actually wanted to *be* a robot too." "Really? Why's that?" "Robots don't have sadness or pain, they aren't egotistical, they aren't narcissistic, they're always fair toward others. . . ." The conversation went on. "Robots are pretty great, don't you think?" she said. She knew a pub nearby, so they stopped in and ordered some sake. Michael smiled, "I seem to recall you're a pretty good drinker." She replied, "I always say, 'Work and liquor, I can handle as much as they dish out,' but every time, I just zonk right out." After a brief pause, she added, "Michael-*san*, did you know the expression 'zonk out' comes from Indonesian?" Michael shook his head in surprise, but then she started giggling. "Just kidding! Made you believe it!" With that, she lifted her glass energetically. They hadn't had much to drink yet, but she already seemed inebriated. Through the opening in the short sleeve of her blouse Michael could see the slack, white skin just below her underarm. The sight of this made him think of Mamoru's armpits—the jet black, thick, and straight hair. He wished he could caress those armpits forever. It was already quite late, but he thought he'd stick it out with this woman for another hour, then call Mamoru. It was past five in the evening in Berlin, so Mamoru would be headed home soon. He could propose they have a drink "together." In truth, they'd just be doing the same thing at the same time. But they probably didn't have the same kind of sake in Berlin that they do here, and they certainly didn't have the same kind of wine here that they have in Berlin. For that reason, the last time they had a drink together, Michael had ordered vodka, even though he didn't especially like it. There aren't too many brands of vodka so you tend to find the same ones all over the world.

He stole a look at his watch. One-thirty. "You'll have to excuse me," Michael said to Kanagawa, and stood up from his chair. The alcohol had gone to her head. She asked in a loud voice, "Huh, what? You need to take a leak?" The man drinking in the next seat looked at her and frowned in disapproval. "No, I just want to go shake hands with a friend," Michael answered, then disappeared into the back of the bar. When he was alone in one of the bathroom stalls, he pulled out his cellphone. Mamoru had asked him for his number so he could call Michael at any time, but he never had. It rang seven times before Mamoru picked up. Michael played the fool, "Hello, this is the aspiring manga artist in Tokyo," but immediately he sensed a stiffness on the other end of the line. He was in high school when he had learned to differentiate silences he'd hear in telephone conversations, and even now, he still thought of it as a peculiar ability. Mamoru asked hesitantly, "Where are you now?" "I'm in a toilet stall in a bar. I'm out drinking with a journalist named Kanagawa. A woman. But I called 'cause I want to have a drink with you. You still have the Moskovskaya you bought the other day?" "Yeah." "At exactly 1:45 a.m. Tokyo time, I'm going to lift my glass to you. Let's both down some vodka at exactly the same moment." "Down some vodka?" "Doesn't have to be a big shot. I'm not talking about an entire bottle."

Michael hung up, went back to his seat, and ordered a shot of Moskovskaya. "This'll be the last one," he declared to Kanagawa Sakurako. "Afterward, I've gotta go home." Kanagawa suddenly seemed flustered. "But go with me back to my apartment at least. It's not far." Her eyes were bloodshot. Michael nodded and glanced at his watch. It was time. He raised his glass into the air and with a *"Kanpai!"* he drank the contents down in a single gulp. The woman with him clinked her glass with his energetically and shouted *"Kanpai!"* too.

Mamoru was planning to go to a lecture, "The Iraq War and Changes in Language in the Media," so he didn't really feel like having a shot of hard liquor. Michael would never find out if he didn't. That reminded him. Hadn't Michael written in one of his emails that, for some reason, he liked the word *bareru*, "to be found out"? If Michael wanted to fly all the way to Germany to check if he had drunk a shot of vodka, he'd have a long flight ahead of him. He wouldn't get as far as Narita Airport before the day would be over in Berlin. Mamoru didn't feel like he'd really be betraying Michael. People far away are powerless anyway. Mamoru poured some vodka into a crystal glass, as if he were participating in some mystical ceremony, then glanced at the clock. It was a satellite clock that automatically adjusted itself to precisely the right time, down to the very second. He watched the numbers until the clock indicated exactly five forty-five, then with a loud, clear voice, he pronounced the word *"Kanpai!"* Instead of pouring the liquid down his throat, however, he poured it on the palms of his hands almost in an act of purification. Then, he washed his hands, hurriedly threw his linen bag over his shoulder, and rushed out of the apartment.

At that moment, Manfred was rushing to his department meeting. With the rise of interest in the Middle East, the decision had been made to hire a teacher of Arabic. Members of the department had been discussing the position for the last month. Should they bring in someone from another country, or should they cherry-pick an instructor from another institution in the States? Should they hire a recent PhD graduate, or should they hire a veteran professor? Manfred had told them candidly he didn't care whom they hired, but no one would forgive him if he missed the meeting. They had whittled down the pool of applicants from over a hundred to fifteen, and each candidate had been asked to send in a video that made the case for why they should be hired, explaining their field of research, their pedagogical methods, and their contribution to the university. Among the videos received, some had distorted images, others had voices that weren't entirely audible, while yet others were so overproduced that the candidate might as well have been a pop star. All the faculty could determine from the videos was how different the candidates' video-production abilities were; it was impossible to tell how they would differ as teachers. Someone made the point that it was unfair to judge candidates this way. There weren't the funds to invite all fifteen candidates to campus for an interview, however. It was decided that the videos and other documents would be used, as much as seemed feasible, to narrow the pool to five people, and those would be the ones brought in for a campus visit. That was where the meeting ended.

Relieved that there had been some conclusion at least, Manfred stood up from his chair. Julia, the creative writing instructor who taught fiction, had been seated next to him again. She always seemed to sit next to him in meetings, eager to chat once the meeting was over. Recently she'd told him she had adopted a child. She invited him to come back to her office to look at pictures. Manfred had no eye for babies, but he went back to her office anyway. She had taped three enlarged photos of her baby to the wall, as if they were posters of an actor. It was just a little baby, but already it had tufts of black hair. "I adopted her in Beijing. Beijing was an amazing place." Manfred hesitated for a moment at Julia's declaration, then asked, "Why Beijing?" "The Chinese government is the only one these days that allows a single parent to adopt a baby. If you try to adopt a baby from South America, you have to be married, living with your husband, and you have to be young to boot. If you want to adopt from Russia, it's okay to be unmarried, but you've got to have a man in the house. It doesn't matter if it's a brother, father, or whatever. The thing is, I don't have a man living with me." "Why don't you adopt a baby from here in the U.S.?" "There aren't too many babies up for adoption in the U.S. When they are available, often there are problems like fetal alcohol syndrome, drugs, and things like that. That's what happened to my sister when she adopted a child. I'm not sure I could handle something like that on my own. Chinese babies tend to have good personalities and totally cute faces. Plus, they're smart too." Manfred grimaced as he remembered Mamoru's face. Mamoru's face had grown smaller and smaller in Manfred's memory, and before Manfred knew it, Mamoru had become like a baby. He imagined Julia changing his diapers. Julia nudged Manfred for his approval, "Cute, eh?" No doubt about it, Mamoru was cute. But as a sexual being, Mamoru lacked something in Manfred's eyes. For instance, Mamoru lacked the stick-to-itiveness and courage to torment him over a long period of time in ways that Manfred really wanted. When Mamoru was the one being tormented, he just lay there and suffered, and that was no fun at all. Manfred wanted Mamoru to become more involved, but he just retreated into his own little cocoon. Compared to Mamoru, Michael was smaller and thinner, but he was tenacious and wasn't at all afraid to bring out whatever cruelty he had inside him. They could sweat together until dawn rolled around, exploring one another's bodies. Even if Michael were to find some blood on his fingers, he wouldn't stop. He'd just as soon lick it off to satiate his appetite.

Manfred suddenly came to, realizing Julia was looking at him quizzically. "But you've got your job here," he said, trying to return to the conversation. "Are you going to be able to raise a baby on your own?" "My girlfriend is a computer graphic designer, and she works at home." "Oh! I see. You're not a single mother, you're double mothers. I envy you—" He stopped midsentence, not quite sure if he should talk about himself. Had Julia tried to get so close to him just by chance, or did her gaydar pick up on him, giving her a feeling of kinship? As he was asking himself these questions, the telephone rang. Julia grabbed the receiver from the phone on her desk. Manfred decided to take it as a cue to leave. He bid Julia goodbye with his eyes and left. Back in his own office, he started pressing the tiny buttons on his mobile: zero one one eight one three . . . He got irritated at this seemingly never-ending string of numbers. He had heard you could store numbers, but it was too much trouble to read the instructions, so he didn't know how. No one answered. It was past two in the morning. Was Michael playing around? Spending the night at someone else's place? Manfred felt dizzy. The skyscrapers outside the window leaned to one side, and he felt an unfamiliar space open below his feet. He was falling into a darkness that rose to envelop him. It was daytime. Why was it so dark? Bright petals of flowers spread over his head like fireworks. What on earth was happening?

Michael had been prone to carsickness ever since he was a child. Even the time his father had promised to take him on a fun trip to Florida with his uncle, the first whiff of gasoline had been enough to make him nauseous. Even so, he had gotten in the car, thinking how much he wanted to see the dolphins. He had never been carsick, however, since coming to Japan. As he thought about it, he realized he'd never taken a long car ride since arriving in the country, but now he was in a cab escorting Kanagawa Sakurako to her apartment. She had lied when she said it was nearby. The taxi had been driving on the highway for forty full minutes. Eventually, it got off at an exit, continued for a little, then finally stopped. She put some money in Michael's hand, winked at him, and got out. That wasn't especially strange, but he realized what she had given him wasn't a ten-thousand-yen bill but a measly thousand yen. Had she just been drunk and made a mistake? He was stuck. He didn't have any choice but to use the same taxi to get back home. The thousand yen plus all the money he had on him would be barely enough. He worried that if he dug out all the cash he had in his apartment, it still wouldn't be enough. Wanting to save the cost of the highway tolls, he asked the driver not take the highway back. The driver nodded without a word. The car wormed its way through dark city streets, passing the lonely lights of all-night convenience stores. One curb replaced another. Suddenly, Michael began to feel the contents of his stomach rise into his mouth. He wanted to say, "Excuse me, please stop the car," but moments after he'd said not to take the highway, the driver had started talking nonstop, hardly even inserting a comma or period long enough for Michael to interrupt. "Sure, this is the kind of work I'm doing now, but I'll show the world when the time's right. I'm trying to get ready for the day when I'm not driving a cab no more. I'm telling you this 'cause I can see you're not a run-of-the-mill kind of guy. Know how I can tell? 'Cause I can see what's behind your head—that light shining there. You were born with it. I've been able to see things like that my whole life, but it took me a long time to realize my appointed mission. Wish I figured out earlier what I was put here on earth to do." "Excuse me, could you stop the car?" "Huh? We're not there yet. And we just started talking." "I feel sick. Please stop. Right away." "As soon as you told me back there not to take the highway, I realized I found someone who'd listen." "Please. Stop. I'm gonna mess up your car."

At the entrance to the auditorium where the lecture was to take place, there were four uniformed guards checking bags and patting down the people who had come to listen. The security guard who stuck his hand in Mamoru's linen bag rustled around for a moment before pulling out the encased sashimi knife. He held it high over his head as if in victory. Mamoru was quickly pulled back to reality and let out a sigh of annoyance. Why hadn't he left it at home? It'd been in his bag since he bought it at the department store last week. "Please come with us, sir." He did as he was told. In the backroom where they led him, there were policemen standing by. One of them, a blond guy in uniform, explained, "Someone telephoned and warned us there'd be an attempt on the speaker's life, so we're being extra careful." His tone suggested they were about done with him, but the other policeman—a guy in plain clothes who had a stack of papers on his desk—glared at Mamoru as if he were a criminal. Mamoru hung his head and instantly realized he'd forgotten to zip up his jeans. If he did it now, he'd only draw more attention. They probably wouldn't notice if he kept his legs tightly together. "Where's your passport?" "At home." "You know you're supposed to have it with you at all times, right?" "Yeah, but no one really does that, do they?" The plainclothes policeman turned over the sashimi knife in his hands and wrote down some numbers. Mamoru realized he was in real trouble. He'd spent his entire life without ever getting involved with the law. He found himself amazed how quickly one could turn into a criminal. As the gravity of his situation sunk in, the tension went out of his knees, and for a moment, everything went black. "This is just a procedural investigation, but you know the time we're living in. We have to follow proper procedures." The man said this as if to comfort him, taking Mamoru by the arm and pointing out the window with his chin. Outside, a car was stopped. It was the same color as an army uniform.

Manfred grabbed at the sill of his office window and breathed in and out. There's nothing wrong, you're in perfect health, the weather is great, everything outside is like always—the words went through his mind clear as day, but he could feel his consciousness slipping away. There wasn't any reason for him to feel faint, but he was aware he was on the verge of passing out. A moment later, he'd be on the floor. His chest was heavy, full of stone, and his legs were growing thinner and thinner. His breath stuck in his throat. He wanted to call out. He caught a glimpse of the telephone out of the corner of his eye, but if he reached out to it, he'd lose his balance. He thought about yelling, but he could not muster his voice. Had his vocal chords disappeared? He heard a siren in the distance. He thought, there was no way it could be coming for me. Or perhaps, just perhaps, could someone out there have already called it for me?

SIXTEEN

"The Playroom" (Mikkusu rūmu)
by Morii Ryō (2014)

Translated by Stephen D. Miller

Biography and Introduction

Morii Ryō (1984–) was born in Chiba prefecture. He lived and studied in France for several years and specialized in modern French literature in graduate school at Waseda University, where he has been an assistant professor since 2016. "The Playroom" (Mikkusu rūmu), his first published short story, won the 119th Bungakukai Shinjinshō (Newcomer's Award, *Bungakukai Journal*) in 2014. He is also the author of two academic monographs on André Gide and Éric Marty, published in 2017 and 2018.

"The Playroom" is about a young gay man, Yumio, who lives, at the beginning of the story at least, in Tokyo. Later, Yumio moves back to his parents' rural home in an undesignated prefecture. There are several aspects to the narrative: cruising for sexual contacts, an unnamed physical malady, the loss of a job, the 3/11 earthquake and tsunami disaster, and finally a long, and sometimes brutal, sexual encounter, that occurs at the end of the story in a *mikkusu rūmu*. There is no simple translation for the term *mikkusu rūmu* ("mixed room"): in English, it could be an apartment in a building used for sexual encounters between gay men, an orgy room, a bathhouse, or a kind of sexual playroom. The story alternates between being partially hallucinatory and partially straightforward narrative with the frequent use of flashbacks. In the end, the story is a literary exploration of a young, gay Japanese man's interiority and his sometimes confused sexual desires.

The Playroom

He didn't even score in the usual spots in Shinjuku. His insides were cold even in the warmth of his faded purple hoodie. With no place to go, his blood pulsed under his skin.

The elevator skipped the odd-numbered floors as it descended. Yumio, who was mirrored by visions of himself on all four sides, got off on the ground floor. He couldn't bear the sensation of his heart floating in space. He rubbed his chest, massaging the area around his heart with the thick part of his palm.

He decided to cruise one more spot, so he jumped on to the Sōbu train heading out of Shinjuku.

He was heading for a place in the eastern part of Tokyo, near where he used to live. If you took the north exit of the train station, walked a few hundred feet straight ahead, and turned right at the first road you hit, it was a little ways down, on the second floor of a washed-out multitenant building clad in tiles. When he used to go there, it was full of college boys and businessmen, but it'd been some years now since he'd shown his face.

He would have to catch the bus back home at 11:15, from the west exit of Shinjuku station. There was still plenty of time, but Yumio knew from experience that nights like tonight were over before you knew it. If he had no luck after a couple of hours, he'd move along. It would be tight, but he could always come back to Shinjuku around 9:00 and rest up for a while . . . While he made these calculations, standing on the train, he wrapped the leather straphanger around left his wrist and rubbed the area behind his ear with the thumb of his opposite hand.

That morning Yumio had arrived at the west entrance to Shinjuku station in the morning on an express bus with only four passengers in total. From there he set out for the red-light district in Kabuki-chō, where he walked around 3-chōme, starting from the Koma Theater. In the afternoon, he cruised the back pathways of Shinjuku Park. With no money, he couldn't go out on the town the way he used to. In the evening, he checked a few spots in the gay district of 2-chōme, but they were dead.

How long had it been since he had this much time on his hands? When he finished calculating how many hours he'd been on the move, he looked up to find the dusky scene outside his window rewinding itself, slow and quiet. It was a little before 7:00.

The scene before him as he descended the stairs of the train station both evoked fond memories and made him weary. Even the fluorescent lights in the station precincts faltered. Once the station was behind him, he was hit by a sharp northern wind. Yumio had to protect his heart.

There was no one in the station square. In the past Yumio remembered children running around bumping into passersby. Middle-school students polishing off popsicles would hang out in front of the convenience store.

He remembered there being one of those big chain stores ahead of him on the square. *Sure enough, there it was.* Yumio slowed his pace. He squinted and peered into the store, and as if signaling that it remembered him, the front door automatically opened wide. A single figure came through the doorway. Over the person's shoulders several more figures appeared, lit from behind.

It was getting dark. There were no longer any customers going into the shopping arcade across the square. Housewives emerged from the chain store, shuffling along with yellow plastic shopping bags. The road ventured deep into the arcade, taking twists and turns; the lights in the stores on either side were dark. He couldn't see anyone down there. He thought about his hometown in the countryside as he walked along dejectedly.

The Sōbu train line was not running according to schedule. Announcements to that effect echoed around the area. People hurried along ignoring them. Yumio joined the rush. With the sleepy arcade in the corner of his eyes, he headed straight toward the intersection. He passed a parking lot, a McDonald's at the corner of a narrow street, a local coffee shop, an old furniture shop with writing so antiquated that you couldn't read the characters on the signs, and a chain pharmacy. It was a little after 7:30.

It would have been better to stick around Shinjuku, Yumio thought regretfully. There was time yet until this place would get really busy. If he went in now, he'd just be killing time. Maybe he could sleep in one of the private rooms for an hour . . . Suddenly at the corner of the street, a crowd of children appeared cheering mysterious words. There were so many that he had to step into the street.

Glory, glory, hallelujah
Glory, glory, hallelujah
Glory, glory

. . . they sang. The middle-school students were wearing their school uniforms, and the elementary-school students were dressed in white. Their song lingered in the air long after they passed by Yumio, in single file. *Because they didn't cover their mouths, I could still hear them even if I put my hands over my ears,* he thought reflexively. Jaywalking, he crossed the street, he crossed the intersection, took a right, and then passed the two alleyways.

There was still a beef-bowl joint on the ground floor. Around the side of the building, next to the entrance to the kitchen that was pumping out dense steam, he opened the glass door and climbed the dark stairs.

• • •

The last time he was here must have been the day before he moved back in with his parents. He had shipped all of his personal belongings ahead and might even have spent that final night here before returning to his hometown. As he scoured his memory, the nape of his neck, numb from the cold, felt painfully raw. Yumio took his wallet out of his bag and opened a thick, black door that had a sign reading "Members Only."

In a low voice, Yumio said, "General admission."

"Fifteen hundred yen please," the man immediately replied flirtatiously.

He spoke in a suggestive, high-pitched voice as he handed Yumio his change. The man gripped a key and a towel with a swarthy hand extending through the opening in the reception booth. Without responding, Yumio accepted them from the glass partition. Yumio took his change in silence, along with his receipt.

"The lockers are through the curtain to the right and all the way down. Have fun!"

Yumio could see part of the T-shirt the man was wearing through the opening to the booth. A string of English words in white against black fabric. Yumio didn't know what it said. He parted the curtain. In the bank of green lockers alongside the wall, he found the one assigned to him and threw in his belongings—bag, coat, shoes, jeans, socks, hoodie, shirt. He took out his wallet again, rolled it up in his socks, and stuffed it into his shoes.

Key band wrapped around his wrist, he passed through the black curtain further down to the left.

As soon as he stepped into the room, he was met with hot, almost stifling, air. He knew he was not alone.

Slipping beyond a partition, he entered a narrow hallway. There were doors to private rooms along one side. The first two rooms were empty. Bedding in disarray, used tissues strewn about. The next room down the hall was locked.

"Occupied," said the person inside with a cluck of his tongue. Out of options, Yumio spun around and went into the "maze" on the other side. His eyes weren't used to the dark so he had to strain to see. He groped his way along, feeling out the hidden doors and corners.

When he stood in the threshold of the first playroom, the heater overhead kicked in. The hot air draped his shoulders, and the darkness got even darker.

He could make out the odor of armpits on an undercurrent of the air. It might have been a lingering smell or a smell from someone who was right beside him. He took a tentative step forward. On the top bunk of a bunk bed, a bottle of lotion someone must have forgotten was tipped over. Other than that, there was no indication that anybody was around. His heart began to flutter.

Beads of sweat collected on his forehead. Concerned that the odor he smelled might be him, he wiped his armpit with his hand and held it to his nose, but there was no smell. He felt relieved, but there was nothing he could do about the stuffy air.

He rubbed the palms over his chest, in an attempt to lessen his anxiety. His heart trembled with abandon.

He fished around the trash can at his feet. From the mass of tissues, he picked out a particularly soggy one, held it to his nose, and groped his crotch.

He was that lonely.

• • •

He recalled something that happened at another playroom from when he was still living in Tokyo.

It was shortly before he returned home to his parents' house.

It was a newly refurbished place that catered to guys in their late teens and twenties. He was already in his late twenties, but he still looked like a student so he went there.

When he went into the playroom beyond two partitions, he heard an animal-like sound off to his left. He let out a quick scream and jumped out of the way.

"You're a little jittery."

Yumio turned around. There was a guy sitting on top of a bull-riding machine fixed to the floor. The machine moved rhythmically back and forth, up and down. The guy on it was wearing a fluorescent bathing suit, with the crotch lit up in yellow.

Yumio was sweating profusely. He adjusted his stance to hide his trembling and let out a slow breath. The guy was directly in front of him.

When his eyes focused, he saw a young man with a fashionable haircut, longer on one side than the other.

The guy–who was actually a kid—was short, but on the muscular side. Because it was dark, he couldn't make out his face. Yumio's thought to himself, *Too young—not my type.*

Yumio's chest was beating rapidly. He didn't know if it was from the surprise of running into this guy or the anticipation of pleasures to come. He moved closer and stared at the guy's impassive face. Yumio couldn't see much of anything but the guy's expressionless face. The guy returned Yumio's look without saying a word as he swung back and forth.

The guy was stone-faced. Yumio didn't know why at first—maybe because it was dark. Yumio looked harder to figure out why the kid had no expression. He tried to remember something, but it wouldn't come to him. When at last he recalled what it was, he let out a shout.

The kid didn't have a nose.

It wasn't the dark that got in the way: the nose just wasn't there. The middle of his face was caved in, and the area around it was stretched as if it had been swallowed up. It had taken on its own unique configuration.

There were two eyes and a mouth, but his upper lip had dissolved into the space where the nose had been. The kid's teeth shined brightly. *That's because there are no nostrils,* Yumio thought. But there might have been two holes. His ears were almost entirely hidden by his long hair.

There was no nose.

As he was about to say that, he stopped himself.

Arrested by the flat, black space in the center of the boy's face, Yumio couldn't avert his eyes. It was like being in water and trying to take a breath. He wanted to scream something, but he couldn't. His anxiety was not connected to anything like pain, anguish, loneliness, or fear. Rather than look away, he felt obliged to . . . *I must find his nose,* was the only thing he knew for sure.

The kid laughed with unflinching eyes. Yumio guessed the kid could see his face. *Look there, he's laughing again.* There was a slit on one side of the kid's half-opened mouth, where a faint puff of air, a gasp, leaked out. *Is he laughing?* But it was the kind of gasp you'd make if you were searching for words to say.

(At that moment, there was the sound of a baby coming from inside the floor—a baby who was calling out for its mother far away. It might have been his imagination.)

Yumio felt his body trembling, but maybe this was caused by his desire.

Yumio touched his hand to the kid's cheek.

• • •

The spit and cum in Yumio's mouth were bitter to the taste.

The kid leapt off the rodeo machine, and watching him head through the curtain, Yumio began to wonder, at that moment, whether he really felt any sexual desire.

But it must have been desire. For some time after that, the kid appeared in Yumio's early-morning dreams, paralyzing him.

He had on different clothes in every dream. If Yumio had boarded a bus, the kid would be sitting directly behind him in a gymnast's outfit. Or he might be part of a group of twenty or more going to a party and wearing casual yet stylish clothes. His hair would be blond. Or he would be dressed as a woman in a semi-long wig sprawled out on a sofa in the waiting room of a bank during the day. The one that lingered with him the most was when—just like at the bathhouse—he was hardly wearing anything at all, and he'd be standing between two subway cars.

Was the kid trying to seduce me? Sometimes Yumio thought he must be. But, in the end, he didn't really know. The kid never had a nose in his dreams, and Yumio didn't understand what the disguises meant. The kid always had two eyes, a mouth, and two ears. They never had sex even in Yumio's dreams—and then he'd disappear just like before. Yumio shivered at the thought that he'd seen something not of this world. But he wondered if there was some other reason he felt cold.

After some period of time, as if to console himself, Yumio thought maybe the whole scenario was just a mistaken impression, a mysterious encounter in the dark. There *had* been a lot going on with him at the time . . .

But what did it mean when he reached out to touch the kid? Yumio tried the same thing even in his dreams. *I'd lost all hope. I was lonely. I just wanted to.* No matter what answer he came up with, Yumio just assented. But it wasn't him who was doing the agreeing—he always felt like it was the kid.

I wonder if he could see my nose?

He had strange, fleeting hunches, but it was ridiculous to dwell on them anymore.

Weren't those kinds of things common in this world? Everybody is devoted to their own desires. I desired him and he just rejected me. It must have been a common occurrence for a kid with no nose. Yumio decided to forget about the whole thing, including the big room where they'd met.

The ceiling heater made a low hum, and the area was quiet. The nerves in his chest tingled from his unspent desire.

The desire to smoke felt like someone was lightly moving their fingers over his lips. His throat was dry, and his spit was stuck behind his teeth. He'd already smoked all the cigarettes he'd bought yesterday, and now he didn't have the money to buy more. *Maybe somebody left some on top of their locker,* he thought.

Yumio started walking toward the lockers when someone pinned his arms from behind. *Shit, was he hiding?* Before he could get a word out, rough lips clamped down on his.

Yumio let his head rest on the guy's outstretched arms.

"Come on, I don't want you to say that." Yumio repeated it and forced a cough, but he sounded pitiful, like a singer whose throat was filled with puke. It even surprised himself, but he felt vulnerable, completely defenseless—also a good feeling.

Sex with that man was fantastic.

He liked how light his body felt after he sweated a lot. The man seemed to feel the same. They didn't go straight to the showers after they finished, but instead sprawled out next to each other, face up, completely spent.

"You're really sexy."

The man was still breathing hard, and Yumio felt the air in his ear, threatening to arouse him again.

"I've been around the block a few times, but it's been about three years since I've had sex like that."

"Me too. Thanks."

When Yumio turned his head, the man kissed him. The kiss was rough, but his tongue was soft and pliant. Bringing his head close, Yumio instantly snuggled up tightly against him.

Yumio was surprised that they kissed right off the bat. There were a lot of guys at places like this who didn't want to do anything *above the neck*.

The man had actually grabbed Yumio, kissing him without hesitation. He licked and bit the nape of Yumio's neck so much that it almost turned Yumio off. The man's tongue was ample, his mouth very warm—like he'd just drunk some hot water. *He's been around—probably 38 or 39.* That's what he gathered while he lay scissored between the man's suntanned arms and thick chest.

"So you've just moved to the area?" the man inquired curiously.

"No, not really."

"Your body is so incredibly tight; you said you didn't fuck, but you've got such a nice dick," the man said—all the while, he was pulling on Yumio's soft cock like he was teasing it.

"It's because it's been a long time."

"I don't think so."

While he enjoyed listening to the man's rough speech, Yumio thought about his own fingers that had just been in the man's asshole.

His hole was looser and bigger than he'd expected.

Yumio let out a smile when he thought, *"This guy too?"*—fooled at first by the man's come-on. It was funny—to fool and be fooled by one's partner. Incredible that with such a hard ass his hole was so soft and loose. Yumio moved his fingers around freely like a child exploring something. How far could he go? He put in more fingers, but stopped at four. The man moaned like a woman, saying, "Any more of that and I'll want to get fucked—"

The man's hand pulled on Yumio's dick harder the more obscenely he talked. Wanting to conceal his own shyness, Yumio tried touching the man's dick, but the man's right arm over his stomach was in the way and Yumio couldn't reach it. Instead, he muttered, "You're much bigger than me," but the man ignored him and kept on talking.

"Licking eyes—and stuff."

"You didn't tell me to stop, right?"

"Licking eyes—that's a first for me." The man laughed for the first time.

"It's just because you're shy."

"Do you ask everybody you do it with?"

"Not everyone."

"Then who do you ask?"

"Guys who seem like they'll let me do it. People who seem like they're sluts."

"Hey! So that's what you think of me?"

"Yep."

Yumio noticed that in the middle of sex he'd lost his left contact lens. The man must have flicked it out when he was licking Yumio's eyelids. The lens probably rolled off onto the pillow, but *since it was the third day on a one-day lens, who cares,* he thought. Strange to think it got stuck to the man's tongue and that he might have swallowed it. At the same time, if that did happen, he found it incredibly repulsive and painful.

"How old are you?"

"Twenty-seven."

"Oh, you're still young."

"Not anymore."

"You must do some rough work."

"Not really."

"You *do.* If not, you wouldn't be this sexy."

"But I said I'm not sexy."

"A slut."

"So what do you do?"

"I work in construction—at a building site near here."

"That's why you have such a good body. Your pecs are incredible."

"You're thin. Skin like a woman's."

"So you always come here around this time?"

"I came a little early today—work let out early. The earthquake meant we couldn't put up the scaffolding, so there was nothing to do."

"I see. That's tough."

"So, how old do I look?"

"Huh?"

"I mean, my age."

"I don't know."

"Take a guess!"

"I don't know—I can't see your face."

"But you have a sense, right?"

"So, about thirty-six?"

"Could be."

"What's that mean? How old?"

"So do you wanna know what I tell people here, or my real age?"

"Are they different? That's awful."

"So which is it? Which one?"

"Huh?"

"Which one do you wanna know?"

"That's ridiculous!"

"Which one do ya wanna know?"

"Okay, your real age."

"I'll tell you."

"Okay."

"Forty-eight."

I wonder what time it is now. When Yumio leaned his face toward the man, his breath suddenly smelled fishy. Or maybe it smelled that way before and Yumio had just now noticed it. But the smell reassured him.

"I'm married."

"Oh."

The man began talking about his children. The older one was a boy in his second year of middle school and the younger one was also a boy in the sixth year of elementary school . . . Yumio listened without saying anything. He put the man's right hand on his dick and moved it slowly back and forth. It felt so good he thought he might disappear without a trace.

• • •

The man persisted in asking whether or not his younger son had beat off yet.

Yumio was sick of what he was talking about. It was absurd to even reply with, "Well, that's the age . . ."

Yumio's lips, once moist from their kissing, had begun to feel parched. He could hear the sound of the ceiling heater revving up and blowing loud on the papered partition. All around them were signs of worn carpet.

Yumio turned and spoke into the man's ear, "There are a lot of people here now."

Yumio drew his head back and the man whispered back, "When we were doing it, did you notice people trying to come into our room?"

"No, I didn't."

"I kicked the door shut to stop them."

"Really? But they might have peeked in through a hole."

"Sure."

"Everybody comes here at this time of day."

"Idiot. They come *because* it's this time of day. They can't wait to get here."

"Really?"

"*Really.*"

"We too . . ."

A single figure who was listening at the door walked off.

Yumio wanted to sink into his own sensations. He wanted to go somewhere so far away that if he screamed, nobody could hear him. The air in the room somehow had thinned out, and he wanted them to embrace passionately again. When he reached out as a reaction to this urge, the man sat up like he'd been waiting for Yumio to do just that.

"Well." The man stood up in one swift motion.

"Yeah." Yumio quickly pulled away. Their eyes came face to face in the dark.

The two of them stood up and looked around the room. Their underpants, scattered tissues, a mat that had slipped out of place, and the lid from some lotion were scattered against the walls. And then . . .

"That was great. See you later."

Yumio was squatting down with his back to the man as he said that. Just then Yumio found the unused condom he'd stuck into his briefs.

"See you around."

The man lightly touched both of Yumio's arms and left the room.

Yumio lingered in the darkness. He shut the door and laid down on the mat. The back of his head was cold.

• • •

The crossbeams on the dark ceiling were like the ribs on a thin woman. He had no sense of time for a while.

He could hear the far-off sound of the showers; it was his turn to leave the room.

Slowly, Yumio slipped out of the darkness.

The area in front of the shower room was bright, but there was only a single light. Yumio felt like his body was glowing. Still not accustomed to the brightness, his eyes hurt like they had pins in them. He knew for sure now that he'd lost his left contact lens.

Yumio could see the man's naked body bouncing back and forth through the opaque glass. He just got a glimpse of him before Yumio turned his back. He wanted to see the man's face in the light. His chest, his thick pubic hair, his thick dick. It was a fair exchange since the man had seen Yumio naked.

Yumio crossed his arms and hugged his shoulders trying to stave off the cold. Rubbing his feet together, he waited for the man to come out.

The man appeared through the door in a fog.

"Ah."

"Ah." Yumio bit down on his lip.

The man looked like a kind father. He had small, narrow eyes with a round nose. His hair was a brownish color that had been dyed with some cheap bleach, and it was cut in a partial Mohican. His chest muscles shined in the light, and his crotch was a deep black.

Yumio's wide-open eyes conveyed his surprise.

The man stood expressionless, as if he had forgotten about Yumio and was thinking about something else. Then, he bowed slightly and in several long steps disappeared into the corridor leading to the lockers. His demeanor was strange, and he appeared lonely.

Yumio opened the door to the shower.

The mist that rose from the hot shower smelled of spit and sweat left over from the encounter with the man. He washed off his body carefully and when he finished wiping it dry, he looked at the hanging wall clock in the lounge.

It was 9:10.

• • •

Yumio didn't know what to do: return to Shinjuku or stick around here.

The two hours of sex he'd had with the man wasn't enough. Most of it was useless chatter, and he didn't know how long they'd actually fucked. But he was sure the sex was good.

His heart beat excitedly.

This occasionally happened, but as he was on his way to the train station from his house, it felt like someone had seized his heart with their bare hands.

Yumio resisted the feeling by bending forward, but the hand was clearly trying to stop his beating heart. He twisted his body sideways with the realization that his heart couldn't be stopped so easily.

Yumio headed for the station with his back hunched over. Just before he went through the ticket gate, he fell to his knees. A man in a dark blue uniform came running up to him. After that men with white helmets and bluish coats gathered around and held on to his body.

Yumio lost consciousness.

The doctor told him *no matter how you look at it, you're lucky.* He explained in some detail how exactly Yumio's luck was good. The doctor's transitions between one piece of information and the next were so polished that Yumio didn't understand how anything connected, and then the topic changed to warnings about his everyday life and how to care for himself. The doctor's hair hung down to his shoulders fluttering back and forth, and his eyes drooped, his gums bluish-black. Just as Yumio was wondering how old he was, the doctor—now using a threatening, irritated tone of voice said, "You got it, right?" Flustered, Yumio had no choice but to smile back.

Yumio went to get what was left of his salary after he resigned: two weeks and four days' worth. His quick-eyed colleague inched closer to him on his way out.

"Honestly I'm so relieved."

That's what he thought he heard, so Yumio thanked her evasively.

His colleague's lips stiffened unattractively; the whites of her eyes looked dirty—yellow. She was an older woman.

They'd been work buddies for a while so there were conflicts. The problems were about the details of their assignments, but whenever they broached the topic, they ended up shouting at each other.

She'd always say, "Let's get out everything we want to say to each other." But it never ended there. The arguments were endless, persistent, and useless. When one long argument ended, he was completely exhausted and hurt and what was left behind was the two of them, one younger than the other, reliant on each other.

"Hang in there, okay? I'll do the same here."

Hearing that, Yumio realized he was crying. The woman didn't say anything else; with sunken downcast eyes, she walked away.

Yumio lit a cigarette he'd pilfered in the locker room at the baths.

Another man went in to the showers. After glancing over at Yumio, who was sitting on the leather sofa in the waiting room, he disappeared into the light of a shower stall with something like a scowl on his face.

Yumio wondered whether the hot water he was listening to was washing over them both.

Yumio looked up at the fluorescent light on the ceiling. He stared up at it for a while as if it could burn right through his left eye. Soon after getting his pay, he cleared out of his Tokyo apartment and returned to his parent's house.

His father, who still had a few years left until retirement, and his divorced older sister were still at home. His older brother—by two years—had returned home at the beginning of the new year and had just started a job at a local real estate company.

Yumio was in the kitchen. And so was his mother, whom he hadn't actually seen face to face in a number of years.

"Your older sister just sits around, and your older brother isn't used to his job yet. And you're not well. I can't sleep at night, thinking about you . . ."

Yumio's mother didn't look at him. She was completely absorbed in cutting the vegetables into star shapes. She pressed the aluminum mold into the thinly-cut carrots. When she finished cutting a number of stars, she threw them all together into some cloudy hot water.

Yumio just looked on from the doorway.

With what looked like great pleasure, his mother began picking out tableware from the cupboard. She wasn't choosing them randomly, but with some plan in mind. She chose the cheap, broken ones and pulled them down with an ear-splitting clatter.

"And then there's the matter of money. After grandpa died, his pension stopped coming in. We've been depending on that up to now. Dad's retirement money will start year after next. And if your brother comes home for good, we'll be okay if he throws some money in too."

She wouldn't ask Yumio to contribute anything. The man came out of the shower room. Yumio threw his finished cigarette into the ashtray.

• • •

It was almost 9:30. Yumio lit another cigarette. He'd have to wait for a while until his unemployment money came through.

Until then, Yumio had to look for a new job. He'd be okay with his savings for the rest of the year. He had nothing to worry about since his food and his living expenses would be covered while he was at home. Yumio thought about this distractedly while he smoked his menthol cigarette.

"There's nothing but emptiness to release you from emptiness," a musician-turned-novelist had written in a magazine essay. Before he knew it, those became Yumio's own words. Maybe it was because of his meds, but he couldn't get fully hard. He worried about whether or not sex with men was included in the doctor's warnings about "strenuous exercise."

He passed by the only gay bar in the prefecture. A few shadows were inside. They all had the same kind of face, and when he spoke to them he realized they were all the same type of person. They exchanged ambiguous stares, not sure if they were trying to keep each other at a distance or draw each other in. The sex he had with them was a mixture of mutual compromise, inexplicable hatred, and a powerful, dark desire.

The men and women were rushing out of the east entrance to the JR line and were cutting across the plaza in front of the Alta Department Store and heading further east along Yasukuni Ave. It was like a picture on TV in which groups of wild oxen in Africa or someplace similar were scattering with a tremendous sense of purpose across a muddy river. This vision was stuck in his mind along with the caption "there is nothing but emptiness to save oneself from emptiness."

Yumio advertised for partners on the internet. The majority of them were one-night stands. He'd meet them in a hotel (if they were rich) or in a car or a public bathhouse or a department-store toilet.

The men liked revealing their lives to Yumio. There was the student preparing for university exams who was an inveterate pervert, the chef's apprentice who wet his pants, the marijuana grower still dressed in his work apparel, and the railroad employee whose hobby was drinking and eating without spending any money . . . They told Yumio a lot, and when they were finished, they asked about Yumio's life as if that were the least they could do to be courteous.

Yumio didn't talk about much of anything, because he couldn't remember the kinds of replies he was supposed to give.

Almost all of them were married with children. And uniformly they all wanted *that*.

And like throwing a bone to a dog, he gave them *that*.

• • •

"Hey, do you care if we use a condom?"

After Yumio nodded, the man took out a condom from a box. He peeled it out of its packaging with a motion that showed he'd done it before and rolled it over Yumio's penis.

Yumio used his hand to get his half-shrunken penis hard again, but the man nonchalantly brushed his hand away. Then he swallowed Yumio's penis deep into his mouth.

Yumio's unemployment insurance ran out so he'd have to cut into his savings.

He quit his part-time job at the convenience store. The medicine he was taking wasn't working, but when he asked the doctor about it, the doctor shot back, "Do you know how many times you've asked this?"

Yumio felt like killing him.

When he stayed in the house all day, he slept past noon. When he'd wake up, sudden conversations made him tense up. He replied as best he could to each voice in turn. He'd stand up and walk around the house. When he looked at his face in the bathroom mirror, which he did numerous times each day, he'd relax a little. On his way out of the bathroom, he never forgot to go to the toilet.

Whenever he verbally responded to something on TV, it made him look bad, but it kept his mother and his older sister at bay. His father didn't say anything simply because he wasn't home in the daytime. His brother returned from work late, and when he did return, he'd shut himself in his room on the second floor.

Yumio's mother got mad at Yumio any number of times, even though she said it wasn't because she was mad. His friend called about once every two weeks; it was only then that Yumio felt he could have an actual conversation.

When he began to take the new medicine that his doctor ordered, his sleep was shallow, and he dreamed a lot.

His dreams were confusing. He had dreams within dreams, and those dreams were superimposed on other dreams. Yumio tried to count how many times his dreams looped around. When he woke up from one dream, he fell back into another, and if he woke up from that dream, he fell into a third. The cycle gradually became faster and finally the speed of his dreams become so dizzying that Yumio wasn't able to keep track of them anymore.

In one, water covered the ground, and to dodge it, he slid on top of it. His feet had become one with the water, and he couldn't feel his toes or heels. He desperately kicked the ground with his round, flabby, ineffective feet.

There might not have been any water resistance. If there was, it was faint. It felt like he was being urged on with the words "if you don't get out of here somehow." Yumio fled, but he couldn't get away, so he got into a taxi, and then the roof came off.

Dark black blood fell from the sky, but it wasn't from above. It sprayed from the side diagonally. That's why the right side of his face was dyed in blood. When he looked outside the window, a horse was running parallel to the car, and then he realized that the blood on his face was from the horse. The *mikan* trees at his house were planted about a hundred meters on the edge of the opposite lane of traffic and something was riding on top of them; his whole body shook violently. He looked back as he worriedly rode right past. When he put his face up to the glass of the back window, he saw that what was on top of the trees were corpses. Recognizing that the corpses were those of his older brother and father, he gagged. But he was able to stop what he was about to puke up with his hands, and before he knew it, he realized there was nothing on his hands. When he glanced outside, blood was gushing from the place where the horse should have had a neck.

Yumio opened his eyes, and when he did, the plaster from the ceiling was melting in drips. That dripping plaster turned into rain falling on Yumio's face. When he realized, *oh, it's milk*, the palpitations began.

Yumio was on a bed in a business hotel in Akasaka with a man who was seven years older than him.

The man said, "I can't mas-masturbate." Yumio asked him, "What do you mean?" "I can't do it with my ha-hand. There-therefore, I can't cum using anybody's hand. Your mouth doesn't work either. So, what can I do? When I went to the doc-doctor, he said it'll get better with the help of a par-partner." "Well, then I'll help you." "Even if you-you help me, it won't work." "So what can we do?" "The doctor said people make up their own ways of doing it." "Well, show me."

The man crawled onto the bed. With a tissue beneath his crotch, he began to move his body slowly while he held on to the edge of the mattress with both his hands. He was going to rub his crotch against the sheets until he climaxed. The bed shook, and Yumio, who lay sideways on it, had no choice but to shake along with it.

That shaking steadily became more intense, making Yumio irritable as it did. When Yumio looked anxiously at the man to his side, the man was looking upward just as he thought he might be, and his eyes were bloodshot. "Won't you stop for a minute?" "N—no—no. It's scary."

No, I'm not scared. Just a little more and I'll come. No, this isn't at all awful." "Won't you stop for a minute?" When Yumio screamed this the second time, the man had already finished, and the bed stopped shaking too.

But actually it was about to get worse.

Yumio didn't think the medicine was helping him, so he requested an appointment with the doctor. Even if he tried saying—*I feel awful, uneasy*—the doctor just threw his words back at him. *What kind of medicine do you want this time?* Yumio searched for something to say, but just like before he couldn't breathe.

This was already the fourth time. With Yumio's dick in his mouth, the man's upturned eyes seemed to be telling him that maybe that's how it would be. Yumio couldn't be sure.

• • •

The top lip of the person curled up when he laughed.

The man was sporting a well-worn black down jacket. His face was a little puffy, and the unshaven part of his face stood out even in the dark. He laughter and movements hadn't changed at all from before.

The man looked at Yumio and said, "You haven't changed."

"I have."

"I've gotten fatter, right?"

"Maybe a little."

"If you scarf down your food and go to bed, this is what happens to you."

"Yep."

"It's really been a long time."

By twisting his body, Yumio brushed off the man's arm, which was about to reach around his back. The man's lip was turned up when their eyes met. Yumio was in a bad mood immediately. "You're still sleeping with men?"

"Sometimes. But I got married."

"When?"

"Just about a year ago now."

"Really? Congratulations."

"My wife is like this." While he made a gesture with his hands like his stomach was distended, his face showed no emotion. Yumio looked at the man's thoroughly domesticized appearance; he knew that his own cheeks were flushed.

"Your wife at home?"

"No, she's not. She's back with my parents."

"If someone's at home, I won't go."

"The house is new, but I'm alone now."

"So you don't get yourself off alone?"

"How sad! My dad and mom put all their efforts into getting me a bride and now just leave me alone."

"You're with your parents?"

"Yeah, two households, but separate entryways."

As he tried to refresh his memory about the man, the as-always neckless horse was running to his side. Yumio averted his eyes from the man to avoid the spray of blood that would shoot his way. The man wore a crimson jersey jacket that he'd purposely shortened and was walking around on indoor slippers. Yumio remembered that he'd colored his hair slightly—just enough so that their teachers wouldn't know. He walked around spitting in the corridors. His spit was white and soft. Yumio wiped it up with a checkered handkerchief.

The man was good at displaying his knowledge of women's bodies, which he'd gotten from magazines and videos. Yet, once they went into a dark room, he lusted after Yumio's body, to which Yumio responded. The man may have been in a soccer club. Yumio often mimicked the way the man lifted his gym bag.

When Yumio shot him a dubious look, the man patted Yumio's shoulders—*let's hurry*—as if to speed him up. The man hopped around saying, "It's cold" as he sucked in his breath between his teeth—these were all indications of his animalistic desire. Even while the thought that this man and Yumio would get down and dirty tonight dampened his spirits, he was also turned on by the smell of the man's sweat and hair gel.

"I work at a funeral home in M city. It's a pretty big place—started four years ago. I was one of the 'first staff' there—now I'm an assistant manager."

The man talked about his job with excitement. The word "first staff" didn't fit with a funeral home. Yumio thought he must have just thrown the word in without thinking, but the man didn't show any sign of being aware of Yumio's thoughts. He was barely listening. The man suddenly shot him a side glance.

"So what are you doing now?"

Yumio put his cigarette out.

"Oh, that's great," the man said. "I'd like to quit my job. The job I'm doing now isn't very popular with my wife's relatives. They say it's a bad omen. The salary's okay though."

"Then that's enough. Work is work."

"If you want to work where I do, just say the word. Did you know that funeral service directors need certification? After you start at the company, you have to do in-service training. I passed the second level and now I'm going to try to get qualifications above that—it's pretty difficult and a lot of guys fail . . ."

Yumio regretted wearing a thin coat. It was past 8:00 at night in December. He wore a knit shirt under his coat, but he'd been overoptimistic. The cold that was piercing through the tear in the nylon was unpleasant. At first the tear was just a few centimeters on the side but now—maybe because he'd worn it so long—the tear had gradually spread to the back. He had to walk scrunched down so that the tear wouldn't open up any further and be exposed to the elements.

"How much farther do we have to walk?" The irritation Yumio felt toward the man was apparent in the tone of his own voice.

"It's right in front of us. That's it—my house." The man raised his voice as if he were drunk. Where he pointed was a new white-walled house.

"Nice," Yumio said curtly.

The man took what Yumio said at face value. For him it was a house he could boast about. His parents bought some of the neighboring land with a thirty-year loan and built a house right next door. The man escorted Yumio to the entrance, saying in a satisfied voice, *What do you think? Incredible, isn't it?*

Yumio was stifled by the smell of hinoki wood when he stepped into the entrance. The room was brightly lit and the walls were completely white. A full-length mirror was propped in front of them, reflecting their bodies. The living room was at the end of a long hallway to the side of the stairs. The man went in ahead of Yumio and turned on the lights: a three-person sofa, a glass table, a magazine rack, a flat-screen television, and light beige curtains. Two tall plants about half his size were placed on the inside of a window that looked out onto the veranda. It looked just like something out of a real estate catalog—a room with no originality.

"Great house."

"Right?" The man's lip was turned up in a lewd manner. If you turned up the lights a little, it was an undistinguished room that looked like it was about to vanish—the sofa, the table, the TV, the curtains, the plants, and . . .

"And the bedroom?"

Yumio pretended to make a joke, but while his eyes darted around the room, the man suddenly came up from behind and put his arms around him. He grabbed him like he was going to bite into the nape of Yumio's neck, and then he pushed Yumio onto the sofa.

"Hold on, not so fast."

"You'll do it with me like you used to, right?"

"Okay, okay."

When Yumio glanced back at the man's face desperately, his eyes were already animal-like. Trying to slow this wild man down, Yumio asked him to turn off the lights. He couldn't catch his breath. The man stood up and ran over to the switch on the side of the door. The lighting changed the room to a warm color. He could see the dark night through a gap in the curtain.

Yumio reached out for the man when he returned. The man's long tongue slid into Yumio's mouth, and he felt the soft spit on his hard tongue. Yumio's tongue shook as if it were convulsing. The man's tongue also quivered, but just for a moment. They kissed without pause. The man's tongue, rougher still, seemed to have no end. Tiring of kissing on the lips, they went after the nape of their necks. Hanging on to each other, they loosened their hold and took off each other's clothes.

"Hey."

"What?"

"You showered?"

"I showered."

"You smell sweaty."

"Shut up!"

"Your skin is salty tasting."

"That's not true."

"You sweat like this when it's this cold?"

"I've got good metabolism."

"Apparently."

Yumio sniffed his armpits; they smelled like pencil shavings. To do this, he had to arch his back like a bow. The man buried Yumio's face in his armpit, and with the other hand he pushed on the back of his head. Jammed into the man's pits this way was uncomfortable, but it also felt so good it made him crazy.

"Harder."

"Like this?"

"More."

"This much?"

Twisting his body, he tightened his grip on Yumio's head from the side and he stuck his tongue into Yumio's right ear. The man's long tongue felt like it almost grazed his eardrum. With his nose pushed into the man's armpit, Yumio moaned under his breath.

He could hear the sound echoing through his head. Yumio's left hand grazed the man's hard nipple.

• • •

Yumio wanted to feel the cold night air.

On the sofa naked, they turned to face each other no matter how uncomfortable they were in this unpleasant room. Now that the sex was over, the lights in the room were too bright.

Yumio could faintly hear the sound of the shower from down the hallway through the open door to the living room. Just thinking about the water washing away the man's strong body odor made Yumio lightheaded.

The man didn't penetrate Yumio, so he sat astride him impatiently. Yumio initiated a change in positions by pushing him down onto the sofa face up. From that position, Yumio couldn't help but see how out of shape his body was. He was too fat around his stomach and his butt, and Yumio noticed the sharp smell of sweat from his crotch. As Yumio swallowed the man's dick and moved his mouth up and down, the man moaned ecstatically, both of them rolling onto the wooden floor. Rimming his hole with his tongue, the man rolled over as if that's what he'd wanted all along, desperately wanting *that*.

Yumio grabbed and held onto him. He knew the guy didn't just do this "sometimes." There's no doubt that he'd been having sex with men for a long time. The thought made his arms grow more powerful. When he pushed his cock in, the man cried out like a woman. And so it ended—that easily.

"When did you learn to do that?"

"Recently." The man was still out of breath.

"Does it feel good?"

"Sort of. . . ."

"It does feel good, doesn't it?"

"You've never thought you wanted to get fucked?" The man's thick lips trembled as if he were being ironic for the first time.

"Undignified?"

"A little. But it's okay. How was it?"

"It was good."

"Really. You're the top then?"

"Usually. I don't bottom often. I don't have any interest."

He was half joking and half telling the truth.

Having finished with his shower, the man began putting his clothes on sheepishly. He moved his hands around as if he were touching his own body but with his clothes on. He seemed to be looking for his cigarettes; they were probably in the pocket of his down jacket, which he'd thrown to the side of the sofa. Not aware that's where they were, the man walked around seemingly ill at ease. One of his eyelids was red and swollen as if he'd been crying.

But there was another reason he was anxious. He quit looking for his cigarettes and sat down on the floor cross-legged and began to talk.

"I lied to you a little while ago." He licked his lips again and again. While Yumio began putting on his clothes, he waited for the man to start talking.

"My wife? She's in the hospital now."

"Okay."

"Yeah, she's in the hospital."

"Really?"

"So, she gave birth yesterday and my dad and my mom went there."

"Really?" His voice was hoarse.

"Haha." The man laughed and his lip began turned up.

"Why are you laughing?"

"Well, maybe because I was so fired up, because it was this time . . . you know, I'm human, and I have . . ."

The man uncurled his upper lip and laughed as if he'd gotten his fill of what he wanted. It was a laugh that made Yumio the man's accomplice. Yet his eyes were still swollen, and he had no expression on his face.

"Let's do this again. You know what they say, renewing old friendships and the like. When my wife isn't around, I'll contact you." Having recovered his spirits, the man spoke in an overly cheerful voice. He patted Yumio's shoulder.

In the end, Yumio promised they'd get together again, and then he left. Yumio had no memory of whether or not he'd ever followed up on that promise.

• • •

Yumio opened the shower door.

The mist whooshed out suddenly as if freed from chains. The light shined in the waiting room. A man was sitting on the sofa. He knew he'd seen him somewhere before.

Even though a year had passed since he'd returned to his parent's home, he couldn't get Tokyo out of his mind. In fact, he longed for it even more. He knew his friend in Tokyo had a blog, but he didn't dare peek at it.

Yumio hadn't even contacted him. But there were phone calls from a few friends. About half the conversations were joking around and the other half were people boasting about themselves.

Any men in your life? How's work? Found a job? The other day I broke up with my boyfriend, ya know?! But I found a replacement for him fortunately. For the first time, I started dating a guy older than me.

Yumio: *Well, I gotta go, I have to get up early;* caller: *Oh, really? Of course. I'll catch ya later*—the last part he spoke in a perfunctory tone before he hung up. In spite of the fact that he had no plans at all, what was left unsaid hung in the air.

I didn't tell my friends anything except that I'd changed jobs, so I was going back to my parents' home and I would study again. Nobody really believed me. One friend sent me some lines from my friend's blog in which he had been gossiping behind my back: Ya know, this is how he's talking about you. I can only imagine what he's thinking about you.

"It's been a long time," the man said to Yumio, rising from the sofa.

"I'm sorry, I don't know you."

Even if his friends had kept in touch for a while, later they tended to stop.

Maybe there hadn't been a connection with any of them from the beginning; Yumio rationalized this to protect his peace of mind. *That's just how things are,* he believed.

• • •

It had been a long time since his cellphone rang. The caller ID read "Hayashi-home."

Hayashi's voice was low and muffled for a woman. Yet, she sounded cheerful.

"It's been a long time."

"How you doin'?"

"Not too bad. You?"

"Okay, I guess . . . After you quit, people got moved around and now I'm in the cognitive-impairment ward."

Hayashi had been assigned to the general ward when Yumio worked at the facility. They would often gossip about new patients and help each other. The cognitive-impairment ward was regarded as a difficult post that everybody tried to avoid. The symptoms varied from patient to patient, but a patient who was calm in the daytime sometimes began wandering about aimlessly, screaming, and behaving violently at night.

Yumio didn't know why Hayashi had been promoted at work. He was jealous rather than sympathetic. *She must have managed to gain the trust of her coworkers.*

Whenever Yumio sympathized with her, she'd just brush his comments off as if they were nothing and say things like, "Well, everybody's calmed down now. They're all just saints. No one has gotten out of hand recently that I can think of."

"Maybe. But you've been promoted!"

"But I've already been here five years."

Then the topic changed to what they were both doing now.

Yumio didn't know anything about Hayashi's private life. She kept her affairs to herself, but she was aware of what was happening in his life. They fell naturally into their usual conversation about the staff or rumors about the patients. A name that Yumio wanted to avoid came up.

"Speaking of which, did you hear about Shōji?" Her voice grew a little tense.

"That's okay—I don't want to hear about her."

"But, she just up and quit."

"Oh, when?"

"It was about six months after you quit. You didn't know anything about it, right?"

"That's because no one told me about it." Hayashi was the first person to have contacted him from work.

"Well, they said she was sick."

"Uh-huh."

"And you know what else? It was bad."

"Oh? What was it?"

"It was cancer."

"Huh?!"

"You know Mr. Hirai from the office? I heard he went to visit her in the hospital. It was awful, he said. She went from being plump to incredibly thin. He said the size of her head was about half the size it used to be. Her coloring was awful, and she had no expression on her face. He said he couldn't really look at her."

Yumio searched for the right response, but nothing came to mind. Hayashi went on to tell Yumio about this and that. It seemed like her voice just got more and more cheerful. There was something strangely innocent about it, like a child who doesn't understand the words they're speaking. Yumio couldn't think of anything to say.

"Not only that but she seems to have been sick even when she was here. She pushed herself when she wasn't feeling good and just kept working. But they said it's not going to be much longer. It's last-stage uterine cancer."

"Really."

"Sorry, Katō. You'll feel guilty now that I've told you this."

"Probably."

"Huh?"

"Did you call me to tell me that?"

"No! I thought you already knew it, so. . . ."

Hayashi's voice pretended innocence. Yumio realized that Hayashi's report was all in the past tense—*it didn't take long*—*last stages of uterine cancer.*

The woman was probably already dead. The person who went to visit her at the hospital was probably Hayashi herself. If that's the case, she knew the woman was no longer alive.

"Yumio, I'm not criticizing you. Don't take it to heart. Ms. Shōji didn't tell anyone it seems—about her cancer."

Yumio wondered why he should feel guilty. He stared into space with his cellphone held to his ear. Had he made the woman sicker? Yumio thought that's what Hayashi was saying.

"To tell you the truth, I'm relieved."

Yumio's memory of Hayashi brought him back to his senses. After passing judgment on Yumio, Hayashi's face popped in and out and then disappeared in a fog.

"Well, I'm gonna hang up now. Take care of yourself, Katō. If you come to Tokyo, let me know. Let's get together for tea or something."

Yumio would probably never have tea with Hayashi in Tokyo. There probably wouldn't be any more phone calls either.

He could barely feel the beating of his heart. He placed the palm of his hand on his chest.

"Yumio, I'm going shopping—would you get the car out?"

His mother was knocking on his door. But what he heard out of the blue was someone saying *keep me company, okay. Fellow traveler, come travel with me, keep me company.* Her voice was strong, but it was so far away that he didn't know whose voice it was. *Should he go with her? I should,* he answered.

He left his room as if someone were pushing him out the door.

• • •

The road home ran along the seashore.

Pointing to something over Yumio's shoulder, his mother said, "Hey, look at that."

He looked out to sea. A flock of a hundred or so seagulls was flying over and then landing on a seawall of large concrete tetrapods.

The birds looked like a huge mound of snow. As he focused his sight on them, they seemed to shimmer a little. There were hundreds of yellow beaks among those white wings. Their colors blended in with the ashy-colored sky and the deep blue of the sea.

The seagulls weren't posed to fly off. Some pressed in and nudged one another while others stared out to sea motionless.

"What are they doing?"

"Really, what *are* they doing? Maybe they're all consulting with each another about something?"

His mom gave a pleased laugh. "I wonder if they're asking each other about what they'll eat later? We're going to have pork cutlets, fish and seaweed salad, green onions in miso soup . . ." She laughed good-naturedly, shaking the full sacks of food she held on her knees. Yumio pressed down on the accelerator and turned the steering wheel into the passing lane.

He opened the window some to let air into the car. The wind from the sea was still cold. He couldn't hear any sounds because the sea was far calmer that it usually was. The flock of seagulls was now out of sight—they'd disappeared behind them.

His older sister in gray sweatpants appeared at the entryway, rubbing her swollen eyes.

"Something terrible's happened."

"What?!"

His mother let the bags she'd been holding fall with a bang to the floor.

They could hear the voices on the TV just over her shoulder. People were screaming and yelling, but he still couldn't see it.

Yumio listened to the sounds and stared at the TV. After a while he could make out muddied waters flowing onto land, gobbling up cars and carrying them along.

The screen changed.

And then there was a scene in Shinjuku where crazed-looking people were coming and going just as they always did.

• • •

Yumio headed for the exit.

It was 9:30. He decided to go back to Shinjuku and hang out somewhere until the bus left for home.

But still he thought that he ought to stick around a bit longer. He might have more luck here than in Shinjuku. The not-so-bad sex he'd already had with the two guys lingered in his mind.

The noise from the overhead heater blew louder and harder, shaking the hanging partition curtain.

I'll stick around a little longer. I can still get back in time for the bus. Having made up his mind, he looped back to the lounge. *It was a waste of time to overthink it.* He went to the bathroom, washed his face, and rinsed out his mouth. He could still taste some guy's spit in his mouth.

He passed through to another room, the partition slapping against his face. He'd been in the light for a while, so his eyes weren't used to the dark. He followed the pathway as his senses perked up again. He could tell that there were guys lurking around. All the doors to the private rooms were locked.

The armpit odor was even stronger than before—like burning wood chips. Feet were shuffling along. The heater roared from the ceiling, emitting a deep, dark sound, and Yumio could make out what he thought might be moans, too.

Yumio held his breath, taking in everything.

He shouldn't have stepped foot in here. Why wasn't he aware of it sooner? But when he became aware, it was too late.

Turning around, he headed down the hallway hurriedly for the exit.

Just then, some guy pulled on Yumio's arm. He staggered as if he were leaning toward them. And then just as he lost his balance, someone else pushed him from the other side. There were a number of bodies already in the room in front of him.

The figures were lined up with their backs to the walls.

They surrounded him on all sides in the pitch dark. He couldn't tell how many bodies there were. They lined up around him in a circular formation. He knew what they wanted.

They grabbed his arms from behind and pushed him down. His skin scraped against the floor, and it hurt. They threw him into the middle of the room, pushing him with their feet. One figure came forward and gave his cheek a sudden kick.

Ouch, he screamed out instantly, but without saying a word the man continued to kick him. They poked at his shoulders with their feet, driving him into a corner, where his hands were scissored to his side. He was lifted up by force and kicked in the cheek again and again.

"Ow, ow!"

They stretched him out on the floor on his back and held his head. Somebody grasped his throat and pulled on him until his face was straight up. *Ok, ok, I get it, stop it.* With Yumio speechless, they raised his body, and when they lifted his head, someone pushed their dick into his mouth. He tried pushing it away, but then they pried his mouth open and now it was filled with both a cock and fingers.

His mouth burned with pain as the person thrust his cock intensely into his throat. With his breath cut off, he started to gag. They lifted his legs and spread his crotch wide; he felt like his lower body was floating.

He thrashed his legs trying to resist, but there were more and more hands that held him. The hands that were holding his legs down were joined by several more, and he couldn't catch his breath. His upper body slid down of its own accord, and his head touched the floor. The body standing right in front of him, lowered itself and sat astride his chest.

Somebody pushed their tongue into his hole. A finger also worked its way in, as if to open him up completely. Fingernails scratched his insides, and he could see more of them out of the corner of his eye. A heel rubbed against his cheek, and suddenly, as if out of anger, it roughly pushed against his cheekbone. Spit dribbled onto his eyelids faster and faster from above; after the drops landed, they made a sound like bubbles bursting. He could smell them. The air in the room was hot, and the dick in his mouth was hard. It pushed straight down his throat, narrowing and then growing thick.

It came back to him—that anxious feeling of dreaming one dream after another. Desperately, he tried tracking the scenes with his eyes one by one as they superimposed themselves.

But, ignoring what he wanted, something besides a tongue pushed its way into his hole—something thicker and more frightful than either it or a finger. The dick in his mouth pulled out, the body on his chest rose up and backed away. They were now joined chest to chest, their arms intertwined, as lips inched their way over the nape of his neck, and from the side, fingers pinched his nipples, and another dick from above tried to push its way into his open mouth, as a new body slid onto his chest, its dick squirming its way into his hole.

This must be a dream, isn't it? But if it was a dream, he was in agony. He felt like he couldn't move. *So, how am I going to get out of this and make it stop?* But then he was again flung into the middle of the room.

Yumio seemed to be surrounded by other figures yet again. *How many bodies were there?* Some stood with their backs to the wall—yet, he could see one of the bodies was getting closer and landed a sudden kick against Yumio's cheek; he didn't know how many times.

The dick was warm, but the palm on his cheek was cool. *Its owner must have a warm heart, right?* The pain in Yumio's body confirmed this belief. Maybe he read it in some magazine. It said something like people with cold palms were deeply tender. *If that's the case, show me some of that tenderness. However much you can in this place, show it to me. Your tenderness doesn't change, does it?* With this sense that change was imminent, his body began to move up and down, sometimes with several bodies on top of him. Then they would melt away and later come together as a single group—vibrating. One, two, three bodies. He was in pain, scared and sad, but yet, he wanted them to be a single group of bodies. *Become a single group of men and don't let me go.* He prayed for more of this, *for me, for everyone, this had to happen*—and then the single group would dissolve, becoming water, becoming sweat, becoming cum—he smelled it.

The figures that left were replaced by others. Yumio hated being surrounded by them all and tried to stay in a corner of the room. But the bodies on top of him were too heavy, and he couldn't move or speak. At last he had an idea of how he could free himself: using his tongue—the only free part of his body—he signaled the person piled directly on top of him. Holding the man tightly with his arms, he held back his tears. How pitiful, asking for help in spite of the fact that he couldn't be assured of it. But it was far better than crawling back to the center of the room and waiting for a new pair of feet to kick him. If he did that, the dreams would also return. He'd be starting all over again—he could see fingernails off to his side, the heels of someone's feet stroking his cheek and then pushing up against his cheekbone obnoxiously. And it would be far better than spit dripping down onto his eyelids . . .

At first glance, Yumio thought that figure squatting down in the corner of the room might be the horse, the young horse with the splendid coat, the horse in his dream that ran through the water, the horse that fractured its leg, resting with its head lowered. But how sad to think that any horse wouldn't have a neck. The dream's endlessness started all over again. Would the neck even be found? Was the horse even there? Did the neckless horse exist? The odor of armpits around him almost made him choke—it was so strong he couldn't distinguish it from the odor of the horse. *Despite being covered in blood now, I am silently crying, not being able to make out the color of blood.*

It looked like the figures in the room were also crying. The sound from the ceiling heater resonated with the sound of my beating heart. It seemed like the shaking was coming from somewhere else—it might be my lust, more intense than ever. Was the horse in the corner of the room trying to stand up? But in the midst of this shaking, somebody's hand tried to snatch away my nose. Yumio cried, for the past. *That kid came for me. He came looking for me on the horse. You must feel the emptiness too. That time I touched your cheek. Before somebody made off with his nose,* Yumio hastily grabbed at the sticky hand, wriggled free, and somersaulted head over heels.

And then, he grabbed that finger . . .

· · ·

Yumio pushed on the shower door. His heart continued ringing like a fire alarm—he didn't know what it was. But this much he did know: *at least I got free of them.*

His head was heavy, and he felt horribly nauseous. His field of vision in his right eye was red. Unless he hunched over, it felt like his insides would spill out from somewhere, so he finally let himself bend forward. He pressed his forehead against the shower tile; *this might support his body.* His knees were weak, so he just trembled in place.

He adjusted the showerhead, closed both eyes, and with his head down, let the hot water roll down his back. *You're really a slut.* He responded to the man's voice immediately. *Yeah, I guess.* The man's thick hand rested on Yumio's back. He came to and when he opened his left eye just a bit, the water had formed a whirlpool of red in the drain. The blood was incredibly beautiful, and before he knew it vomit fell from his mouth into that eddy of water. The blood and vomit slowed the water in the whirling drain.

Retching, he vomited on and on. He couldn't stop so he just gave himself over to it; sobbing, he vomited up everything he had inside, on and on. Every time he vomited, the area behind his balls constricted like the air had been sucked out. The constriction caused his insides to contract. *So this is it:* anxious that his whole body might turn itself inside out, he couldn't help but double over. But when he did so, his asshole ached, rendering him motionless.

It felt like a second fire had started inside the one that was already smoldering. His hole was so hot and quivering that he might have mistaken it for desire. But then it changed into burning charcoal and collapsed all at once into ash. Yumio despaired of hoping the ash would soar away into the air. He tried to stand up shakily, but his whole body was in intense pain, and everything in front of him turned white. When he tried to shut his eyes, his right eyelid wouldn't close all the way, and the edge of his lip curled up—he hurt and ached, and he felt alone—he screamed out as if to hang on to someone, anyone.

What kind of medicine do you want this time?

Yumio came out of the shower room shaking off the doctor's voice in his head. He didn't look in the mirror of the bathroom because he knew how horrible his face must be. He cut through the lounge and headed to the corridor that led to the locker room. He could hear the voices of people moaning through the curtain. That was the world he had just been in, and now he'd escaped from it. The sound of ligaments and muscles straining, the sound of supple skin and the soles of feet rubbing along the carpet, the smell of sweat and saliva, the driving sound of the heater . . .

Yumio walked to the lockers. With his towel over his mouth, he groped along the wall and slowly made his way through the layers of curtains. It was a muddy river, a river of mud. But was the river this long and dark—just to cross the second floor of this building, here in a corner of Tokyo?

When he got to the lockers, Yumio sank down into a cheap leather sofa. *I really can breathe.* That was not an audial hallucination; it was actually Yumio's own voice.

• • •

How long have I been like this?

Maybe he'd been sleeping. He couldn't tell what was a dream and what wasn't.

What time is it now? He searched for a wall clock, but he couldn't find one. *How much time had passed after all that?*

I've got to get home. What time was the bus again? 11:00? He tried getting up, but his legs wouldn't move. It was as if all his joints were dislocated. It was the same for his arms and his neck. His face burned, and he could tell that his lip was swollen.

Supporting himself with his hurt hand, he slid his hips up the wall and slowly stretched his legs to the floor. Once he was up just for a moment, he felt like his strength was returning. He stepped ahead lightly as if familiarizing himself with the ground, and he registered that sensation on the soles of his feet.

While his body was acclimating itself, he searched for his locker. #25. *Fourth from the right on the top. There it was.* But he didn't have the key.

The key he expected to find around his left wrist wasn't there. He stared at it, his thin wrist covered in abrasions and bruises.

I couldn't possibly go back in there. I don't want to go back in there.

He sank into the sofa again. He couldn't think about anything. He felt a pleasant sense of fatigue and pain fill his body. The countless figures were calling out on the other side of the curtains.

You don't have to go home, someone said.

That may be so.

• • •

When he'd floated up out of the fathomless depths a number of times, he noticed the black curtain swaying to his side.

"Hey, what're you doing?"

A deep, firm voice descended on him from above. Instinctively, Yumio stiffened his body. As he opened his eyes and turned his head, the man was looking down at him.

"Hey, what's going on?"

It was a face he recognized. Narrow eyes, cheap bleached hair, a figure from the deep . . . He laughed while he flicked the waist of his pink swimming trunks. The laughter was clearly pretending to be a partner in crime.

"Huh."

"Why are you plunked down here? You haven't had enough, have you?"

"Yeah."

"Which is it—you wanna do it or not?"

"Huh."

"You know, you were amazing."

"Oh."

"I watched you the whole time."

"Huh."

"I was in there. Don't you remember? I climbed up on top of you in the middle of it all."

Yumio closed his eyes.

"Really. I was getting fucked, and you were busy over there so I couldn't do anything, but . . . you were crying, and you grabbed onto me."

"Huh."

"You *are* a slut."

"Yeah."

The man flashed his teeth when he laughed, and pinched Yumio's nipple. He said, *You were into that, weren't ya, when you called out in a low voice?* Then he patted Yumio's shoulder.

Yumio closed his eyes again. *Which dream was this?*

"What's with your face? Look in the mirror. Incredible."

The man pulled out his dull-colored work pants and work boots from his locker and quickly put them on, but he was barely visible. He was humming a tune. Before he could even register a feeling of surprise—*how naïve I was!*—Yumio couldn't fight off the feeling of sleepiness that came over him.

When the man finished putting his clothes on, he came back. He was waving something in front of Yumio's face. It sounded like a muffled bell.

"This is yours, right?"

"Huh."

"I snatched it from your wrist."

"Why?"

"Because I thought it would get in the way."

He threw the key down, and it landed on Yumio's crotch. The feel of the cold metal ran through the lower part of his body. The number 25 was clearly visible above the white band. It was definitely Yumio's key. The man laughed and put his mouth to Yumio's ear, telling him, "I'm just kidding you. I picked it up." *You probably took it while I was being shoved around.*

"Why?" Yumio asked, barely able to make a sound. It seemed as if he were both complaining and acting like a spoiled child.

"Are you telling me you forgot about it while you were wallowing in ecstasy?"

That's what he heard. That's what the man said as he turned away and started to leave. Yumio immediately stood up. He couldn't focus on anything, and overwhelmed by something he didn't yet understand, his eyes filled with tears.

"Wait," he said running up to the man and trying to grab his arm. The man turned around.

"Wait."

Still wobbly, Yumio ran into the lockers sideways. He slid down onto one knee with his cheek against the cold locker. When he came around, before he knew it the man was walking away. Just like he was a new species of animal.

"So, you're just putting on an act."

The man grabbed Yumio's ass with both hands and shook him roughly. *See ya.* With that, he strode out the exit without looking back. Yumio was about to make a miserable sound, but it caught in his throat. He raised his face when he tried to speak and stand up, but the man was gone.

Yumio screamed at the man who was on the other side of the door. He was mad and miserable, but a smile broke out on his face despite the lingering pain in his cheek.

• • •

The area was quiet after the man left.

He couldn't hear either the sound of the heater or the moaning. He could just barely hear the rustling of clothes in the distance. He felt as if everything was far away now. Yumio silently rubbed the area around his heart with his hand. Like a pendulum, he began swaying from side to side.

Is that all there is? He had no choice but to think it was. That was the answer that came to him again in his own voice.

With the key the man had given him, Yumio opened his locker. Even that felt strange. He took out his hoodie, his jeans, his bag, his coat, and his shoes.

While putting them on, he glanced at the display on his wristwatch that he'd thrown into the back of the locker. 11:06. Yumio doubted his own eyes. He couldn't believe it. The dream continued.

When he finished dressing, he hurried out the exit. The pain in his body that he thought he wouldn't ever forget dissipated bit by bit.

"Thank you!" said the man's voice coming from the reception center, and Yumio dashed outside running down the dark stairs.

Once he'd opened the glass doors and got downstairs, he let his eyes wander over the trees in the night. He knew his own eyes were just a bit luminous. *Right? Left?* As it was, he still couldn't see clearly out of one eye, but his line of vision grew even worse once the steam from the kitchen of the beef-bowl shop enveloped him. And beyond the steam was just complete darkness.

He fixed his eyes on that darkness. He thought he heard somebody's voice say, *over here* but Yumio ran off along the road opposite to the one going to the train station. The lingering wind on this still-cold March night blew unforgivingly through the holes in his coat. But it wasn't cold at all. Rather, he felt propelled forward. Of that he was certain.

The palpitations of Yumio's heart echoed loudly in his ears. His legs ran helter-skelter and little by little he curled his back as if it were trying to protect himself from something. But he pretended not to notice and hurried along the street. In order to meet up with the construction worker again . . .

Please, you can't go home. Tonight, just for one night, be with me? If he could get to him in time, that's what he wanted to ask.

Acknowledgments

Acknowledgments are how we recognize our interconnectedness to others. There are many people to whom I am grateful for supporting me with this project.

First, my gratitude to Markus Nornes at the University of Michigan Press, for seeing the worth of this project, and to Christopher Dreyer, Anna Pohlod, Daniel Otis, and Mary Hashman, for helping me enormously to finalize the manuscript.

Numerous people lent their support in deciphering difficult sections of Japanese texts, including Minori Murata and Taka Muraji. Thank you to Sachi Schmidt-Hori, who made the trip from Dartmouth to Amherst for a stimulating discussion about *chigo* in my Queer Japan course.

I'm grateful to Sam Bett for suggesting the English title for my translation of "The Playroom," and to Professor Nakagawa Shigemi for alerting me to the short story by Morii Ryō and for putting me in touch with the author.

Thank you to the students in my "Queer Japan in Literature and Culture" courses, whose insights helped me finalize the table of contents and propose questions for the translators.

Thank you to the University of Colorado, Brown University, Smith College, and the University of Massachusetts Amherst for encouraging me to develop and teach Queer Japan.

Jeffrey Angles's advice and support were, and continue to be, invaluable. I feel honored that he agreed to let me include three of his translations in this volume.

I'm indebted to all the translators (many first-time translators) for their immense contributions.

My gratitude to those who read stories and novels, helping me decide what works to include. Some became co-translators: Akira Kohbara,

Anthony Chambers, Jeffrey Angles, Sam Bett, Steve Snyder, Chelsea Bernard, and Amanda Seaman.

Thank you to Professor Jason Webb at the University of Southern California, who invited me to present this material in 2020. I'm especially grateful to Joseph Hawkins, the director of the ONE National Gay and Lesbian Archives, for attending that symposium, and for lending his expertise to the proceedings.

Personal thanks to Tom Duffy, Keith Gresham, and George Bealer, whose support and friendship sustained me during this work. Finally, I thank my husband, Patrick Donnelly, whose indefatigable generosity to me and love for me throughout this process was lifesaving.

Contributors

Mio Akasako is a multidisciplinarian. She is a neuroscientist, data visualization developer, and seemingly everything in between. Currently, she is co-founder and VP of Design at Ash Wellness, a healthcare company enabling providers and businesses alike to enable at-home diagnostic health testing for the communities they serve, ultimately with a mission to provide inclusive and accessible healthcare for all. Her foray into translation began as a child growing up in a traditional Japanese household in California, which required seamless transitioning between Japanese and English languages. At Brown University, she spent time formally learning translation practices, and has engaged in a number of projects since. She is constantly looking to merge her many interests, most recently succeeding when a colleague asked her to translate an experimental protocol he obtained from researchers in Japan.

Nicholas Albertson (PhD, University of Chicago) is an assistant professor of Japanese at Colgate University where he teaches Japanese language, literature, and film. His research focuses on gender and nature in Japanese poetry from the late nineteenth and early twentieth centuries. Recent articles include "Supernatural Longing in Yamakawa Tomiko's *Tanka*" (*Japanese Studies*, 2019) and a translation of Yamada Bimyō's short story "Butterfly" (*Review of Japanese Culture and Society*, 2017).

Jeffrey Angles is a poet, translator, and professor of Japanese literature at Western Michigan University. His collection of original Japanese-language poetry *Watashi no hizukehenkōsen* won the Yomiuri Prize for Literature, a rare honor accorded only a few non-native speakers since the award began in 1949. He has translated into English dozens of translations of Japan's most important modern authors and poets. He believes strongly in the role of translators as activists and has focused on translating socially engaged, feminist, and queer writers. Among his recent translations is Orikuchi Shinobu's modernist classic, *The Book of the Dead*, and Itō Hiromi's tale of Japanese-American life, *The Thorn-Puller*.

Chelsea Bernard is a technical and creative Japanese translator based in California.

Sam Bett is a fiction writer and Japanese translator whose credits include *Star* by Mishima Yukio (New Directions, 2019). His translation work has won the Japan-U.S. Friendship Commission Prize and been shortlisted for the International Booker Prize.

Davinder L. Bhowmik is an associate professor of Japanese at the University of Washington, Seattle. She teaches and publishes research in the field of modern Japanese literature with a specialization in prose fiction from Okinawa, where she was born and lived until the age of eighteen. Other scholarly interests include regional fiction, the atomic bombings, and Japanese film. Her publications include *Islands of Protest: Japanese Literature from Okinawa* (co-edited with Steve Rabson, 2016); *Writing Okinawa: Narratives of Identity and Resistance* (2008); and "Temporal Discontinuity in the Atomic Bomb Fiction of Hayashi Kyōko (in *Ōe and Beyond: Fiction in Contemporary Japan*, 1999).

Joseph Boxman is a translator currently living in Brooklyn, New York. He received his BA in Japanese studies from Earlham College and spent a year at Waseda University through Earlham's Japan Study program. He completed an MA in Japanese literature at the University of Washington where he finished this translation of Orikuchi's "Whistle."

Stephen Dodd is Professor Emeritus of Japanese Literature at SOAS, University of London. His many articles related to modern Japanese literature include "The Significance of Bodies in Sōseki's *Kokoro*" (*Monumenta Nipponica* 53 [4], 1998). He is author of *Writing Home: Representations of the Native Place in Modern Japanese Literature* (Harvard University Asia Center, 2004), and *The Youth of Things: Life and Death in the Age of Kajii Motojirō* (Hawai'i University Press, 2014.). His translation of Mishima Yukio's *Life for Sale* (*Inochi urimasu*, 1968) was published as a Penguin Classic in 2019, and his translation of Mishima's sci-fi novel, *Beautiful Star* (*Utsukushii hoshi*, 1962), came out with Penguin in April 2022. His present research includes the work of Mishima and Nagai Kafū. In 2011, he was awarded a UK Arts and Humanities Research Council (AHRC) Fellowship, and a Japan Society for the Promotion of Science (JSPS) Fellowship. His one-year Visiting Research Scholarship at Nichibunken, Kyoto, began from April 2022.

Paul McCarthy received a PhD in East Asian Languages and Civilizations from Harvard University with a dissertation on Tanizaki Jun'ichirō. He has taught Japanese and English language and literature and comparative literature at universities in the United States and Japan, and he was Visiting Professor at the International Center for Japanese Studies in Kyoto. He is Professor Emeritus of Comparative Culture, Surugadai University, and lives in Tokyo. He has written studies of Tanizaki, Mishima Yukio, and Nakajima Atsushi and has translated numerous works including *Childhood Years, A Memoir* (University of Michigan Press) and *A Cat, a Man, and Two Women and Other Stories* (New Directions) by Tanizaki, as well as *The Word Book* (Dalkey Archive) and *Oh, Tama!* (Stone Bridge Press) by Kanai Mieko, and *101 Modern Japanese Poems* (Thames River Press) compiled by Ōoka Makoto. He was a co-translator of two multi-volume historical novels by Shiba Ryōtarō in recent years: *Clouds Above the Hill* (Routledge) and *Ryōma!* currently available as an e-book). A co-translation of three Tanizaki stories, with Anthony H. Chambers, is forthcoming in January 2022 from Columbia University Press:*Longing and Other Stories.*

Scott Mehl is an assistant professor of Japanese at Colgate University. Trained as a comparatist with a specialization in modern Japanese literature, he works on the intersections between Japanese literature and literature in other languages, often with a focus on the history of literary criticism. His published essays and translations have appeared in *Comparative Literature Studies, Monumenta Nipponica, Japanese Language and Literature, Japanese Studies,* and other venues. He is the author of *The Ends of Meter in Modern Japanese Poetry: Translation and Form* (Cornell University Press, 2021).

Stephen D. Miller is associate professor of Japanese language and literature at the University of Massachusetts Amherst. Miller is author of *The Wind from Vulture Peak: The Buddhification of Japanese Waka in the Heian Period* (Cornell East Asia Series, 2013). He is translator of *A Pilgrim's Guide to Forty-Six Temples* (Weatherhill, 1990), and editor of *Partings at Dawn:*

An Anthology of Japanese Gay Literature (Gay Sunshine Press, 1996). Miller lived in Japan for nine years between 1980 and 1999, in part as the recipient of two Japan Foundation fellowships for research abroad. Miller, with poet Patrick Donnelly, is co-translator of the classical Japanese Buddhist poems in *The Wind from Vulture Peak: The Buddhification of Japanese Waka in the Heian Period* (Cornell East Asia Series, 2013), which were awarded the 2015–2016 Japan-U.S. Friendship Commission Prize for the Translation of Japanese Literature, from the Donald Keene Center of Japanese Culture at Columbia University. Miller and Donnelly's translations have appeared in numerous poetry and translation journals, including *Cha: An Asian Literary Journal, Circumference, The Cortland Review, The Drunken Boat, eXchanges, Inquiring Mind, Kyoto Journal, Metamorphoses, New Plains Review, NOON: The Journal of the Short Poem, Poetry International,* and *Transference,* and their translation of the sixteenth-century Japanese Nō play *Shunzei Tadanori* appeared in *Like Clouds or Mists: Studies and Translations of Nō Plays of the Genpei War* (Cornell East Asia Series, 2014).

Janet Poole is an Associate Professor in the Department of East Asian Studies at the University of Toronto. Her research focuses on the relationship between aesthetics and formations of colonialism and postcolonial national division, explored through literature, art and material culture, on theories of translation and literary translation. Her exploration of Korean modernist writers' response to Japanese fascist occupation during the Pacific War appeared as *When the Future Disappears: The Modernist Imagination of Late Colonial Korea* (Columbia University Press, 2014) and was awarded the 2015 Modernist Studies Association Book Prize. A dedicated literary translator, Poole has translated many works by the mid-twentieth century writer Yi T'aejun. A collection of his anecdotal essays written during the Asia-Pacific War was published as *Eastern Sentiments* by Columbia University Press in 2009 and a selection of his short stories written during the Pacific War and the early years of the Democratic People's Republic appeared as *Dust and Other Stories* (Columbia University Press, 2018). The latter was awarded a residency fellowship from the Banff International Literary Translation Centre. Her most recent project, "Going North and the History of Korean Modernism," looks at the writings of Korea's modernist writers and artists who crossed the 38th parallel into what was to become the Democratic People's Republic in the late 1940s.

Amanda C. Seaman teaches at the University of Massachusetts Amherst, where she is a professor of modern Japanese language and literature. A scholar of modern women's literature, genre fiction, and gender studies, she is the author of *Bodies of Evidence: Women, Society and Detective Fiction in 1990s Japan* (2004) and *Writing Pregnancy in Low-Fertility Japan* (2017). Her other publications include translations of Japanese women's literature, writings on Japanese popular culture and Japanese food culture. Her current research explores the representation of illness and the afflicted in postwar Japanese literature, film, and popular media.

Kristin Sivak received her PhD from the Department of East Asian Studies at the University of Toronto. Her dissertation, "Serving Stories: Servant Characters in 20th Century Japanese Literature," discusses the ways in which servant characters inhabit, structure, and challenge their employers' narratives in the works of Natsume Sōseki (1867–1916), Tanizaki Jun'ichirō (1886–1965), and Mishima Yukio (1925–1970). Via close examination of the structural roles played by servant characters in both upholding and unsettling the text, she proposes new ways of thinking about issues of representation, power, and authority in modern Japanese fiction. She received an Ontario Graduate Scholarship Visa Award in support of her work at the University of Toronto, as well as a Japanese Studies Fellowship through the Japan Foundation, which funded a year of research at Hokkaido University in Sapporo, Japan. She is also the translator of Miyazaki Kazumi's "Camellias and Vampires: Reading the Spermatic Economy in Natsume Sōseki's *And Then,*" published in the 2017 special issue of *Review of Japanese Culture, Reading Sōseki Now.*

Bruce Suttmeier is Dean of the College of Arts and Sciences and Associate Professor of Japanese at Lewis & Clark College in Portland, Oregon. His recent publications include works on Kaikō Takeshi's high-growth-era foodie novel (in *Devouring Japan*, published by Oxford University Press in 2018) and on Okuda Hideo's alternate history novel "Olympic Ransom" (in *Tokyo: Memory, Imagination, City*, published by Lexington Books in 2018). His current research involves counterfactual narratives in both literary and historical narratives, exploring the genre's complex connections to memory, contingency, and the fixity of historical facts themselves. This work has been supported by research grants from the American Philosophical Society (2019) and the Japan Foundation (2020).

Robert Tierney is professor of modern Japanese literature in the East Asian Languages and Cultures Department at the University of Illinois at Urbana-Champaign. His recent publications include *Monster of the Twentieth Century: Kōtoku Shūsui and Japan's First Anti-Imperialist Movement* (University of California Press, 2015); "*Othello* in Tokyo: Performing Race and Empire in Early Twentieth Century Japan," *Shakespeare Quarterly* 62(4), December 2011; and *Tropics of Savagery: The Culture of Japanese Empire in Comparative Frame* (University of California Press, 2010). He is currently working on a study of Nakae Chōmin and a monograph on death writings in modern Japan. He may be contacted at rtierney@illinois.edu